PENGUIN BOOKS

MRS JORDAN'S PROFESSION

'Riveting … conjures up a rich, alluring period which, in its brittle decadence and love of scandal and flamboyance, often seems closer than the nineteenth century to our own times … the most haunting biography I have read this year' – Jackie Wullschlager in the *Financial Times*

'The strangest and most sensational story she has told so far … a miraculously detailed portrait – as brisk, unsentimental, good-humoured and fairminded as its subject' – Hilary Spurling in the *Daily Telegraph*

'Tomalin triumphantly succeeds in saying – and in seeing – much that is new and worth while. In part she does so by her mastery of the context, brilliantly recreating Dora's milieu … a *fin de siècle* atmosphere heavy with assignation, infidelity, betrayal and revolution … above all, she takes Dora seriously as a woman in ways that previous royal writers never did' – David Cannadine in the *London Review of Books*

'Enthralling … Ms Tomalin's biography is as enchanting as its subject. It brilliantly brings to life a historical and theatrical epoch and a saga in which the nineteenth-century House of Hanover foreshadows the House of Windsor today' – Michael Arditti in the *Sunday Express*

'Only Claire Tomalin could have *found* this story – for such narratives have to be excavated … and only Claire Tomalin could have written this story with the same scrupulousness and sheer imaginative sleuthing that distinguished her last book [*The Invisible Woman*]' – Neil Paraday in the *Guardian*

'Claire Tomalin's biographies hum with love and anger – an anger civilized and well researched, and all the more effective for that … she has never found a more appealing subject than Dora Jordan' – Loraine Fletcher in the *New Statesman & Society*

Claire Tomalin worked in publishing and journalism for many years. She was literary editor first of the *New Statesman* and then the *Sunday Times*, before devoting herself to writing full time. She is the author of eight highly acclaimed biographies: *The Life and Death of Mary Wollstonecraft*, which won the Whitbread First Book Award; *Shelley and His World*; *Katherine Mansfield: A Secret Life*; *The Invisible Woman: The Story of Nelly Ternan and Charles Dickens*, which won the Hawthornden Prize, the NCR Book Award and the James Tait Black Memorial Prize for Biography; *Mrs Jordan's Profession*; *Jane Austen: A Life*; *Samuel Pepys: The Unequalled Self*, which was the 2002 Whitbread Book of the Year; *Thomas Hardy: The Time-Torn Man*; and, most recently, *Charles Dickens: A Life*.

She lives in London with her husband, the novelist and playwright Michael Frayn.

CLAIRE TOMALIN

Mrs Jordan's Profession

The story of a great actress
and a future King

PENGUIN BOOKS

PENGUIN BOOKS

Published by the Penguin Group
Penguin Books Ltd, 80 Strand, London WC2R ORL, England
Penguin Group (USA) Inc., 375 Hudson Street, New York, New York 10014, USA
Penguin Group (Canada), 90 Eglinton Avenue East, Suite 700, Toronto, Ontario, Canada M4P 2Y3
(a division of Pearson Penguin Canada Inc.)
Penguin Ireland, 25 St Stephen's Green, Dublin 2, Ireland (a division of Penguin Books Ltd)
Penguin Group (Australia), 250 Camberwell Road, Camberwell, Victoria 3124, Australia
(a division of Pearson Australia Group Pty Ltd)
Penguin Books India Pvt Ltd, 11 Community Centre, Panchsheel Park, New Delhi – 110 017, India
Penguin Group (NZ), 67 Apollo Drive, Rosedale, Auckland 0632, New Zealand
(a division of Pearson New Zealand Ltd)
Penguin Books (South Africa) (Pty) Ltd, Block D, Rosebank Office Park,
181 Jan Smuts Avenue, Parktown North, Gauteng 2193, South Africa

Penguin Books Ltd, Registered Offices: 80 Strand, London WC2R ORL, England

www.penguin.com

First published by Viking 1994
Published with a new Afterword in Penguin Books 1995
Reissued in this edition 2012
001

The acknowledgements on pp. xii–xv constitute an extension of this copyright page

Printed in Great Britain by Clays Ltd, St Ives plc

ISBN: 978-0-241-96329-6

www.greenpenguin.co.uk

Penguin Books is committed to a sustainable
future for our business, our readers and our planet.
This book is made from Forest Stewardship
Council™ certified paper.

ALWAYS LEARNING   **PEARSON**

For my children
Josephine, Susanna, Emily and Tom
and for Rosa

Contents

CONTENTS

List of Illustrations

LIST OF ILLUSTRATIONS

Drawing by Henry Edridge of Richard Ford (by permission of Sir Brinsley Ford/photo: Eileen Tweedie)

The Duke of Clarence in 1788 (National Portrait Gallery Archive)

John Hoppner's portrait of Mrs Jordan as Viola in *Twelfth Night* (Kenwood House © The Iveagh Bequest, English Heritage)

Mrs Jordan as Hippolita, engraving of a scene from *She Would and She Would Not*, undated (The Royal Collection © Her Majesty Queen Elizabeth II, 1994)

Silhouette by Mrs Millicent Brown of Mrs Jordan as Hippolita, once in the collection of Lady Dorothy Neville and reproduced from E.N. Jackson's *History of Silhouettes*, 1911 (British Library)

SECOND INSET

James Gillray's 'The Lubber's Hole', 1 November 1791 (British Museum)

James Gillray's 'Neptune reposing after Fording the Jordan', 24 October 1791 (British Museum)

William Dent's 'The Flattering Glass, or Nell's Mistake', 28 October 1791 (British Museum)

James Gillray's 'La Promenade en Famille', April 1797 (British Museum)

Engraving from Steeden's drawing of Mrs Jordan as Nell in *The Devil to Pay* (by permission of Sir Brinsley Ford/photo: Eileen Tweedie)

George FitzClarence, from *The Great Illegitimates*, 1832 (British Library)

Isaac R. Cruikshank's '*Cl----ce's Dream: or, Binnacle Billy Receiving an Unwelcome Visit From ye Other World*', April 1821 (Theatre Museum by courtesy of the trustees of the Victoria & Albert Museum)

Statue of Mrs Jordan by Francis Chantrey, 1834 (The Royal Academy of Arts/The Royal Collection)

George Henry Harlow's painting of Frederick, Eliza and Adolphus FitzClarence at Bushy, *c.* 1805

LIST OF ILLUSTRATIONS

TEXT ILLUSTRATIONS

Acknowledgements

By gracious permission of Her Majesty the Queen I have been allowed free access to all the material in the Royal Archives at Windsor and permission to reproduce certain pictures from the Royal Collection.

I was fortunate in having the help of Lady de Bellaigue, Registrar of the Royal Archives, at many points, including the deciphering of some difficult readings of Mrs Jordan's hand, and should like to express my particular sense of indebtedness to her for her meticulous checking; also to all her staff.

I am grateful to the Huntington Library, San Marino, California, and its Curator, Sara S. Hodson, for providing me with microfilms of its collection of Mrs Jordan's letters, and for permission to reproduce extracts from them. My warm thanks also to Judith Flanders for finding me a microfilm reader which enabled me to study the Huntington letters at my own pace at home.

I have met with much kindness while working on this book. Among the living descendants of Mrs Jordan, the present Earl of Munster was the first to give me advice and assistance. Mr J.U.C. Birkbeck and Miss Mary Birkbeck, Viscount De L'Isle and Viscount Falkland were all generous with their time and in showing me papers, letters, pictures and memorabilia. Mr Birkbeck has allowed me to reproduce from family papers, and I have also been granted permission to reproduce from the De L'Isle Manuscripts, a private family archive held at Maidstone in Kent. Others who prefer not to be named have also offered me substantial help, which is by no means forgotten.

Sir Brinsley Ford generously allowed me to study his family papers and pictures and to take copies and photographs of them. General Sir Victor FitzGeorge-Balfour gave me more than the usual assistance by allowing me to take away his family papers to study and copy. Dr P.B. Clapham, Director of the National Physical Laboratory, together with Mrs Clapham, took me into every corner of Bushy House from cellar to attic to garden, instructed me in its history, located pictures and entered enthusiastically into my interest. Dr Nicholas Penny led me to the hitherto unknown Beechey portrait of Mrs Jordan as Rosalind, and gave me the extraordinary story of the destruction of Chantrey's casts. Christopher Lloyd, Surveyor of the Queen's Pictures, offered much useful information and took me to see Chantrey's statue and Hoppner's allegorical painting; and the Hon. Mrs Jane Roberts, Curator of the Print Room, Windsor Castle, also went to considerable trouble on my behalf. I had kind help from the Rt. Hon. Sir Robert Fellowes, Keeper of the Queen's Archives, and from Sir Oliver Millar.

Susan Palmer, Archivist at Sir John Soane's Museum, was exceptionally helpful, as was Jonathan Franklin at the National Portrait Gallery Archive. Nicholas Savage and the staff of the Library of the Royal Academy; Janet Birkett of the Theatre Museum; Ian Dejardin, Curator at Kenwood; Norman Fenner of Richmond Theatre and Richard Mangan of the Raymond Mander & Jo Mitchenson Collection all gave me substantial assistance.

I should also like to thank Dr Mary Beal of the Government Art Collection; Dr John Whiteley of the Ashmolean Print Room; the Very Reverend Michael Mayne, Dean of Westminster; Mr Jo Wisdom of the Library of St Paul's Cathedral; Miss Betty Beesley, Secretary to the Works of Art Committee of the Garrick Club Collection; Roger Beacham of Cheltenham Public Library; Brian Allen and Elizabeth A. Powis at the Paul Mellon Centre for Studies in British Art; Rosamund Griffin, Keeper of the Collection at Waddesdon Manor; the Municipal Archivist of Saint-Cloud; David Learmont of the National Trust of Scotland; Betty Muirden of the Yale Center for British Art; Michael Roberts and the Hon. Georgina Stonor at Brooks's Club; Kay Mowlam of Sotheby's; Oliver Cyzer and Paul Obrey of Christie's; Iris Rhodes of Gallery 90, Guildford; Joy Ashby, Curator of Fenton House for the National Trust; G.W. Oxley, Archivist for Hull City Council; Brian Dyson, Archivist at the University of Hull; Miss M.J. Swarbrick, Chief Archivist to the City of Westminster; and Mark Ballard of the Centre for Kentish Studies, Maidstone. In New York, Kristine Puopolo kindly sought out the death notice of Fanny Alsop for me.

The British Library was, as always, both haven and place of discovery, its staff unfailingly helpful. The same is true of the London Library. Humberside Libraries were also of assistance.

Mary Kift provided me with much information about Mapledurham and Augustus FitzClarence. Richard Holmes assisted me greatly in investigating Coleridge's interest in Mrs Jordan. Dr Christopher Mallinson and Dr Michael Price both devoted much time and thought to considering

ACKNOWLEDGEMENTS

her symptoms and final illness. Christopher Bland sent me a useful stack of information relating to the earlier generations of the Bland family. Mr Francis Atkins, Churchwarden Emeritus of St Mary the Virgin, Hampton, was a wonderful source of information both about the church where George Munster is buried and the general history of the area. Professor Harold Tedford shared his knowledge and enthusiasm for Mrs Jordan with me; and the expertise of Diana B. Joll enabled her to establish the name of her silhouettist for me.

Jill Grey did some brilliant research and also located copies of rare books for me. I had help too from Philip Ziegler, Flora Fraser, Tom Pocock, John Carey, Graham Storey, John Hayes, Robert Holden, Alan Cowie, John Kenworthy-Browne, David Mannings, Marie Cooper, Messrs Dorling Kindersley, Richard Chapman, John Wilson, Aileen Ribeiro, Peter Holland and the late R.L. Bayne-Powell.

Both my English and American editors, Tony Lacey and Charles Elliott, have made substantial suggestions for improving the text for which I am grateful, as I am to Donna Poppy; this is the third of my books to be copy-edited by her, and to owe much to her scrupulousness and eye for detail.

My husband has shown patience and forbearance with my obsession with Dora Jordan's history, which has taken several years to unravel. While busy with his own writing, he cheered me through bad patches, shared my jubilation over discoveries of letters and pictures, and gave excellent advice at all times.

* * *

The paperback edition incorporates some new material.

Peter B. S. Davies and David W. James, both of St David's, Pembrokeshire, have generously shared with me their discoveries relating to Mrs Jordan's mother and her Welsh family.

Diana Daniell showed me her precious collection of letters written by the FitzClarence children to her great-great-great-uncle James William Daniell, tutor to the boys at Bushy, who remained on friendly terms with them until their and his deaths in the mid-1850s.

Philip Jones of Ewell drew my attention to the parish register held in the Surrey Record Office in which are entered the baptisms of Mrs Jordan's daughter Lucy Hester (Ford) in August 1792 and her son George FitzClarence in May 1794.

Foreword

Books do not always obey the author's orders, and this book, first planned as a general study of actresses working in Britain in the late eighteenth and early nineteenth century, quickly became obstreperous. As I absorbed myself in collecting material I soon realized that there was far too much for one volume. Then – and this was more important – came the realization that I had found, in one of the earliest of the actresses I planned to investigate, a character so strong and a story so extraordinary that she demanded a whole book to herself. Dora Jordan is not an entirely unknown figure, but she is at best half known: most people have heard of Mrs Siddons, few respond to the name of Mrs Jordan, although in their lifetime they were equally celebrated. Mrs Jordan has been written about occasionally over the two hundred years since she reigned at Drury Lane, sometimes abusively, sometimes admiringly; but I do not believe justice has been done either to her story or to her personality. There is a special tone that creeps into eulogies of actresses, presenting them as lovable, wayward creatures and striking them stone dead in the process; and an actress whose private life connected her with the royal family presents particular difficulties. Mrs Jordan has evoked embarrassment, jocularity, reverence and abuse, according to the writer's prejudices.

Most actresses have to sit down under whatever treatment critics and biographers hand out to them. The first well-established one to challenge the idea by producing an autobiography, Elizabeth Inchbald – a contemporary and friend of Dora – lost her nerve and destroyed her manuscript on the advice of her confessor: she was a Roman Catholic, and this was 1821. None of the great actresses of the eighteenth century – Peg Woffington, Frances Abington, Susanna Cibber, Kitty Clive – left memoirs, although a failed one, Charlotte Charke, did; nor, in the next century, did Lucia Vestris, Maria Foote, Fanny Stirling or Fanny Kelly, all highly intelligent and effective women. Only in the second half of the century did it become acceptable for them to give their private histories to the public, and then only up to a point; Fanny Kemble, Madge Bancroft and Ellen Terry all tidied themselves and their families up to appear more presentable. Dora Jordan produced no autobiography, but we have something almost as good, at least for twenty-five years of her life, and that is her letters. A few, treasured by theatrical friends, were published in the decades following her death, in memoirs, and by her first biographer, James Boaden, but most remained unpublished and unknown. None of her daughters seems to have kept any, or if any did, later generations destroyed them; but two of her sons preserved theirs, and passed them down through the family. These were the eldest, George, and the fourth, Adolphus, who was only fourteen when she died; forty letters to him are still in private possession. George also kept a good many; and he also preserved letters written by his younger brothers and sisters.

Many hundreds of letters from Mrs Jordan to the Duke of Clarence, later King William IV, and the father of most of her children, have survived. They were preserved in the first instance by Queen Adelaide, who found them after the King's death; she was kind enough to keep them and bequeath them in turn to Frederick, Dora's eldest surviving son at the time of the Queen's death. He clearly intended them to be kept together as part of his estate – there is a note to that effect, written not long before his death in 1854 – but he died in India, his only daughter did not marry, and they were somehow scattered. During the first three decades of this century letters appeared in various sales. Some were acquired by George's great-grandson, the fifth Earl of Munster, who presented about 270 of them to the Royal Archives; and about 600 more went, in two batches, to the Californian collector Henry Huntington. In California they have sat, and as far as I know only one scholar has looked at them.

This was Arthur Aspinall, Professor of Modern History at the University of Reading. In 1951 he produced an edition of Mrs Jordan's letters at the request of the fifth Earl. Aspinall had already achieved the colossal task of editing the complete letters of King George III, and was engaged on an edition of the complete letters of his son, first Prince of Wales, then Prince Regent, then King George IV; also those of Princess Charlotte, granddaughter of George III and daughter of George IV. All these letters were published in full, with copious notes, and are a mine of information for students of the period; they fill many stout volumes. But when Professor Aspinall came to edit and publish the correspondence of Mrs Jordan he adopted a different style. To begin with, he made a great many unexplained cuts; and as well as being cut, the letters were incorporated into a curiously unsympathetic narrative. There are mistakes – for instance in giving the dates of the children – and Aspinall also omitted without explanation a crucial letter in the Huntington collection which proves that Mrs Jordan was innocent of accusations made against her in royal circles that she threatened to blackmail her royal lover.

Aspinall's cuts do her other disfavours and distort the picture of her character. He removed, for instance, much of the good and sensible advice she gave the Duke. He also removed all her warm expressions of sympathy for the troubles of the royal family – the King's madness, the illness and death of his youngest daughter. He removed a mass of evidence of her conscientious care of her children and descriptions of daily life at Bushy, their house and estate near Hampton Court. He removed most of her humour. Professor

Aspinall, so at ease in the world of politics and the royal family, was clearly not at ease in the world – or the mind – of Mrs Jordan.

His approach is also generally condescending, which seems misplaced, for although she was no more highly educated than other women of her generation, her letters are intelligent and full of good sense, and she was by no means uncultured. She was able to write correct and charming verse. She knew Shakespeare and the chief dramatists, naturally, as well as Milton, Goldsmith, Sterne, Defoe and Shenstone. She read and appreciated Coleridge and Wordsworth and she mentions Dr Johnson and Hogarth; she recommended books to the Duke, read with her children and sent her sons books when they went off to school, and the army and navy. She composed, performed and published music. She employed talented artists to paint her children, as well as sitting herself to many leading painters.

In certain respects Aspinall was a superb editor. His knowledge of the period was enormous, and he provides a lot of background information. He was working under the constraint of having to fit the material into one volume – not for Mrs Jordan the stately spread of royal correspondence – and some of his cuts are justified, because there are boring and repetitious passages in her letters; although it must be said that the same is true of those by royal personages. Still, it is surprising to find how much failed to interest Aspinall; and the only biography to appear since he edited the letters – Brian Fothergill's of 1965 – relied on his edition, and did not use the originals in the Huntington.

History – and biography, which is a branch of history – is always a matter of choice and control. The writer or editor decides what is history and what is not. Percy Fitzgerald, the 1884 biographer who entirely omitted to mention Mrs Jordan in his two-volume *Life and Times of William IV*, took an attitude that seems extreme to us but was perfectly normal for its time. Professor Aspinall allowed her to exist, but ignored or devalued large areas of her expèrience, notably the dom-estic side of her life.

My own prejudices make me devote much less attention to her theatrical performances than previous biographers have done; I believe it is hard for the general reader to follow detailed accounts of past productions, however fascinating to the theatre specialist. So I have not attempted to list every performance she gave. An appendix does what it can in this area. In the main text I have only tried to show, through the comments of her fellow players and the critics, what an incomparable actress she appeared to them, and through her own words what her profession meant to her.

Shakespeare's woman: Dora Jordan. – Charles Lamb

... real solemn history, I cannot be interested in ... the men all so good for nothing, and hardly any women at all. – Jane Austen, *Northanger Abbey*

Arrah, now, honey ... won't I sit in the gallery, and won't your Royal Grace give me a courtesy, and won't I give your Royal Highness a howl, and a hiss into the bargain! – Irish cook to Mrs Jordan

... abomination! The full moon came thundering down from Heaven, like a Cannon Ball; & seeing that nothing could be done went quietly back again! Dreamt these words before daylight, May Morning, 1804. Put 'em into a Mrs Jordan's mouth, ridiculing some pompous moral or political Declaimer. – Samuel Taylor Coleridge

Serious Reviewer, interrupting: But, my good sir, suppose some of your female readers should take it into their heads to be Mrs Jordan?
Author: Oh, my good sir, don't be alarmed. My female readers are not persons to be so much afraid for, as you seem to think yours are. The stage itself has taught them large measures both of charity and discernment. – Leigh Hunt, in his *Autobiography*, published 1850

Prologue:
'Beside the monuments of the Queens'

At six o'clock in the morning of 26 June 1830, an elderly gentleman of no great distinction, sleeping peacefully in his country house in Middlesex, was woken by his manservant and told that two doctors were waiting to see him. The old man got up, put on his dressing-gown, and went downstairs. The doctors were bringing him some good news. His elder brother George had died in the night, and they had ridden over from Windsor to Bushy in the early morning sunshine to tell him so, and to be the first to salute him as the new King of England. He was sixty-four years old, had spent a large part of his life unemployed and made a hash of the jobs he had been given: now he found himself King William IV.

William was the third son of King George III and his Queen Charlotte, and had not been expected to succeed to the throne, or educated with it in mind. He had been sent to serve in the navy as a boy, with the idea that it should become his profession; when that proved a mistake, he was given a dukedom, an income and an estate, and left largely to his own devices. He had married, at the age of fifty-three, a German princess, Adelaide; she was less than half his age, but they had no living children.

The new King was not known as a patron of the arts, but one of the first acts of his reign was to send for the sculptor Francis Chantrey and commission a work. Chantrey was the leading sculptor of the day and an established favourite of the royal family. He had made busts of George III and Queen

Charlotte as well as of most of the distinguished figures of his generation: Wellington, Pitt, Walter Scott, Wordsworth, James Watt and many more. George IV, a notable patron, had also commissioned a bust of himself, and paid three hundred guineas for it. But the new King was not on this occasion asking for a bust of himself or his Queen Adelaide. What he wanted was a life-size representation of an actress. King William wept as he explained to Chantrey exactly what he had in mind.[1]

The subject of the statue had been dead for fifteen years, but Chantrey agreed to attempt the work and began by producing a small terracotta model, showing her, as the King had asked, with two of her children. The model is faceless, and all three figures are bare and rudimentary – to a modern eye they look like little figures by Henry Moore – but evidently the King approved it. For the features Chantrey had to work from portraits, of which there were fortunately many. He felt confident enough to ask a fee of two thousand guineas. The King agreed to these terms, and there was a formal commission early in 1831. It can still be read in Chantrey's ledger, under the heading 'Mrs Jordans Monument': 'Recd an order from His Majesty William IV to create a Monumental Groupe in memory of Mrs Jordan to be erected in Westminster Abbey . . .' The line of writing continues, crossed through in ink, but deciphered quite easily through the deletion: '. . . beside the monuments of the Queens'. So the King's intention was clearly to have the statue not only in the Abbey, but also in a place of special honour.[2]

It took Chantrey several years to produce first a plaster cast and then the marble monument itself; in the summer of 1834 it was finally finished. It is a magnificent and touching work. The subject is shown life-size and, as the King wished, with two of her children, one a curly-headed small boy, the other a fat baby, also a boy. She is seated on a plain block, knees apart and ankles crossed, looking down at the infant on her lap, and draped in the simplest and lightest of classical gowns, held on her right shoulder by a single large button and edged with an embroidered band. Her left shoulder is uncovered, and her hair falls forward in loose curls. The mask of comedy and a set of musical pipes representing music and poetry lie beside her bare and beautiful feet, but her pose, in its simplicity and tenderness, makes one think less of an actress or a muse than of a Renaissance madonna.[3]

The King was pleased. He made a personal friend of Chantrey, conferred a knighthood on him a few years later, and even offered him a baronetcy, which the sculptor modestly refused.

But there were problems. The Dean of Westminster at this time was John Ireland, an ailing scholar in his seventies. His own bust had been made by Chantrey, and he had held the crown at the coronations of both George IV and William IV.[4] Ireland was not prepared to allow Chantrey's monumental statue into the Abbey, either among the queens of England or indeed anywhere else. If he even troubled to look at the statue, the Dean may well have thought it too secular and celebratory of its subject's beauty for a religious setting; but fundamentally his refusal must have been on moral grounds, because Dorothy or, as she preferred it, Dora Jordan, had a double stain on her character. She had lived with the King when he was Duke of Clarence, and borne him ten children over a period of twenty years. At the same time she had never given up her professional career in the theatre. She was the best-loved and most admired comic actress of her time, hailed by fellow actors, critics and public alike as a uniquely gifted performer, fully the equal in comedy to Mrs Siddons in tragedy: for several decades they were generally referred to as the Muses of Comedy and Tragedy. George III, Joshua Reynolds, Coleridge, Hazlitt, Byron, Mrs Inchbald, John Kemble, Fanny Burney, Madame de Staël, Leigh Hunt, Charles Lamb, Benjamin Haydon and William Macready were all among her admirers. Lamb, looking at her portrait some years after her death, described her simply as 'Shakespeare's woman', the highest praise he could accord.[5]

Whatever stain the church might perceive on her character, it was a lesser stain than marked the King himself, or the previous King, his brother George, known to be a bigamist and adulterer, or indeed a significant number of men in public life honoured in the Abbey. Other actresses, virtuous and otherwise, were buried or commemorated there: from the seventeenth century Mary Saunderson, from the eighteenth Anne Bracegirdle, who had been Congreve's mistress, Susanna Cibber, who had been divorced, the rackety, much married Ann Barry, the blameless Hannah Pritchard and Anne Oldfield, interred without a monument, on account of her two illegitimate sons. David Garrick and Samuel Foote were also buried there, and Sarah Siddons's statue appeared in the following decade.[6] But, despite the King's wishes, Mrs Jordan was not allowed into Westminster Abbey.

When the Dean of St Paul's was approached, he reacted in the same way. Other suggestions seem to have been made, and rejected as unsuitable, by the eldest son of the King and Mrs Jordan, the little boy represented in the statue, now Earl of Munster. So the nation was deprived of an outstandingly beautiful monument, and the rejected group remained in Chantrey's Pimlico studio. It was still there in 1839, two years after King William's death, and had become something of an embarrassment.[7] The young Queen Victoria, who had a passion for the theatre, was curious about Mrs Jordan, whose children were after all her own first cousins. Her diary records several conversations with the Prime Minister, Lord Melbourne, in which she asked about her.

At the end of December 1838:

Lord M talked of Mrs Jordan; I thought he couldn't remember her, but he said he did perfectly, and remembers going to see her act in '13 with Madame de Stael, who was delighted with her; she had a beautiful voice, and sang all those songs without music delightfully; exceedingly lively, and seemed always in the highest spirits on the stage; Lord M continued, that her real forte was in such characters as a 'Chamber Maid', though she acted latterly Lady Teazle and even Juliet, but it wasn't the same thing ... Her singing 'used to produce an electrical effect' ...

Lord M [also said] it was a very curious thing, her acquaintance with the late King, which he thinks began as early as '82, for that he was not very fond of the Theatre, though he always used to be there when she acted; and Peak, the Treasurer of either Drury Lane or Covent Garden, told Lord M, that the King used always to come himself to receive her salary – which was paid regularly to him; Mrs Jordan was very good natured, Lord M said, and George IV liked her, and used to go and dine with them.[8]

In January 1839 the Queen had two more conversations about Mrs Jordan with Lord Melbourne. She noted that he

had seen all Chantrey's works in his studio; and he said, 'I saw Mrs Jordan's statue'; the late King, Lord M told me (Chantrey told him) sent for Chantrey about 4 or 5 days after he came to the Throne, and desired him to make this statue, which he had *always* intended to have done when he had the means for it; [WIV] wished to place it in Henry VII's Chapel, which Lord M said is Crown property, over which the Dean has no power, so that no one could refuse or prevent its being put there; but Munster (why, he don't know) would not let the King do it, and thwarted the King amazingly about it; and the King's Executors tell Chantrey it belongs to Munster, but Lord M said Munster doesn't know what to do with it; it's too large for a house. Said I thought it was rather odd to put it in Henry VII's Chapel; 'I think it's rather odd,' said Lord M, 'as she wasn't even buried there.'[9] Then Lord M said, they didn't know what to write under it, so they called it, 'Sacred to the memory of an affectionate Mother, Dorah Bland.'[10] But I asked Lord M, why shouldn't it be Dorah Jordan? Bland was her maiden name; Lord M said he had no idea who Mr Jordan was, or if she was married to him.[11]

The Queen continued to be curious. Her questions may have arisen as much from a desire to understand the marital and extramarital histories of her uncles and her father as from an enthusiasm for cultural history, although this is what Lord Melbourne mostly offered her. Later, her diary reads:

> Talked again of Mrs Jordan ... 'She was beautifully formed,' Lord M said, 'her legs and feet were beautifully formed, as this statue is'; and she used to be fond of acting in men's clothes; she used to act Hippolyta in *She Would and She Would Not*, and Rosalind in *As You Like It*; 'a lovely play,' said Lord M, 'the prettiest play in the world; and her acting in that was quite beautiful.' 'She had a beautiful enunciation,' he added. She was an Irish girl.[12]

Interested as she was, and enthusiastic about the theatre, Queen Victoria did not want the statue herself. Nor did its rightful owner, Lord Munster, who suffered cruelly from taunts in the press about his shameful birth, which may be why he wanted nothing to do with the commemorative piece. It remained in Chantrey's studio, 'never having been settled during the King's life', and it looks as though it was still there at Chantrey's death in the autumn of 1841.[13]

The subject of Chantrey's statue, Dora Jordan, and her tangled and tormented relations with the royal family with whom she became so closely allied, make the subject of this book. Her life was one of extremes: extremes of poverty and misfortune, extremes of success and riches. For over twenty-five years she was probably the most popular actress in Britain, based at the Theatre Royal, Drury Lane, under the management of Richard Brinsley Sheridan, with whom she was closely connected both professionally and personally. Her fame was immense and sometimes scandalous, and she was one of the first women to fight back against the power of the press and make it serve her purpose instead of accepting that she must always be its victim. She was intensely serious about her work, and revered by several generations of her fellow professionals. She also bore thirteen children who lived to adult life, and involved herself deeply and lovingly in their care and upbringing while continuing her acting career. As an unmarried working mother, she crossed every social barrier, going from penniless provincial to royal intimacy in a few years, without ever growing affected or pretentious. Although she never married, five of her daughters entered the British aristocracy through marriage; her sons, all of whom went into the services, had more curious and in some cases much sadder fates.

If she moved through her early years like the passionate heroine of a picaresque novel – Fielding's *Tom Jones*, say – in which morality is developed through experience, trial and error, she lived to see her children enter the more circumscribed world of Jane Austen, with its backdrop of army, navy and colonies, its insistence on prudent and advantageous marriage and its tight, confident social structure that simply obliterated those who, for one reason or another, failed to fit or conform. Her name and reputation were partly suppressed and yet covertly fascinating to the nineteenth century. To those who knew her story she became a symbol of the strength a stage career could confer on a woman, and a warning of its dangers: independence, yes, and professional satisfaction, but also the risk of degradation, and of crashing from the brilliant pinnacle of fame to poverty and humiliation.

She was painted by some of the best artists of her time, and caricatured by the cruellest; the range of images is startling, and a rich source of information. The first three decades of her life can be traced only through outside evidence. There is no shortage of this, because she was born with the knack of attracting attention; but from the age of thirty we have her own voice in her letters. Against the odds, many hundreds have been preserved. Very few of them are formal, or carefully composed. Almost all were written in haste and without a thought of posterity, dashed off in the dressing rooms of provincial theatres, or in nurseries, or in lodging houses and inns, in her various town houses, in St James's Palace, and in the home in which she passed her happiest years, Bushy

House. Most were addressed to her royal partner, the future King.

If Dora's letters give a voice to her statue, the most curious thing about the statue itself is that the King was memorializing his own victim. Like Leontes in *The Winter's Tale*, William first honoured and then destroyed the woman he loved; and hoped to make amends to a statue for the wrong done to a living woman. Only Dora's statue could not come back to life as Hermione's did; and it suffered the further indignity of being treated by the nation as she had been treated by William: rejected and consigned to oblivion. This book seeks to tell the story of both the statue and the woman, and to do what it can to distinguish between image and truth. 'On doit des égards aux vivants; on ne doit aux morts que la vérité.'

I

The Sins of the Fathers: 1761–1782

In retrospect King William and Dora Jordan make a very unlikely couple. In prospect they would have seemed even more improbable. He was born to legitimate splendour and riches in 1765, she four years earlier to a marked lack of any such advantages. They shared a birthplace, London; beyond that there was nothing to link their fates. All the royal circumstances of William's birth are recorded, down to the length of the Queen's labour (an easy four hours), the midwife's meals and the yards of stuff purchased for the wet nurse's nightgowns; but doubts and uncertainties cloud Dora's birth and early history.

Although Lord Melbourne said she was an Irish girl, her mother was Welsh and her father came from a Protestant Yorkshire family settled in Ireland for less than a century; and although they usually lived in Dublin, she was born somewhere in the neighbourhood of Leicester Square, Covent Garden and the Strand. What were her parents doing in London in 1761? They may have been looking for work, judging it a hopeful time as the capital prepared itself for the festivities surrounding the coronation and wedding of the new King, George III; or they may have been simply visiting friends or family. What we know for certain is that Francis and Grace Bland registered the birth of their daughter Dorothy as having taken place on 22 November 1761, and that she was baptized at the church of St Martin-in-the-Fields on 5 December.

The baptismal register is clear enough; but her parents' marriage was not legally valid; Grace Phillips was not really entitled to be set down as Mrs Bland, and Dorothy should perhaps have been given Phillips as her family name. Against this, Francis and Grace both considered themselves as good as married, and Dorothy was not their first child. They may have gone through some sort of ceremony somewhere; less than perfectly legal marriages were not hard to arrange in the middle of the eighteenth century. The problem was that Francis had not asked for his father's consent. He had not asked because he knew he would not get it; he had been under twenty-one at the time of the 'marriage', and Grace was not the heiress his father hoped for, but a working actress. She was nothing like the sort of actress Boswell picked up outside Drury Lane, with a murky history of false marriages and lovers, but a respectable and well brought up young woman, the daughter of a clergyman; and she put her whole trust in young Bland as a gentleman, in spite of his father's feelings.

The Bland family had done very well out of their adoptive country. Francis's father Nathaniel became a doctor of divinity, a vicar-general and a judge of the Prerogative Court in Dublin; and he acquired a castle at Derriquin in County Kerry for good measure. Judge Bland expected his sons to build on these achievements, and his disapproval of Francis's marriage, or half-marriage, was implacable. He had already disinherited his eldest son John for becoming an actor and marrying an actress: what was it about these young men that made them involve themselves with the stage? After Grace had borne two children to Francis, Judge Bland had their marriage declared void on the grounds that his son had been a minor at the time. It was one of the old man's last acts; he died in 1760, before the birth of his granddaughter Dorothy.

The young couple continued to pass as Mr and Mrs Bland in Dublin and London and also, it seems, with Grace Phillips's family. Her father, George, one-time rector of St Thomas's,

Haverfordwest in Pembrokeshire, had died when she was only seven, but her spirited cousin Blanch Williams – married but childless, and sixteen years older than Grace – kept a welcoming home at Upper Trelethyn, her farmhouse set high up above St David's Head. There were other branches of the family in Bristol, where Grace spent some of her girlhood, and where she acquired the polished manners of a city girl, and the ambition to make something of herself. Bristol was the second city of the kingdom, and supported a particularly successful theatre. There was hardly a town in the land that did not welcome strolling groups of players at this time – apart from church-going it was the chief entertainment – but the Bristol theatre was a fine, formal building, regularly visited by leading London players.[1] Grace and her sisters were stage-struck, and, with remarkable strength of character, she and her elder sister Maria set off together for Dublin in the mid-1750s determined to become actresses. The Irish players may have been familiar – they came touring in the west of England in summer – and the Phillips sisters were greeted in Dublin as 'two young ladies lately arrived from England (sisters) to perform at the Theatre Royal who have never yet appeared on any stage. As they have all the requisites to make a figure in that sphere, added to a polite education and a knowledge of the Beau Monde, it is hoped they will prove shining ornaments to the Theatre.'[2] And they did shine, brightly enough at least to be accepted as fellow professionals by the thriving theatre community of Dublin.

Their success encouraged a third sister to follow. She also found work and married a fellow actor, Usher. All three appeared at the Smock Alley Theatre under the management of Thomas Sheridan, whose skill and dedication as an impresario raised the reputation of his theatre close to the level of the great London houses, and brought their stars across to play for him. The Phillips sisters did not become stars, but they had their triumphs. Grace played Juliet to the Romeo of Sheridan, and Maria appeared as Jane Shore, both in November

1756.[3] In the 1758 season Grace was Desdemona to the Othello of a young actor called Tate Wilkinson, who went on to become the most famous of all provincial managers, and to play a crucial part in her daughter's life. This was also the year Francis Bland became Grace's husband.

If Francis entertained any passing hopes of following his elder brother in a stage career, he was disappointed. Grace continued with hers, while he received an allowance from his family, and on this the couple managed. A daughter Hester was born, and a son George. Then in the winter of 1760 the Smock Alley closed down after Thomas Sheridan decided to desert to England, and many of the company followed him in search of work; the Blands and Maria Phillips were among those who went.[4] Sheridan was in London, lecturing, writing and making occasional appearances at Drury Lane, and he may have tried to help them. He and his wife, who was as clever as he was, and busy writing novels and plays, lived in Henrietta Street, Covent Garden; they had left their ten-year-old son, Richard Brinsley, behind in Dublin, but now they brought him over too, and sent him to Harrow school.[5]

London was packed and busy throughout the autumn of 1761, as the coronation approached. The two big theatres, Drury Lane and Covent Garden, both prepared 'Coronation Spectacles' to be put on after the main plays, in which large numbers of players dressed as the King and Queen, courtiers and other grandees paraded against elaborate backdrops. These shows were popular enough to run for forty nights, so that Londoners could take their pick of two royal processions on stage as well as the real festivities taking place outside, in which the members of the royal family paraded in still more elaborately artificial costumes.[6] On the afternoon of 8 September – a day of intense heat – crowds assembled in St James's Park as the King's bride, Princess Charlotte of Mecklenburg, arrived at the garden gate of St James's Palace to the sound of gunfire. It must have been a fine sight, as she was handed down from the coach, hair elaborately dressed, wearing a white and silver négligé trimmed with gold lace; she threw herself at the feet of her future husband, who raised her up, greeted her courteously and led her indoors to examine the heaps of jewels and ceremonial robes prepared for her. What she felt, a girl of seventeen from a quiet little German principality, educated by Lutheran nuns, and speaking not a word of English, is another matter. Bride and groom had never set eyes on one another until this moment. Her mother was dead and she came without even a sister; she had just endured a long, stormy sea passage, finally forced to put in at Harwich and finish the exhausting journey by coach. As the coach came over Constitution Hill, one of the English ladies accompanying her remarked that there was scarcely time to dress for the wedding. 'The wedding?' asked Charlotte, turning pale. She had not been told that it was to take place that very evening.

No matter, this was a public ritual, and she had been most carefully vetted for the role she was to play. She was the King's third cousin, with the all-important royal blood in her veins. She was no beauty, but passable-looking and – of course – Protestant and a virgin. She was also thought likely to be a good breeder; her elder sister had been rejected as too old at twenty-five.[7]

And at ten o'clock that evening Charlotte was married to the King in the Chapel Royal, wearing the crown especially made for her. Its pendant diamonds swung and sparkled, and the bridegroom was dressed in stuff of silver with embossed plate and frostings. The effect was admirable, although she was so burdened by the weight of her clothes and jewels she could hardly bear them; she trembled, and was able to say nothing but the words 'Ich will'. The next day there were two court drawing rooms and a ball, and on the following Monday she made her first official public appearance, going with the King to Drury Lane Theatre – not to see themselves represented, but David Garrick in a performance of the popular satirical comedy *The Rehearsal*.[8]

As the theatre crowds pressed forward to look at her, the

new Queen was frightened for a moment, because she had never seen so many people gathered together in one place; but once inside Drury Lane and installed in the royal box, she became noticeably cheerful. She had never seen a theatre before either, and she could not understand a word, but she liked everything about it. Perhaps the company of two thousand people laughing and enjoying themselves in the brilliantly lit space was more fun than being closeted alone with a plain, dullish young man who had suddenly become her absolute lord and master.

Happily the King shared her new enthusiasm, and a whole series of royal command performances was quickly arranged. They ran steadily through the autumn and winter: *Much Ado about Nothing*, *King John*, *Macbeth*, *Henry V*, *Cymbeline*, *The Beggar's Opera*, *The Jealous Wife*, *Comus*, *Rule a Wife and Have a Wife*, and many musical entertainments. The theatre became a lifelong passion with the Queen.[9] Forty years later, she still talked with great animation about plots and actors, and said she preferred 'plays to all other amusements'.[10] All her children were taken, from the early age of five, to Drury Lane, Covent Garden and other theatres in London and the provinces; she also enjoyed having them dressed up in specially made theatrical costumes, togas, tunics, Harlequin suits, frocks, feathers and tiny swords, as though they were little actors. Their portraits were painted wearing these fancy-dress outfits, and sometimes they put on performances of their own.

Queen Charlotte's life must at times have seemed to her to be largely given over to performance, even though it was the performance of duties that she did not question for a moment. She had been required to give up her native speech and customs, and to conduct most of her activities in the public eye, wearing ceremonial costume; a leading part but a lonely one, as the King told her he did not wish her to have any friends. Apart from theatre-going, her first English months were almost entirely taken up with ceremonies. In the gaps between them she and the King established intimacy as best they could; it was a good thing he could speak German, and both of them knew French. Their coronation took place on 22 September in Westminster Abbey. On 10 October she started to learn English with a tutor. On 9 November there was a state entry into the City of London and a great banquet at the Guildhall, given by the Lord Mayor, with crowds lining the streets and heads looking out of every window. By now the Queen was pregnant. On 2 December she went with the King to the Palace of Westminster where he was to give his royal assent to a bill providing for her support: she was to have £100,000 a year should she outlive him, a palace in London and a lodge in Richmond Park.

Although her English progressed only slowly, and she refused to give up her habit of taking snuff, in all other respects her performance was beyond praise. The following August, 1762, her first child, Prince George, was born. Almost exactly a year later a second son, Frederick, appeared; and two years after that – there was a miscarriage in between – a third Prince, the William of this story, was born, once again in August, at Buckingham House, usually known as the Queen's House, because she preferred its modern airiness to St James's Palace with its maze of old rooms. At this point she was just twenty-one.

The Bland family also continued to grow, although things did not go well for them in other respects. Soon after Dorothy's birth they were back in Dublin. Whatever Grace's family in Wales thought of her career and behaviour, her cousin Blanch offered a haven for her children when they needed one, at Trelethyn, near St David's. Blanch's affection for her young Bland cousins led her to give several of them a home, and in due course to bequeath her farmhouse to two of them, Nathaniel and Hester.[11]

Certainly the young couple had all the appearance of a settled family. Children were born, year after year – one account says there were nine – and Grace sometimes used the name 'Mrs Francis' for her stage appearances. Like other actresses, she was accustomed to working throughout her pregnancies; audiences must have been so used to the pregnant shape that they hardly expected anything else. Maria did not marry, and moved to England to join Tate Wilkinson's company in Yorkshire, but the young Blands stayed in Ireland, and Dorothy often spoke of herself as Irish, although she also said she detested the country, and had not a good word for any of her relatives there.

Actresses often put their children on stage at an early age, and the taste for child performers was well established in Dublin; but there is no record of Mrs Francis doing so, or of Dorothy appearing in public before she was in her teens. Her father was not, after all, a stage manager but a gentleman, as were both her grandfathers. Sometimes she went to stay with her Welsh cousins. We know she was in Wales in 1771, because years later she met a man who remembered how she had chastised him for 'drownding a mouse' when he was five and she was a commanding ten-year-old.[12]

If she and her sisters had little formal schooling, there was nothing unusual about that, and their mother at least 'had received a finished and accomplished education', which gave her something to pass on to her children.[13] Dorothy learnt enough to become a vivid letter-writer and a decent occasional poet; her literacy compares quite favourably with, for example, that of Princess Charlotte, the daughter of the Prince Regent, when she was being educated for the throne forty years later. And one of Dorothy's brothers, Nathaniel Phillips Bland, got an education good enough to go on to Oxford, where he took his BA in 1790.

So she grew among brothers and sisters. We know the names of George, Francis and Nathaniel, and of Hester and Lucy. They had the care of a loving if busy mother and a father who seemed a fixed feature of their world. But when Dorothy was thirteen, in 1774, this fixed feature disappeared.

Thirteen is not a good age to lose your father. Nothing is known of how his behaviour was explained to his children.

What is certain is that he abandoned them and went back to London, where he made a perfectly legal marriage at St Botolph's in Aldgate to an Irish heiress, Catherine Mahoney of Killarney. Soon he had another family, a son and a daughter. He paid out something to his first family, but their situation became increasingly precarious. Grace's stage career had been good but not outstanding, and now that she was no longer young she could not expect to earn much; and she was devastated by the behaviour of the man who had been her husband for so many years, and who now treated her with a contempt and cruelty she had done nothing to deserve. Dorothy wrote later of her mother's 'silent anguish' and 'curb'd resentment', which suggests that she kept her pain to herself as much as she could.[14] To add to her worries, at least one of her daughters, Lucy, was ill. She was sent to Trelethyn to be cared for. The elder children had to turn their hands to work. Dorothy shouldered the role of the good daughter, determined to protect and help her mother. She wrote, much later: 'from my first starting in life, at the early age of fourteen, I have always had a large family to support'.[15] Her first job was not very demanding, but not very interesting either: she became a shop assistant, selling hats for a Dublin milliner. With this, her childhood was over.

Once she was of an age to choose, she became Dora rather than Dorothy. Others referred to her as Dorothy, or Dorothea, but she was Dora to herself; she signed her letters 'Dora', and later had her seals made with 'Dora' – so Dora she will be in these pages from now on. The further complications of her second name are still to come.

How long she worked as a milliner's assistant, and whether she tried her hand at anything else, are things we don't know. Many years later she recalled that she had received a proposal of marriage from a young man called Smith, said to have been very much in love with her, and that his father, a clergyman, considered her far too young to marry. He made no comment about her being an actress, so she was probably still working in the shop; and she does not say what she thought of the proposal, which suggests it meant little enough to her; but after young Smith had died, she took some pleasure in the memory of his proposal, and visited his sisters.[16] Meanwhile her own absent father's new life turned out less well than he had hoped. His health began to break down, and in 1778 he decided to travel to the South of France, the traditional destination for the well-to-do invalid. He got only as far as Dover, and there died; and with his death, the small sums he had sent to Grace and their children dried up completely. Later something was again sent for the children, possibly by Francis's widowed mother, but for the moment things were very bad. In this miserable situation news came from Trelethyn of the death of Dora's younger sister Lucy: she was fourteen. A decade later Dora gave her name to a child of her own, as it happened the kindest and most loyal of all her daughters.

About the time of her father's death Dora left the milliner's shop and made her first appearance on the stage. There is no doubt that Grace had divined her talent and guided the first steps of her career. She did not begin at her mother's old theatre but at the rival one in Crow Street, and she was billed as 'Miss Francis': if her father had done little else for her, he could at least provide her with a stage name. By her own account, when the time came for her to go on for her very first entrance, she fled, terror-struck, through the wings, and had to be caught and pushed on to the stage; but once on, with the blazing candlelight above her and the swarm of faces in front, her courage came back.[17]

Her first appearance was in a farce, traditionally put on after the main play of the evening. She had the lead, as Miss Lucy, in Henry Fielding's *The Virgin Unmasked*, playing a girl who accepts proposals of marriage from a succession of suitors sent in by her rich father, and who at the end sends them all packing with the words, 'By Goles, I will tell you – I hate you!' and announces she has secretly married a handsome footman. One of the earliest engravings of Dora shows her dressed as Miss Lucy and is labelled 'The Comic Muse, by Goles!' Mockery of marriage was the staple fare of stage comedy – marriage as a trap, marriage between incompatible partners, marriage by fortune-hunters – although it may not have seemed so funny considered in the cold light of the Bland household; but the pert, innocent part suited Dora, and she made the Dubliners laugh.

She was never considered a beauty. There was too much nose and chin about her face for that; but she had a charming and expressive face, with great sweetness in her smile and vivacity in the dark eyes under their dark brows: 'sable eyes', one poet called them, suggesting they were black – 'keen' he wrote too, but he was wrong about that. Dora was short-sighted; the world was always slightly blurred for her, and she carried spectacles on a chain.[18] She was neatly made, not tall, with a small waist and what the eighteenth century called a symmetrical shape. Her most striking feature was probably her great mop of brown curls. Fashion dictated that they should be powdered when she was a young actress, so that, rather confusingly, she sometimes appears in paintings and prints as white-haired in her youth, and gets darker as she grows older. Her legs naturally went unnoticed until she appeared in male costume on stage, when they were found to be exceptionally beautiful – the finest ever seen on stage according to one connoisseur – and thereafter in constant demand.[19] She was not vain, but not bashful either. There was altogether something natural, humorous, wholesome about her: she was seductive, not as a fine, elegant woman, but as one who simply made men want to put their arms around her.

The way she would take a friend by the cheek and kiss her, or make up a quarrel with a lover, or coax a guardian into good-humour, or sing (without accompaniment). . ., trusting, as she had a right to do, to the sole effect of her sweet, mellow, and loving voice – the reader will pardon me, but tears of pleasure and regret come into my eyes at the recollection, as if she personified whatsoever was happy at that period of life, and which has gone like herself,

wrote one who cherished her memory.[20]

At this time she also played her first Shakespeare, as Phoebe, the simple-minded shepherdess in *As You Like It.* Thomas Sheridan's daughter Betsy, who must have known the whole family, saw her perform and claims to have predicted that she would one day become 'the first comic actress in England or Ireland...For her chastity of acting, *naïveté*, and *being* the character she represents, young as she is, she surpasses what could have been expected; but mark my words, she will one day or other be a favourite and the first in her line of acting.'[21]

When the Dublin theatres closed for the summer, the companies toured. Dora went to Waterford, where she met a young army lieutenant, Charles Doyne, who fell in love with her. His intentions were honourable, and he was well born and educated, though not rich; and he felt hopeful enough to make a formal offer of marriage. It was her second proposal; but whatever she thought of him, her mother decided he would not do, and 'worked upon her daughter to decline the proposal'.[22] Grace had her own unfortunate marital history to brood on; and she was still in a sense stage-struck, now on her daughter's behalf, and believed in her gift. Why should it be sacrificed to domestic life and perpetual child-bearing? So Doyne was sent packing. He said his heart was broken, but he found another bride, this time with a fortune, which may have helped to mend it.

Miss Francis went back to Dublin and the pursuit of theatrical success. It was not a bad place to make the attempt. Anglo-Irish society revolved round the lord lieutenant, always an English aristocrat – Lord Chesterfield, the Earl of Northumberland, and the Dukes of Rutland, Dorset and Richmond all held the post – and he presided from his Castle in the city centre over a brilliantly fashionable and pleasure-seeking set. Life was very pleasant, if pleasure went with scores of servants, lavish eating and drinking – the men were rarely sober after dinner – gossip and quarrels, picnic parties and private theatricals; and everyone went to the theatre and the opera, to hear music and watch the dancers. As in most aristocratic societies, the great fear was boredom. The rich demand to be amused, and then amused again, and better; they like to be tickled and surprised. There was an appetite for sophisticated entertainment. In this climate the manager of Crow Street, Thomas Ryder, hit on the idea of adapting a comic opera by the young Sheridan, *The Duenna*, and of turning it into an entirely transvestite performance, all the male characters played by women, and vice versa. Miss Francis was cast in a leading part.

She was at once seen – and heard, for she had to sing – to be extraordinary: a perfect girl-boy in her young man's breeches that showed her slim waist and pretty legs. She was not shy, and she was not bawdy; she was easy and natural. Her face was finely expressive, her singing voice untrained, and all the more captivating for it. Either she had learnt her art quickly and without effort, or – as people preferred to think – she had simply been born with the gift for comedy. Her laugh bubbled up 'from the heart', they said; and when she laughed the audience laughed back, helpless and delighted, like a whole house full of lovers, and her charm infused the theatre from pit to upper gallery.

Not surprisingly she caught the attention of a young rival manager, newly appointed to the Smock Alley Theatre. Richard Daly came from Galway, had studied at Trinity College, Dublin, and turned to the stage only when his personal fortune ran out. He regarded himself as a gentleman, and was the perfect type of the Irish buck, tall and elegant, always beautifully 'embroidered, ruffled and curled'.[23] He was also a frequent and ferocious dueller with sword and pistol, and equally enthusiastic and brutal in pursuit of women. His face was strikingly handsome in spite of a terrific squint. This was a positive asset in a duel, his opponent being unable to guess where he intended to strike from the direction of his eyes; and it hindered him no more than it did John Wilkes in his sexual conquests. On stage, though, it may have been disconcerting. He failed in England as an actor, and had to return to Ireland, joining a company in Cork and then moving to the Crow Street Theatre. Here he first met Dora; and here he married a widowed actress in 1780, and turned his thoughts to becoming a manager.

The following year he was established at the Smock Alley. He relished the power his position gave him. 'He was said to be the general *lover* in his theatrical company; . . . the resistance of the fair to a *manager* may be somewhat modified by the danger of offending one, who has the power to appoint them to parts, either striking or otherwise; and who must not be irritated, if he cannot be obliged.'[24] Another account of Daly says he made a habit of advancing money to young actresses and then, when they were unable to repay the loan, suggesting they should make it good in a simpler way. If they were unwilling, he would threaten to have them arrested for debt, or resort to violence. Whatever Dora and her mother knew of his reputation, his professional offer was too good to turn down, and in 1781 she joined his company.

There are various accounts of what happened between them. It may have been what is these days called sexual harassment and in those days had no name at all; or it may have started as outright rape: 'the Irish gentleman of 1782 considered himself beyond [the reach of law]', wrote Dora's friend James Boaden, and added, 'Who would have believed in the virtuous resistance of an actress?'[25] Another reliable witness, Elizabeth Inchbald, who joined Daly's company the following year, reported that he tried to seduce her and, when she refused him, at once dismissed her outright. Mrs Inchbald was not a young girl but a widow, highly intelligent and capable, and a well-established actress; if she could hardly cope with Daly, it is not surprising that Dora, younger and more dependent on his favour, managed less well and suffered worse treatment.[26] He may have entangled her in debt, though it is curious that her careful mother should have allowed this to occur. It is even possible that Dora was fascinated by him, and fell in love: such things can happen, and her subsequent loathing by no means rules it out. He was the king of his court, with the sexual charisma that goes with that power. And whatever he did to her, or whatever passed between them, she did not immediately fly from him and turn her face to the wall, as moralists considered the proper course. She was no Clarissa Harlowe.

We know that his wife was in an advanced state of pregnancy in 1781; her appearance on stage in November indicated that she was about to give birth.[27] We also know that Dora conceived a child by Daly in February 1782, presumably while Mrs Daly was busy at home with her new baby. Dora was now twenty, and had just been allowed to take leading parts opposite John Kemble. In February she was Adelaide to his Count of Narbonne; in April Lady Anne to his Richard III. Kemble was not yet the mighty star he was to become, but he was rising rapidly, helped on his way by the established fame of his sister, Mrs Sarah Siddons. On his tour of Ireland, he noted the 'idleness, drunkenness and dirt' of the Smock Alley, but was glad of the princely £10 a night they paid him. Dora's salary is unlikely to have exceeded a few shillings, on which she had to keep her mother, brothers and sisters. Later, Kemble was to quarrel with her more than once, but finally her sheer perfection in performance won even his resistant heart.

At first she must simply have hoped and prayed to whatever power might be listening that she was not pregnant. Her prayers were not answered, and easy-going as the Smock Alley regime may have been, when Mrs Daly returned to the stage from her confinement, and Miss Francis's pregnancy began to be suspected, her prospects in the company cannot have looked very good. If she hoped for anything from Daly – affection, moral support or financial assistance – it was not forthcoming. In early May she was playing Maria in *The School for Scandal*; but she made her last appearance on 16 May. Her mother was ill. Perhaps it was illness that had distracted the maternal eye, or perhaps the illness was caused by anxiety at the frightful turn of events; now Dora began to feel ill herself. There was nothing her aunt and uncle Usher could do for them. Dora had been the hope of the family, and now they were all sliding into the abyss with her; and the abyss in Dublin was as murky and as deep as you could go.

June was a blank, for Dora a time of shame and terror combined with hatred of the man whose love had proved even less reliable than her father's. If the family cast about for help – from Trelethyn, from the Blands – they got none; but Grace kept a flicker of faith in the future. In July she, Dora, Hester and George packed up their few goods and embarked for Liverpool, on their way to Leeds, where Grace's sister Maria, who now worked for Tate Wilkinson's Yorkshire company, was thought to be.

In Leeds they found no Aunt Phillips, just the news that she was seriously ill in York, and could do nothing for them. They went to an inn and sent a message to Wilkinson. Obligingly he set off to see them, more perhaps for old times' sake than anything else, and at a distinctly unconvivial early hour of the morning. The sight of the little party dismayed him: 'when I first met them at the inn, I cannot say they were so well accoutred, as I could have wished for their sakes or my own'.[28] One look at Dora inclined him to turn down Grace's suggestion that he should give her work. She had no money, no clothes apparently but those she stood up in – good clothes were a first necessity for an actress – and no friends from whom to borrow; England was to her a strange country and, although Tate was too polite to spell this out in his memoirs, she was visibly pregnant, and without any sign of a husband.

This lack was made more troubling by the obvious dependence of the others. And so, early morning as it was,

> the mamma, like other mammas, and in particular *actresses'
> mammas*, talked so fulsomely of her daughter's merits, that I
> was almost disgusted, and very near giving a flat denial to any
> negotiation; knowing the disagreeable weight of a large family,
> which with moderate talents, I feared, even with economy,
> the young lady would not by any means be able to support.

Worse, he could not discern 'the least trait of comic powers in the features or manner of the young lady; indeed quite the reverse, dejected, melancholy, tears in the eyes, and a languor, that without the help of words pleaded wonderfully for assistance'. Wilkinson excused himself for half an hour, and went away to think how best to turn down Grace's embarrassing professional offer of her daughter. But he was a good-hearted man, blessed with the kindness the theatre breeds in its own out of the very precariousness of their lives. He went back to the inn and asked if Dora could manage to speak a few lines.

To his surprise, she refused. She said she wanted a 'fair trial on the boards'. Disconcerted, and perhaps as a final gesture of friendship before leaving, Wilkinson ordered a bottle of Madeira and sat down to talk stage gossip with mother and daughter; after a while he again suggested that Dora should recite something. This time she agreed, and spoke some lines, rather appropriately from *The Fair Penitent*, a tragedy centred on a rape, with a hero called Lothario and a heroine Calista, on which Richardson had drawn for his Lovelace and Clarissa. This was interesting to Wilkinson, and when he heard her voice he felt surprise and delight; at first he kept it to himself, and then he burst out with a compliment. Dora, her natural charm beginning to work, answered that if she pleased *him*, she did not fear an audience.

The situation was transformed. According to Wilkinson's

account, 'we complimented and flattered, and flattered and complimented, till we really found a sudden impulse of regard, and parted that noon with mutual good wishes and assurances'. Dora's own account goes one better. She says Wilkinson asked her whether she went in for tragedy, comedy or opera; to which she answered, her confidence now fully restored, with one word, '*All*.' 'I never saw an elderly gentleman more astonished,' she added, which was a little hard on Wilkinson, who was not yet forty-five.[29]

Between them they wasted no more time. Dora appeared as Calista in *The Fair Penitent* on 11 July 1782; perhaps Wilkinson, like some modern managers, enjoyed matching his actress to a part with which she could identify. No doubt intending to be tactful to her mother, he advertised her as Miss Bland, only to have Grace insist on changing this to Miss Francis on the playbills. She had another suggestion, that Dora should sing a song after the tragedy. Wilkinson thought this an absurd idea, but gave way, and it turned into a triumph; the public and the manager were equally delighted with her song, 'The Greenwood Laddie', delivered in 'a frock and a little mob-cap'.

He offered her a salary of 15s. a week, and a benefit – a performance for which she would drum up support, and get most of the profits – on 5 August. For this the theatre was packed. Wilkinson was now sure enough of her value to insist that she sign an article of agreement tying her to his company.

The next move was to York for the season of the race meetings, always relied on to bring in good audiences. Here Grace and her children were able to visit Maria Phillips, who was clearly dying, some said of drink, possibly of laudanum addiction, perhaps simply of an undiagnosed illness. A sad family reunion took place around her bed. She expressed her faith in her niece's talent in the most positive way possible, by bequeathing her entire stage wardrobe to her. Unfortunately, it turned out that the pawn-shop had already claimed it.

Perhaps Mr Wilkinson obliged here. Aunt Phillips was also prompted, after one look at Dora, to a piece of practical advice. Whatever name she intended to appear under, it should now be prefixed by 'Mrs' rather than 'Miss'.

But 'Mrs' what? Grace had vetoed the use of Bland, for fear it should injure her daughter in the opinion of her father's relations – something that suggests they did take some interest at least in the family. Wilkinson agreed that there were 'obvious and pressing reasons for a change of name', and he later claimed the credit for inventing her new name. He was the son of a clergyman, albeit one who had been threatened with transportation for conducting just the kind of illegal marriages that Dora's parents had made and that had left her name in doubt; and as the son of a clergyman he made a biblical allusion to the passing of the River Jordan, out of slavery and into freedom, comparing it with her escape from Daly across the Irish Sea. 'Why, said I, my dear, you have crossed the water, so I'll call you Jordan.'[30]

Both the joke and the name pleased her, and she became 'Mrs Jordan'. It was not by any means the last name she used, and it was sometimes rudely turned against her; but it was also the one that represented the fame and success that came to her, and it is the one by which she is remembered.

2

The Yorkshire Circuit: 1782–1785

For the next three years, Dora walked round Yorkshire. She was a tough woman, and she needed to be. Travelling was an essential part of the lives of most actors and actresses, and Tate Wilkinson's company made their way annually over a cross-country route of about 150 miles; it was roughly triangular in shape, its three points being York in the north, Sheffield in the south and Hull on the coast. The journeys could be arduous over the high and desolate moors or across the flat, windswept east riding; a few of the men might go on horseback, the company's scenery wagon might take a few of the women with children. Rides might also be begged from farm or even coal carts. The players would cheer one another on as best they could; walking was part of their way of life.[1] Sometimes Wilkinson, travelling ahead in his carriage, would stop and order a meal to be ready for them at an inn. He enjoyed good food and offering it to others; and he presided over the Yorkshire circuit like the kindly head of a large, talented and quarrelsome family. A look at their playbills shows it numbered at least thirty adults plus assorted children: they must have made an impressive sight when they arrived in town, 'the horse and the foot', as Wilkinson said.[2] They included eight married couples in which both partners played regularly, some with children already performing: the Lengs, Dancers, Cumminses, Chalmerses, Powells, Smiths and Kaynes. There was the chief comedian Mr Creswell, the young male lead, George Inchbald, the prompter Earby, the carpenter Bearpark and the treasurer Swalwell. When Dora joined the company all the other adult women were billed as 'Mrs' whether they had a husband or not: it may have been a safety measure of Wilkinson's. He was devoted to his ladies, but disconcerted by their frequent habit of becoming pregnant.

Wilkinson was a short man with a plain face and awkward movements from a crookedly set leg, broken in a fall on stage. He had made his name in the theatre as a superb mimic, the toast of his audiences, but not of the actors and actresses he took off with such sprightly malice. These antics were past, and he was long since settled into being a company manager, with a comfortable Yorkshire wife and a family of five children; one son, John, was already working with him. He had been running the circuit for fifteen years, and although he still acted occasionally – Dora played Emilia to his Othello, for instance – his reputation now rested on being known as the best of all the provincial managers, admired for the efficient running of his company and envied for his undoubted ability to spot a future star. Wilkinson valued this reputation, and enjoyed playing the character he had established for himself: wise, eccentric in his conversation, humorous, gruff and whimsical. He was a busy, worldly, tolerant professional, with the manners of a gentleman, and generally accorded the respect due to one. This is the personality that comes through his memoirs, in which Dora makes many appearances; he was quite obviously fond and proud of her, and defended her against all comers while reserving the right to tease her himself.

She had already discovered that he was kind and uncensorious. He looked his actresses over carefully to see how they would appeal to the public, but these were entirely professional inspections. He was not another Daly. And although he might tease, his control was more velvet than iron. Wilkinson knew everyone in the theatrical world. He travelled about, to Scotland and London and the other provincial circuits, to keep an eye on what they were doing. In turn he attracted the London managers, who came regularly to see his shows, and regularly poached his best players. At Dora's very first appearance in York she was seen by a visiting actor from Drury Lane, William Smith – known as 'Gentleman' Smith on the grounds that he always took Mondays off to go hunting – who was there looking out for talent. Smith liked what he saw so much that he came back to watch every performance she gave during his stay in the north, and Wilkinson realized he had been wise to sign her up securely, or she might have been carried off on the coach to London with Smith when he left.

Another admirer appeared, this one less dangerous to Tate: a very old man with the charmingly old-fashioned name of Cornelius Swan, a critic and Shakespeare scholar, who kept an eye on the theatre in York. He was delighted by Dora and offered to give her some coaching. According to Wilkinson, he visited her in her lodgings when she was ill in bed – this was during her pregnancy – and was admitted to her 'little bed-chamber where, by the side of the bed, with Mrs Bland's old red cloak round his neck, he would sit and instruct his pupil'. The picture is touching, and Swan forecast a great future for her. She was wonderfully quick to pick up his tips, he said, and every bit as good as any of the great stage ladies he remembered from his youth. He did something else for her. When Daly found out where she was, he tried to have her arrested for breaking her engagement with the Smock Alley and failing to repay money she owed him. Mr Swan paid off the money. He said he now regarded her as his adopted child.[3]

Even with this encouragement and help, Dora's first year on the northern circuit was a severe trial of her strength and spirit. However well Wilkinson understood his business and ran his company, conditions were testing, and his actresses needed their good health and energy at least as much as acting skills. It was not only the travelling across unfamiliar country while preparing to give birth. She also had to face jealousy, disapproval and malice.

At the start of Wilkinson's Yorkshire venture his company had often found itself playing in 'theatres' that were nothing more than rooms over the stables attached to an inn; he had changed that by his energy and enthusiasm. He knew how to make friends with high sheriffs, local landowners, mayors and aldermen, and work on their civic pride as well as their desire for entertainment. Since 1770 he had opened the new Theatre Royal in York and, observing that both Leeds and Wakefield were 'opulent and genteel' places surrounded by splendid new villas, built further theatres of his own in both these cities. Doncaster corporation put up a theatre in 1776. Pontefract also had one; so did Beverley, only nine miles from Hull. Dora had the good luck to arrive at the high point of a brief theatrical golden age for Yorkshire. The circuit was carefully planned to coincide with race meetings, assize weeks and markets, when the country gentry and farmers travelled into town and swelled the audiences. Local regiments were also important patrons and, at the lowest social level, the sailors of the Hull whaling fleets could fill the gallery, if not always to the benefit of the rest of the audience below, as food, drink and worse showered down from above.

Wilkinson had a house in York, but it is unlikely that anyone else in the company could afford a settled home. So they lived on the road – players and their children, scene painters, prompter, musicians – carrying everything they needed with them from one lodging to the next. Inns were mostly too expensive for regular use; players found lodgings, as close to the theatre as they could. In Hull we find Dora installed 'at Mr Dunn's, in Myton-gate': rooms over a shop. Perhaps Mrs Dunn obliged with some food, or it was brought in. With luck, the place was clean and not bug-ridden. Once settled in lodgings, there were lines to be copied and learned, costumes to be made or repaired, rehearsals in the mornings and sometimes the afternoons too. The theatre doors opened at four, and performances usually lasted from six until midnight. There would always be a main play and a farce, and often an extra short entertainment, and interludes of dances, songs and recitations: hard work all round. Of comfort and privacy there was little; of rivalry and spite there could be a good deal. The moral support and protection of her mother was very necessary to Dora under these circumstances. She earned the bread, but she depended on Mrs Bland for comfort.

She had the trick of learning her lines fast. Wilkinson speaks of 'her uncommon labour and study for the Theatre', and another friend says she was 'so indefatigable in her application, that she studied a new character and played it between day and day'.[4] Not only played it, but played it better than anyone else. Her immediate success made some of the other actresses suspicious of her, and they decided Wilkinson was favouring her. There was always jealousy about stealing parts; and in the nature of things she was bound to do just that.[5] During her first months with the company Mrs Smith, who was more advanced in pregnancy than Dora, was so worried about losing 'her' part of Fanny in *The Clandestine Marriage* that she insisted on getting up too speedily after the delivery of her child, and taking strenuous outdoor exercise to prepare herself for the eighteen-mile journey from Doncaster to Sheffield, due to take place only eleven days after her confinement. The result was that Mrs Smith did herself an injury, and the very thing she feared came about. Dora played Fanny; but the respectably married ladies of the company decided to use her pregnancy against her, and they agreed upon a campaign intended to drive her out of the company.

Before it could take effect, while they were still in Sheffield, Dora was nearly killed by a piece of heavy stage machinery falling from the roof. It missed her by inches, but she kept her nerve, as she always did on stage; she was equally calm when, years later, her costume caught fire. She also found herself another admirer in Sheffield, in the shape of a local land-owner, Charles Howard, currently MP for Carlisle. He was a man in his thirties, with radical ideas, and greatly interested in the arts; he was also son and heir to the Duke of Norfolk, moved in the highest circles in London, and was friendly with the Prince of Wales. Howard was generous to those whose work he liked, and befriended both Sheridan and Shelley later; and from now on he took a benevolent interest in Dora.

The company left Sheffield at the beginning of November, moving to Hull for the Christmas season. Hull was a prosperous and cheerful city, richer than either Manchester or Liverpool, and one of their most important and reliable bases. Its money came from the whaling industry, which gave employment to the men and huge profits to the shipowners. They spent lavishly on their pleasures, hunting, horse-racing, gambling and entertaining; it was 'as gay a place as could be found out of London. The theatre, balls, great suppers and card parties were the delight of the principal families of the town.'[6] Wilkinson called it 'the Dublin of England' for the liveliness of its society, and the whole company looked forward to its season there; but little of the gaiety appeared to Dora at first, because after the journey from Sheffield she retreated into her lodgings – Mr Dunn's in Myton-Gate, or some similarly modest place – where, in November 1782, round about the time of her twenty-first birthday, she gave birth to her first child; or, as Wilkinson put it tactfully in his memoir, she 'despatched her business'.[7]

She had her mother to help her through the ordeal, and everything went well. The child was a girl: and now, whatever her feelings for Daly, she loved her daughter with a painful, protective love, not least because she could identify so closely with her, as another illegitimate and fatherless daughter. She named her Frances. It was not a family name – unless she was thinking of her father – but it was one of the most popular of the period. Dora always used the affectionate form of Fanny, and she had just been playing a Fanny in *The*

Clandestine Marriage, a girl who was misunderstood and turned out of her home, but finally won through to happiness: perhaps it seemed a good omen. No registration of her birth or baptism has come to light, so whatever second name Fanny was given is lost: Daly? Bland? Phillips? Jordan? At the time it hardly mattered. For nearly five years little Fanny would have no real rival in her mother's love.[8]

While Dora remained indoors with the baby – 'in the straw' was Wilkinson's phrase – her character was being blackened by Mrs Smith and her fellow actresses among the people of Hull, especially the ladies. They found unexpected support from a tide of religious enthusiasm – Methodist and Evangelical – that was advancing across the north of England with great speed and force. Soon, even in merry Hull, it would direct strong disapproval at the theatre; and already, although audiences were still large, they were liable to engage in the pleasure of delivering judgement on erring players from their seats.

Wilkinson decreed that Dora should reappear on the Hull stage on Boxing Day, playing Calista in *The Fair Penitent*. Both choice of play and casting turned out to be a mistake. The story is a shocking one, since it hinges on forbidden sexual pleasures, and until the last scene Calista herself is shown as far from penitent. She has been seduced by Lothario, and fallen in love with him despite his dishonourable behaviour. His description of the seduction makes it clear she was a willing victim; she is torn between anger and love, and they continue to enjoy themselves ('let us melt the present hour in bliss'). He refuses to marry her, and she is desperate to preserve her good name, accusing another character of treating her 'like a common prostitute'. All this was too much for the good people of Hull. A murmur ran through the house: the part of Calista was only too appropriate to what they had been told so assiduously by the good married ladies of the company. 'There was a cold and sarcastic application of the character of the heroine (Calista) to the performer, among the ladies, which chilled the actress,' wrote Wilkinson.[9]

Through the chill Dora played on to the end, when she appeared in black velvet asking for heaven's mercy and stabbed herself. In the wings her infant daughter was certainly waiting to be fed, held in her grandmother's arms. Black velvet discarded, baby comforted, Dora resurrected herself and went back on stage to sing her song 'The Highland Laddie', which could be relied on to bring the house down; instead, she was hissed. It was a frightening moment.

Now Wilkinson showed his strength. He at once came warmly to her support. To her, he made light of the incident: she was not to be discouraged. Better, he set about countering the hostile gossip running through the town by putting out a kinder version of her history. People were asked to observe that, although she had a child and no husband, there was no sign of any lover either. She lived with her mother. She was a victim, not a trollop. Everyone could see that she worked extremely hard and conscientiously. She also had good manners, and was evidently a nice young woman.

A little grudgingly at first, the ladies of Hull decided to forgive her. 'Mrs Jordan uniformly distinguished herself by propriety in her domestic conduct, and the untaxed modesty of her manners; thus rendering herself the more amiable and distinguished by supporting and firmly protecting a breach which had been so lately assaulted and violated' – as one commentator delicately put it.[10] Such was Wilkinson's success and Dora's grit – for she continued to play – that, by her benefit night in the middle of January 1783, she had won over the theatre-going population of Hull. The plot had failed, and although there were further sporadic attempts in the company to upset her and spoil her performance, they were also put down. The company returned to York. Recovered from childbirth, Dora put on boy's clothes again to sing the part of William in a rustic operetta, *Rosina*. With this, she and Tate had the satisfaction of finding the theatre sold out, night after night, as long as she appeared.

She settled into the routine of the circuit. Roads and lodgings grew familiar, and she learnt all the standard repertoire, from Shakespeare, Fletcher, Steele, Dryden and Cibber to the young O'Keefe. No letters from this time survive, and our picture has to come from Wilkinson, from playbills and from what she told her later friend and first biographer, James Boaden. She said nothing to him about the day-to-day detail of her life at this period, either because it all seemed obvious or because she did not want to relive a difficult time. What she did choose to talk of was how much she learnt about her profession from her fellow players, and particularly the women. There was the terrible example of Mrs Baddeley, who came from Drury Lane, where she had been acclaimed by the King and Queen for her beauty and charm, become enormously popular and earned herself a small fortune; on her way to Edinburgh she stopped off to act with the Yorkshire company and, to their dismay, dosed herself so heavily with laudanum before the performance that she could scarcely speak, and the audience decided she was drunk. Not long afterwards her addiction ended both her career and her life; she died at forty, in mental distress and without a penny left of all her earnings.[11] At the opposite end of the scale was the shining example of Wilkinson's earlier favourite, Elizabeth Inchbald, a Norfolk farmer's daughter who began her theatre career by running away to London. She and her husband acted on the Yorkshire circuit, and when he died suddenly she went south; this was two years before Dora's arrival, but the company still spoke of her charm, beauty and wit, which she turned to good use by writing plays of her own. George Inchbald was her stepson; before she left she offered to play Hamlet to his Horatio. Hamlet is a part many actresses covet but few achieve, and this was a typical piece of bravura by a woman who matched Dora in force of character, and was to

36

become her friend and collaborator. For the present their link was George, acting regularly opposite Dora; if she got to play Hamlet too, there is unfortunately no record of it.

As the young male lead George made love to Dora twice a week on stage, and backstage there was gossip that she was fond of him, and even had hopes of marriage; but he was wary of committing himself to a young woman with a child. So he lost the chance to emerge from obscurity, and remains nothing but the actor who had the good luck to work closely with two of the most remarkable women of his time, and failed to make anything of his opportunity.

Patience was not Dora's virtue, and during 1784, her third year on the circuit, she showed she had had enough, and became careless and difficult. There were days when she simply did not bother to give her best performance; then other actors criticized her, reasonably enough, and the public grew less warm. She would say she was ill; Wilkinson had to put pressure on her to sing the songs she had made popular, and sometimes to appear at all. She felt she had served her apprenticeship, and was ready for something different.

Another actress gave her an idea. In the spring of 1785 Wilkinson put on a comedy called *The Country Girl* in York. It was a polite adaptation by Garrick of a rude old Restoration play, Wycherley's *The Country Wife*. An experienced actress, Mrs Brown, took the title role, that of a nineteen-year-old girl who, through very innocence, makes a fool of her guardian. Dora saw the performance and was impressed by Mrs Brown's technique. She went away, studied the text, and thought hard about it; said nothing to anyone, but decided privately that she would make the part her own. This was a crucial moment for her. When she became celebrated, she was always talked of as a natural actress, one who simply appeared, more or less, in her own character; on or off stage, she *was* the country girl, or so people liked to believe. The truth was quite different. She planned her most 'natural' part with the care, foresight and strategy of a general mapping out a

37

campaign that will carry him from a skirmish in the provinces to a triumphant taking of the capital city.

The most formidable actress in the country, Sarah Siddons, came from London on a visit to York and her old friend Wilkinson that August, and while she was there naturally went to see his leading lady perform. Dora was playing one of her popular boy's parts, a soldier in a farce by O'Keefe, but she failed to amuse Mrs Siddons. Her verdict was that Mrs Jordan would do better to remain in the provinces; she was simply not up to London. The remark was made to Wilkinson, but it certainly reached Dora's ears. No doubt he softened it with a reminder that Siddons was notoriously jealous of other actresses, and lacked any glimmer of comic talent herself. Yet her words must have wounded, especially coming from a sister in arms.

Siddons was only six years older than Dora, and knew all about the hardships of their profession. She came from a poor acting family and had worked as a child performer. She had been a lady's maid and when she married, against her family's wishes, her husband turned out to have little talent. So she was the breadwinner, acting through her pregnancies, on one occasion even going into labour on stage. Ten years before, given the chance of a trial season at Drury Lane, she had been rudely rejected by Garrick, and sent back to provincial touring. The Siddons style was noble, statuesque, command-ing, in every way opposed to Dora's; and while Siddons was now at the very top of her profession, her success had been achieved only in the past three years. She had been forced to wait for a summons from Garrick's successor at Drury Lane, Richard Brinsley Sheridan, the son of Mrs Bland's old friend.

Young Sheridan's faith in Siddons was justified, and he now depended on her to bring in the public, but privately he described her as a 'magnificent and appalling creature', adding with his own special brand of cheek that he would as soon think of making love to the Archbishop of Canterbury.

Not that Mrs Siddons would have welcomed Sheridan's advances. She was a strict moralist, and her reputation was such that she had recently been appointed 'Preceptress in English Reading to the Princesses' by the King and Queen, and gave regular readings to their elder daughters, now in their teens. It was an official court appointment. Such a position demanded perfect discretion, and might make her unwilling to show sympathy or approval to less well-behaved female colleagues.[12] However spotless Dora's current behaviour, her history and the existence of her child could not recommend her to the Preceptress; and she would have heard her brother John Kemble's eyewitness account of Dora's troubles with Daly in Dublin. Kemble was also now established at Drury Lane; like his sister, he excelled in tragedy, and much preferred it to any other form of theatre. Dignity was important to them both in their determination to raise the status of the stage, and with it their own status in society; and Dora was an unlikely ally in this ambition of the Kemble clan.

Before Dora had time to brood on Mrs Siddons's opinion of her any further, William Smith also arrived from London. This time he came with a firm offer of £4 a week to abandon the northern circuit for Drury Lane. She took it. Wilkinson may have felt some chagrin, but no surprise. He knew that every ambitious young player felt the draw of the capital like a magnet. However well you did in the provinces, you were still a strolling player; whereas you had only to look at Sarah Siddons to see what success in London could do for you. He gave Dora his blessing.

She gave her last performance with Wilkinson's company on 9 September 1785 at Wakefield, then made her farewells, packed up her precious costumes and books, gathered her family about her and set off south. With her went two-year-old Fanny and Mrs Bland, sister Hester, who made herself useful at the price of a temper, and brother George, hankering after a stage career of his own and ready to believe London might give him the opportunity he had somehow missed so far. According to Wilkinson, Dora did not go in high spirits, but 'with a doubtful heart': she knew it was a gamble. There were two days in the public coach to be endured, dusty, bumping, rattling hours of discomfort and heat punctuated by stop after stop at the inns along the Great North Road; one of those journeys when you ache to arrive, but also dread the moment of delivery into the unknown. At last they were on Highgate Hill, the city in its veil of smoke below. The final two miles took them through fields and brickyards, a farm here, an inn there, a green-edged stream, a scatter of houses, building sites. Then the streets closed round them, and there was din and confusion as the coach approached Holborn; and they were set down.

3

Drury Lane

Hundreds of hopeful young women arrived in London every week all through the eighteenth century, but most of them came alone. Hardly any can have brought with them a burden anything like Dora's, at twenty-three head of a family of three generations, and responsible for its provision and welfare. London was for the hopeful and ambitious; there was no safety net for failures. To succeed she had to prove herself as an actress in front of her new colleagues, the best in the profession, and before London audiences, far more demanding than any she had yet faced, and not given to making allowances for newcomers. She must learn her way about town, master its customs and manners, and, whatever she felt inside, put on a show of confidence.

To begin with, lodgings had to be found. Mrs Bland may have recalled that Thomas Sheridan lived in Henrietta Street in Covent Garden at the time of Dora's birth, and the memory served. They were able to rent rooms at No. 8, Henrietta Street; the house is still standing, one of a handsome four-storeyed terrace, with a broad door and windows, a fine staircase, barley-sugar banisters and wood-panelled rooms.[1] At the back they looked out over yards to Maiden Lane; the front faced towards Inigo Jones's barn-shaped church, St Paul's, Covent Garden, with a glimpse of the pink columns of Lord Orford's mansion beyond. Just along the street was Covent Garden Piazza, a clutter of market stalls and sheds in the centre, hotels, coffee-houses, bath-houses and taverns in the arcades; and a step further away, Drury Lane theatre. The area was naturally popular with players. Kitty Clive, one of Drury Lane's chief comic actresses for forty years, had lived in Henrietta Street; Charles Macklin, the Irish actor and playwright, now in his eighties, was the founder of the Piazza Coffee House, and Garrick himself had owned a house in Southampton Street, just round the corner.*

But the London Mrs Bland remembered from the 1760s had taken on a new look. Prosperity and civic pride had turned up the lighting: at dusk, elegant double-branched oil lamps were lit along the streets, so bright that strangers thought they must be celebrating some special event. But no, they were for the ordinary citizens going about their business: the shops were open from seven in the morning until ten at night. The old mud streets were now paved and cleaned, there were sewers beneath, and the first piped water. A third bridge crossed the Thames at Blackfriars, where families could take the air and admire the view on a fine Sunday; there was an embankment on the river where the Adelphi terraces stood, and near by, on the Strand, was Somerset House, also newly built, a civic palace intended as a home for a whole collection of official and academic bodies, from the Royal Academy to the Navy Office. To the west, squares and streets were being laid out and houses raised as fast as

---

* Kitty Clive, born in 1711, was still alive when Dora arrived in London, but no longer in Henrietta Street. She moved on her retirement in 1769 to a house on Strawberry Hill offered to her by Horace Walpole who, like Dr Johnson, was a close friend. She had been briefly married to a lawyer, but separated from him and lived with her brother. Generous and modest, she was a leading actress at Drury Lane from 1728, and excelled in what was called 'low comedy'; she also wrote several farces. She died in December 1785, three months after Dora's first appearance at her old theatre. Macklin founded the Coffee House in the 1750s, and left it when he became bankrupt. An Irish actor and playwright, he was best known for his performance as Shylock, for his comedy, *The Man of the World*, and for his violent temper.

builders could get the work done: Bedford and Portman Squares, and Portland Place, opening on to the fields of Marylebone. Money, and the confidence of money, was the message of all this paving, lighting, bridging, sewerage, brick and stucco. The same message came from Hyde Park, where London's richest and most powerful men, extravagantly and exquisitely dressed, paraded with their ladies, in their carriages or on horseback. They may have been 'taking the dust' as Dora's witty new employer, young Sheridan, put it; but they were taking it in the most expensive and elegant fashion possible.

Behind this splendid frontage there were also warrens of slums unblessed by paving, sewers or lighting; and their most wretched inhabitants were notoriously the Irish, the most despised of the immigrant groups. Some had begged their way to London, some came as seasonal visitors; they did the heaviest and dirtiest work, squashed into dirty rooms that they shared by ancient tradition with the pigs they kept for food. What they earned they spent on drink. They fought constantly among themselves, and set their children to thieve and beg. This at any rate was their reputation, and even the charitable were inclined to see them as a lower form of humanity; though they were undoubtedly useful, and the more amenable ones were given better jobs, as cooks, maids or footmen. To more aspiring Irish immigrants they offered a particularly depressing and disquieting spectacle. Dora voiced her dislike of all things Irish more than once, and it may not have been only her memories of Dublin that fuelled this feeling. The London Irish were tangible evidence of that fearful abyss into which you could fall if you had no money, and no one to protect you. People still died of starvation in London, and especially women.

For the moment, young Mrs Jordan had enough with her £4 a week to keep her family in a satisfactory way. Rent would be at most 8s.* A joint of beef cost 2s., a pair of shoes 5, a good beaver great coat 25; a washerwoman worked for twenty-four hours, getting through several weeks' worth of the family's laundry, for half a crown – 2s. 6d. Mrs Bland could be comfortable, Hester would have nothing to complain of; George might smarten himself up, and Fanny could be spoilt. She could be shown all the splendours, from St Paul's to Westminster Abbey, St James's Park and Palace, the Mansion House and the Monument; she could enjoy boat trips on the Thames to Greenwich or Richmond, and go on a Sunday to a tea garden in the fields at 'New Tunbridge Wells' (Sadler's Wells), Gray's Inn Lane or Kentish Town. She might also be taken, under most careful supervision from her grandmother or aunt, to the theatre, to visit her mother's dressing room and the dark, cavernous mysteries of backstage Drury Lane, where children hardly older than her were already employed: the son of the ballet master, Giuseppe Grimaldi, had been performing since the age of two and a half. But there was no question of Fanny working. She was not being reared for the stage.

The back of the theatre was the usual maze of stairs and dim passages, some sloping to take wheels and animals, with wooden planks nailed across to stop them slipping. There was a general ladies' dressing room, with a candle and a mirror assigned to each person, chalk marks on the floor to divide the space, and babies being tended while their mothers were on stage; Dora was used to all this, only now, as a principal player, she had her own room, to which her maid would

---

* Compare Boswell, who as a young gentleman about town had an allowance of £25 a quarter in the 1760s; Dora's initial London earnings were twice that at £200 a year. Even deducting money from weeks when the theatre was closed – say twelve weeks – her earnings equalled those of a shopkeeper, a farmer, or a minor clergyman. Jane Austen writes of a country living being worth £140 a year, which she thought not much to marry on, but still possible. Note too that Francis Place's brother-in-law earned £4 a week as a chair-carver in 1788, but never saved a penny, drinking it all away as soon as he earned it.

carry her costumes in a large milliner's basket. The hairdresser also came to her there. The only make-up consisted of powder of different colours, into which liquids could be mixed; you might rouge, or white yourself, not much more. At rehearsal time the prompter would be sitting with his books in the wings near the stage box; carpenters and scene painters, in their blouses and forage caps, moved about taking instructions, actors stood gossiping and going through their cues. Rehearsals were done with hardly any lights. One morning a friend of the proprietor, coming backstage to arrange for a box the next evening, settled down in the dark to watch, and found himself sitting in a pot of paint: it was Charles James Fox, a politician with a passion for the theatre; he 'damnd the Prompter and disappeared'.[2] During performances the stage lighting came from chandeliers in the wings – Garrick had moved them from their traditional place above the stage – and from oil lamps set along the edge of the stage, another of his innovations. No manager had yet turned down the house lights during the performance, because everyone knew that people came to see each other as well as the play.

Reputations might be made or broken on the stage of Drury Lane, but its significance was far greater than the success or failure of any particular performance. The oldest and largest theatre in the country, it had become an institution that gathered in many different strands of the life of the nation, and wove them together with a power shared only by its sister, the Theatre Royal, Covent Garden. Physically, the Drury Lane seen by the public was always magnificent, as befitted its status; 'the gay, gilded theatre' Boswell called it in the 1760s, when he was ready to sit on a bench in the pit, packed from four in the afternoon until curtain-up at half past six, to make sure of seeing Garrick's *Lear*. In the 1770s the building was remodelled for Garrick by the Adam brothers, with a sober, classical façade; inside was a great airy space, gold and white walls and a geometrically patterned ceiling. Three tiers of boxes ran along each side, three of benches along the back, and there were slender pillars inlaid with glass over crimson and green paintwork. The stage, edged with spikes as well as floats, extended forward in an apron, the stage boxes beside it, lined with crimson-spotted paper. Above the proscenium was a painted head of Shakespeare, with the Muses of Comedy and Tragedy – Thalia and Melpomene – on either side. Two thousand could crowd in, and often did. No other theatre in the world was so big, so splendid, so conscious of a long and great tradition. Since 1780, when the Gordon rioters had damaged the building, it even boasted its own company of Guards, posted outside every evening to protect the precious national institution.

The names of Dryden and Garrick – the former resident playwright and first poet laureate, the latter joint manager and leading actor from 1746 for thirty years – suggest Drury Lane's particular combination of intellectual eminence and popular appeal. Historically, the company was closely associated with the sovereign; from 1660, when Charles II welcomed the revival of the theatre, its leading actors were sworn servants of the crown, some of whom were appointed Grooms of the Chamber, and supplied with scarlet and crimson livery that proclaimed them 'His Majesty's Servants'; and they had to sign themselves into the theatre books by order of the Lord Chamberlain.[3] More important still than this formal link was the continued enthusiasm of the King and Queen, so firmly established at the time of their marriage, maintaining itself over the decades into their middle age, and shared with the Princes and Princesses: the Prince of Wales was now twenty-three, and there were twelve younger ones.

Drury Lane was one of the chief places in which the different classes of society came together to share an experience: royalty, the aristocracy of both sexes, the squirearchy and Members of Parliament, professionals and intellectuals, City merchants and their wives and children, provincial visitors, undergraduates on vacation from Oxford and Cambridge, young men about town, soldiers and sailors on leave, whores both expensive and cheap, and the rest of the poor right down to the apprentices and other common Londoners. Everyone felt they had a stake in Drury Lane: it was in reality what we hopefully call our great building on London's South Bank today, both a royal and a national theatre.

Its surroundings mirrored the social mixture inside. A century earlier it had stood amid the mansions of the aristocracy; then London gave one of its heaves and the rich all moved westwards, leaving their houses and courtyards to dwindle into disreputable warrens, gambling and drinking dens. People complained that the whole district had become dirty, immoral and unsafe; but no one stayed away from the play on that account.

It also served as a cosmopolitan centre and provided a link with the continent. Plays and operas moved about freely, and so did players and musicians: many of the works put on were translations, many of its singers and dancers came from or journeyed to Paris, Vienna, Venice, Naples and even St Petersburg. Mrs Garrick was a Viennese-born dancer. Marie-Thérèse De Camp, the daughter of a Frenchman, born in Vienna, brought to England as a child performer, remained to become a leading actress at Drury Lane, write plays in her adopted language, and marry a Kemble. Michael Kelly, who composed, borrowed and arranged much of the music at the theatre, was born in Dublin, trained in Naples, Palermo and Florence, and worked in Austria with Mozart. Sheridan's other close musical associates, with whom he shared a house at one time, were Stephen Storace and his sister Nancy, and they were also Mozart's friends; she was his first Susanna in *The Marriage of Figaro* in Vienna. Next to aristocrats, theatre people were the great travellers of the age; and until the war that began in 1792, isolating Britain for over two decades, Drury Lane was part of a common European culture.

British aristocrats had always behaved as though they owned the theatre, but Garrick, Thomas Sheridan and other determined proprietors beat down their pretensions firmly. They were no longer allowed on stage, and at Drury Lane visits to the green room – the actors' common room – could not be made merely at whim; special passes had to be agreed and provided by the management. And although the social standing of actors remained uncertain, Garrick raised himself to a point where no one condescended to him. As he grew older his company was sought by dukes and earls, and when he died they were pallbearers at his funeral.

Actresses might also conquer the aristocracy, but they always presented more of a problem. Because they were thrilling to look at, and provoked speculation about the nature of the real woman, mysteriously concealed inside the role and the costume, they became a focus for doubts about the morality of the theatre. People agreed that it was a place of enjoyment, entertainment and relaxation, but worried in case it slid too far in that direction. So there were periodic outcries against its immorality, the improper jokes, the actresses who appeared on stage unnaturally and provocatively dressed as men, showing their legs, and against drunken behaviour and the presence of prostitutes in the audience. As part of the anti-vice campaign, Garrick rewrote the bawdy Restoration plays, removing the coarsest (and the best) jokes. He also gave up his mistress, the greatest actress of the mid-century, Peg Woffington, and settled down as a sober and faithful husband, on the model of the King. The Theatre Royal justified itself as a place dedicated to moral and cultural uplift, with a great tradition of national pride and high thinking. Yet without its Peg Woffingtons it would have been a poorer place; and she continued with her career after she and Garrick parted, and went on living as she pleased. Art and public morality do not always face in the same direction. But when the sixteen-year-old Prince of Wales plucked a mistress, Mary Robinson, from Drury Lane – in 1778, after Garrick's day – the public was as put out as the King, and her career remained blighted even after the Prince dropped her.

Garrick had kept the balance pretty well; under his rule, which lasted until 1776, Drury Lane flourished as the meeting place of the rich, the well-born, the beautiful and the clever.

Dr Johnson brought his only tragedy to be performed there, and earned more from it than from anything else he had written. For the first night he even kitted himself up in the scarlet and gold livery; then he took a taste for sitting in the green room and talking to the actors, and although he too announced himself disturbed by 'the white bosoms and silk stockings' of the actresses, he kept an interest in the profession. In his old age he was a friend of another great actress, Mrs Abington, as well as John Kemble, whom he questioned curiously about acting. Did Kemble ever feel himself actually *transformed* into the character he played? No, answered Kemble, he was always conscious of his craft; and Johnson approved. He also hailed young Sheridan as the author of the two best comedies of the day, *The Rivals* and *The School for Scandal*, before Garrick passed on the proprietorship to him.

It was Sheridan's theatre to which Dora was summoned. In his hands Drury Lane looked set to shine with more brilliance than ever; since he was a playwright, the son of an actor-manager, with a father-in-law who was a renowned musician to take over the musical directing, and a wife of rare gifts, prepared to read texts, do the theatre accounts, interview singers and advise on productions. He was as clever as anyone of his generation, and possessed of a charm few could resist. Garrick retired a wealthy man to his Thames-side house at Hampton; there seemed no reason why Sheridan should not make his fortune too. Yet, unlike Garrick, he was always ambivalent about the theatre's role and status, and his own situation within it.

He had a particular difficulty with actresses. A year before taking over from Garrick, he wrote what must be the most hostile private account ever penned on the subject. It was in a letter intended to prevent his sister-in-law Mary from accepting an offer of work from Garrick, whom he accused of being a liar and corrupter of innocence. He said Mary would be forced to play the Coquet, the Wanton, to retail loose innuendoes in Comedy, or glow with warm Descriptions in Tragedy; and in both to be haul'd about, squeez'd and kiss'd by beastly pimping Actors! ... everything around them is unchaste – their Studies are Lessons of Vice and Passion. – Like Wretches who work in unwholesome Mines, Their senses are corrupted in the operation of their Trade.[4]

Sheridan himself was never averse to illicit squeezing and kissing; it was the idea of it happening in the theatre to a woman in his own family that he disliked so much. He claimed that he himself 'had always an Instinctive Abhorrence' to the theatre as 'the greatest Nursery of Vice and Misery on the Face of the Earth'; said he was convinced that most actresses were unhappy in their work, and that none could hope to marry decent men. It is an altogether extraordinary diatribe to come from a man who went on to make his living in the theatre, even in a private letter. They were not views he could ever make public; and it was as well that Dora could have known nothing of them when she arrived to work for him.

She was asked to make her first appearance in a revival of *Philaster*, an old and sentimental play by Beaumont and Fletcher, her part that of a page who turns out to be a girl in disguise, behaves nobly, and loses her lover. It was announced in the press, with a puff explaining that Mrs Jordan was not a novice. Then she suggested her own, better idea. The fact that she had never faced a London audience in her life, while the manager and his men were all experienced, and trained by Garrick, did not deter her. She was determined to choose her own vehicle. She asked to appear in the play she had been preparing privately, *The Country Girl*: which, while it was Garrick's own adaptation, had flopped badly when he put it on fifteen years earlier, and not been played in London since. Some of the company had actually played in Garrick's production and seen it fail. Still, she insisted.

In rehearsal they began to think she might be right. The company talked together: 'I think she *is* clever. – One thing I can tell you, she is like nothing you have been used to. Her laugh is good! but then she is, or seems to be very nervous. We shall see.'⁵ Good-naturedly, they surrounded her with as solid a comic cast as could be found in the country. Almost all of them were old enough to be her parents. Tom King, who led the cast, had known Mrs Bland in Dublin in the 1750s; James Dodd, the fop, had been a crony of Tate Wilkinson for years. John Palmer and Mrs Wrighten were old troupers too; and among all these theatrical uncles and aunts, even the one player of her own age, her leading man, John Bannister, had been trained by Garrick.

The opening was set for Tuesday, 18 October 1785. The theatre was not full by any means, but the audience included Sheridan's sister-in-law, Mary Tickell, the same Mary to whom Garrick had offered a job, provoking Sheridan's furious outburst; and the next morning she sat down and wrote a vivid appreciation of what she had seen and heard to her sister Elizabeth Sheridan, who was away in the country:

> I went last night to see our new Country Girl and I can assure you ... she has more genius in her little finger than Miss Brunton in her whole body.⁶ ... little she is and yet not insignificant in her figure, which, though *short*, has a certain roundness and *embonpoint* which is very graceful. Her voice is harmony itself ... and it has certain little breaks and undescribable [*sic*] tones which in simple archness have a wonderful effect, and I think (without exception even of Mrs Siddons) she has the most *distinct* delivery of any actor or actress I ever heard. Her face I could not see, owing to the amazing bunch of hair she had pulled over her forehead, but they tell me it is expressive, but not very pretty; her figure is such as I have described, and uncommonly pretty in boy's clothes, which she goes into in the 3rd act. Her action is *odd*; I think there is something foreign in it, at least it is a little *outré*, which

however was probably affected for the character – for nothing could suit it better. Tickell was in raptures, and, indeed, I think Sheridan would be almost tempted to give us the poor *Forresters* if he saw what a pretty boy Mrs Jordan makes.[7]

The bunch of hair over her face, the little breaks in her speech, the superb delivery with something foreign in her action – Mary Tickell's letter does conjure up a real person and performance. There was no doubt of Dora's success. Everyone in the theatre responded to her and, while the farce that followed filled it with music and laughter, the best of the night's gaiety had been hers. She went home knowing she had sailed over the first hurdle. The newspapers had their say, favourable on the whole, if rather grudging, but it was word of mouth that brought in the audiences.* Her second appearance, on 21 October, already showed its effects; at the third, a week later, the Prince of Wales was in his box, with his uncle the Duke of Cumberland. Lord North, the former Prime Minister, was also there, and was observed to laugh. By now one would expect Sheridan to have seen his own leading lady, but it is not at all certain that he had. His attendance was erratic, and he was distracted both by his friend the Prince of Wales and political business; for Sheridan was also a Member of Parliament. So it was Tom King, acting as his manager, who announced that she would play Viola in *Twelfth Night* next.

The first performance, on 11 November, was as successful

---

* Among press comments were that she was not a beauty, more agreeable than handsome, though intelligent-looking; that she was rather short, but with a neat and elegant figure; that her voice was not particularly sweet, but strong and clear; and that she had vivacity and self-possession. She was said to be 'a most valuable acquisition to the public stock of innocent entertainment'; and another critic wrote, 'Upon the whole, we congratulate the public on such a valuable acquisition, that will greatly contribute to the support of the comic muse, and give an importance to the dramatic exertions of Old Drury.'

as *The Country Girl*, although Mary Tickell had a few reserva-
tions this time:

> Now for Mrs Jordan. I dare say I am wrong in my opinion, as
> everybody else likes her very much indeed, but I own I do not
> *entirely* approve of her Viola; to me she was too precise in her
> manner of delivery, too like tragedy, and, by-the-bye, she (I
> am sure) would make a sweet tragedian, for her voice in the
> pathetic is musical and soft, and she has the Siddons' 'Oh!' in
> perfection . . . You can't conceive how she was applauded,
> and really deserved it.[8]

The Prince of Wales came twice to *Twelfth Night* and spoke
publicly of his pleasure.

Mary Tickell continued to monitor Mrs Jordan's progress,
and to report to Elizabeth Sheridan. On 21 November,
having seen her again, she gave the last of her critiques:

> Well, ma'am, all I can say, now that I *have* seen her [as Imogen in
> *Cymbeline* and Priscilla Tomboy in *The Romp*] is that I think her
> by much the best comedian on either stage, or that I ever saw, the
> Imogen was but la la, that is, by way of anything great . . . the
> *Romp*, however, made amends for all, and very great applause
> indeed she very deservedly received . . . The Papers did not
> praise her half enough. I saw Mrs Siddons after the play . . . She
> had been in Dr Ford's box and was delighted with Mrs Jordan.[9]

So Mrs Siddons was honest, and generous, enough to change
her mind, and to one of the theatre's proprietors: the Dr Ford
who entertained her shared the ownership of Drury Lane
with Sheridan and his father-in-law, Thomas Linley. The
Doctor's investment in the theatre was large, but his interest
was that of an enthusiastic amateur; he worked as an obstetrician at the Middlesex Hospital. He had become so successful
and eminent that the Queen invited him to deliver her last
child, Princess Amelia, in 1783, and he may have been
preparing to do the same for Mrs Siddons, who had only a
month to go before the birth of her next child.[10]

Dora was happily free from any anxieties of this kind. It was just as well; she was working so hard she scarcely had time to appreciate her own fame, as it spiralled and grew from day to day. Already, at the stage door, small crowds gathered to watch her arriving for rehearsals; she could not go on foot any longer, but had to hire a coach. Her picture began to appear in prints and magazines: at the start of December there was one showing her as the Romp, and a few weeks later the *Lady's Magazine* published an engraving of her as the Country Girl. When the death of Kitty Clive was announced on 6 December, Horace Walpole was prompted to write a poem lamenting that the comic muse was now dead; he was swiftly answered by Peter Pindar, the best known of the satirical poets, who pointed out that, on the contrary, she was alive and well, and appearing at Drury Lane.

For several months Dora had hardly more than a single day off in the week, and often she was in both play and farce on the same night; in this whirl Fanny's third birthday and her twenty-fourth passed. On 16 December the management triumvirate, Sheridan, Linley and Dr Ford, showed their delight in their astonishing acquisition by signing a new four-year contract with her. They did not forget to write in the usual penalties – no pay if she was sick, forfeits if she failed to come to rehearsals or performances as required, £105 to be paid in before each benefit – but they doubled her salary on the spot and promised her a benefit each season.

In the new year (1786) she played Miss Hoyden in Sheridan's *A Trip to Scarborough*, acting for the first time alongside the elegant Elizabeth Farren, an established star.*

---

* Elizabeth Farren was about the same age as Dora, the daughter of an Irish surgeon turned player, who died young, leaving his family penniless. She worked as a child actress, often carrying the drum ahead of her group of strolling players. She was courted by Fox and by a fellow actor, John Palmer, but rejected them both, and won the love of the Earl of Derby. He was unhappily married; she refused to become his mistress, and when Dora met her he had been devoted to her for eight years. She moved in aristocratic circles, and was extremely sensitive about her early life.

Sheridan's sister Betsy, and his wife too, came to see her in this. The King also came. After this even Mrs Montague, learned, dignified and a little remote from the world, took notice of her in a letter, saying society was divided between Mrs Siddons's admirers and Mrs Jordan's, and that 'all who have much frequented the theatre, speak of Mrs Jordan as the best actress in parts of humour that ever was seen on any stage'.[11]

All through January, February and March, with the energy Wilkinson had admired so much keeping her at full blaze, she took on new parts and brought out ones she had played in the north to dazzle London. One more woman, Elizabeth Inchbald, summed up the achievement of Dora's first season in London like this:

> She came to town with no report in her favour to elevate her above a very moderate salary, or to attract more than a very moderate house when she appeared. But here moderation stopped. She at once displayed such consummate art with such bewitching nature, such excellent sense, and such innocent simplicity, that her auditors were boundless in their plaudits, and so warm in their praises when they left the theatre, that their friends at home would not give credit to the extent of their eulogiums.[12]

So, one after another, the disbelieving friends came to see her and went away converted. For her first benefit at the end of April she earned over £200. These were riches such as neither she nor her mother had ever known; and there was more to come. The members of Brooks's – the Whig club in St James's, to which Sheridan belonged, and Fox, and the Prince of Wales, and many more rich, fashionable lords and aspiring politicians who liked to get drunk and gamble and gossip in fine rooms away from home – made a pretty gesture and presented her with a purse containing £300.[13] The rich paid generously when they were amused, and she amused them. London's money was flowing towards her in a deep, glittering, almost miraculous stream.

4

Proprietor and Prince

When Dora signed her new contract with her three employers, Sheridan, Linley and Ford, on 16 December, she may have expected some friendly gossip with Sheridan, as the principal proprietor, the youngest, and the son of her mother's old friend and Dublin manager, Thomas Sheridan. Some compliments on her performances were in order, even perhaps a hint of the play he might write for her; but it is unlikely she got much talk of this kind. He must have been aware of the chorus of praise that had greeted her and heard the glowing accounts from his own family; but he himself hardly ever sat through a complete performance of a play – he said so quite openly – and his attitude towards actresses, if not so fixed in disapproval as it had been ten years before, remained cautious. When he did occasionally appear in the green room, his presence was felt to cast something of a cloud; on one such visit Miss De Camp told him to his face that he made them all uncomfortable.[1] He was also on bad terms with his father, who was known as 'old Surly Boots' in the family; Richard, unlike Thomas, disdained to act himself and took no responsibility for the day-to-day management of his company. When Dora joined Drury Lane, its affairs were of very much less interest to Sheridan than his parliamentary career. He needed the income from the theatre, but relied on a series of managers to do most of the work; it was an unsatisfactory state of affairs for everyone concerned.

Neither Dora nor anyone else would ever find Sheridan

easy to know; he was too complex and various. Yet they were to work together at Drury Lane for the next quarter of a century, their lives running strikingly parallel outside the theatre as well as in. Each was a brilliant performer, she on stage, he both in Parliament and in society; and both dazzled the watching world by taking risks, as good performers do. They were not such different creatures as he liked to think, and must at times have recognized their kinship. Their Irish background gave them a first point in common; both disliked it, but it was inescapable. His Dublin experiences were less catastrophic and painful than hers, but he had some grim years to remember when, still a small child, he was left behind in Ireland with only the servants to care for him, while his parents stayed away in England – leaving a first scar on his sensitive skin. Then, although there was nothing to be ashamed of in his family origins – scholars and writers on both sides, and his father's work in the theatre more than honourable – he felt them as a profound humiliation. This sense of shame was learnt partly at Harrow, among the boys who could take money and privilege for granted. Sheridan suffered when his school fees went unpaid, as often happened, and when he was not provided with the proper clothes. Clever as he was, he found himself slighted by the masters and tormented by the boys as a 'poor player's son'. Such was the English educational system; and when he was fifteen, still struggling through its cruelties, he took another blow when his mother died, far away in France.

Again like Dora, Sheridan put aside his griefs and relied on his skills, his wit, his charm, his toughness, to make the world do his bidding; and he rose with unprecedented speed and grace through the layers of English society. He was proud, and believed in his own power to succeed; as a young man, he wrote his own proclamation of the virtues of meritocracy:

I shall one of these days learnedly confute the idea that God could ever have intended individuals to fill up any particular

57

stations in which accidents of birth or fortune may have flung
them ... As God very often pleases to let down great folks
from the elevated stations which they might claim as their
birthright, there can be no reason for us to suppose that He
does not mean the others to ascend.[2]

So, without a penny behind him, he ascended.

After Harrow he studied law for long enough to qualify as
a barrister. He was quickly recognized as a prodigy. At
twenty-five, just a year after writing the letter abusing Garrick
for his bad faith, Garrick chose him as his successor. Sheridan
took on Drury Lane and, still in his twenties, his plays made
him famous all over the country; no one had written comedy
like him for a hundred years. Then he met Fox, his equal in
brilliance, charm and eloquence and a good deal more
fortunate in his circumstances. Fox, born to riches and privilege, and possessed of complete social confidence, loved the
theatre, and had none of Sheridan's anxiety about actresses;
he pursued several, then lived with and finally married an
even lowlier woman, a theatre dresser. Despite this difference
in their sexual tastes, the two men were instantly drawn to
one another, each seeing something to envy in the other: Fox
loved Sheridan's wit and his power at Drury Lane, and
Sheridan saw that Fox could carry him into the world of
politics. By 1780 Sheridan was in Parliament, and in the
same year he was elected to Brooks's Club: of the two, the
club was possibly the more difficult to enter, for getting into
Parliament depended mostly on bribes, but Brooks's on
overcoming the snobbery and prejudice of its existing
members. It became one of the centres of his life; you could
run up your credit indefinitely with Mr Brooks, and stay all
night drinking and playing whist with men who were
splendidly careless about lesser things but passionate for
politics. Within two years Sheridan was under-secretary for
foreign affairs, then secretary to the Treasury.

But there were no more plays from his pen, only fragments,
translations and unfulfilled projects. This was a tragedy for

him, for his players, and also for the English theatre. Good plays last better than even the most splendid parliamentary oratory. A Sheridan devoted to turning out serious comedies – an English Beaumarchais, a more intelligent O'Keefe, an early version of Granville-Barker – might have changed the dismal face of the nineteenth-century theatre in Britain. He had the benefit of an outstanding team of actors and actresses to work with, but they found themselves obliged to appear in a mixture of revivals and indifferent new stuff. It meant that the theatre depended heavily on its virtuoso performers – among them Dora – to attract audiences; they were perpetually redeeming thin farces and sentimental rubbish, and appearing in revivals. In due course Dora did perform both Sheridan's Lady Teazle and his Lydia, but he never gave her a good play of her own, as he should have done.

None of this was yet clear in 1785; on the contrary, it seemed there was still everything to hope for. Sheridan planned to finish his *Foresters* at last (he never did) and write more, if only because he needed money to maintain his way of life. The plays he had already written had earned enough to make him rich, but the income slipped somehow through his fingers. He rented too many houses, entertained too many friends, took too many hackney cabs, drank too much claret, spent too much at his club: all absolute necessities in the world he chose to inhabit.

Whatever Dora expected of him, he would clearly not be another Tate Wilkinson: not an uncle, or a brother, with a ready shoulder to lean on. Measuring him up with a shrewd eye, she saw that she would have to forge her way in the company without favour or special support. She quickly learnt to be tough in her financial dealings with him; at Drury Lane, players who were not tended to go unpaid. None of this prevented her from expressing admiration for his genius, and affection too.[3]

Mrs Sheridan certainly saw the value of Mrs Jordan and

59

insisted on it to her husband. She too had been brought up as a professional performer – a singer – by her father, Thomas Linley; and she too had committed an early indiscretion, not so serious as Dora's but damaging enough. At sixteen she had allowed Sheridan to persuade her to elope with him to France. They were separated by their angry parents, and Sheridan fought two duels on her behalf; they were not allowed to marry for another three years, and some of the shine may have gone from their early love by then. Elizabeth was beautiful – as can be seen from her portraits – and elegant, good and clever. Her background was exceedingly modest; the Linleys were all working musicians, and her grandfather was a carpenter; and she had the same impulse as Sheridan to escape into a grander, more spacious world. The fame of her beauty and the beauty of her singing voice were such that Garrick had tried to persuade her as well as her sister to join his company as an actress; but whether from her own instinct, or tutored by Sheridan, she felt public performance as a degradation. Indeed, she soon became unwilling even to continue as a professional singer in oratorio, for which her father had trained her.

Elizabeth Linley's last public performance before her wedding was made before the royal family at Buckingham House. The King was enchanted by her and presented her father – not her – with £100, a telling transaction: she was the chief breadwinner for the family. Once married, Sheridan supported her in her wish to give up her profession altogether. Instead she helped him with his work, in the theatre and sometimes with the drafting of parliamentary speeches. They had one son; her frail health was a problem – there was tuberculosis in the family – and her father warned her husband, 'You must absolutely keep from her, for every time you touch her, you drive a Nail in her Coffin.' It was a hard admonition.

The young Sheridans started their married life in a gently Bohemian way, sharing a Soho lodging with the musicians

Stephen and Nancy Storace, who were on the point of departing abroad to Italy to continue their music studies, then to Vienna, where they worked with Mozart. When you consider the Sheridans and their story, it is most often a Mozart comic opera that comes to mind, with its bright promising surface, the jokes, the fancy dress, the breaking of class barriers, the sentimental protestations; and then the cruel underside of jealousy, the games of power and adultery – on which the Sheridans too embarked. Long before Dora knew them their life had lost its simplicity and become a sophisticated, almost feverish progress, unsettled and extravagant. Elizabeth attempted to keep some order and calm, but he always had too many ambitions, too many desires, too much to do. He could not be punctual; he failed to answer letters, and became famous for not bothering even to open them. For a while whatever he did added to his fame; he became one of the most famous men in England, but he could not settle his bills or pay his employees what they were owed. He simply never had any money.

They were always on the move, from one half-furnished rented house to another, never anywhere but in smart streets or attractive suburbs. Dora's early patron, the Duke of Norfolk, lent them a house in Surrey; and they visited the Whig families in their London and country mansions. Elizabeth's sprightliness and unaffected sweetness of character made her as much admired as her husband. They enjoyed being so popular, but they both remained vulnerable to the caprices and arrogance of the great people who became their playmates: it is hard to see them as true friends.

The Sheridans were asked everywhere. Elizabeth would sing at private parties, and he would make everyone laugh. They went to the beautiful Duchess of Devonshire's – after her initial hesitation about whether you could possibly invite a player's son – and to her clever and still more ravishing sister, Lady Duncannon (later Countess of Bessborough). At Devonshire House Sheridan first met the Prince of Wales.

The Prince was eleven years his junior, and clever enough to appreciate Sheridan's abilities as well as his wit; soon he was the Prince's confidant and adviser.

How the world gaped. The Prince enjoyed singing with Mrs Sheridan. The Sheridans were invited to still more great houses, and to the villas and mansions of other beauties, Mrs Crewe, and Mrs Bouverie, well read and clever, though short of occupation. With several of the ladies he flirted sentimentally, and sometimes he was more dangerously involved. Elizabeth suffered from his absences and infidelities. Reading the couple's letters – the few that survive – and the comments of their contemporaries, one sees how they were admired, and how they were used, in the careless way of the rich. Sheridan was a snob; he loved these people, and he knew he had the capacity to be something more than any of them. He was quicker, cleverer, wittier, more charming. And finally he was not accepted as an equal. They thought him delightful and amusing as long as he did not try to pursue his own ideas or desires too far. He was a toy, a favourite, a flattering jester.

No one could organize a party, or a picnic, or write a love letter, or devise an impromptu set of verses, or a practical joke, as Sheridan could. Staying with grand friends in the country, he once persuaded a whole house party to act out a Civil War battle in the open air, using cows and donkeys strategically entrenched in ditches; everyone joined in and, better still, everyone enjoyed it. He would prepare a dish of his own *al fresco*; Irish stew was his speciality, a small joke against himself. People passed round Sheridan stories: after being wounded in one of the duels over Elizabeth, they said, he had asked for the newspaper next morning 'to see whether I am dead or alive'. One day in London, finding he could not pay off a hackney cab he had already kept waiting for hours, he ordered it to drive about until he saw a friend; he hailed his friend and invited him to join him, then skilfully picked a political quarrel, swore he could not stay in such company and leapt out – leaving his friend to settle the huge bill with the driver.

People remembered these tricks with pleasure; and also how he looked – his peculiarly lustrous eyes, his thin arms and delicate hands, his brightly coloured clothes, a red waistcoat and a cocked hat, a blue coat with metal buttons – and how he talked, mimicking, joking, bringing tears to everyone's eyes in his speeches, arguing over the dinner table until drink made him inarticulate. He was 'tall, and very upright, and his appearance and address are at once manly and fashionable, without the smallest tincture of foppery or modish graces', wrote Fanny Burney, surprised to find herself liking him so much.[4] There was a Shakespearean turn to his head, declared John Kemble. His charm won him invitations, affection, love: the Prince of Wales was sincerely attached to him, almost as far as he was capable of real attachment to anyone but himself. 'The upper part of his face was that of a god, while below he showed the satyr,' wrote Byron later; both the god and the satyr had their appeal in the great world.

In Parliament Sheridan was sometimes teased for being a theatre manager, just as he had been teased at Harrow for being a player's son. There was a celebrated exchange with Pitt, who taunted him with his 'dramatic turns', adding that 'if they were reserved for the proper stage they would no doubt receive the plaudits of the audience'; to which Sheridan responded with a stinging reference to Pitt's youth, comparing him to 'the Angry Boy', a character in Ben Jonson's *The Alchemist*. The ability to score points in debate was highly prized, and exchanges of this kind in the House of Commons were reported throughout the clubs and drawing rooms of London society, so that there was a sense in which the House doubled with the stage as a place of entertainment, and those who triumphed in the House were regarded as star performers. On the other hand, the reproach of the theatre connection was used against him again and again, not only by Pitt in the House, but also in private, and in the press. He was attacked for his origins, and for moving away from them: 'that a young man, the son of a player, should refuse though in very distressed circumstances to let his wife sing at a royal concert because it would degrade his character as a *gentleman*', was found deplorable enough. That he 'should desert the comic muse for politics' was still worse.

Sheridan was stung by these gibes, but his own behaviour sometimes played into the hands of his attackers. When, at the peak of his political career, he led the prosecution in the Warren Hastings trial of 1788, the proceedings at Westminster Hall were as thoroughly stage-managed as any celebrity concert. Tickets were sold at inflated prices up to £50, people sat up all night to get in, and the crush in Palace Yard on the day he was due to start speaking was such that ladies lost their bonnets and shoes. Everyone wanted to be there, including the royal family. Many hardened politicians cried 'heartily and copiously' with emotion; so did Mrs Siddons; and at one point Elizabeth Sheridan, sitting next to her, fainted. Her husband spoke on four separate days, and it was generally agreed, even by his political opponents, that he gave a superb account of himself; but it was seen as a performance. The historian Gibbon, who was there for the last speech, could not resist a touch of malice in his account: 'Sheridan at the close of his speech sank into Burke's arms; – a good actor; but I called this morning, he is perfectly well.'[5]

If Sheridan had been happy in the theatre, as Garrick was, such teasing and attacks would hardly have hurt him; sadly, he felt himself demeaned by his theatrical connection – more demeaned than by his services to the Prince of Wales. Dora must have been struck by the oddity of a man who ran a theatre while disliking so much about it; for she never in her life felt ashamed of the theatre.

Sheridan was especially distracted throughout her first weeks at Drury Lane because the affairs of the Prince were in acute crisis. In fact it was on the very evening before she signed her new contract that the Prince did something especially unfortunate, and from some points of view disastrous: he got married, secretly and in defiance of the law of the land. It was secret, because he was forbidden, by the Royal Marriages Act, to marry without the consent of his father, the King; and had he sought his consent, it would not have been given. It was dangerous as well as illegal, because the woman he married was a Roman Catholic, and if it were known that the heir to the throne had married a Catholic there would be trouble throughout the country – and possibly not just trouble but the threat of civil war, for it was less than a hundred years since the Stuarts had been driven from the throne for their suspected Catholicism.

The Prince had bullied his bride into the marriage with every sort of false and outrageous statement and action. He had been hysterical for months. There had been difficulties with previous mistresses, including the Drury Lane actress, Mary Robinson, and others had come and gone, but this time everything was different. His present love, Maria Fitzherbert, a young woman of good family, twice widowed, was sensibly resistant to his pleas and promises, and held out against his wooing for two years. In July 1785, when he was twenty-two, the Prince attempted suicide. He was bandaged up, and then threatened to tear off the bandages unless Maria came to him at St James's and promised to marry him. She prudently insisted on being accompanied by the young Duchess of Devonshire, a friend to both parties and regarded as a 'sister' by the Prince. Under his repeated threats, Maria accepted a ring – he had none of his own and had to borrow one from the Duchess – and signed a paper saying she would marry him. The two women left, and the Duchess at once wrote a deposition to the effect that Mrs Fitzherbert knew that a written promise extracted under such threats was invalid. Maria went abroad the next day and remained there for four months while the Prince raged and plotted, unable to follow her without his father's permission.

During this period he 'cried by the hour . . . rolling on the floor, striking his forehead, tearing his hair, falling into hysterics, and swearing that he would abandon the country, forgo the Crown, sell his jewels and plate, and scrape together a competence to fly with the object of his affections to America'.[6] As we know, he also relieved his feelings by visits to the theatre, and perhaps felt a special affinity with the unhappy lovers in *Twelfth Night*. The Prince turned to words too, and composed a letter of over forty pages that he sent by express messenger to his Maria in Paris, swearing lifelong fidelity, calling himself a liar and a scoundrel should he ever fail her, reminding her of her promise, telling her the King believed him to be married already and had accepted it – a lie – and urging her to return.

Mrs Fitzherbert, who seems to have been in love with the Prince, unwisely believed his words, softened, and came back to England. It is possible that Sheridan was one of those who helped to set up the wedding: he certainly knew about it. The ceremony took place behind locked doors, and was conducted by a clergyman brought out of the Fleet prison for the purpose, and grossly bribed: his debts were settled, and he was promised a bishopric.[7] So although the marriage was illegal, it was valid in the eyes of the church, which meant that any children would be illegitimate by English law, but legitimate by canon law. The Prince and his wife, or not wife, went to Ormeley Lodge on Ham Common to enjoy their honeymoon.

Having got his way, the Prince denied the marriage in public, because he thought it might cost him the succession to the throne, and he was not prepared to sacrifice the prospect of becoming king. When the matter was raised in Parliament the following year, Fox stated categorically on the Prince's behalf that no marriage had taken place. Maria wept and protested at this insulting lie, and Sheridan was required by the Prince to make a further statement to the House, intended to soothe her feelings and at the same time to save him from any danger of losing the income that Parliament had to approve for the heir to the throne. Sheridan's performance did the trick. No wonder the Prince loved and depended on him; but it is a shoddy story.

George, Prince of Wales, was clever and remarkably handsome, but morally he was damaged goods. He had been petted and paraded in public from infancy, and in private reared by courtiers, mostly away from his busy parents, and subject to a strictly regimented routine – a walk at the same time every day, for instance, regardless of the weather. Queen Charlotte always insisted on the rigid observance of etiquette, possibly as her way of confronting the fact that she was used, year after year, as a breeding machine; the King wanted as large a family as possible, and she was still enduring regular pregnancies when her eldest son was conducting his first love affairs. Court life as conducted by his father and mother was of no interest to him, but he hardly knew how to occupy himself. For several years now he had been lurching from one callow and callously conducted affair to another, running up spectacular debts the while, and falling out with both his parents. He had his own households, at Carlton House and Windsor (and later at Brighton), and took pleasure in horses and paintings, clothes, furniture, food and drink, as well as women. When he began to think of politics, he chose his friends from the opposition; as long as his father believed in the sober, careful, Tory Pitt, George allied himself with Fox and the Whigs. The King, never having been much tempted by luxury or women himself, settled into a baffled and chilly disapproval, and was inclined to blame the Prince's friends, rather than the royal method of upbringing, for his son's behaviour; but while it is true that Sheridan and Fox also drank too much, ran after women and got into debt, the Prince needed no corrupting, and Sheridan was no Mephistopheles.

The King undoubtedly brought many of his troubles on himself. Having accepted the necessity of making an arranged marriage himself, he became determined to control the marriages of his children, and introduced the Royal Marriages Act, a piece of legislation that made it impossible for any member of his family to marry without his approval before the age of twenty-five, and difficult thereafter.* The King saw it as a way of protecting the dignity of the royal family, but the results were almost precisely the reverse of what he had intended, as one after another of his sons found himself unable to marry the woman he cared for, or went through dubious ceremonies, or simply lived a profligate life; while the Princesses pined for husbands into their thirties. The spectacle became deplorable.

To Dora the behaviour of the royal family was of no great concern in 1785 except when one of them came to the theatre to see her perform; professionally, she hoped to please these powerful and glamorous figures, and was satisfied when she did. There must have been plenty of gossip and speculation in the theatre about the proprietor's dealings with the Prince of Wales, but she had other things to occupy her, principally the hard labour of taking on leading parts in twelve different productions through the winter and spring. Later, things would change: London society was small, and the number of royal Princes launching themselves into it disproportionately large. Nine sons were born to the King and Queen, of whom seven survived into manhood: after George came Frederick, then William, Edward, Ernest, Augustus and Adolphus. Busy as Dora's working life kept her, she found herself drawn into circles in which the Princes would appear, not as remote, emblematic figures, but as human creatures, flesh and blood like herself.

* The Royal Marriages Act of 1772 was brought in by George III – and passed without a murmur in Parliament – when his brothers made marriages he disapproved of. It barred all members of the royal family from marrying unless they had the King's consent declared in council and signified under the great seal, or unless they were over twenty-five years of age and had given twelve months' notice to the privy council.

5

Admirers: 1786–1787

Among the new pictures on display at the Royal Academy in May 1786, was a very large, elaborate, allegorical painting with a large, elaborate, allegorical title to match: 'Mrs Jordan as the Comic Muse supported by Euphrosyne, who represses the advances of a Satyr'. It was seen by everyone who counted for anything in London society, and greatly admired; and it was the work of John Hoppner, a young artist who had just carried out a royal commission to paint portraits of the three youngest Princesses, Sophia, Mary and Amelia. Hoppner was a clever artist and a witty and ambitious man. He knew all the gossip, what was in and what was out, and he and his American wife, also an artist, went in for entertaining the fashionable world in their house off St James's Square. This is where Dora went for sittings; and where Hoppner, in the many drawings and paintings he made of her, helped to make her into an icon of that world. One of his first studies of her was sent round as a gift to Lady Duncannon, friend of Sheridan and the Prince of Wales. It showed Dora pensive, with powdered hair, modestly frilled collar and stiff black belt round her narrow waist, a small hat piled with flowers on her pretty head: a delectable pastel, full of sexual allure. Hoppner had the measure of the society he served. To further his career, he encouraged a rumour that he was the illegitimate son of King George III. The truth was less glamorous, and more to the credit of the King: Hoppner's modest German parents had made him a chorister in the royal chapel, where the King had taken a fancy to him and paid for his training as an artist.

For the Academy show Hoppner decided to give Dora a grand and formal treatment, and to paint her on the same large scale as Reynolds's portrait of Mrs Siddons as the Tragic Muse. The result is original and striking – and also odd. The meticulously painted canvas is full of movement and colour. Dora appears, full length, in the centre, her body twisting dramatically as she flies from the satyr lurking in the bushes behind her into the sheltering arms of Euphrosyne. Euphrosyne – one of the three Graces, given a fine Grecian profile and auburn hair – is a commanding figure, holding out an arm to banish the satyr. The satyr was Hoppner's bold stroke: who was he meant to represent? The obvious answer must surely be the male theatre-goer, who regarded actresses as sexual prey; and since this was a characteristic commonly found among the artist's patrons, Hoppner was either deliberately teasing or he must have reckoned that a little classical distancing would go a long way to remove any offence. The satyr is ugly, and he is leering evilly at the Comic Muse in her filmy green muslin dress, embroidered with stars; but she is smiling too sweetly and serenely to suggest she feels in any real danger, as though she knows she is safe because this is only an allegory. The mask of comedy is in her hand, there are gold sandals on her feet, and her heart-shaped face is framed in loose dark curls.

No two paintings of Dora make her look the same, and Hoppner was a glamorizer of women; he was attacked in the press for flattering his subject to please the '*Jordan Mania* of his poor countrymen'.[1] Yet he evidently caught something of the shape and suppleness that were so much admired; and the picture was such a draw that he immediately advertised for subscribers for an engraving. It was made the following year. This particular image of Dora became one of the most popular, and it was sometimes copied with the figure of Euphrosyne cut out, leaving her alone with the satyr, and turning it into a much rawer representation of lust and danger than Hoppner can have intended.[2]

Other painters were laying siege to her now. Many tried to catch her likeness quickly, working from the auditorium or the wings as she acted; but a few months later she began sittings with one of the great portraitists, George Romney, at his studio in Cavendish Square. Romney was at the height of his fame as a painter of the aristocracy and the theatrical world, and his usual fee for a full-length portrait was eighty guineas; he clearly chose to paint Mrs Jordan for his own interest and pleasure, and without a fee, confident that a buyer would be found later – and of course he was right. She went for the first sitting in the simple costume she wore for *The Country Girl*, a plain white dress with a blue sash, her hair unpowdered and tumbling loose down her back. The story goes that she and Romney could not agree on a pose, each rejecting the other's suggestions, until Dora pretended to have had enough, sprang out of the chair in which Romney had sat her, went to the door and turned her head to say she was leaving. The truth was that she had used this pose on stage and knew how effective it was; and when Romney saw it he exclaimed, 'That will do!', and so painted her, in twelve sittings.[3] He did not glamorize her as Hoppner did, but made her look like a real woman, with something gentle and vulnerable about her dark eyes and nut-brown hair.

Going about London, she could hardly miss her image or her name. There were the theatrical engravings in print-shop windows, and the sheet music of the songs she sang at Drury Lane, inscribed 'as sung by Mrs Jordan', to be sold to the countless young women who entertained their families from the piano at home. Picking up the *Morning Herald*, she could read, 'There is no company where Mrs Jordan is not named with uncommon applause'; in other papers find herself praised for her energy, her skill and her good humour.[4] Her world expanded round her like a bright bubble. The narrow lodgings, her little family and its demands remained at the centre, rehearsals and performance continued as usual, but there were constant visitors and invitations. Men and women of all sorts and ranks tried to attract her attention and came to see her, offering to help her or asking to be helped. As well as painting her, they wanted to compose songs for her, or cook for her, or make hats for her; they wrote poems about her and discovered family connections with her. A cousin of her father's, and a baronet too, suddenly decided she was worth knowing: Sir Francis Lumm and his lady invited her to a party. When they found she not only passed muster socially but was a success, they followed up the first invitation with another; she became a regular guest.

Her fame in London quickly filtered out to the provinces. In Yorkshire those who had doubted her abilities had to change their tune and those who had believed in her nodded wisely. George Inchbald, still walking the circuit with Tate Wilkinson, began to think again about his rejection of her offered love. Now it seemed he had lost a pearl of great price. He took a few days' leave to go to London, called at Henrietta Street and, with more optimism than finesse, explained that he had come to make a proposal of marriage after all. Dora was human enough to take satisfaction in this, as we know from her telling the story later, but the time it had taken him to have second thoughts had changed things for her too. She turned him down politely; in her mind he had already faded into the man who had missed his chance. He went away and was not heard of again.

There was a further reason. At some point during this first year in London she met a man who wiped out the image of George entirely. It may have been through the Sheridans, or even in Dr Ford's own box that she was introduced to his son Richard. Richard Ford became the second villain in her life, but he did not come on like a villain. A drawing of him preserved in his family shows a slim, sensitive-looking and elegantly turned out young man, remarkably handsome, with dreamy eyes and neatly arranged dark hair. He was twenty-

The most childlike image of Dora, acting the part of Miss Lucy in Fielding's farce *The Virgin Unmasked*, which she first played at the Crow Street Theatre in Dublin in November 1779, when she was eighteen, calling herself Miss Francis, and simply dressed in 'a frock and a little mob-cap, and her curls, as she wore them all her life'.

'Her face I could not see, owing to the amazing bunch of hair she had pulled over her forehead,' wrote Sheridan's sister-in-law, praising Mrs Jordan's performance at Drury Lane: this print suggests the effect, and gives an impression of her vigour on stage. It is dated 1 November 1790, and entitled 'The Comic Muse, by Goles!' ('Goles' being a euphemism for God).

'Mrs Tomboy and the Irish Manager' in *Town and Country* magazine's series 'Histories of the Tête-à-Tête' are Dora Jordan and Richard Daly. He seduced, or raped, her in Dublin in 1782, forcing her to flee, pregnant, to England. The print appeared in London in January 1787, when her success made her an object of ever increasing interest to the press.

Tate Wilkinson, the great and good Yorkshire manager who in his youth acted with Dora's mother and aunt, and took her into his company in 1782. It was Tate who suggested her new name of Mrs Jordan: 'Mrs' because she was visibly pregnant, 'Jordan' because she had passed across the waters from slavery in Ireland under Daly to freedom in Yorkshire with him, just as the Israelites crossed the River Jordan into the promised land. Wilkinson defended her against disapproving audiences and jealous theatrical rivals, remained her friend and was immensely proud of her success.

THE ROMP.

An action picture of Dora on stage in 1785 as Priscilla Tomboy in the operatic farce *The Romp*, which she played for Wilkinson in Yorkshire, at Drury Lane and then all over the provinces on her tours.

Henry Bunbury, courtier, passionate theatre-goer and amateur artist, dedicated this 1795 engraving of Dora in boots and feathered hat to her 'in gratitude for the Pleasure receiv'd from her Inimitable Performance' in *As You Like It*. It shows Act III, Scene v.

The fashionable and ambitious John Hoppner's earliest portrait of Dora, done soon after her arrival in London in 1785: a delicate pastel drawing showing her dressed as smartly as the great Whig ladies, the Duchess of Devonshire and her sister Lady Bessborough, who came to admire her at Drury Lane. On the back of this picture is written 'Given to Lady Friedrich Bessborough' in an eighteenth-century hand, probably that of Hoppner himself.

Note the spectacles: they are not merely a prop – Mrs Jordan was short-sighted. This is Hoppner's portrait of her as Hippolita, the high-spirited Spanish heroine of Colley Cibber's *She Would and She Would Not*, in which she and her maid are both dressed as young men throughout the play, she in full military uniform, with sword and plumed hat; she controls the whole action, going through a marriage ceremony with another woman, and challenged to a duel by her own lover. It was among her most popular roles, and 'one of the parts on which I used to pique myself', she told the theatre historian John Genest at the end of her career. This picture belonged to her daughter Elizabeth, who married the eighteenth Earl of Errol in 1820.

A tremendous hit at the Royal Academy in May 1786, Hoppner's large, elaborate, allegorical painting with a title to match: 'Mrs Jordan as the Comic Muse supported by Euphrosyne, who represses the advances of a Satyr'. Did the Satyr represent the male theatre-goer, who regarded the actress as legitimate sexual prey?

Richard Ford, slim, sensitive-looking and elegantly turned out, trained as a lawyer, and with his eye on a seat in Parliament, was the son of Dr James Ford, part-proprietor of Drury Lane and obstetrician to the Queen. Young Ford fell in love with Dora, old Ford disapproved; young Ford promised marriage and referred to Dora as 'Mrs Ford'. They set up house together in Gower Street and three children were born, but he failed to make good his promise, and she grew angry at the insult.

Another admirer appeared: Prince William, the third son of King George III, created Duke of Clarence in 1789 after spending his boyhood in the navy. William was 'handsome, as are all the Royal Family, though he is not of a height to be called a good figure'. He was boisterous, lonely and affectionate, and longed for domestic comforts; but when he offered to help out his elder brother with his debts by marrying 'someone very rich', the Prince of Wales sneered, 'Who would marry *you*?'

Another Hoppner showing Dora as Viola in *Twelfth Night*, disguised as the boy Cesario and wearing a hussar's hat. In this performance, said Joshua Reynolds, she 'combines feeling with sportive effect, and does as much by the music of her melancholy as the music of her laugh'. Charles Lamb also praised her 'plaintive' Viola: 'There is no giving an account of how she delivered the disguised story of her love for Orsino. It was no set speech, that she had foreseen . . . [but] some growing (and not mechanical) process, thought springing up after thought . . . She used no rhetoric in her passion; or it was nature's own rhetoric.'

Dora was particularly admired for her assured impersonation of young men. Here she is with her sword up: 'she drove everything home to the mark, and the visible enjoyment of her own power added sensibly to its effect upon others. Of her beautiful compact figure she had the most captivating use – its spring, its wild activity, its quickness of turn . . . '

This silhouette, cut by a Mrs Millicent Brown whose other subjects included the Duchess of Devonshire and the historian Edward Gibbon, shows the detail of one of Dora's military costumes, with short boots, legs revealed to mid-thigh, ribboned uniform, plumed hat, sword and rapier: a sensational effect for the 1790s.

seven (two years older than her) when they met, interested in the theatre, but not the sort of man who hung about the green room to see what he could pick up; not at all of the breed of satyrs, but gentle, well educated and serious. The Fords were a Sussex family, solidly established in the professions, and not only through Dr Ford's medical eminence; there was a brother, and a brother-in-law, in the church – one on the way to a bishopric – and Richard had trained as a lawyer, like Dora's grandfather, and like Sheridan. Now he had his eye on Parliament.

There was nothing strange about his finding her adorable: half the men in London shared his view. But he had a better chance, as the son of one of the proprietors and the friend of another, of getting to know her privately; and soon they were evidently absorbed in one another. He was old enough to know his own mind and plan his life accordingly: or so it must have seemed to her. Each had a good deal to offer the other. His involvement in the theatre through his father allowed him to understand her work and encourage her in it; and she in turn could help him with her earnings, for he had still to establish himself as a barrister. He seemed likely to do well; his father's court connections could do no harm, and his own abilities were soon to win him his seat in Parliament.

Anyone observing them together – two handsome and gifted young people – might have seen the prospect of a fine professional, social and domestic life opening before them. It would not be lived at the dazzling level of the Sheridans, because Ford had none of Sheridan's brilliance; on the other hand he was altogether steadier where debts, drink and women were concerned, and Mrs Ford would not expect to suffer the troubles of Mrs Sheridan. Dora let herself dream of a prospect of joint success and happiness that would allow her to obliterate the painful elements of her past; Fanny would be absorbed into their family. They exchanged lovers' vows and agreed they would marry: or so it appeared.

Dora did not intend to hurry matters. At the end of her

first season, in June 1786, she left Ford in London and travelled north with her mother, Hester and Fanny. Their destination was Scotland, and Tate Wilkinson welcomed her on both north- and southbound journeys, with offers of benefit nights and star treatment. 'Instead of a suppliant she came splish, splash, dish, dash, to the Leeds play-house, and tossels dangling, &c – Oh! it's a charming thing to be a woman of quality, – and in lieu of her asking me for an engagement, the case was greatly altered, for I was obliged to solicit the lady who formerly solicited me,' is his account of their transaction, which obviously gave him great pleasure. He loved his protégées to succeed; there were profits too, as the lady played to overflowing houses in Leeds, York and Wakefield.[5] Then she went on her way to Edinburgh, where she found the other black sheep of her father's family, her uncle John Bland, now the treasurer of the theatre there; and she played opposite his son in *The Country Girl*. They may well have laughed at the thought of Judge Bland turning in his grave as two of his grandchildren disgraced themselves together; but Edinburgh applauded.[6] Her triumphs continued in Glasgow, where she was presented with a gold medal. Then she turned south again.

The Sheridans, who had been away for the summer in Weymouth and Plymouth, were now back and busy preparing a new musical entertainment from Paris, *Richard Coeur de Lion*, with a central part for Dora. Elizabeth Sheridan was doing most of the work, adapting the music as fast as she could, because Covent Garden was putting on a rival version; Drury Lane got in first, opening in September, with Dora as Queen Matilda, disguised through most of the action as a blind boy minstrel – pathetic, but in breeches. They scored a success and wiped out the Covent Garden production, even though John Kemble, singing Richard, was tone-deaf. Only Horace Walpole grumbled that 'Mrs Jordan was quite out of her character', having hurried to Drury Lane to see her: she had become the actress nobody wanted to miss.

74

Both Richards kept her busy through the autumn. In November the season was interrupted when the King's aunt died. Two weeks' closure of all the theatres was ordered while the court mourned; for the actors the mourning period had an extra edge, because it meant no pay. Dora could bear this without hardship; and the enforced holiday allowed her to resolve things with Richard Ford. What happened now was that she moved, with all her family, from Henrietta Street, and set up house with him in Bloomsbury: a whole house too, newly built and tall, where four-year-old Fanny could run up and down the stairs from attic to basement all day if she chose. No. 5, Gower Street, is just north of Bedford Square, then the northern edge of London: the country started beyond their backyard. There were friendly neighbours with children for Fanny to play with: Dora's leading man, John Bannister, also lived in Gower Street, with his wife and their young family. Hester and Mrs Bland came with her to run the domestic side of the household, but the dynamics between them changed, because Dora now took on the dignified semblance of a married woman.

Many people assumed she and Ford had been discreetly married. Ford never gave his side of the story, but he certainly referred to Dora as his wife in writing as well as in conversation, and allowed some very respectable friends, including her cousins the Lumms, to believe they were married, and to entertain them on that basis. So she went by the name. She also believed he intended to legalize the situation as soon as possible. Her friendship with his sister, attested to by letters exchanged after the separation, shows that Miss Ford took the relationship to be an entirely serious one.[7]

Dora said later that Ford promised marriage before she agreed to live with him, and that he excused the postponement on the grounds of his father's disapproval. The excuse was such an old one – Dora must have been in a dozen plays in which the seducer trots out a version of it – that she might have doubted its validity. But she did not; and perhaps Ford did mean what he said at the time. His father's disapproval was genuine and must have put the Doctor into some difficulties; he was obliged to be tactful, since Mrs Jordan was bringing good money into his theatre, and it would not do to offend her. Nonetheless he is said to have threatened Richard with disinheritance if he went ahead with the marriage.

Sexual arrangements are always mysterious, powered by forces that defy logic and prediction. The one bit of basic training all girls received in the eighteenth century, along with their needlework, was that they must be strict sexual bargainers. Any other woman could have told Dora not to trust her admirer, however much in love she might be, but to keep him at bay and hold out for a ceremony. Her colleague Elizabeth Farren did as much with the Earl of Derby, year after year, while they waited for the Countess to die, and was much admired for her cool determination. Dora was not so cool. She was not an easy conquest. She was prudent, sober and well behaved, and had lived chastely ever since the disastrous episode with Daly; but she allowed herself to warm up too soon, and failed to make the necessary hard bargain.

There is an account of what it is like to be the lover of an actress that suggests there is something erotic in the alternation between her public triumph and her private submission:

> it was a dream of rapture to ... take her to the theatre in a warm shawl, to stand at the wing and receive her as she came radiant from the dressing room, to watch her from her rear as she stood like some power about to descend on the stage ... and hear the burst of applause that followed ... to take her hand when she came off, feel how her nerves were strung like a greyhound's after a race, and her whole frame in a high even glow ... And to have the same great creature leaning her head on his shoulder, and listening with a charming complacency, whilst he purred to her of love and calm delights.[8]

To have what other men desired, to command his own private performance, to possess the secret of the difference between Dora in private and Mrs Jordan on the stage, was intoxicating for any young man. As for Dora, she had no experience of tenderness from a man, or of domestic happiness. This, at least as much as passion, was the irresistible bait. Richard Ford would make everything good and safe for Fanny as well as for her.

From Fanny's point of view it may not have seemed such a good arrangement to be deposed from the centre of her mother's attention, and no longer so welcome in her bed. And no sooner had they moved to Gower Street than Dora became pregnant. Now the press was on her heels. *Town and Country* magazine took notice of her move, confidently claiming that she did not love Ford but had taken him for reasons of 'prudence' (i.e., money), adding insultingly – and far from the mark – that she had always been 'prudent in her amours'. Later it printed pictures of Dora and Daly together in its 'Tête-à-tête' series, labelled 'Mrs Tomboy and The Irish Manager'. A more kindly paper, in order to explain the presence of Fanny, assured its readers that Dora had been 'married to a sea-faring man, who left her next morning'. Ford may have winced, but they could have expected worse.

The Drury Lane season kept her busy through the rest of 1786 and into the spring of 1787. The repertory system of alternating productions meant she did not have to appear every night; but she might be in either the main play or the farce, or sometimes both, the hours of performance as punishingly long as in the provinces. She continued to be greatly in demand in the parts she had made her own, the Country Girl, Viola, Miss Lucy, Hippolita and Matilda; and she added new ones, among them Miss Prue in *Love for Love*, in which she and Bannister were particularly admired in the comic love scenes.[9] In April, half way through her pregnancy, she played Rosalind in *As You Like It* for the first time; this too became one of her most popular roles, and one she played to the end of her career. Several paintings show her as Rosalind, disguised as a boy, in yellow knee breeches, ruffled shirt and – sometimes – feathered hat. One, by an ambitious young portraitist, William Beechey, who moved on to many royal commissions, is the most beautiful of all the portraits of her.[10] Another lively picture, showing her on stage surrounded by other characters from *As You Like It*, was the work of Henry Bunbury, a gentleman amateur and equerry to Frederick, Duke of York, the King's second son.

The season ran for the ten months from September to June, but the theatres always closed for Passion and Easter weeks, the traditional actors' holiday; the summer was for touring – by no means a rest. Over the next few years Dora travelled north three times, and once to Cheltenham. To have somewhere to relax, the Fords took a country house by the Thames, at Petersham, near Richmond, a quiet but fashionable retreat for well-to-do Londoners who had to stay within reach of town; but soon this too became less restful than they had intended, as she was drawn into appearing at the Richmond Theatre. Work was her pleasure, and she found it hard to resist these invitations.

In May 1787 she set off northwards once again. This time her family party included her 'husband'; just as well for the Yorkshire audiences, given that she was visibly pregnant. Her admirer the Duke of Norfolk was in Leeds, 'which did not make her profits less at her benefit' according to Wilkinson, delighted to welcome his dear Jordan again on her way to Edinburgh. There, discreetly far from home, she gave birth to her second daughter. Fanny was almost five when Dorothea Maria – often known as Dodee – was born, in August. Inevitably word got about, and in September the *Public Advertiser* announced to its readers, 'Homeward Bound ... The Jordan from Edinburgh – a small sprightly vessel – went out of London harbour laden – dropt her cargo in Edinburgh.' And small and sprightly, she was back on stage in September, and playing the lightest and airiest of parts.

6

A Visit to Cheltenham: 1788

In the summer of 1788 the novelist Fanny Burney saw Dora Jordan acting in Cheltenham. She wrote in her diary for 25 July, 'We all proceeded to the playhouse, which is a very pretty little theatre. Mrs Jordan played the "Country Girl", most admirably; but the play is so disagreeable in its whole plot and tendency, that all the merit of her performance was insufficient to ward off disgust.'[1]

Fanny Burney was there with 'the Royals', as she usually called them in her diary. She meant the King and Queen and, on this occasion, the three eldest Princesses, Charlotte, Elizabeth and Augusta, all now adult but still kept firmly under parental discipline; and she was with them as a keeper of robes to the Queen, an official position at court. There were no Princes in sight: they had all fled the rigidly respectable court as soon as they were old enough. Cheltenham was chosen for a summer visit because the King, who was now fifty and had been on the throne for twenty-eight years, had been feeling unwell, and his doctors decided he would benefit from a few weeks at a spa, taking the waters in peaceful surroundings. The arrangements were made as informal as possible. This meant the whole party setting off from Windsor at five o'clock in the morning in a procession of carriages, the royals stopping for breakfast with a conveniently placed aristocrat, Miss Burney and her fellow courtiers taking theirs at a Henley-on-Thames inn. They went on through Oxford, changed horses at Burford, and the journey was done by evening. It had not gone unnoticed: all along the road the towns and villages were crowded with people who had walked in from the surrounding countryside in the July rain to see the royal family pass by. People were as closely packed together as the audience in the pit of a playhouse, Burney noted; 'every town seemed all face', and every few miles there would be another band of fiddlers, tuneless and timeless but enthusiastically loyal, scraping out 'God Save the King'.

Cheltenham consisted of hardly more than a single street. It was extremely long, clean and well paved, and lined with inns – the George, the Plough, the Swan, the York Hotel; it had its newly built theatre and assembly rooms, but no building considered suitable for the reception of the royal party. A local landowner, Lord Fauconberg, offered them the use of his house, Bayshill Lodge, a short way out of town. Even there, space was so tight that all the male courtiers, the pages and the housemaids had to go back into town to be lodged; the only man sleeping in the house was the King himself. Burney was up at five with her duties, having no maid of her own to help her; but she found time to keep up her diary.

Like Dora Jordan, Fanny Burney had a career of her own. She had published a novel, *Evelina*, when she was twenty-six, which brought her immediate fame, and followed it up with a second, *Cecilia*, four years later, no less successful; she had been the darling of Dr Johnson and the friend of Garrick. She had plans to write more novels, as well as plays – for years Sheridan had been pressing her for a comedy – but at present her writing career was stalled. All her energies were going into her work for the Queen.[2] Her family – and especially her father – had encouraged the court appointment because it brought the likelihood of a pension, for she was not now expected to marry: too clever, too shy and, in her mid-thirties, too old. She was indeed quiet and delicate; and she found her work at court, which meant almost constant attendance on her mistress and the almost constant company of other courtiers, not all of them congenial, exhausting. She pined for freedom, and to be able to return to her chosen profession; but although her diary makes it clear how desperately she suffered from the confinement, boredom and brutal hard work at court, she allowed herself not a breath of criticism of her employers. Sometimes she let slip a sad phrase about the effect of life at court on her spirits – 'dreary vacuity of heart and of pleasure' is one – but she prided herself on her submission to what was deemed necessary. When regrets arose or criticisms occurred to her, she repressed them; it may have made her fiercer over the things she did feel free to criticize. She had been at court for two years when the Cheltenham visit took place.

The Queen, her early enthusiasm for the theatre as great as ever, must have intended to be kind when she sent Miss Burney off to the playhouse, and was quite unaware of her disapproval because a few days later she gave her some more tickets. The second visit was still less to her taste than the first.

> In the afternoon I went again to the play ... It was 'Sir Harry Wildair' and Mrs Jordan performed it extremely well, but very little to my satisfaction. It is a very disagreeable play, and wholly abounding in all that can do violence to innocence and morality ... It was for the benefit of Mrs Jordan; and all our household had taken tickets.[3]

Fanny Burney's disapproval was not generally shared. In fact Dora was almost as great an attraction in Cheltenham as the royal party. 'Mrs Jordan's popularity has been so great at Cheltenham that next to the eagerness of the people to see the Royal Family has been their expectation of this comic heroine,' reported the local newspaper, and went on, 'Her success has not fallen in consequence of this highly raised desire, for she has performed to crowded houses, and her fame has even increased since her theatrical appearance.'[4] Cheltenham may have considered itself particularly lucky to see her in the role of Sir Harry Wildair, because she had just played it for the first time at Drury Lane, where she carried it off with such style and conviction, 'charmingly dressed and provokingly at ease', that shouts of applause had followed her when she left the stage in London.[5] The part was not written for a woman, and the plot turns on the joke that Wildair, a rakish but good-hearted young man about town, mistakes the respectable heiress he is meant to be courting with a view to marriage for a high-class prostitute. You can see why Burney was shocked. The joke is broad – the play is by Farquhar and dates from the Restoration – but it is not just coarse; there is a redeeming wit and good humour to it. Before Dora, Peg Woffington, the greatest actress of her day, had chosen to play Wildair, and made it one of her popular roles; and according to Elizabeth Inchbald, Dora was 'no less admired and no less attractive' in it than Woffington.

Miss Burney's distaste was not conveyed to her royal employers, and they were all very keen to see Dora. The local paper announced that 'their Majesties do not honour the playhouse till Mrs Jordan makes her appearance'. They saw her on the 28th of July in play and farce, as Hippolita and the Romp, and the King sent his Colonel Digby round with a gift to her benefit ('all, all, and much more, she deserves' proclaimed a local enthusiast).[6] Theatre fever was increased when the King's second – and favourite – son, Frederick, Duke of York, arrived on a flying visit to his parents with his equerry, Henry Bunbury, already a champion of Dora. Bunbury announced himself 'languishing to see the play', the Duke seconded him, and another royal box was at once arranged. At the same time the King insisted on having a wooden house moved out from the centre of Cheltenham to accommodate his son as close to him as possible during his brief stay. It was a gesture the locals may have taken as typically royal, although in truth it was more likely another sign of his impending mental collapse.

Dora appeared in a further command performance on

9 August; it was O'Keefe's *The Poor Soldier*, and out of respect for royal decorum she gave up her usual part as the Soldier and appeared as the heroine, in a skirt. She then went off to the Worcester Theatre for a few days, returning to play Mistress Ford in *The Merry Wives of Windsor* before the King and Queen on the last night of their visit. They declared themselves delighted yet again, and before they set off the next morning the King gave permission for the playhouse to be known as the Theatre Royal.

Fanny Burney also saw Dora as Mistress Ford, and on this occasion did not express any disapproval; in any case her earlier distaste was for the plays, not the player. Burney was fastidious, but also far too conscious of the barriers set up in the paths of all clever women not to rally to the defence of a sister worker. She spoke up as a staunch supporter of Mrs Jordan's powers as an actress, defending her skilfully when a gentleman of the court said he did not care for hoydens and suspected Jordan of being in life what she played on stage. Burney answered that although she too had *begun* to feel disgust when she first saw her as the Romp, she changed her view as the performance proceeded, because 'afterwards she displayed such uncommon humour that it brought me to pardon her assumed vulgarity, in favour of a representation of nature, which, in its particular class, seemed to me quite perfect'.[7] The tribute is so intelligent that one groans at the thought of Burney having to waste her time among such dim, supercilious courtiers. Provoked, she was able to speak honestly and even boldly; she knew that to express admiration for tragedy, and Mrs Siddons, was always safer ground than to praise comedians, but this time she said what she really felt. Another time she confessed to laughing so much at a farce that she was 'almost ashamed', an avowal read with some relief, coming from someone so rigidly self-controlled.

Fanny Burney and Dora Jordan stand about as far apart in their experience of life as two women could: the one carefully protected – in intention at least – and docile and decorous in all things, reluctant to question the attitudes imposed on her by family and court; the other unprotected, self-motivated and willed, forced to fend for herself and her family. Yet Burney was too wise and clear-headed not to recognize and respect in Jordan what she shared with her – her professional skill.

And Mrs Jordan too, robust as she was, would have preferred not to shock Burney. Dora liked a joke, but she did not set out to challenge the moral order, and her attitude towards the court and the royal family was as reverential as that of the people who came out to line the streets to express their loyalty. She took royal patronage and approval seriously: with a twinkle in her eye for the young Duke and Mr Bunbury, perhaps, but a very thorough and proper respect and gratitude towards King George.

There is another curious entry in Fanny Burney's Cheltenham diary. It contains her first reference to the King's third son, Prince William, absent at sea during the Cheltenham jaunt – he was serving in the navy – but soon to reappear. A few days after Burney's second visit to the theatre, she was sitting with another of the Queen's ladies, Miss Planta, and a court clergyman called Fairly, when he suddenly asked her how she managed to cope with the boisterousness of the royal Princes; because as far as he was concerned 'there was something in the violence of their animal spirits that would make him accept no post and no pay to live with them. Their very voices, he said, had a loudness and force that wore him.'[8] Burney was so embarrassed by this sudden and unprovoked criticism of members of the royal family that she could hardly speak, but just managed to explain that she scarcely knew the Princes, for the good reason that they were almost never at court. Mr Fairly congratulated her on this. If they had been, he said, 'they would have come to you, I promise you; and what could you have done – what would have become of you? – with Prince William in particular? Do you not think,

Miss Planta, the Prince of Wales and Prince William would have been quite enough for Miss Burney?' Miss Burney answered again, still more faintly, that she would have avoided them.

> 'Impossible! They would have come to your tea-room.' 'I would have given up tea.' 'Then they would have followed you – called for you – sent for you – the Prince of Wales would have called about him, "Here! Where's Miss Burney?"' 'O, no, no, no!' cried I; 'I would have kept wholly out of the way, and they would never have thought about me.' 'O, ho!' cried he, laughing, 'never think of seeing Miss Burney! Prince William, too! what say you to that, Miss Planta?'

Miss Planta agreed there was no probability of such an escape; and Miss Burney's July diary ends with an expression of relief that her time at court had not coincided with that of the Princes. Mr Fairly was then summoned by a page to play backgammon with His Majesty, putting an end to the torment. Fairly was usually a kindly man, yet he obviously enjoyed teasing Burney for her primness on this occasion; perhaps the idea of her being confronted by the boisterous, rakish Princes came into his head after seeing her shocked reaction to Sir Harry Wildair, just such a rakish youth as one of them. And as it happens, his warning was timely, for within a few months she did find herself face to face with Prince William at Windsor, and was able to discover for herself whether Mr Fairly's account was exaggerated, or whether he was indeed another Wildair.

If Miss Burney noticed that Mrs Jordan was with child at Cheltenham, she was far too well bred to mention such a thing in her diary. The pregnancy was not very far advanced, but it may have been partly responsible for Dora's decision to give up her male role in *The Poor Soldier*, a very unusual concession for her. She was billed as Mrs Jordan, of course, but was often now called Mrs Ford; the coincidence of the name when she played Mistress Ford must have been one of the jokes of Cheltenham that season. Richard Ford accompanied her on some of her out-of-town engagements, so he may have been with her for some of her stay at least. Her brother George was certainly there, because he was acting alongside her; and very likely the two little girls were also taken along for the country air, with Mrs Bland and Hester, all packed into a comfortable lodging, near the theatre but also close to the fields and hills surrounding the smart little spa town.

The success of this summer season was very important to the owner of Cheltenham's theatre, an Irishman of many talents called Boles Watson: he had been its builder and was now its manager too. As things turned out, he was so grateful to Dora that when she left in September he presented her with a locket of blue enamel, set with pearls and brilliants, with a picture of the Comic Muse 'after Reynolds' inside and an inscription, 'Presented to Mrs Jordan, Thalia's Sweetest Child', in gold letters: a charming tribute, although the picture, rather tactlessly, was not of Dora. She had not yet sat for Sir Joshua, as the Comic Muse or anything else. On the other hand he may have planned to paint her, because his 'Sitter Book' shows that she visited him early the following year. He also expressed his admiration for her in unusually warm terms, saying 'she vastly exceeded everything that he had seen, and really *was* what others only affected to be'.[9] He was especially struck by the fact that she could play both fashionable men like Wildair and women who pass as men, 'the tender and exquisite Viola of Shakespeare, where she combines *feeling* with sportive effect, and does as much by the music of her *melancholy* as the music of her *laugh*'.[10] Sadly, his tribute was made only in words, and neither her melancholy Viola nor her elegant Wildair was put on canvas by Reynolds to stand alongside the Mrs Siddons he painted that year.

Cheltenham took up Dora's summer. She had been almost continually busy at Drury Lane until mid-June, and was immediately back again in September, playing the Shakespeare heroines she had already made her own, and more of the Restoration dramatists whose women's parts seemed to have been written especially for her: Congreve's Miss Prue, Corinna in Vanbrugh's *The Confederacy*, Miss Hoyden in *A Trip to Scarborough* (which was Sheridan's toned-down version of Vanbrugh's *The Relapse*). In all these plays she appeared with her neighbour John Bannister as her leading man, and they could do no wrong in the eyes of the audience when they appeared together, clowning or sentimental as lovers, fast and funny as a pair of rakes.

Yet when John Kemble took over the management of Drury Lane this autumn he and Dora quarrelled like cat and dog, sometimes over her salary, sometimes over her occasional refusals to appear. He fully understood her value to the theatre, but she maddened him. 'Mrs Jordan again fancied herself ill. I spent above Two Hours in coaxing her to act . . . she was as well as ever she was in her life, and stayed when she had done her part to see the whole Pantomime,' he wrote angrily on one particularly trying occasion.[11] She would never give ground when she was fighting for a pay increase or an extra benefit. This shocked and embarrassed both Kemble and Sheridan, because it was so unlike the behaviour expected of a lady; and it was precisely her strength that she was prepared to embarrass them. People noticed that Sheridan was sometimes 'as afraid as a Mouse of a Cat' when faced with Dora in one of her fierce moods.[12] She knew she had to be as tough as the toughest of the men she was dealing with, and she used whatever weapons came to hand to achieve what she believed to be her due.

Some of her pleas of illness may have been put on to make a point, but others were certainly genuine; Kemble, childless himself, was not likely to take much account of pregnancies or of the demands made by sick children on their mothers' attention. After a year of almost unceasing work, Dora gave birth to her third child during the autumn of 1788. This was the first to be born in London, and her first boy, but there was no rejoicing. He may have arrived prematurely; he did not live long enough to be given a name. A son and heir might have tipped Ford towards legitimizing his domestic situation; the disappointment did not encourage him. But whatever gloom fell upon Gower Street, Dora quickly gathered her energies and was back on stage in late November.

7

Carnival: 1789–1791

The waters of Cheltenham did not save the King's health. In the autumn of 1788 he fell ill with a fever; the fever turned to madness. Sometimes he wept, sometimes he talked on and on until he was raving uncontrollably; sometimes, it was said, he even barked like a dog. The Queen was naturally distraught, many doctors were called in, and the most intimate details of the royal illness were publicly discussed. The Prince of Wales expected to be made Regent, which modified whatever distress he felt. Charles James Fox, getting the news in Italy, came back at all speed. Parliament was thrown into more severe conflict than usual, the Whigs supporting the Prince, Pitt and his followers seeking ways of limiting the power he might have to be granted. One clause of the Regency Bill made it impossible for him to create peerages or to appoint his friends to offices for a period of twelve months; Pitt was pinning his faith on the recovery of the King. Another clause would deprive the Prince of all authority if – it was carefully phrased – he should marry a Catholic.

Sheridan, summoned at all hours to Carlton House to administer advice and comfort to the Prince, and often kept there half the night, did his best for his cause both in and out of the House. He asked Members of Parliament not to inquire into the matter of Mrs Fitzherbert; the Prince did his bit gallantly by putting it about that he was tired of her. Sheridan was also able to get a handbill relating to their marriage suppressed; and he took on Pitt fiercely, accusing him of insolence in his dealings with the Prince. The Prince said to his friends at Devonshire House that 'he must crush Pitt or Pitt him'.[1]

Devonshire House in Piccadilly was one of the places where the Duchess of Devonshire and Lady Duncannon regularly entertained, gossiped, gambled, flirted and presided over the Prince's party. Sheridan was there as often as he was at Carlton House. Both Whigs and Pittites gathered at Drury Lane in the evening. Sheridan's appearances were more likely to be in the front of the house with his political cronies than backstage, while Kemble was allowed to get on with the running of the theatre. When Sheridan was at home he was often too distracted to talk to his family. In November his sister Betsy wrote from his house in Bruton Street, 'Dick with us but so engaged in thought he hardly seemed to hear or see us, and so we went to the play, – *Confederacy* and *Sultan*, Mrs Jordan delightful in both. The usual intimates came home to eat oysters.'[2]

Mrs Jordan could have been among the oyster eaters, but she is more likely to have gone home to Gower Street after her strenuous double bill. She was pregnant again, not so many weeks after losing the baby boy; not that she let it curtail her appearances. In December, for her benefit, she played Rosalind in *As You Like It* and Nell in the farce *The Devil to Pay*, 'exquisitely well – nothing could be better' wrote the clergyman critic, John Genest.

In February the King began to show signs of recovery. Fanny Burney, meeting him unexpectedly in the gardens of Kew Palace, was frightened and tried to run away, but then found him gentle and sensible; he took hold of her and kissed her. Something about the gesture, which suggested his need for affection and reassurance after his ordeal, touched her heart. Soon the news went out and the country as a whole rejoiced with her. The Queen presented Miss Burney with a fan ornamented with the words 'Health restored to one, and happiness to millions'. The claim was scarcely exaggerated;

the King had never been so popular as his illness made him. The town of Windsor subscribed forty guineas for fireworks to greet his return to his castle, and clergymen sent up thanks to God; one country parson gave his two servants a bottle of gin between them to celebrate.[3]

The Prince of Wales and the Whigs were thought to be slow to share in the general jubilation, an attitude judged unsporting at the very least. A cartoon by Rowlandson depicted Sheridan, Fox, Burke, the Prince, Mrs Fitzherbert and several others, all visibly put out at the royal recovery. The inclusion of Mrs Jordan in this group – the only Drury Lane performer who figures in the drawing – suggests that her sympathies were believed to lie with them.[4] It is extremely unlikely that they did; Dora wrote many times of her affection for the King in later years, and he had just praised her at Cheltenham. Of course she may have been caught up in a prevailing mood; she may even have been given lines with topical jokes and allusions, often put into the prologues and epilogues of plays, that identified her with the Whig cause. More likely the fact that everyone knew her face made her a good subject for cartoonists. It was a penalty of success; she could be depicted at the centre of events in London, and people would feel in the know, and laugh.

In the spring the King and Queen attended a service of thanksgiving for his recovery at St Paul's. There were illuminations, command performances and balls; Mrs Siddons impersonated Britannia for the Brooks's ball, held at the opera house, and soon the Queen was seen again at the opera and the King at the play. Less happily, Dr Ford sold out his share in Drury Lane. Under Sheridan's casual system of management, it had lost him a great deal of his money, and one way and another he felt obliged to go abroad for a while. He was not reconciled to his son's domestic arrangements.

In July Dora was engaged to appear in Scotland again, and she set off northwards with her mother, stopping in Leeds on the way to visit their old friend. Wilkinson had broken his leg for a second time, and it had set badly. She offered to play a benefit for him; unfortunately the 'precise ladies of Leeds' were shocked by her acting Sir Harry Wildair while visibly pregnant, and they gave her a cool reception. In nearby Harrogate the public was altogether less delicate; the guests staying at the various hotels there clubbed together to make up enough money to persuade Mrs Jordan to give them a few nights' entertainment.

This made her late for her Edinburgh engagement. The manager there, a Mr Jackson, was annoyed by such high-handedness, reasonably enough, and here she again had less than her usual success. 'We were all to the play last night to see Mrs Jordan, who is to act six nights at Edinburgh,' wrote the Duchess of Buccleuch at Dalkeith House to Lady Louisa Stuart. 'She always delights me, and as the House was not very full, I was not so hot as I expected. She acts again tomorrow, and I see a strong inclination in the young part of the family to go again, to which, I believe, I must give way.'[5]

So with cool, half-filled houses Dora had to be content; but Jackson was not, and they fell out. There was more on her mind than thin audiences. In Edinburgh Mrs Bland was taken ill; it must have been a sudden attack, because she would scarcely have made the long and tiring journey to the north if she was already feeling unwell. Within the space of days she was dead. Dora was with her to nurse her, and held her in her arms as she died. The pain of losing the one constantly loving and beloved person who had been with her all her life, and on whom she had always relied for support and advice, was hard to bear.

Grace Bland cannot have been older than her mid-fifties. Her life had not been easy, although the last years, in which she was able to enjoy and participate in her daughter's good fortune, must have made up for some of her sorrows. Dora was not so sure. The mourning poem she wrote for her mother insists squarely on the injury done to her mother by her father. She calls her mother a 'suffering saint' and a 'patient wife', stresses the cruel usage she endured, and emphasizes, along with her fidelity, her gentle acceptance of the wrongs done to her: her 'silent anguish' and 'curb'd resentment'. The poem goes on to say that any comforts that came to her arrived too late to make much difference.[6]

The verses praise her mother, but their very existence shows just how determined Dora was not to be like her. *She* would not curb any resentment or be silent in anguish; and she intended a public statement as well as an expression of personal grief. The poem was offered to an Edinburgh newspaper, where it appeared. Dora's diction was wholly conventional, but she wrote effective couplets:

> Thus silent anguish marked her for her own,
> And comfort coming late was barely known;
> It, like a shadow, smil'd and slipp'd away –
> For churlish Death refus'd to let it stay;
> A two-fold dart he levell'd, to destroy,
> At once, both mother's life and daughter's joy.

Even as she mourned her mother, she embarked on a public quarrel with the Mr Jackson of the Edinburgh Theatre. For him, the last straw was her request for a break in the arranged programme while she nursed her mother. He withheld some promised payment; she protested. When he attacked her in the press, she answered in the press, giving as good as she got. Her letter accused him of failing to pay her according to their agreement; the £100 bill he finally gave her in Glasgow, she wrote, bounced when she tried to cash it.

Dora had by now acquired a pretty good understanding of the power of the press. Her ability to make use of it to defend herself and advance her own arguments is striking. Few women of her generation had the strength of mind to try such brazen methods. Letters by women might be charming, self-deprecating, cajoling, hesitant, gentle or wryly humorous; they were rarely combative. Dora was different. The conclusion to her letter about the Scottish manager goes like this: 'I have now entirely done with this subject, and, thank God, with Mr Jackson, who I hope, by his punctuality, to pay his *at present protested note*, will not compel me to resume any acquaintance with him, by the methods the law points out!'[7] Apart from her verses, this is the first time we hear her authentic voice, and its harshness is disconcerting; it is a tough Dora who appears before us here, fully armed, to remind us irresistibly that her grandfather was a judge, and a fierce old fellow, and that she had his genes in her.

Her diminished party travelled south through Chester and she was back in London for the birth of her third daughter, christened with names chosen not from the Ford family but from hers: she was called Lucy Hester. Dora did not hurry back to Drury Lane; there was the baby to enjoy – this time strong and healthy – and her mother to mourn. There was rejoicing over Ford winning a parliamentary seat at East Grinstead; and there were also quarrels with John Kemble over the terms of her engagement. She did not appear on stage again until February 1790. Then she persuaded Kemble – a bit of hard bargaining – to let her brother George act Sebastian to her Viola. It was only a moderate success. He was small enough to be a credible twin brother, but there was little else to recommend his performance. He remained a steady drain on her patience and her purse; but at this moment her ascendancy was such that she could carry him easily enough. When Covent Garden tried to poach her away from Drury Lane this winter, she had only to mention it to Sheridan for her salary to be put up: now she was paid the same as Mrs Siddons, £30 a week for three performances.

At this point Dora's life looks as though it might be settled into its final shape. She was approaching thirty, was at the summit of her profession, and could expect perhaps another ten years on stage. She had three much loved little daughters, lived in a desirable part of London and could always get away to Petersham when they needed a change of air for a few days. Her 'husband' had achieved his ambition by getting into Parliament; they could feel pleased with themselves and with one another.

Yet it was not quite like this. They lived surrounded by a society that was growing almost frenetic in its pursuit of excitement and pleasure. The great revolutionary events taking place in France thrilled, dismayed and divided people in Britain too, and even those who were not very interested in ideas felt the fever; some behaved as though gratification must be pursued to extremes as well as political theories. Serious happenings have never brought light behaviour to a stop, of course, and did not then. People continued to go to the theatre, fall in love and behave badly while the rights of man were debated, great polemics written, constitutions changed. The theatrical world overlapped with the world of politics, of the Whig aristocracy, of royalty; in the years 1789, 1790, 1791 they made up a social merry-go-round that span and whirled faster and faster, always drawing some into the brightness at the centre, and casting others out into the darkness. It was a frivolous, seductive, dangerous carnival. The Sheridans were deeply drawn in; the Fords were still at the edge, although Dora's presence in the Rowlandson cartoon suggests that she was already associated with it.

A few reports from Drury Lane, Carlton House and Devonshire House reveal the carnival atmosphere. They are not edifying, these tangled cat's cradles of adultery and snobbery, but they do suggest the tightness of the interlocking circles and the steamy atmosphere of London. At Drury Lane a close colleague and friend of both Dora and the Sheridans was the musician Michael Kelly, who wrote most of the music for their productions after his return from Vienna in 1787. He fell in love with another singer, Mrs Anna Maria Crouch – she played Olivia to Dora's Viola – and set up house with her, first as a *ménage-à-trois* with her husband, then without him. As a quasi-incestuous Drury Lane tangle, theirs was notable, since Mrs Crouch had earlier been on the point of marrying John Kemble; now, with Kelly's complaisance, she became the Prince of Wales's mistress briefly. Dora disliked her, and was friendly with the Prince's earlier theatrical mistress, Mary Robinson, who had also spent some time under Fox's protection; she was now ill and embittered, and had turned to writing plays, one of which Dora championed. It was a satire on society ladies who became compulsive gamblers, something for which the Duchess of Devonshire was well known. In this one tangle Dora could see the theatre and the great world outside enmeshed together.

She got another view of the Prince of Wales from John Bannister, who was sometimes invited to dine at Carlton House. He was a well-educated man, counting among his friends both Fox and Gainsborough, but he found that, in the Prince's dining room, the 'public performers, sat all together, as all guests took their places according to rank ... we never mixed in that [conversation] of the general party, further than to answer questions'.[8] In other words, an invisible barrier was set firmly in his face. The Prince was unpredictable in this way. The Sheridans moved through most of his invisible barriers easily enough; they could and did invite him back to whichever house they were currently living in. The Prince and Elizabeth Sheridan were also on terms intimate enough to attend together sessions with the fashionable hypnotist Dr Marmaduke, and be thrown into fainting fits, while the Duchess of Devonshire had hysterics beside them.[9]

The Duchess, Georgiana, and Harriet Duncannon, great ladies as they were, played out their own farces and tragedies; both became involved in scandals quite as murky as the ones based on Drury Lane during these years. They were Dora's contemporaries, and, comparing their lives, they appear at first glance supremely fortunate and easy; but looking closer, you see they had been confined and limited to a degree she had never known. They were married at sixteen and nineteen to men chosen by their parents, and told by their mothers that absolute obedience to their husbands, religious observance and a quiet existence, preferably passed in the country with their babies, should be their complete programme for life. Both resisted. They cared about books, ideas, politics, pictures, the theatre, as well as clothes and parties. Georgiana wrote the music for one of Sheridan's verses, and it was used at Drury Lane. Harriet wrote witty, well-informed letters; but they had no satisfactory outlets for their talents. Fox did something to enliven them by allowing them to play a part in his electioneering, though it could not be much more than a decorative role. Georgiana's compulsive gambling was surely an expression of boredom; it meant she lived in terror of her husband discovering the extent of her debts, and staved off disaster by borrowing from anyone who would lend. She also lived in a *ménage-à-trois* with her husband and his mistress, who was also her best friend. Both the children of this liaison were born in France, and left there under false names; and Georgiana's daughter by her lover, another Whig grandee, was similarly born abroad and kept successfully hidden. The great were skilled at shielding one another from public disapproval when they chose, though it meant sacrificing the children.

Harriet Duncannon was not a gambler; she was more beautiful, better read and more intelligent than the Duchess, and Sheridan fell distractedly in love with her. His earlier flirtations and infidelities had shaken his wife without turning her seriously against him, but the affair with Harriet did real damage to all concerned. In 1790 Lord Duncannon threatened divorce and a 'criminal connection' suit against Sheridan: this would have meant humiliation, dirty linen washed in public, law reports in the press. Emotionally, things were so bad for Elizabeth Sheridan that she too talked of a separation. Harriet, appalled, became seriously ill: it was supposed to be a stroke, unlikely at her age, and considering that she made a complete recovery. Perhaps Duncannon pushed her downstairs in a rage. Whatever it was, she was ordered abroad, the standard resource for great ladies in trouble, and duly disappeared for a time.

Elizabeth Sheridan had no such resource. 'The World, my dear Hetty,' she wrote to a friend,

> is a bad one, and we are both Victims of its Seductions. Sheridan has involved himself by his Gallantries and cannot retreat. The Duplicity of his Conduct to me has hurt me more than anything else, and I confess to you that my Heart is entirely alienated from him, and I see no prospect of Happiness for either of us but in the Proposal I have made him of Parting.[10]

Elizabeth's often stated preference for life in the country, her reluctance to be too much at Devonshire House, her warnings to her husband not to give too much of himself to politics and Brooks's Club, and not to expect too much back from them, were all expressions of a sense that she and her husband were taking – had taken – a dangerous path. Now she was proved right.

Elizabeth had her own temptations. She was being pursued by a new admirer, and a royal one, the Prince of Wales's younger brother William. Elizabeth found him appealing: he was more than ten years younger than her, fresh faced and enthusiastic. She confessed to her woman friend that she was far from indifferent to his 'devoted Attachment for me, and have thought more favourably of him still since I have had reason to make comparisons between his Conduct and S's'.[11] Later she told the same friend that she would probably have run away with William had he been nearer her age; adding wryly that she would also probably 'have hung myself a Week afterwards' had she done as he wished. Her letter goes on to describe his 'importunate passion' and her strong inclination to yield to it; she was at least a little in love with him.

Before Lord Duncannon's suit against Sheridan could proceed in Doctors' Commons, the Duke of Devonshire intervened to have it removed, and succeeded in calming the injured husband. At the same time Fox begged Elizabeth not to insist on a separation from her husband and to accept his 'Oaths and Professions' of contrition graciously. She agreed to 'throw off' the attentions of her princely admirer, and the Prince of Wales, allying himself with Sheridan's interests, spoke firmly to his brother on the subject.

Elizabeth accepted that her marriage might be patched up after a fashion: 'we are both now descending the Hill pretty fast . . . and perhaps we shall meet at the Bottom . . . and then our Wanderings and Deviations may serve for Moralising in our Chimney Corner some twenty years hence,' she wrote.[12] Things settled down – or rather they half settled down, because Sheridan was interrupted in the middle of seducing a governess called Miss Ford in a bedroom in Crewe Hall even as Fox was in the process of persuading Elizabeth to forgive him.

There were many of these moments when princes, players, politicians, duchesses and governesses met on roughly equal terms, and many forms of entertainment that allowed social boundaries to be crossed for a few hours at least. Great ladies sometimes imitated the costumes of actresses, and sought their advice on clothes. One of the Prince of Wales's social accomplishments was mimicry, and he particularly enjoyed imitating John Kemble. What was work for actors became a game for the aristocrats who set up their own amateur theatricals, which became very popular at this time. So was dressing up of all kinds.[13] The Prince of Wales adored planning and appearing in extravagant costumes, from Van Dyck hats and suits – black velvet, with spangles, pink lining and pink heels to his shoes, or white satin with pink satin knots – to his own version of the tartan of a Highland chief, in which he and his brother William made an entrance at one o'clock in the morning at a party in Hammersmith in the summer of 1789, after which he invited Elizabeth Sheridan to sing trios with him.[14]

On another evening the Sheridans were involved in a

fancy-dress party in which all the women appeared masked and made the men try to guess their identities. The next night there was a return match when the men disguised themselves as a group of Turks, wearing masks and sitting silently around a table. With much laughter, the wives made their choices. At this point there burst in through a half-open door the real men – lords, princes, Members of Parliament, theatre managers or whatever – gleeful and triumphant at having tricked their women so thoroughly: the Turks round the table, they revealed to their ladies, were only servants, got up to deceive them.[15]

The episode reads like a London version of *Così fan tutte*, and makes Europe seem small for a moment; *Così* was written in 1789 and first played in Vienna in 1790.* Something of the bright intensity, the sheen of the opera, which promises pure laughter only to give us a glimpse of darkness and cruelty beneath the surface of its silly lovers' games, finds an equivalent in the London society in which Dora and the Sheridans and the royal princes met. There was pleasure, there was luxury, and most of the players were capable of putting on magnificent virtuoso performances; but there were victims, and prices to be paid in due course, as Elizabeth already saw clearly enough. She sent Prince William packing. In any case he already had his eye fixed on someone else. He had seen her in the theatre: her name was Dora Jordan.

---

* The link is quite close. Michael Kelly was intimate with Mozart in Vienna; both he and Nancy Storace, who had shared a house with the young Sheridans in London, and gone on to become the first Susanna in *The Marriage of Figaro* in Vienna, returned to Drury Lane in 1787. Da Ponte, the librettist of *Così*, also turned up in London a few years later.

8

A Royal Education: Prince William

The admirer of Mrs Sheridan and Mrs Jordan was the same boisterous Prince William whose pranks Fanny Burney had been warned against in Cheltenham. William had not enjoyed a sheltered upbringing. In Chapter 1 we saw him born to the very young Queen at Buckingham House, on 21 August 1765, the third child and third son, and almost at once life was hard for him. As was normal for royal children, he was put in the charge of a wet nurse; he was also weaned at four months, perhaps because his wet nurse, Mrs Sarah Tuting, was found unsuitable by the Queen. Although highly recommended by one of her court ladies, the Duchess of Ancaster, Mrs Tuting turned out to be the mistress of the Duchess's father, who also ran the royal stud at Newmarket; her departure must have been a bad moment for baby William.

His earliest cheerful memories were probably of Richmond Lodge, the house on the Thames, just south of Kew, used by his parents in summer; he always liked living close to the river. There he tumbled about on the grass, and ran and shouted with his brothers and sisters – Charlotte, Edward and Augusta arrived in 1766, 1767 and 1768 – and the royal nurses, who could be cuddled one minute and bullied the next. The children followed a healthy routine, were bathed once a fortnight and vaccinated in batches. In the early days their father sometimes got down on the floor to play with them, but their mother's strict etiquette meant they were not usually allowed even to sit down in her presence, and sometimes they fell asleep on their feet. There were toys, among them twenty-one small brass guns on travelling carriages for George on his fifth birthday, and a specially made 'Chamber Horse to Carry four Children at once' for the nurseries. There was also much music and dancing, fireworks on their father's birthday, and presents on New Year's Day. In public the children were shown off in Roman togas and other fancy dress; and William, still in petticoats, played 'Mademoiselle' to Frederick's Harlequin in a little entertainment.

So far so good; but when he was seven, William saw his two elder brothers, aged ten and nine, formally installed as Knights of the Garter at Windsor Castle, and after this their familiar world was broken up. George and Frederick were given an establishment in London, and William was put into a separate household of his own on Kew Green, shared only with five-year-old Edward, whom he did not much like. He was allotted tutors, middle-aged clergymen and retired army officers; he copied out pages of copperplate improving sentiments, and studied Latin, French and German, mathematics, riding and fencing. More to his taste, he was allowed to help with the running of a model farm set up for the royal children. It was a curious life for a boy. He saw that he was special and set apart, and he lacked equal companionship and love.

He continued to idolize his handsome and clever eldest brother at a distance. George charmed most people, although by the age of twelve he was incurring parental disapproval for his lack of application and 'bad habit of not speaking the truth', and at sixteen he was embarked on a way of life entirely disapproved by his father.[1] Frederick was destined for the army; and when William reached thirteen, the King decided to put him into the navy. It was a wholly original plan, and not William's idea, but he does not seem to have raised any objection. Other boys went into the navy as early as eleven, leaving everything familiar behind them; he was treated more gently in that he was nearly fourteen when he joined his first ship as a midshipman, and he went accompanied by a tutor. He took his meals at the admiral's table, was allowed to go home for Christmas, and was shielded from the grosser discomforts and cruelties midshipmen could expect to encounter. He was small for his age, with straight fair hair, pouting lips and an oddly elongated head; he was also bold and sociable.

The first year in the navy was by far his best. It brought him approval from his parents, and made him briefly famous and popular with the general public. He was with Rodney's fleet when it captured a Spanish flagship, immediately renamed the *Prince William* in his honour; a full-scale battle followed and William, who behaved courageously throughout, became a national hero.[2] This was in January 1780; on his next leave he was taken to Drury Lane for a celebratory evening, and his presence threw the audience into such excitement that there was almost a disaster: pressing forward to see the Prince, people were half crushed and had to be hauled out of the pit on to the stage.[3] Verses were written in his honour and a glorious future was predicted for him as a naval leader.

Nothing so good happened again. He went to sea and learnt his profession, but there were no more battles. He began to feel neglected and unloved by his parents. They wrote rarely, and when they did their letters were admonitory, and dull. As time went by they made it clear that the navy was not acting on his character as they had hoped: they were surprised and displeased to find he picked up the sailor's amusements of swearing, drinking and worse, and lost whatever princely polish he had once possessed. He resented his parents' disappointment and disapproval, the more so since no one else dared to criticize him, because flattery was the routine approach to all members of the royal family. As he grew up, William received it from almost everyone but his parents and siblings. Even naval discipline was oiled and diluted with it. When fellow midshipmen or senior officers disapproved of his actions, their criticisms were not made to his face. If they disliked him, they concealed it, avoided him or were kept out of his way. The sternest admirals used unctuous phrases when they wrote to him: he might, after all, be king one day. The effect was baffling and isolating; he could not learn how to get on with people because he rarely saw their true faces.

He also remained powerless to order his own life. When he was seventeen his father decided to take him out of the navy and send him to the court of Hanover; the idea was that he should pick up some manners from his German cousins. It was another plunge into a wholly strange environment, and William hated it from the start. He preferred the middle-class families of Hanover, but when he tried to make friends with them he met with disapproval. He fell in love, first with a princess, then with a bourgeois girl, but was not allowed to court either. Bad reports went back to his father. In his loneliness the young man took to the brothels, and to writing crude and angry letters to the Prince of Wales. He complained of his boredom at being forced to remain in Hanover, 'this damnable country, smoaking, playing at twopenny whist and wearing great thick boots. Oh, for England and the pretty girls of Westminster; at least to such as would not clap or pox me every time I fucked.'[4] He was also increasingly bitter about his parents: 'Yesterday morning I received a set down from the two persons that were concerned in begetting me. The female was more severe than the male. I do not mention names for fear the letter should be opened.'[5] After two unprofitable years in Germany he was allowed back into the navy and promoted to lieutenant; but he still complained that his parents 'keep me under like a slave'.[6]

During the next years, as he sailed the Atlantic, he got into scrapes of various kinds. He ran up debts, a failing shared with his mother and brothers, but still disapproved by his father. When he became a captain, he overdid the discipline aboard his ship to a ludicrous degree, inventing unnecessary rules and punishing minor infractions with disproportionate severity. He got into every sort of trouble with women. His one artistic talent lay in designing uniforms for his midshipmen, but they were more theatrical than practical: the breeches split when the boys climbed the rigging. Above all he still failed to develop a sense of how to get on with his fellow officers. He made friends with the young Horatio Nelson in the West Indies; but although Nelson, a fervent monarchist, said he grew fond of Prince William, and did his best to keep up in his round of dancing and feasting in the islands, even he could not support him in all his professional behaviour. Gradually William lost favour with the sea lords as well as with his father. Early in 1786 he wrote to his brother saying he was not sure whether he wanted to remain in the navy, but 'what is to become of a young man of one & twenty years old, who has neither a profession nor money? A pretty situation indeed: add to all this a King's son. What shall I do?'[7] It was a reasonable question. In September 1787 he threatened to resign.[8] To the admiralty lords, it was obvious that the King's plan for his son had failed. He would never have made an outstanding officer, and the upbringing he received went a long way towards obliterating the good qualities he had.

On hearing of his father's illness, he hurried back from his station in the West Indies, dispensing with the necessary formality of seeking permission from his commanding officer. Instead he simply wrote to his elder brother, under the impression that he was already Regent, asking to be recalled. He sent no letter of sympathy to his mother, telling his brother he lacked words, and it is true that he found language awkward to handle. 'The poor Queen: what a situation for her ... Permit me to express myself strongly. I follow the dictates of my heart. Sincerely do I love this good and worthy man and long may he yet with his usual firmness reign over us.' Admirable sentiments, though he also assured the supposed Regent, 'I am attached to you of all other of the family in the strongest manner.'⁹ William hoped his brother would either appoint him to the Admiralty or make sure he was given a high command.

When he arrived in England at the end of April 1789 it was to find his brother with no more power than before, and the Admiralty strongly opposed to his continuing in the navy at all. The King passed on this verdict, and grumbled about his unauthorized return; but he saw that something had to be done for William. The immediate answer was a peerage. He was made a duke and an earl too, for good measure: Duke of Clarence and of St Andrews, and Earl of Munster in the Irish peerage. From now on he ceased to be known as Prince William and became the Duke of Clarence, the first since the unfortunate Clarence who was drowned in a butt of malmsey in the Tower, under orders from his brother, Richard III.

The new Clarence got £12,000 a year and a set of rooms in St James's Palace. It was about as bad an arrangement as could have been made, for none of this gave him an occupation. He had not lived at home for ten years, hardly recognized his own sisters, and found his parents cold towards him; they made it clear that his manners, mostly acquired at sea, were not up to scratch. He had been systematically forbidden to marry any of the young women he had fallen in love with, and, without moral or social guidance, had resorted to loose women on a scale even his naval companions found spectacular. He wanted to be liked – this is clear – and he wanted to belong, but he did not know where he belonged. He was already half sickened by his years of debauchery, and his boisterousness was partly the defence of a lonely boy.¹⁰

The best descriptions of him at this time come from Burney's careful pen. In May she heard he was back, and of his parents' disapproval, and then on the same day, as she sat with a group of courtiers at Windsor, found herself face to face with him as he burst suddenly into the room. He greeted everyone civilly and 'began to discourse, with the most unbounded openness and careless ease, of everything that occurred to him'. He was, she thought, 'handsome, as are all the Royal Family, though he is not of a height to be called a good figure' – which means he was short, something that does not appear in his portraits. What won her over was his knowing that she had a brother in the navy. '"I am very happy, ma'am," he cried, "to see you here; it gives me great pleasure the Queen should appoint the sister of a sea-officer to so eligible a situation. As long as she has a brother in the service ... I look upon her as one of us. O, faith I do! I do indeed! she is one of the corps."' And he stayed for an hour, chatting about what a reformed character he had become, and about his sisters, and how Princess Augusta interested him particularly because 'she looks as if she knew more than she would say; and I like that character'.[11] Miss Burney was to see more of him, when he came to the play readings she gave at court the next spring, and on other occasions when he appeared among the courtiers, teasing them by insisting they drink his father's health in champagne, boasting about his fine new carriage, and altogether 'gay, and full of sport and mischief, yet clever withal as well as comical'.[12] Although he was not at all the sort of young man she admired or approved, she clearly found something likeable in William.

He must have noticed Dora properly for the first time in May or June 1789. Bannister, playing Ben in Congreve's *Love for Love*, has a story about Clarence coming backstage to offer his naval expertise over the way to wear a sailor's handkerchief; Dora was his Miss Prue. So the Duke saw her at Drury Lane, and at Richmond Theatre too, where she was acting during the early summer that year. He may also have seen her out and about in Richmond, with her children and her handsome 'husband', because he took a house there himself. The Fords' house was outside Richmond in the meadows, while the Duke's house, Ivy Lodge, was in the centre of the town, in a terrace close to the Thames, with what Horace Walpole described as only a little green apron of land between it and the water.

Walpole, who kept his sharp eye on everything from the other side of the river, and was usually ready with a gibe, dismissed Ivy Lodge as a house fit for an old gentlewoman interested in nothing more than playing cards. William quickly showed he did not meet this description. He brought down a handsome young woman to keep him company, who was obviously not going to be invited to any card parties in Richmond. She was known as Polly Finch, and she usually plied her trade in London.

While Richmond and Twickenham gossiped about the Duke's affairs, the Fords were away in the north. They were still away when he celebrated his twenty-fourth birthday in August, appearing on the balcony of the Castle Tavern to survey a regatta. Polly Finch was soon back in London; it was put about that she was bored by the Duke's reading aloud from the *Lives of the Admirals*, which sounds, like much good gossip, too funny to be true. He was quickly forgiven his *faux pas*. Walpole decided to praise his sobriety, his regular domestic habits – he locked his servants in at night – and, most surprisingly, his punctual settlement of bills with the Richmond tradesmen, all departures from princely habits. He began to take an interest in local life. Early in October he organized a command performance at the Richmond Theatre, asking for two farces, *Chapter of Accidents* and *Animal Magnetism*. The theatre had been one of his few pleasures in Hanover, and he had been an actor himself, in amateur shipboard productions, and in Shakespeare too; he had been Prince Hal on one occasion, and Mistress Page on another when, to add to the verisimilitude, he had arranged for his Falstaff to fall into some real pitch.[13]

The Sheridans, on the move as always, also had a house in Richmond at this time. William was delighted to find such congenial neighbours. 'The Duke of Clarence lives within a hundred yards of me and he generally pays me a visit most mornings,' wrote Elizabeth to a friend.[14] The Fords too arrived back in September, but Dora was mourning her mother, and awaiting the birth of Lucy, and is less likely to have taken part in any social life.

In November (1789) the Duke returned to St James's. Dora stayed at home with her baby and was not seen at the theatre until February; but once back at work she picked up her usual momentum very fast.[15] In March she was in a new farce called *The Spoiled Child*, playing a mischievous boy, Little Pickle. The plot is extremely simple; Pickle's tricks run to tying people's clothes together, and substituting a pet parrot for the chicken being prepared for dinner. This type of humour, entirely devoid of sexual innuendo, and interspersed with songs, appealed strongly to the Duke. The general public shared his taste, Little Pickle was the rage, and every seat at Drury Lane was filled whenever it was on. Audiences who came expecting to see Dora as Pickle rioted and asked for their money back if she failed to appear; and provincial actresses were soon reproducing her performance all over the country.[16] The rumour went about that she had written it herself; it is certainly the work of someone who knew exactly what they were about technically in constructing a farce. Ford's name was also suggested; he seems an unlikely author. Dora might have put it together when she was at home with the baby during the winter, to amuse herself, and as a vehicle for a range of stage effects she knew she could bring off; but she never claimed to be the author, and the attribution remains uncertain.*

One of the things the Duke particularly enjoyed in *The*

---

* A printed version sets her name to it, but Boaden, who knew her well enough to ask, mentions the attribution only to dismiss it. He says it was probably by Isaac Bickerstaffe, an Irish farce writer driven into exile on the continent under the threat of the death penalty for homosexual acts. I am inclined to believe Boaden. If Dora were the author, she had no reason not to say so. On the other hand, she could write, and was later credited with helping Mary Robinson to write *Nobody* (see p. 145).

Spoiled Child was a song about the navy ('What girl but loves the merry Tar'), delivered of course by Dora. He was often seen at Drury Lane; but so was the rest of his family. One of the Queen's ladies who was also a childhood playmate of William, Charlotte Papendiek, described this period in the aftermath of the King's recovery, when 'Miss Farren, Mrs Siddons and Mrs Jordan filled the house every night to overflow ... the stage was in its zenith ... Their Majesties gave every encouragement to it, by appearing every week at one or the other house.'[17]

Dora had another success, with Kemble and Bannister, in Aphra Behn's *The Rover* (renamed *Love in Many Masks* – it was another Peg Woffington role), which had not been revived for thirty years. Just about every part she touched turned to gold, and everyone at Drury Lane appreciated the fact. In April Elizabeth Sheridan wrote to her husband, 'I am very glad *The Rivals* is to be got up at Drury Lane. I dare say it will bring very good houses especially if you alter Lydia Languish for Mrs Jordan. Is that to be done or how? [*sic*]' Whether Sheridan wrote alterations to suit Dora or not – if he did, they have not survived – she duly appeared as Lydia Languish, with Miss Farren as Julia.[18] And she managed to put in an appearance at the rival house, Covent Garden, too, doing *The Country Girl* in a benefit performance for widows and orphans.

The London season was a particularly festive one. The revolution rumbled on in France, but still seemed more benign than threatening to many of the English; it did not, for instance, prevent the Duchess of Devonshire from visiting Paris that summer. At Carlton House the Prince of Wales gave a series of levees and balls. A respectable lady complained that, 'not satisfied with asking all the W—s at this end of town, [he] sent into the City for more Ws'; but then her name had been left off the Prince's list.[19] The round of the young royals' pleasures was not going to be slowed down by disapproval. In May William was obliged to tear himself away. The navy was on alert; someone at the Admiralty remembered that the Duke was a sailor, and he was summoned to Portsmouth to take command of the *Valiant*. He busied himself about his ship as best he could, but was only half pleased to be given another command just now. He read enviously in the newspapers of the masquerades, fêtes and balls he was missing, and wrote complaining to his brother that there was 'not a woman fit to be touched with tongs' in Portsmouth.[20] As the Admiralty officials had rightly judged, being a royal duke and being in command of a frigate were not easily compatible pursuits.

Dora did not make the journey north or west this year, but kept Fanny, Dodee and baby Lucy with her in Petersham. It was easy and agreeable to go across the meadows to Richmond Theatre, where she did her summer season in June and July. She was also looking for a new house in London; whether Gower Street was too small, or too sad in its associations with her lost mother and her lost baby son, she had decided to move. She found a more central and fashionable house between Portman Square and Oxford Street, in Somerset Street. (It ran from Orchard Street to Duke Street, and has disappeared beneath Selfridges.) Ford naturally moved with her; but it looks as though the choice was hers, and the house belonged to her, either outright or on a lease in her name.

In mid-September she was back at Drury Lane for the first night of the season, starring both in the Aphra Behn and the farce; in October she was in a new five-act farce by Frederic Reynolds, *Better Late than Never*, which the grateful author said she saved single-handed from total disaster.[21] She was full of energy, with the bonus of not being pregnant for nearly a year. Whether this was chance, care or coolness on Ford's side or hers, she must have enjoyed her freedom. On her return to the stage after the birth of Lucy the press had, for the first time, commented on what they called her 'bulk';

Dora was not a particularly vain woman, but nobody likes to be described as bulky.

November brought her twenty-ninth birthday. It also brought the Duke back to London, very pleased to be dining at Carlton House again rather than in a cabin with the Admiral; in one of his letters he spoke of having been long enough at sea to hate it, and expressed his unwillingness to serve except in war conditions. He also mentioned his desire to be back in 'the quiet and peaceable regions of Richmond'.[22] His two elder brothers welcomed him, not least because they wanted him to join them in a scheme for raising a loan of £300,000 that they saw as a means of paying off their current debts. Anxious to be accepted as one of them, he did as they asked, involving himself in their financial tangle with disastrous long-term results. Trying to be still more helpful, he is supposed to have suggested that he might 'do something for the family' by marrying 'someone very rich': an offer greeted by the Prince of Wales with one of his special sneers: 'Who would marry *you*?'[23]

Fantasies of marriage did not prevent William from pursuing ladies he could not hope to honour with the offer of his hand. A son was born to him at about this time, acknowledged by him and called William; we are left wondering who the mother was, and what became of her. Could it have been Polly Finch? It seems unlikely that the Duke would have taken into his own care the child of a woman of her reputation. Since he also claimed never to have debauched an innocent woman, little William's mother may have been a married woman. Whatever her status, 'natural' children were regarded as natural mistakes made by men. Even Jane Austen, a clergyman's daughter, refers to them without embarrassment. Unmarried mothers often willingly handed over their children if the fathers were rich enough to offer them a better chance in life than they could; and in any case the law denied such mothers any rights over the child after the age of seven.

The father might claim them, if he chose to; but he was under no obligation to do so.[24]

If we are to believe the Duke's statement to his brother, he began to court Dora on his return from Portsmouth in November 1790. He wrote to the Prince the following October (1791) saying, 'Mrs Jordan, through a course of eleven months' endless difficulty, has behaved like an angel.'[25] Perhaps his memory was at fault, because in the winter of 1790 he was, as we have seen, vigorously pursuing Elizabeth Sheridan. Her letters about him date from January 1791, and mention his age as twenty-six, and hers as thirty-seven.[26] The fact that she took him seriously and found him attractive is a real — and rather surprising — testimonial to his ability to charm. If, after two decades with the wittiest husband in Britain, she could find herself 'not indifferent to his [i.e., the Duke's] devoted Attachment for me', it certainly suggests he could transform himself into a different person from the man his brother mocked and the great ladies found 'heavy to have *sur les bras*', as Lady Duncannon put it.[27] Elizabeth might welcome a blunt man for a change, but she would surely not have liked a boor or a complete fool, even with the dazzle of royalty about him. Another voice in his favour was Horace Walpole's: he found William lively, cheerful, talkative, manly, well-bred and sensible.[28]

He did not take Elizabeth's dismissal entirely easily. There is mention of his 'persecutions' later. They were brought to an end as her delicate image was blotted out by the bolder one of Mrs Jordan.

It was an image hard to avoid in London in 1790. She was visible in the theatre, in prints, in paintings and engravings: as Rosalind and Viola, her most popular Shakespeare roles, both of which she was playing through that spring; as farcical chambermaids, Romps, Hoydens and Pickles; as the dashing Hippolita, with military sword and feathered hat. Hoppner painted her again in this role, with her spectacles in her hand.

A fine silhouette of her dressed as Hippolita in her soldier's costume was also cut about this time, with the high plume of feathers on her head, carrying a sabre, and showing her legs up to mid-thigh.[29]

In February 1791 Dora was visited by her friend Tate Wilkinson. He put up in a hotel in Gray's Inn Lane, on the other side of town. The weather was terrible, the Thames had risen over its banks, and he had to struggle through rain and flooded streets with his bad leg to Drury Lane; to get him to *Twelfth Night* and back, his servant had to bribe a private coachman waiting outside Brooks's, who took the job because he could rely on his master not coming out until four or five in the morning – a point noted by Wilkinson with a mixture of horror and amusement. So the old manager managed to see her in her glory, both as Viola and as Hippolita; and when he had seen her, he persuaded her to promise another visit north in July, and went away well satisfied.

The Duke's serious attentions began after Wilkinson's visit. In March he decided to move from his small place in Richmond and bought Petersham Lodge, a comfortable house set in its own grounds; he renamed it, a trifle self-importantly, Clarence Lodge. It was of course close to the Fords. Both he and Dora were now dividing their time between Petersham and London. He was having his rooms in St James's Palace redesigned and decorated by the architect John Soane; she was working at full tilt, and more often at Somerset Street. But someone got an inkling of something, and although there were no babies in question – as far as Dora was concerned at least – a curious print appeared in the middle of March called 'Mrs Pickle's mistake', showing a baby held at the window of a house in 'Sommers St', with the Duke, Richard Ford and Dr Warren, the Prince of Wales's doctor, also present. It is inexplicable unless it is an allusion to the Duke's baby son, by a misinformed cartoonist.[30]

Dora said afterwards that she did nothing to encourage the Duke, and that her wish was to remain with Richard Ford.

Her behaviour confirms this, right up to the autumn; but she must have been flattered, and amused. She may have enjoyed people speculating about William's attentions, and she may even have thought it was good for business. One of her roles was that of a noble girl who spurns a royal seducer in fine words: 'Feed on the scum of sin? . . . Dishonour to the noble name that nurs'd thee . . . There, take your jewels; let 'em give them lustres/That have dark lives and souls; wear them yourself, sir.'[31] If he was offering her jewels, she was not accepting them at this point. On the other hand, when she played this part, a modern epilogue was attached for her to speak, which suggests the theatre management was happy enough to stir up speculation about a royal admirer:

> How strange! methinks I hear a critic say,
> What, *she* the serious heroine of a play!
> The manager his want of sense evinces
> To pitch on *Hoydens* for the love of Princes!
> To trick out *Chambermaids* in awkward pomp –
> Horrid! to make a Princess of a *Romp*.

The public could read what they liked into this demure declaration.

On 4 June she was chosen to lead the last performance ever to be given in the Drury Lane built by the Adam brothers. Sheridan had made his ill-starred decision to rebuild the theatre again, on a much larger scale, hoping to increase his revenue; he invited Henry Holland, the architect employed by the Prince of Wales to remodel Carlton House, to undertake the project. Meanwhile the company would have to move to the opera house in the Haymarket, where they remained until 1794.[32] On this final night in the familiar theatre Dora was in both *The Country Girl* and *No Song, No Supper*, and the house was bursting at the seams, with people packed and squeezed into every one of the two thousand seats.

On the same day the Duke was at St James's, celebrating

his father's official birthday; 'this is the first day I have ever dined with the King at St James's on his birthday', he told a group of courtiers. He was in high spirits, boasting of the beauty of his new carriage and saying he had to hurry off to see his tailor, but he ordered champagne and insisted on them all drinking toasts to the King and Queen, and refilling the glasses of the most reluctant. Clearly he was already drunk himself, and his behaviour was not endearing. He was rude to one of the Queen's faithful old German ladies, calling her 'potato-jaw' and then trying to make amends by kissing her hand clumsily. 'Dat Prince Villiam – oders de Duke de Clarence – bin raelly ver merry – oders vat you call tipsy,' grumbled another of the ladies.[33]

His approaches to Dora must have been more circumspect. In July the press was printing reports of his infatuation, but said it was unrequited: 'Mrs Jordan has withstood the unbounded offers of a certain personage . . .' 'Little Pickle has been besieged at Richmond by a certain exalted youth, whom at present she has managed to keep at bay . . .' There was renewed speculation as to whether she was really married to Ford or not, opinion inclining to her being Mrs Ford; no one could resist punning on the situation: 'The Ford is too dangerous for him to cross the Jordan.' She herself did not tell the Duke whether she was married or not at this stage; why should she? The royal princes were not noted for constancy. Lady Lumm advised her strongly to keep him away and to stick to Ford. Hester was also a Ford partisan, regarding him, for all his faults of omission, as a gentleman.

Even if Dora was half pleased by William's very public attentions, her first intention was to follow Lady Lumm's advice. By her own account,

The declared attachment of the Prince weighed at first no more with her than to take the opportunity of ascertaining, whether Mr Ford was sincere in his devotion to her; in which case she thought herself every way entitled to his hand; and, in fact, even upon a mere worldly estimate of the matter, a desirable match, in possession of a positive, and progressive fortune, the honourable result of superior, indeed unequalled talents.[34]

The Duke, that is, was at this stage hardly more than a lever to be used on Richard Ford. The events of the summer bear out this remarkably frank admission. William came to a benefit she gave at the Haymarket on 2 August. The next evening she played at Richmond Theatre to a full house: 'scarcely a family of any rank or consequence in Richmond, and the adjoining Villages, but paid a tribute to the abilities of this charming Actress'. The Duke then let it be known that he would be giving a splendid fête, to which the charming actress was invited. Perhaps he chose this moment to press his suit with a serious declaration.

Dora turned down his invitation. The fête was cancelled. Not only that, she escaped altogether, leaving both Richmond and London. Five days later, on 8 August, she and Ford were in York. She had promised Tate Wilkinson; the trip also allowed her to tackle Ford about his intentions, and to test the Duke's fidelity.

Wilkinson's detailed account of the Fords' visit makes it clear it was an edgy experience for everyone concerned. To begin with, it was not a good moment for the theatre; there had been political riots, with houses burnt down in Birmingham, only a few weeks before, and the whole country was disturbed by the news of massacres in Paris and the imprisonment of the French King and Queen after their attempted flight. There was also a blistering heat wave, punctuated by thunderstorms, which discouraged audiences. The High Sheriff came to see Dora's Rosalind, but the people of York decided *The Country Girl* was rude and vulgar. Some of the same tribe who had hissed Dora in Hull eight years before shouted insults when she appeared on stage. Wilkinson says they were about her living openly as Ford's mistress, but rumours of the Duke's attentions may have filtered through as well. He himself teased her by calling her a 'theatrical duchess'. 'She did not deign to reply, but reddened and looked angry.'[35] Then the Wilkinsons gave one of their splendid dinner parties for the Fords, and she recovered her good humour. Michael Kelly and Mrs Crouch were in York too, and John Kemble arrived, and was put up by the Mayor; the city was abuzz with parties and entertainments.

But Dora was not happy. She resented the position she was in, and she was not used to a hostile reception. One evening, at the end of *She Would and She Would Not*, she showed what she thought of the lukewarm Yorkshire audience: instead of bowing towards it – she was dressed for Hippolita, and always bowed when she wore male costume – she turned her back and bowed the other way, 'as much as to say, kiss—', wrote Wilkinson, somewhat taken aback, but also amused by such fighting spirit.

Whatever Ford thought of this, the next day he wrote to Wilkinson to say Dora was ill and could not either come to dinner again, as had been arranged, or continue to perform. Kemble went round to see her, but she would not budge, and Ford carried her off on a trip to Castle Howard. If this was meant to give them a breathing space to enjoy each other's company, it was not a success. Her distress as the mistress of the man who had been living with her and promising marriage for five years had turned to anger. How could he pretend to be looking after her, when he was the very cause of her troubles? Their relations soured from day to day; and now escape from her current situation began to look attractive.

Wilkinson sent to say she must pay a £30 indemnity. She returned a formal note: 'I agree with pleasure to your proposal of giving you thirty pounds, rather than ever perform in York. I shall return tomorrow and settle the balance of the account.' It was signed, firmly, 'D. Ford'.[36] But in her mind D. Ford was occupied with questions that excluded R. Ford altogether. They returned to York together to see Kemble as

Othello – not the most tactfully chosen entertainment – in the continuing heat wave, then took themselves off to Newcastle. She expected to act there, but the arrangements, which depended on Kemble's brother Stephen, fell through. Altogether it was a very bad month for Wilkinson's 'truly admired and beloved Mrs Jordan'. It was also the last trip she and Ford made together.

In Twickenham at least, Walpole was finally convinced that the Fords were married: he wrote to a friend on 16 September, 'Do you know that Mrs Jordan is acknowledged to be Mrs Ford?'[37] But by the time she and Ford arrived back, he had failed his test and she had understood he was never going to make good his promise of marriage. She told him that, if she had to choose between being his mistress and the Duke's she might as well opt for the Duke; or, as she put it later to the sympathetic Boaden,

> She at length required of Mr Ford a definitive answer to the proposal of marriage; and, finding that he shrunk from the test, she told him distinctly, that her mind was made up, at least to one point, THAT, if she must choose between offers of *protection*, she would certainly choose those that promised the fairest; but that, if he could think her worthy of being his *wife*, no temptations would be strong enough to detach her from him and her duties.[38]

Although this is her own version, intended to justify her behaviour, its effect is unfortunate because it suggests she gave up one lover for another on financial grounds, settling for the one who 'promised the fairest'. She was trying to put the blame on Ford, and to emphasize her own sense of duty; but the effect was to make herself look mercenary. She could simply have said she chose the one who loved her best; and that Ford's failure to demonstrate his love gradually destroyed her belief in it, until her own feelings changed. The talk about being willing to do her duty as his wife was irrelevant by then, because she knew she never would be. They were on the point of separating.

Meanwhile, on 22 September, she opened the season at the Haymarket. The following evening both the Duke and the Prince of Wales were there to see her. Nothing was settled yet; but three weeks later, on 13 October, the Duke wrote to his brother from Petersham triumphantly,

> you may safely congratulate me on my success: everything is arranged: they never were married: I have all proofs requisite and even legal ones. I have as quiet, full and ample possession of the house in Somerset Street as if I had been an inhabitant for ten years. No letter could possibly contain the particulars: suspend then judgment till we meet. In your way to Windsor come here Sunday ... I am sure I am too well acquainted with your friendship to doubt for a moment you will, my dear brother, behave kindly to a woman who possesses so deservedly my heart and confidence, and who has given me so many unequivocal and steady proofs of the most uncommon steady attachment.[39]

9

Scandal: 1791

Dora was accustomed to public attention, but the storm of abuse that broke about her when she was known to have accepted the Duke's advances was unlike anything she had experienced before. It seems obvious that neither an actress nor a prince could hope to conduct their affairs in private, and that journalists and cartoonists, offered such an opportunity, should seize on it for all it was worth; even so, the savagery and ribald fervour with which they went for her shocks. The ferocity of their attacks could of course be justified in the name of public morality, on the grounds that it was the duty of the royal princes to set an example to the nation in their private lives, and that Mrs Jordan's behaviour now associated her with their vices. The indignation may even have been genuine in part; but there is another strong whiff arising from the whole affair – the whiff of the satirists' glee at getting hold of such a perfect story.

The Duke was not a delicate man, and Dora was used to standing up before an audience and delivering broad jokes, but she winced and he protested when they saw themselves savaged in the windows of the print-shops, and mocked with the special relish that greets revelations of delinquency in the famous and privileged. Some of Gillray's and Cruikshank's drawings can still make you wince today. She had been teased in the press because of the question marks over her past and her private life, although usually with affection; but the love affair with a prince changed the perception of her disastrously for the worse. She was suspected of using her professional success to rise socially, and even with a view to leaving the stage. Some thought she was selling herself cynically; others were driven to particular spite because she and the Duke seemed to be enjoying themselves too much. Day after day, they were held up to the nation's contempt.

Dora made as splendid a leading lady for the satirists' purposes as she did on stage; and their fun could be much more outrageous than hers. She was irresistible, and the Duke was quite as good a subject, not least because he lacked any notion of discretion. The spectacle of a second of the King's sons blatantly following in the footsteps of the Prince of Wales, and with a woman he had stolen from another man, provided them with one glorious opportunity after another. Cruikshank drew 'The Pot Calling the Kettle Black', setting Dora alongside a Mrs Fitzherbert who strives to look superior. Venereal disease and drunkenness, both rightly thought to be attributes of the royal brothers, could be invoked in a cartoon showing the Prince of Wales sitting in a box, watching Dora on stage, and saying, 'I'll clap her' while his brother administers gin from a large, leaky bottle.

Gillray drew Dora and William together in a tumbled bed, he in post-coital slumber, she sitting up proudly and reflecting on her success. In one cartoon they were made to represent 'Debauchery'. In another, captioned 'A Burning shame and Adulterous disgrace', Dora was shown with her breasts bared. A third set her on horseback, leading the princes to ruin, William riding behind with a chamber-pot on his head.

'Jordan' was a common term for a chamber-pot, so her name came in very handily. Just as the words 'Little Pickle' were understood by everyone to refer to her, the chamber-pot became an instantly recognizable visual symbol. Sometimes it was put over the head of the Duke; sometimes he was shown standing in it, with her prettily draped round the edge, naked and mermaid-like. In other drawings the pot reverted to its domestic function under the bed; the words 'Public jordan open to all parties' were written round one of these. The most effective and cruellest was Gillray's simple picture showing Dora as a giant chamber-pot, cracked and with a vagina-shaped hole into which the figure of William is disappearing, giving a nautical shout of pleasure as he does so. His braided coat is hanging on a peg to one side, and her ankles and feet in dainty slippers appear below the pot. The caption reads 'The Lubber's Hole, alias The Crack'd Jordan'. It was bad luck for Dora that Gillray was a genius, and that he struck off here a brilliant surreal image that imprints itself on the eye at once, and stays. It must have haunted her: an image to make its victim reluctant to face friends, enemies, family – Fanny was old enough to be aware of written words and pictures – colleagues, servants, or even strangers in the street; that could wake her at two in the morning in a cold sweat of humiliation.

There were political as well as moralistic elements in these attacks. With the French reforming their society across the channel, a significant number of the English were sympathetic to egalitarian ideas and efforts, and the spectacle of a brood of idle princes living extravagantly at the expense of the nation evoked strong disapproval. When it was rumoured that William was making a financial settlement on Dora, she could be presented as yet another drain on the nation's purse. Since actresses were routinely accused of being mercenary, and of using their public appearances to get rich lovers, some suggested she had set out to entrap the Duke. Others mocked their financial arrangements from the opposite end. One paper reported that Little Pickle's 'new FRIEND . . . actually received her *week's salary* from the *Treasurer*, on Saturday last' at the theatre.[1] This story was so good that it was taken up by the comic versifier Peter Pindar:

> As Jordan's high and mighty squire
> Her playhouse profits deigns to skim;
> Some folks audaciously inquire
> If *he* keeps *her* or *she* keeps *him*.

This version remained in the mythology. Those who thought she was the one who had been fooled warned her of the risks she was taking; the usual attention span of the princes did not inspire confident predictions for her future. Her mistake in thinking she might become a duchess was mocked in a cartoon showing her gazing into the mirror in her dressing room, which gives a false reflection in which she is wearing a coronet.

There was sympathy for Ford, who had seen his mistress and the mother of his children pinched by a rival with advantages that owed more to social position than merit. In mid-December a newspaper reported that a '*Naval Officer*' (i.e., the Duke) was infesting the Haymarket Theatre to the annoyance of everyone working there, and that he had asked 'Mr S' (i.e., Sheridan) to forbid Mr Ford from going backstage. 'Mr S very properly told the naval officer, that Mr Ford's *behaviour*, as a *gentleman*, precluded such a prohibition; and that in point of *right*, Mr F had as much pretention as (Mr S) himself.'[2]

The Duke busied himself trying to stop attacks that were sometimes precipitated by his own behaviour. He even applied to Sheridan for advice about how to silence the press, not stopping to think that there might be something awkward about going to the husband of a woman he had quite recently attempted to seduce. Sheridan, understandably enough, passed him on to the Controller General of the Post Office, John Palmer, who was a former theatre manager, and knew Dora; and the Duke's lawyer urged Palmer to try to silence the *Morning Herald*, which had been particularly vicious in its attacks. Whether this had any effect or not is impossible to tell; the Duke went on agitating, and urged his lawyer to prosecute the publishers of a scandalous book that revived the Daly story. But more books and pamphlets followed, with titles like *Little Pickle or the Pretty Plotter*.[3]

She continued at the Haymarket while the punishment went on until, at the end of November 1791, she became so distressed that she refused to appear. This precipitated further mockery and abuse, and she was accused of faking illness. The Duke called in the royal physicians, who said she must remain at Petersham for at least two weeks.

Dora suffered, but not in silence for long. When she was attacked for abandoning her children – 'To be mistress of the King's son Little Pickle thinks respectable, and so away go all tender ties to children' wrote *Bon Ton* magazine[4] – she reasonably enough asked Ford to write a letter stating that she had not done so. He obliged with a statement declaring that

> her conduct has ... been as laudable, generous, and as like a fond mother as in her present situation it was possible to be. She has indeed given up for their use every sixpence she has been able to save from her theatrical profits. She has also engaged to allow them £550 per an. and at the same time settled £50 a year upon her sister. 'Tis but bare justice for me to assert this as the father of those children.

He wrote a further note, again at her request:

> In gratitude for the care Mrs Jordan has ever bestowed upon my children, it is my consent and wish that she should, whenever she pleases, see and be with them, provided her visits are not attended by any circumstances which may be improper to them or unpleasant to me.[5]

Now, in order to silence the attacks on her in relation to the children, Dora gave Ford's statements to the press. This made him so angry that he wrote in turn to the *Morning Post* to say he had not authorized their publication; though one wonders what he thought the purpose of the letters was if they remained private. He then took himself across the channel to recover; his father was still in France, keeping clear of the financial tangles of Drury Lane in which he still feared involvement. According to Sheridan, this was 'a meer matter of unnecessary caution', but Dr Ford preferred to stay safely away. Father and son, feeling themselves to be fellow victims of the conduct of their one-time theatrical idols, licked their wounds ruefully together in Rouen.[6]

Dora also used the press at the end of November when she was attacked for failing to appear at the Haymarket. She wrote a letter from the theatre that she sent to several newspapers, including *The Times*, making the point that the public had no right to concern itself with anything outside her professional life.

> I have submitted in silence to the unprovoked and unmanly abuse which, for some time past, has been directed against me; because it has related to subjects about which the public could not be interested; but to an attack upon my conduct in my profession . . . I think it my duty to reply.
>
> Nothing can be more cruel and unfounded than the insinuation, that I absented myself from the theatre, on Saturday last, from any other cause than real inability, from illness, to sustain my part in the entertainment . . . I would not obtrude upon the public an allusion to anything that does not relate to my profession, in which *alone* I may, without presumption, say, I am accountable to them; but thus called on, in the present instance, there can be no impropriety in my answering those who have so ungenerously attacked me, that if they could drive me from that profession, they would take from me the *only income* I have, or mean to possess, the whole earnings of which, upon the past, and one-half for the future, I have already *settled* upon my children.

She went on to say she had been 'injustly and cruelly traduced' in the matter of her children; otherwise, she did not attempt to defend herself.

It is a good letter, clear and businesslike. Boaden says it was greeted with sneers, and certainly *The Times* first failed to print it and then commented rudely, 'she declares that if driven from the stage, she shall be deprived of the only income she has, or means to possess. If this be the case, we cannot help saying there are certainly more fools than one in the world.'[7] The insulting implication was that her career was of no account and could easily be given up; and that she should as a matter of course rely on the Duke to support her and her children in future.

She did accept a financial settlement from the Duke on 4 November, but she had no intention of giving up her career. The settlement was made through lawyers, and by its terms she received £840 a year from the Duke, paid as a quarterly allowance; his income, it will be remembered, was £12,000 a year. At the same time she transferred her entire savings, invested in government stock, to her sister and Richard Ford, for the future provision of their daughters, and promised to give them an annual allowance of £600. She also continued to be responsible for Fanny, and for her house in Somerset Street. So it is not surprising that she felt indignant at the accusations levelled against her. The difference between her arrangement with the Duke and the settlements made when the daughters of the rich married was that theirs were made by their fathers or brothers; whereas Dora had to make her own terms for herself and her children.

She was back on stage earlier than the doctors permitted, on 10 December. The audience was hostile. There were shouts, boos and hisses. Instead of leaving or showing she was angry, she came forward and spoke to the house. She was unsmiling and straightforward. She said she had never absented herself for one minute from the duties of her profession except when she was ill; and that as a result she considered herself 'under the public protection'. Only when she saw she had won the audience over did she allow a smile to appear. The effect was perfect. Boaden, who was present, said nothing in the play that night was quite so good as that moment. In the theatre at least she was victorious over her enemies. Even Kemble wrote in his diary, 'Mrs Jordan made an Apology this Night, and all is well again.'[8] But it was not an apology: it was a claim upon the loyalty of the audience and their solidarity with her. She worked for them, and − contrary to the view taken by *The Times* − she took her work seriously; and she expected them to be on her side.

10

'The only rival you can ever have'

Was the blundering Duke worth the commotion? Uncouth, uncultivated and prone to take up bad causes – he was a keen supporter of slavery, for example – he looks all too much of a royal Bottom to Dora's Titania. But she found him lovable; and although we can see, with hindsight, that it would have been better if she had never met him, she was drawn into the carnival, found herself at the whirling centre, and could not stop to consider or get away. Her first letters to him are sometimes tremulous, as though she felt she were indeed living through a fairy story, and he might sprout wings or carry her off in a magic pumpkin. How was it possible for a hardened Drury Lane actress who had seen the Prince of Wales at work on her colleagues to react like this? The answer is, as easily as for Elizabeth Sheridan, or Fanny Burney, or Mary Robinson, or almost anyone else. Royal blood confers charm, wit and even profundity on its lucky possessors. Even historians are sometimes vulnerable to it – Roger Fulford claimed that 'all the sons of George III had abilities far above the average' – so it is not too surprising that Dora Jordan found an irresistible glamour in being loved and courted by a real prince of the blood.[1]

The magic of royalty was not the only thing: for all his faults and deficiencies, he was a warm, outgoing creature, and she had been living with a man who had turned chilly. The Duke was energetic, passionately in love with her, and burning to display his love. He wanted to protect her; he called the best doctors when she was ill; he did his utmost to silence the press when it snarled and growled. He was kind and jolly with her daughters. He showed an interest in her working life and was proud of her professional reputation. He had an easy-going temper. He was not clever, or smart, like the Prince of Wales, but much more of an innocent, as much in need of a mother as a mistress. At twenty-six he longed for affection, and for the warmth of domestic life. Dora could give him both; and may have been encouraged by knowing she could supply what was needed.

And her effect on him was tonic. Not only was her dedication to her work exemplary, she also provided a centre and order to his life. She gave him good advice. Under her tactful guidance he largely gave up drinking – the exception being when he visited the Prince of Wales, which meant being on what Dora called 'hard duty' in that department. She teased him and even quarrelled with him, but she was loyal and constant. As one satirist wrote, congratulating him on his good fortune,

> She's in truth the best feather you have in your cap.
> How you got her, to me, I must own, is a wonder!
> When I think of your natural aptness to blunder.[2]

There was no question of marriage. All the Princes were under the constraint of the Royal Marriages Act, which they dealt with according to their temperaments. The Prince of Wales pursued his own duplicitous course. Frederick, Duke of York, obediently married the German princess selected for him and then lived mostly apart from her and had no children. The fourth son, Edward (later Duke of Kent), invited a young Frenchwoman, Julie de Saint Laurent, to live with him and settled down to decades of complete domestic happiness; whether they were married, and whether they had children, remains uncertain. Prince Ernest (later Duke of Cumberland) lived a generally profligate life, and had one known illegitimate son, FitzErnest; he was also suspected of making incestuous advances to one of his sisters. Prince Augustus made an illegal marriage in Rome, and fathered two children of uncertain status. The Princesses pined for husbands into their thirties and forties, or in vain.

Dora was disqualified as a possible royal bride, not only by being illegitimate, and an actress, and the mother of three children, but because she had not the right type of blood flowing in her veins: royals were supposed to marry other royals. The Duke's letters have not survived, and hers to him make no mention of the subject of her status, so there is no way of knowing how he explained his position to her; and perhaps no explanation was necessary, seeing what promises of marriage had done for her and her mother. But Dora was not a Mrs Crouch or an Emma Hamilton, ready to have a fling and then forget it, or to be passed from one admirer to another; and there was nothing casual about the setting up of the terms on which she and William were going to live together. There could be no church blessing, but there was a settlement, in its way a serious thing that acknowledged her dignity. In the eyes of the world the Duke became her 'protector', a word wonderfully unsuitable, but understood by everyone.

Ford's version of his parting with Dora was never given, and his silence leaves many questions unanswered. According to Boaden, he 'resigned her with legal composure'; but Boaden was a hostile witness, the best he could find to say of Ford being that 'of all the men it has been my chance to know, I never knew a man of whom there is so little to tell', and that none of his legal colleagues had anything to say about him.[3] So perhaps he was more upset by the public humiliation than by the break itself; he could, after all, have married her, and by doing so prevented the whole messy business. Yet other accounts suggest he was distressed. Hester Bland thought he had been ill-used, and wrote of Dora doing 'so much to make him unhappy'; and another observer said he 'seemed to enjoy no very enviable state of mind'.[4] But we shall never know whether he kept his lips sealed as a perfect gentleman who felt he should say nothing either against the mother of his children or against the King's son, or as a guilty fellow who knew he could not defend his own behaviour.

He was deeply attached to his four-year-old daughter Dodee, as is clear from the offer he made at one point to forgo seeing little Lucy altogether if only he might keep her.[5] Hester's letters paint a woeful picture of wrangles over the children. When the Petersham house was given up, Dora leased and furnished another house in Brompton for them, giving Hester the furniture and Ford the lease. He insisted on paying all expenses there, but then tried to stop Dodee going to stay with her mother at Somerset Street. The Duke intervened to insist that Somerset Street should be Dodee's home, and she should only visit the Brompton house. At this Hester threatened to withdraw altogether from the care of the children. Her allegiance went entirely to Ford; she said she pitied Dora and spiritedly asked her to 'tell the Duke *from me* that I will not be consider'd as *his nurse and housekeeper*, nor will I continue in a house of which he is *master*'.[6] Hester at least was immune to the royal glamour.

The disputes over the two girls continued in a dispiriting way for several years. There is a letter accusing Ford of non-payment of an allowance for them, and another in which Dora offers to let him have them entirely in his care provided he will guarantee that she can see them regularly and often.[7] This did not happen; by 1795 Ford was married and had a legitimate son, and seems to have become quite detached from Dodee and Lucy, who grew up very close to their mother – and the Duke. Ford became a favourite of the King; he was often at court, and received a knighthood. He also gave up Parliament, and became a police magistrate. When he came to write his will in 1798 he at first assigned his large holding of shares in Drury Lane to 'the use of my two illegitimate children by Mrs Jordan of Drury Lane Theatre', but did not even name them; and a few weeks later he rewrote the will, reassigning the shares to his wife, and cutting out his daughters altogether.[8] Perhaps he felt they were well enough provided for by their mother and saw no need to make any paternal gesture; he had also turned to religion, and may have felt his Dodee and Lucy represented the sinful side of his nature. Still, it leaves a sorry impression.

The first of Dora's private letters to survive are her letters to the Duke, written during the winter of 1791. It is a shock to hear her intimate voice after knowing her from the outside, through other people's accounts, for so many years; and to be eavesdropping on such purely personal letters. Some are touching, some embarrassing; but then love letters are not written to be judged as literature. These contain the phrases you might expect – 'never two people loved so well', 'you are dearer, far dearer to me than life' – but also suggest that the lovers' approach to one another was made with considerable awkwardness, and through a barbed hedge of difficulties and uncertainties. Sometimes he is 'love', sometimes 'Your Royal Highness'. The writing is noticeably smaller than her later hand ever was, suggesting stress, and it is used to convey pain and embarrassment as well as excitement and pleasure.

Although his side of the correspondence is missing, some of it can be guessed from hers.[9] 'What a task you give me when you desire me to tell you how much I love you,' she writes, conjuring up at once the William who has suffered so long from feeling unloved and unappreciated, and is desperately seeking reassurance. She thanks him for sending her presents, prints and drawings, and a picture of himself; in a display of generosity he is at his most confident. She does assure him of his power over her heart and feelings, and of the happiness she feels at his 'dear enchanting professions of love'; but she also worries about what the servants will think.

She 'could dye with shame', and asks him not to come round. She has the worst headache she has ever suffered; then she is sick, too sick to eat dinner. She advises him – 'permit me for the first time to take the liberty of offering you my advice' – not to come out to meet her when he too falls ill. She begs him to delay moving into her house; she is 'of a very shy disposition'. Could they meet in the country, '*any where out of town*' rather than in the public eye? She goes out to meet him, but is turned back by the traffic after two hours' struggle: a very modern love affair, this.

She thinks of moving house at one point because 'I have gone through so many cruel scenes in it, that there is a constant gloom hangs over my mind whenever I am in it'; but he does not encourage her, and she remains in Somerset Street. She tells him about her sister's illness, and apologizes for her brother George, 'whose uncommon affection for me made him more violent than he ought to have been': you wonder whether he threw a punch at the Duke. She says she has been crying for two days, complains about enemies in the acting world, tells him she has been warned 'that you never liked any woman above half a year'. Like most people in love, she is sometimes absurd, and at her silliest suggests she should have an anchor – symbol of the navy – painted on the panels of the carriage he has given her; and he, at his most sensible, vetoes the idea.

At the same time she is wholly sensible and practical about the conditions and demands of her working life. When he expresses dislike of some of her roles, she replies tactfully that she has always disliked those too, 'but the managers will study their own interest', and she must do as the managers direct. She also explains that, while she can be relatively free in summer, in the winter months she must live in London, and near the theatre; it does not cross her mind for an instant that she should give up her career.

She is feeling her way, in these letters, sometimes delightedly, sometimes nervously and uncertainly, towards a *modus vivendi* with the Duke. He is still a largely unknown quantity: one day a pleading boy, the next an overbearing man; sometimes generous, sometimes gross. There are several references to his delicacy and refinement: is she praising a virtue in the hope of producing it? Then the reader is drawn up short when she writes of her children, 'How good, how humane you are, in not wishing to prevent my seeing those dear little things.'[10] Did she ever for one moment think he would try to separate her from them? Perhaps she was led to expect he would; but it was not a condition she would have allowed.

The deepest and truest notes in these letters are struck when she speaks of her daughters, and especially the eldest and most vulnerable. 'You ask me kindly in what manner you can afford me relief and assistance. There is but one way; which is through my dear little Fanny – set my mind totally at [ease] with respect to her, and I will be yours for ever.' In another letter she tells him, 'A dear and amiable little girl made doubly dear to me by mutual misfortune, shall be taught to bless you as her only friend and generous benefactor.' Then, 'I will allow you to be jealous of my poor Fan; as she is the only rival you can ever have in my heart.'[11] Fanny had seen that Ford was quite indifferent to where she was; the Duke was friendly, and she decided to like him.

Once Dora and the Duke were known to be living together, press interest began to flag. The relief of escaping from the pressure of constant observation and ridicule must have been great. In other ways her life was not much easier – and in some ways probably harder – because she had to divide herself between so many places and people, lover, children and theatre all making their conflicting demands on her attention. She was constantly travelling between Somerset Street – she did not get rid of it, and William and the children both used it – Brompton, where Hester was based with the children, William's house at Petersham, and the Haymarket, where Sheridan was sometimes heard to express his aversion to her powerful friend.[12] William also used his rooms in St James's Palace, and sometimes took Dora there too. Even buoyed up by love, she must have found the arrangement tiring.

*

In March 1792, after two and a half years of freedom, she was pregnant again. It made no difference to her working programme; she acted steadily on until the summer. Sheridan's friend Joseph Richardson, a Member of Parliament and a Whig journalist, wrote a comedy called *The Fugitive* especially for her. He put in some fashionable references to women's rights, inspired by the bestseller of the season, Mary Wollstonecraft's *A Vindication of the Rights of Woman*. One character complained that woman was 'a creature with regard to whom engagements lose their faith, and contracts their obligations'. As for men, their love was fiction, their real behaviour bad: 'in your fictitious characters, as lovers, you endeavour to make us believe that we are exalted above human weaknesses; but, in your real characters, as men, you more honestly demonstrate to us, that you place us even below your own level, and deny us the equal truth and justice that belongs alike to all intelligent beings'.[13] The comedy nudged her with a reminder of the painful truth: Ford had failed to keep faith with her, and she could have no certainty that her new lover would behave any better. At the same time she herself was a one-woman vindication of her sex's energy. She put a new song into *Twelfth Night*, played *The Country Girl* yet again for her benefit, making £540 in the one evening, and on 7 June closed the season as Rosalind. Then she retreated to Petersham for the summer; only, with her customary good grace, agreed to come back into town to appear in a benefit for her old friend Mrs Bannister, who – unlike Dora – was retiring to devote herself to her family. This was at the end of July. A few days later she had a miscarriage, at Petersham. For some hours, her life was in danger. Perhaps this acted as a reminder that her youngest child, Lucy, remained unbaptized at nearly three years old; for on 11 August the omission was made good by Thomas Lloyd, curate of Ewell, soon to become Chaplain to the Duke.

For the Sheridans, 1792 brought no comedy at all. Against all advice – 'every time you touch her, you drive a Nail in her Coffin' – Elizabeth was expecting a second child. But her son was already seventeen and away at school, and the new baby was not her husband's. She had at last lost patience with him, and allowed herself to fall in love with one of his political friends: Lord Edward Fitzgerald was a cousin of Fox, a vehement radical, dashing, impetuous and unreliable. He became her lover in 1791; and even before she bore his child, Sheridan was called on to console her for Lord Edward's flightiness. The baby was born in April. From that moment Elizabeth's health slipped away fast. It was tuberculosis, but not only tuberculosis: as she wrote to a friend, she had eaten forbidden fruit and could not return to the 'old Haunts and ways of Happiness and Innocence'.[14]

Sheridan accepted and loved the child, defended Elizabeth against all criticism and devoted himself to her care with a patient tenderness he had not shown her for years. He told his grief to Harriet Duncannon in a series of letters that begged her to comfort him even as they mourned for Elizabeth: 'I am just returned from a long solitary walk on the beach. Night Silence Solitude and the Sea combined will unhinge the cheerfulness of anyone, where there has been length of Life enough to bring regret in reflecting on many past scenes . . .' He blamed himself: 'the irregularity of my Life and pursuits, the restless contriving Temper with which I have persevered in wrong Pursuits and Passions makes . . . reflexion worse to me than even to those who have acted worse.' He felt his bad conduct was responsible for his wife's approaching death, and tried to find some consolation in religion; Harriet's letters urged it on him, and Elizabeth turned entirely to her child-hood faith, but he looked 'in vain into my own mind for assent to her apparent conviction that all will not perish'.[15] He entreated Harriet to keep writing to him. She was abroad, with serious problems of her own to cope with, helping her sister to escape the jealous fury of the Duke of Devonshire, and to conceal the birth of the Duchess's child, whose father was another of Sheridan's political friends, Charles Grey.[16] This child, born at Aix-en-Provence a few weeks before Elizabeth's, was sent back secretly to England to be brought up in her grandparents' house, under a false name and ignorant of her parentage.* The Duchess returned and was forgiven; but Elizabeth went to her grave in June. Her infant daughter lived little more than a year; she became ill while Sheridan was giving a party, and he was informed of her death at the very moment the dancing was about to begin. The world of *Così fan tutte* had come to a bleak curtain.

---

* Eliza Courtney (the name given to the Duchess's daughter by Charles Grey) was brought up at Fallodon, calling her grandmother 'Mama'. The Duchess wrote to her, and worried about her, but was not allowed any close contact.[17]

I I

Nell of Clarence: 1792–1796

Dora spent the autumn of 1792 recovering from her miscarriage at Petersham. It was not quite the life of wicked luxury imagined for her by the curious world; nor had she floated free of her past and family. Her awkward brother George still put pressure on her to find him work and, when that failed, he asked for hand-outs; while Hester, rigidly disapproving in Brompton, had to be trusted not to impress the sinfulness of their mother too strongly upon Fanny, Dodee and Lucy. Whenever possible, Dora had her little girls with her, or went to them, often with the Duke in attendance; and sometimes she abandoned him in order to be with them.

Petersham was as delightful as ever, but Clarence Lodge made a somewhat precarious home. The Duke held it on a mortgage, and his financial problems meant there was considerable uncertainty from month to month as to whether they could remain there; and it was small, with only eight rooms, hardly enough for the existing children, let alone any more. As soon as Dora started acting again she returned to Somerset Street, which remained the centre of their scattered life; during the next four years more than half her time was spent there while she worked, fitting in as best she could the births of two more children — she chose Somerset Street for both — and enduring two more miscarriages.

Even during absences from the theatre, she remained intensely involved with it. Like all who live by the public, she worried about it at least as much as it thought about her; the memory of that moment when the Haymarket audience had turned against her in December 1791 made her determined not to risk losing it again. She spent the winter of 1792 writing, or helping to write, a play. It became the cause of one of the many quarrels that raged in a company full of strong-willed people with conflicting ideas: Kemble, a traditionalist; Sheridan, ready to try a novelty; Jordan, rather surprisingly appearing now as the assertive voice of female power. She wrote *Anna* in collaboration with another woman, a Miss Cuthbertson, who has left no other trace; and Tate Wilkinson credited it all to Dora, and reported that 'the whole town was on tiptoe for Mrs Jordan's New Comedy'.[1] Sheridan gave his agreement to the production; then Kemble threatened to resign as manager if it went ahead. Dora accused him of wanting to put on nothing but revivals – a fair criticism – and the battle of wills flared up more fiercely because it was also a battle about the male manager being attacked by a female member of the company. Then Sheridan and Dora began to wrangle too, about money. As she rehearsed *Anna* in January 1793, everyone was at loggerheads over politics, over money, over the repertoire. She threatened Sheridan with a lawyer's letter when he seemed to withdraw his support, and sent off another letter to the press accusing Kemble of trying to prevent her from appearing in new characters. Under this pressure, Kemble gave way.

The story would come to a better conclusion if *Anna* had been a success; but it was a flop. Even her friends found it derivative, a mere juggling of stock ingredients. It was played once and then, in Tate's Wilkinson's good, vulgar phrase, 'dropped like an unfortunate young lady's pad' – what we call a hair-piece today. Dora had apparently wasted her energy, and Kemble was vindicated; and we cannot dispute the verdict now, for the text, like so many others, has disappeared.

The trials of *Anna* took place against great events in the real world; indeed, they may have helped to kill it. England

and France were moving towards war; even Sheridan's support for the revolution was somewhat shaken by news that the French king was to be put on trial. Mourning his wife as he was, Sheridan was deeply involved in calls for parliamentary reform in England, and in setting up a radical club, the Friends of the People; he mocked the fears displayed by so many of his countrymen and women as French *émigrés* arrived with tales of horror, and the English began to imagine their own society turning upside-down in the same dangerous way. He was right in believing the British would not behave like the French, and could have reform without violence, and his teasing voice was a voice of sanity. At the same time his personal behaviour was becoming more self-destructive. For instance, he could not resist placing bets on reform, one hundred guineas that it would pass into law in two years, five hundred on three, and so on: he could not afford the bets, the sums got bigger as he drank more, and the drinking got worse as he grieved for Elizabeth. At least he found a distraction during the autumn, when he fell in love with Pamela Egalité, a French girl who came to England to meet the British reformers; she was the adopted daughter of two prominent French radicals, the writer Madame de Genlis and the Duke of Orleans, and reared to show that nurture counted for more than blood. Pamela was also said to resemble Elizabeth Sheridan, and her beauty caused a brief sensation. Sheridan danced attendance and everyone in London wanted to know her. She was even introduced to the Duke of Clarence, who escorted her both to Carlton House and to see the King in Parliament; and in December she married Mrs Sheridan's lover, Lord Edward Fitzgerald, neatly closing the circle, but leaving Sheridan no happier. Later Fitzgerald took her to Ireland, where he became an active revolutionary, and the Duke became quite nervous when he realized how close he had been to someone so dangerous.[2]

Another quarrel broke out between Sheridan and Kemble when he shut the Haymarket as a gesture of respect on the day the news of the French king's execution reached London, 24 January 1793. Sheridan complained angrily that the gesture was both unnecessary and expensive: he was having enough trouble funding his new theatre, rising slowly in Drury Lane, without losing receipts. Dora was absorbed in her rehearsals and avoided politics; and the Duke missed the whole thing because he had slipped on a frosty step outside Somerset Street, fallen and broken his arm, and was at once carried off by a protective Prince of Wales to St James's Palace, to be tended by the royal doctors.

This meant he missed *Anna* as well – perhaps a relief to Dora – and he was still at the palace when France declared war on England at the beginning of February. As soon as his arm mended he asked to serve his country by being given a command in the Home Fleet; but he immediately lost whatever chance he might have had by announcing in the Lords that he thought the war should be ended. The Prime Minister, Pitt, told the King he could not have a 'political admiral'; and William remained torn between his desire to serve his country at sea and his anti-war feelings, which developed as the year went by. In November he wrote, 'If ever, unfortunately for this country, I should by Providence be commanded to wear the Crown, my greatest desire would be to be considered *a peaceful Monarch*.'[3] It is one of his more appealing remarks, because it suggests genuine modesty. It shows too that he sometimes allowed himself to imagine a future in which he occupied the throne; which was a reasonable enough prospect, since neither of his elder brothers had children – or at least avowable children.

When the Duke wrote this letter, Dora was again expecting a child. Did he consider its future when he wrote of becoming king himself? Probably not. As the birth approached, in January 1794, she stayed in London and he was away a good deal visiting his brothers. His money problems were particularly acute, and he thought he might be about to lose the Petersham house. The Prince of Wales, largely responsible for his difficulties, was trying to help by asking the King to get Pitt to agree to 'purchase the whole of Petersham for the sum of four-and-twenty-thousand pounds', and to allow William to remain there. 'I am afraid the Prince will not succeed,' he wrote to Thomas Coutts. He was right; there was no reason at all why Pitt, who had more serious matters to attend to, should agree to the proposition. Still William remained optimistic. When Pitt turned him down, he asked the King to buy the house; the King also refused. William managed to raise money through another financier; then he assured Coutts that 'seven thousand pounds will, I am sure, settle difficulties and then by economy I hope to be once more free'.[4]

While these inglorious negotiations were under way, Dora's and the Duke's first child made his appearance at Somerset Street, at seven in the morning of 29 January 1794. The birth was difficult and Dora even thought she might die; but although she was weak and ill for a few days, she soon recovered, and the boy was pronounced 'a very fine one and in the most perfect health' by his proud father. He was not baptized until 10 May, when Thomas Lloyd, the same curate of Ewell who had christened Lucy, now Chaplain to the Duke, went to Petersham to perform the office privately. The child was set down as George FitzClarence, 'son of His Royal Highness The Duke of Clarence and Mrs Dorah Jordan'; at some later date he was given two extra names, Augustus Frederick, for good measure. Little George was adored from the start by both his parents. Dora fed him herself, and he grew into a handsome, high-spirited small boy; he was much indulged, and much loved by his half-sisters.

Engaged in nursing her son, Dora did not appear when the new Drury Lane opened in April, with Mrs Siddons as Lady Macbeth and Miss Farren displaying the glories of the iron fire curtain. Henry Holland had designed a colossal building, with seats for 3,600, but the sight lines were bad and the gallery so high that its occupants found it hard to hear. Sheridan called it his Grand National Theatre, but it was in trouble from the start because he could not manage the finances; actors and staff went unpaid, there were strikes, people left, and the house was never full.

Over the next three years the Duke, despite his disapproval of the war, continued his efforts to get a naval appointment, while England was drawn into one military and naval disaster after another. Three of his brothers were seriously involved, the Duke of York being forced to flee for his life, and the Dukes of Sussex and Cumberland both wounded in battle. The Prussians and the Spaniards made their peace with France; the French crushed the English-backed rising in the Vendée, built up a great revolutionary army, fought off all comers, and became masters of the Dutch coast. Still William was refused any role in the struggle. He was fobbed off with an honorary promotion to vice-admiral; and he was mocked in the prints – unfairly in this instance – which show him holding a baby and saying he'd rather creep into a Jordan than fight the enemy. Cruelly, his naval expertise found its only outlet when Sheridan organized a grand benefit for naval widows at the new Drury Lane in July 1794. The whole thing was written and rehearsed in three days flat – this was very much Sheridan's hallmark – and, since it involved the representation of two fleets in tanks of water on the stage, the Duke was called in to give technical advice. At least the satirists missed this opportunity for further mockery.

Dora, after nursing George quietly for five months, made her first appearance on the new stage at this benefit. Then she began to talk business with Sheridan and, after long negotiations, signed a fresh contract with him on 1 September, engaging herself to 'act, sing and perform any and every character for five years at thirty guineas a week'.[6] It was a generous arrangement for her, but a demanding one; Sheridan may have thought – or hoped – she had enough children, and could now give herself to her career full time. In fact she was already pregnant again. 'Mrs Jordan is shortly expecting to produce *something*, whether a young Admiral or a Pickle

Duchess it is impossible yet to tell,' *Bon Ton* magazine announced to its readers.[7] She did not let this interfere; after a short holiday in Brighton, where she stayed with the Duke and baby George in Mrs Fitzherbert's house, she was back at Drury Lane to work through the autumn and winter. George was always with her; the Duke was not. She sent him reassuring notes: 'your dear little Boy is perfectly well'; she was 'perfectly happy' with him; or she was delayed at a rehearsal with him. It is obvious that she took him into Drury Lane with her, in the time-honoured fashion, making him into a thoroughgoing theatre baby even if his grandfather was the King.[8]

Sheridan was now wooing Hecca, half his age and well connected: she was the daughter of the Dean of Winchester and would become his second wife. But he did not neglect Dora, and even thought of her interest in women playwrights. He asked Elizabeth Inchbald, who had a string of successful plays at Covent Garden, to write something especially for Dora; she seized the chance and wrote a farce mocking male vanity, *The Wedding Day*, in which an elderly widower is on the point of marrying a young girl when his supposedly dead wife returns unexpectedly. Dora's Lady Contest became another of her regularly repeated successes; and encouraged by this, she made another attempt of her own to help a woman playwright by offering to appear in a satirical comedy about gambling, *Nobody*, the work of Mary Robinson, loved and abandoned by the Prince of Wales fifteen years earlier. Some of Dora's colleagues feared that the satire would anger the very ladies on whose patronage the theatre depended – not to mention the Prince – and refused to be involved in the production, so that she found herself championing a play with little support once again; but Bannister at least was loyal. As soon as the curtain went up, ladies in the audience hissed through their fans, while their servants in the gallery were under orders to express themselves as loudly as they could. Dora played on against the interruptions, and was only just able to get through the evening. The Duke was not there to support her, and she sent him a note afterwards, telling him the play had been '*damned* most unfairly . . . I send these few lines to anticipate the newspapers,' she added.[9] But she was back in the theatre the next night, and a brave third. The audiences grew rowdier, and Mrs Robinson decided Mrs Jordan had done enough, and withdrew her comedy. Plays were damned for different reasons, and the text has again disappeared; but Dora's determination to give it a fair trial, her bearing the brunt of the hostile reaction, was an admirable and unusual piece of solidarity with another, less fortunate woman.

After this came a different trial. Twelve-year-old Fanny fell ill, Dora went to nurse her, found she had a high fever, and would not leave her. When the Duke suggested she should at least meet him in the park for a walk, she refused, saying she was too tired to go so far on foot, and would not use the carriage for fear of infecting it with whatever Fanny might have. She called in one of the royal family's physicians, Dr Turton, who diagnosed putrid or scarlet fever. Dodee caught it too, and both children were seriously ill; Dr Turton said Fanny's life depended on her being able to keep down the bark he prescribed. Dora was up for three nights, 'half distracted', and Turton too was anxious enough to remain with the children all through one of them. He was also watching Dora for signs of illness, and though she showed none, he counselled her to keep entirely away from the Duke and from George. This advice she obeyed. 'I should never forgive myself if I was the cause of giving you any pain either of body or mind,' she wrote; 'Love and kiss my dear little boy and let him (independent of the claim he has on *you*) have some interest in your heart because he is mine also.' Whether Dr Turton's bark or their mother's nursing was responsible, the girls slowly recovered; first Fanny, then Dodee was declared out of danger, Dora expressed her gratitude to the doctor, and things settled down into a more normal pattern.[10]

Or at least, she was able to return to Somerset Street for the birth of another child: at two in the morning of 4 March 1795, the Duke's first daughter was born. He gave her the name of his seventeen-year-old sister, Princess Sophia. A month after this Dora was back at work, though sometimes 'very much exhausted and languid'; she was feeding the baby, and found the constant travel between their different houses tiring. There was something else to worry her in April. The Prince of Wales, his debts now amounting to over £600,000, had finally agreed to follow his father's wishes and marry his cousin Caroline of Brunswick. He went through the whole thing reluctantly and in a spirit of total cynicism, simply in order to retrieve his financial situation; although he had long been faithless to Mrs Fitzherbert, he still regarded her as 'the Wife of my heart and soul'.[11] Since Dora was on terms of friendship with her, she could not fail to feel sympathy for her position, and to ponder the royal family's notion of acceptable behaviour.

The Duke naturally attended his brother's second and more public wedding; how the marriage was discussed between them is not on record. We do know that the Prince, who separated from the Princess almost as soon as they were married, came to Petersham the following summer to discuss his marriage problems with his brother, and stayed for two weeks, with Dora as his hostess. She also entertained the Prince of Orange to dinner that summer, putting off a performance at Richmond in order to do so. Horace Walpole, still keeping an eye out on the other side of the river, observed that 'she did the honours at the head of the table' and added slyly, 'no, the Princesses were not there'.[12] The rules of royal behaviour must have seemed as bizarre as the antics of Greek gods on a painted ceiling. The Prince might smile and scatter his favours, or show a cold face and withdraw them, without being asked for a reason from below; and he could share a house with his brother and Dora, but not bring his sisters; and they could watch her across the theatre, but not speak to her.

There were quarrels between her and the Duke this summer of 1795, perhaps precipitated by the royal wedding. The gossip was that William had flirted with a lady at a ball; Dora was not invited but she had gone into the gallery where the band was playing to observe them. Everything about the story was humiliating for her, the social snub she was subjected to, her jealousy, the fact that it seemed justified; only the Duke's response salved the hurt, as he simply refused to consider the separation she proposed in her anger. He had no wish at all to give up his pleasant domestic arrangements with her. His account of the quarrel, reported by a later dancing partner, is more endearing than not:

> Mrs Jordan is a very good creature, very domestic and careful of the children. To be sure she is absurd sometimes, and has her humours. But there are such things more or less in all families. I daresay you and Mr Sutton have your little disputes. To be sure she made a strange, foolish business last summer . . . but then she repented and was sorry for it. You heard of it, I daresay.[13]

The very good creature was also appearing in half a dozen plays in the spring of 1795: one adapted from Madame de Genlis; a revival of Mrs Inchbald's *The Child of Nature*; a farce called *The Adopted Child*, done to music by Mozart (tantalizingly, we do not know which music); other new farces, including *The Welch Heiress* by Jerningham, a friend of the Prince of Wales and Horace Walpole, which failed after one night; and the success of the season, a very up-to-date play about a girl whose parents die in the French Revolution, *First Love*, by Richard Cumberland. The sheer number of lines to learn in one season, alongside all her old parts, must have made considerable demands. No modern actor has to carry anything like such a burdened memory; the nearest equivalent is the old provincial repertory system, but even that did not alternate revivals with new plays, or run two plays every night. Most of the farces in which Dora excelled also demanded considerable physical agility; her letters mention falls, bruises and sprains. Then there were songs to learn and deliver; and counterpointed against the rhythm of learning, performing, consolidating and discarding different parts, was the other rhythm of her life, the pregnancies, the babies, the breast-feeding, the miscarriages. She and the Duke proved an almost indecently fertile couple. It became a subject of amusement to others but probably not to her, although she never complained either. In the busy season of 1795, with Sophia only a few months old and unweaned, she was pregnant again; it was not too surprising that she miscarried in July. The same thing happened the following January, in the middle of an equally hard-working winter.

There was a further piece of unpleasantness to deal with in July, when Richard Daly appeared in London. Not the man to lose an opportunity, he asked Dora if he could see his daughter Fanny, at the same time letting her know he would pay her a hundred guineas a night if she would make the trip back to Dublin to perform at his theatre. Dora was neither touched nor flattered by the sudden interest in Fanny or the recognition of her own cash value. It is unlikely she consulted Fanny, and she refused him on both counts.

She kept up her appearances at Richmond Theatre in August and September. Walpole turned an elegant Shakespearean phrase in her honour: 'Nell of Clarence plays Ophelia tonight at Richmond.'[14] Why did he call her Nell? It was one of her best-known parts, as a poor wife magically transported to riches, in *The Devil to Pay*; but Walpole may also have intended a reference to her famous predecessor as royal theatrical mistress, Nell Gwynne.

After the winter miscarriage she was quickly back at Drury Lane, playing with Kemble in Wycherley's *Plain Dealer*. Their feud had burnt itself out for the moment, and they allowed themselves to be friends; and he found her performance as Fidelia to his Manly so irresistible that he quoted his favourite author, Sterne, in her praise: 'I could have taken her into my arms, and cherished her, though it was in the open street, without blushing.'[15] Kemble may have been softened by some troubles of his own. He had been caught on the point of raping Miss De Camp in her dressing room: she screamed for help, and a crowd gathered and rescued her. Kemble was often drunk, and probably so on this occasion, an acceptable excuse to most of his circle. His wife forgave him, and his grand friends laughed it off as 'more a jest than ... an enormity', but he was obliged all the same to make a public apology in the newspapers, because she was a respectable young woman, who later became his sister-in-law.[16]

Kemble and Jordan were together again in *Vortigern*, one of Sheridan's most misjudged dramatic ventures. The play, which ran to nearly 3,000 lines, was brought to the attention of the world by a father and son, Samuel and William Ireland, who claimed to have discovered some Shakespeare manuscripts. They were authenticated by many eminent people; Boswell, for instance, fell on his knees at the sight of them. The Prince of Wales and Duke of Clarence both asked to see the manuscript of *Vortigern*; and according to young Ireland, who showed it to the Duke and Mrs Jordan, they questioned him about its origin, and made several objections, which he was able to answer. Covent Garden and Drury Lane then competed for the honour of putting it on; Sheridan got it for £300, only a hundred more than he paid Mrs Inchbald for her farce, but promising the Irelands half the profits for the first sixty nights. As it turned out, it was not too disastrous a bit of bargaining, because as soon as the play went into rehearsal, everyone began to have doubts about it. Sheridan, never a Shakespeare enthusiast, pronounced it an early work. Mrs Siddons found she was not well enough to appear. Kemble suggested 1 April as an appropriate opening date. The press was divided about its authenticity, but agog, and the theatre was besieged for the first performance, on 2 April. *Vortigern* was of course a forgery. William Ireland had been inspired by Chatterton; having convinced his own father with the first forgeries he attempted, he found himself carried along on their momentum. He confessed afterwards that he had written the play with parts for particular actors and actresses in mind; Mrs Jordan, for example, had a 'Shakespearean' song, was put into male attire, and given the epilogue, because he knew this was what the public liked. As playwriting policies go, it was not a bad one, but it did not go far enough. Dora did her best, and went out of her way to speak kindly to the eighteen-year-old author as he sat backstage, hearing the packed house begin to shout and jeer as the evening proceeded, while Kemble encouraged the audience from the stage by gesturing to show which side he was on. The evening ended with people howling and throwing oranges, and the sixty nights of half profits remained a dream for the Irelands: *Vortigern* was never played again.

After this there was another row between Kemble and Dora, when they both wanted to put on *Hamlet* for their benefits. Kemble invited her to play Ophelia to Mrs Siddons's Gertrude, and she refused, although it is unlikely she wanted Gertrude for herself. Sheridan, called on to arbitrate, told them neither could have *Hamlet*, at which Kemble performed his old success, *Coriolanus*, and then resigned and went off to Ireland. Dora, more boldly, tried something new and played Juliet. It was not one of her triumphs, but went well enough to be repeated several times; and at least she had just managed to fit it in between pregnancies.

Sheridan was now struggling with the theatre's finances, growing worse from month to month, and he found Dora's pregnancies particularly exasperating. He wrote to William Adam – who acted as her lawyer and the Duke's – in September 1796, when she was once again in this condition, to point out how much time she missed on their account: 'It is to be observed (tho' perhaps out of the Spirit of Chivalry) that when Mrs Jordan's *time comes* to play according to the Letter of her article she will be unfit to perform anything worth her salary.'[17] He need not have grumbled; Dora worked

Playbill for the only performance of *Vortigern*, the Shakespeare forgery, at Drury Lane on 2 April 1796. Note the musical entertainment following, with Mozart's friend, Anna Storace, in the cast.

all through the autumn and into December, when she made a very pregnant Ophelia. She and Sheridan wrangled over the arrears of salary due to her, and her refusal to play parts she disliked. Once he went out to Richmond to 'remove an impediment to Jordan's playing tomorrow' only to find 'she does not return with her Duke till – *ten o'clock* – being gone to see her children'.[18] It was bad luck for Sheridan, left to wander round the fields of Petersham; but we can be pleased to think of Dora and her Duke taking the babies to spend the day with their sisters, not unlike a busy late-twentieth-century career woman trying to fit the various elements of her scattered family together. The new manager of Drury Lane, Richard Wroughton, advised Sheridan to use 'more soothing Terms' when he dealt with Mrs Jordan, and bits of her salary were dribbled out to her: she got £20 on one day, £120 on another, then ten guineas on account in December. The winter settled into a cold spell. The weather was too much for Horace Walpole; he fell ill and was taken to London, and failed to return. Twickenham, Petersham and Richmond felt the loss of his watchful eye and witty pen, and so do we.

Was Nell of Clarence happy? Partly, though she had her bleak times. Sometimes she felt the need to see more friends from her professional world. In such a mood she wrote 'without ceremony' (as he put it) to a newspaper editor and aspiring playwright, James Boaden, inviting him to visit her to discuss scripts, and to consider how she might extend her range. They became friends, and he took to calling regularly to talk about the theatre, often while the children played around them. For her it was useful to have a sympathetic journalist on call, and for him it was flattering; and there was genuine warmth on both sides too. The best result of this initiative of hers was one she could not possibly have foreseen, when, forty years later, Boaden became her first biographer.

Other young men who were to become her champions in later years were coming into the theatre to see her for the first time in the mid-1790s. One was a Cambridge undergraduate and aspiring poet and playwright, Samuel Taylor Coleridge: 'Have you seen the Siddons this season? Or the Jordan?' he asked a friend.[19] Another was William Hazlitt, a minister's son preparing for the ministry himself, but on the brink of abandoning his studies for a career as a critic and essayist; he was struck especially by the beauty of her voice, both singing and speaking – 'like the luscious juice of the ripe grape', he recalled – and by the impression she gave of enjoying whatever she did on stage, and sharing her enjoyment with the audience. There was never anything contrived, 'dexterous or knowing' about her performance, he said; it was all warmth and generosity. Another admirer, a young clerk, fresh out of Christ's Hospital, was Charles Lamb, who particularly admired her in Shakespeare: as Rosalind, Ophelia and Helena in *All's Well*. Hazlitt and Lamb became friends, but each cherished a quite different aspect of Dora's playing. Lamb believed her plaintive parts outdid her much more popular comic ones; in particular he never forgot her sad Viola, telling her love to Orsino as though each line, each idea, had only just come into her head freshly as she spoke it.[20]

When audiences rose to her with appreciation and understanding of this calibre, she became exultant, even ecstatic.[21] The natural converse was that when she failed, or had to fight over productions and parts and money with the management, she became wretched. There is a note to the Duke this winter of 1796 from her dressing room after one such row:

> they are distracted about my refusing to play four times this week – Wroughton says it is their intention if I refuse, to leave me out of all new pieces. I said with regard to that they might do as they thought proper – tho' between ourselves I should be very sorry if they did ... I wish I was at home, when I am here I feel like a person deserted by the whole world, and open to all kind of unpleasant situations.[22]

Only where was home? Another letter from Somerset Street

to the Duke, who was at Windsor, on a dark morning, suggests she was weary of uncertainty on this matter:

> I returned last night at half past ten very much tired as you may suppose after playing in both Play & Farce . . . George is very well tho' his cold is rather troublesome. You will let me know tomorrow whether you wish we should go to Richmond on Saturday or not. I could wish for the child's sake more than for my own that we did not, as I fear he has caught this cold in going backwards & forwards so frequently. I wish you were come home as poor George and I feel quite alone in the world without.

Dora was subject to sudden attacks of melancholy and panic all her life; they were the down side of the high spirits, the exuberance and energy she put into everything she took on – work, love, quarrels, child-rearing. She continued her letter about George: 'I don't know what I should do without him – he wont be a moment away from me – the first thing he did this morning as soon as he was awake was to pull open the curtain and call to me.' Then, in the abrupt style of her letters, she finished, 'I could almost wish you stayd at Windsor today, it is so very dark.'

12

The Man of the Family: Bushy, 1797

By the winter of 1796, against all the odds and confounding the gossips, Mrs Jordan and the Duke of Clarence had become a comfortably settled couple, mutually dependent and devoted. Smart society was disappointed: Hoppner, staying with them at Petersham, judged the Duke to be 'illiterate' and was appalled to be carried off for ten- or twelve-mile walks daily after dinner; and he complained that 'Mrs Jordan affords very little entertainment in Company. Her thoughts seem to be engaged abt. something not present' – which was almost certainly the case.[1] Their way of life was sober and decorous; the Duke was a fond and delighted father; and she was pregnant once again. Both Somerset Street and Clarence Lodge began to feel rather cramped. The prospect of children and nursemaids bursting out of every room drove him to action. He sent for John Soane, the architect who had already fitted up his apartments in St James's Palace, and asked him to prepare plans for a new wing to be added to the lodge. Soane produced drawings with obliging speed; but before things could go any further, in January 1797, William was summoned by his father and offered something that made the enlargement of Clarence Lodge unnecessary.

It seemed that the King had overcome his disapproval of his third son's way of life enough to give him a helping hand. He was presenting him – *unasked*, as William proudly noted – with one of the many royal estates at his disposal: Bushy, a part of the Hampton Court Palace estates. Hampton and

Bushy are not far upstream from Richmond and Petersham, on the opposite, Middlesex bank of the Thames, where Garrick's villa also stood. Bushy House was set back at some distance from the river, and surrounded by more than a thousand acres of parkland, quite flat, but green and wooded. It was only two hours by coach from St James's, and not much more from Drury Lane, though it is unlikely the King had Dora's convenience in mind; it was also easily large enough for their family.

There was talk about such an unusual display of tolerance from the King towards his son's domestic arrangements: 'the Duke of Clarence has managed so well that the King jokes with him about Mrs Jordan'.[2] To the ageing monarch almost anything may have seemed preferable to a repetition of the Prince of Wales's marital behaviour: better one well-established mistress than two unsuitable wives. Even the Queen, who had once written to William that she could not 'bear the idea of your being only Mediocre' and urged him to aim at perfection, may have grown more reconciled to his mediocrity as a public personage, and concluded that a quiet life at Bushy would suit him well enough, for the time being at least.[3]

William's behaviour shows how entirely he now felt himself to be a family man; his first thought was to take Dora and the children to inspect Bushy. On 30 January 1797 they were observed looking it over with 'a boy, like herself but less ugly, and a little girl,' noted one diarist, sour, but intensely interested.[4] George was just three, Sophy not yet two, neither of an age to appreciate the splendours of their future home, but the Duke regarded this as an excursion for them all to enjoy together. Driving into the wintry park through the gates opposite Hampton Court's Lion Gate, they first passed a large, frozen ornamental pond, presided over by a statue of Diana, then proceeded along the triple avenues of leafless but still splendid chestnuts and limes planted by Christopher Wren, catching glimpses of ponds and a stream, and great patches of bracken in which deer were settled. There were scattered cottages, pheasant coverts, a hare warren and stable buildings. When they had almost reached the gates on the Teddington side of the estate, the house itself appeared. Cold and empty as it was, it must have delighted them.

Bushy House was – and still is, though it can only be glimpsed from the park today, and has been almost surrounded by ugly modern buildings – a singularly attractive place.[5] Once a royal hunting lodge, it was enlarged into a comfortable mansion in the 1660s, and stood, a good square block of red brick, with seven tall windows set across each side at each of its three levels and, beneath, great vaulted basements. The special charm of the plan was in the curving corridors – called quadrants – that sprout from the four corners of the building, each leading to a pavilion. When Dora and William first saw the house, the corridors were open colonnades; even closed in, as they are today, they give it a light-hearted appearance. They suggest summer and easy living. You can imagine parties, and children at play running along them between house and garden with shouts and laughter; as indeed a whole tribe of boys and girls was to run and shout and laugh throughout the fifteen years in which Dora lived there. It was to become her most settled, happiest and best loved home: 'dear Bushy' she often called it in her letters, always longing for it when work took her away.

She had never lived in anything on this scale before. The main entrance, on the east front, was reached by a shallow flight of steps: inside you came into a large classically proportioned hall, marble-floored and pillared. From this opened all the great ground-floor rooms, most of them with tall windows on to the gardens. There were two drawing rooms, a dining room, a parlour, a study and a book closet. At the ends of the colonnades, the two pavilions on the south side of the house served as a ball room and a greenhouse. The northern ones housed the kitchens, offices and servants' rooms, keeping them away from the house: it meant colder food perhaps, but greater intimacy for the family. The basement was for the storage of beer and wine, and provided more quarters for the large numbers of servants needed to run such a place.

Through the whole length of the first floor ran a wide central corridor, lit by a south window that filled the house with sunshine; opening off it were a picture room, a magnificent ladies' dressing room and the master's and mistress's bedrooms and dressing rooms. Again, the rooms for valet and maids were away from the house in the north wings. The top floor was obviously the children's domain: two wide passages intersecting in the middle, and seven airy bedrooms with smaller ones attached for nurses; and two skylit storage and laundry rooms. On the plan drawn up by Soane that February a water closet is shown on each floor; at this date baths were still portable, although Dora and the Duke installed both bath and shower later.* From every upstairs window there were views over the parkland; and the rooms were all well proportioned. Some had ceilings ornamented with plaster work, patterns of garlands, ribbons and flowers, and delicate friezes.[6] Dora was to reign over a household and estate as beautiful and grand as that of a true duchess, with dozens of staff and every sort of provision for comfortable living made on the premises and the estate.

With the house went an official, though hardly taxing, position for the Duke. He was now the Ranger of Bushy Park, a title that meant as much or as little as its possessor chose. He could farm, frivolously or seriously; there were no duties so demanding that they would prevent him from taking up a naval appointment should one ever turn up. Earlier Rangers had included two Earls of Halifax; one had walled the park

---

* John Soane made a detailed survey of Bushy House in February and March 1797, presumably at the request of the Duke, that allows us to see the exact state of the house when he and Dora moved in. The plans can still be seen at the Sir John Soane Museum in Lincoln's Inn Fields. There are references in Dora's later letters to the bath and to missing the shower when she is away.

and attempted – and failed – to abolish a public right of way through it. The Duke's immediate predecessor was Lady North, wife of the Prime Minister the King had favoured; the Norths had spent their summers at Bushy for over twenty years. Now Lady North was dead, the Duke expressed his sympathy to her daughter, and urged her to stay on in a smaller lodge in the park. She did not avail herself of the offer. Unmarried, she could hardly live on neighbourly terms with an irregular household, however domestic, however royal.

She was not the only lady to be troubled by Clarence's occasional tendency to blur the distinction between wife and mistress; Fanny Burney – now Madame D'Arblay – also complained that 'the Duke had carried *Mrs Jordan* to Chesington' and that one of her friends had innocently 'received her [Mrs J.] as an honour, & accompanied her about the village, &c ! –'. The mistake was explained to the unfortunate woman, and shuddered at, later. Madame D'Arblay's indignation could be expressed only in a private family letter: meeting the Duke at court, in the room of his sister Princess Augusta, she was all respect, and mentally put the blame for the episode on his aide-de-camp.[7]

The Duke, like many of his family, became an ambitious builder and decorator, with extremely lavish ideas. He found there was little he enjoyed so much as making alterations and 'improvements', ordering walls to be put up and knocked down, windows to be filled in, stairs and doors moved, rooms restructured, gardens redesigned. Bushy was quite habitable as it stood, and he entirely lacked the resources to set about altering it, but he decided at once that the old stables must be rebuilt and a second stable block put up. Some of the exterior steps must also be moved, and the colonnades altered. Soane was accordingly invited to breakfast and asked to transfer his attentions from Petersham to Bushy; his workbook records several visits to the Duke and to Bushy, and the making of drawings by his assistants, during February and March.

Soane also submitted estimates for this work to the Treasury. The Duke's grasp of financial matters was loose; he had been brought up to feel almost totally detached from any sense of personal responsibility, the notion that someone would provide always with him. This time his hope was that the work on Bushy would be paid for out of public funds, but he also immediately asked for a loan of £2,000 from his friend Coutts. Once again he declared that he intended from now on to live with 'the strictest oeconomy', adding that the money he hoped to borrow from Coutts was to go towards new furniture, and stock for the Bushy farm.[8] There was also the matter of the Richmond shopkeepers with whom he had gradually fallen behind and who, on hearing he was going to move from Petersham, very sensibly began to ask for settlement of their accounts. He could not manage that without Coutts's help; and a new house must have furniture and improvements, debts or no debts.

The improvements were soon under way. Unfortunately Soane did not continue to supervise the work, and it seems to have progressed in a haphazard way. Later, called in by the Treasury to look at the bills, Soane put in a report which suggested that neither the Duke nor his advisers knew how to control the operations, and that almost everyone concerned was ready to seize any chance to profit by his, or his steward's, carelessness or gullibility. Soane provides the most vivid demonstration of just how vulnerable Clarence could be to cheating, and helps to explain how debts piled up for him, and for Dora too. Both were clearly regarded as ripe to be swindled wherever possible. The meticulous Soane found that the builders had often charged twice for both materials and work; he reduced the bill, item by item, by many hundreds of pounds.[9] Unfortunately there was no equivalent of Soane watching over their other expenditure. The royal brothers treated money like children at play; a bet made between William and the Prince of Wales this year put a stake of £500 on whether Dora had ever acted in London before 1785. Having thought things over – or perhaps discussed the bet with Dora – the Duke offered to withdraw from it, on the grounds that it was a little too easy for him to win. He may have reflected too that the transfer of £500 from his brother's debts to his own was in any case hardly more than notional.

Now that Bushy House was his, who exactly was to live in it? Obviously, William himself and Dora; obviously too, George, Sophy and the next baby, with their train of nurses. The Duke's chaplain, the Revd Thomas Lloyd, was also installed in an estate house with his young family. Dora's maid and the Duke's valet headed the list of servants; there would be a butler and a housekeeper, cooks, kitchen maids, parlour maids, still-room maids, footmen; and all the outside staff for the gardens, the stables, the dairy, the greenhouse. This was straightforward enough. Less so was the question of the extended family.

There were four other children to be considered: Dora's Fanny, now fourteen; Dodee and Lucy, nine and seven; and the Duke's eldest son, William, aged about seven. The girls were still not to be permanently lodged under the Duke's roof, and Hester remained with them, but Dora wanted them as close as possible; she found Gifford Lodge – once the home of Mrs Fitzherbert – on Twickenham Green, close to Bushy, and installed them there. As for William, the Duke took responsibility for his education, and Dora was kind and motherly to him. He is rarely mentioned except by her, and whether he lived in Bushy House itself, or was lodged in a cottage in the park, or perhaps only came as an occasional visitor, remains uncertain; but he certainly grew attached to her, to the place and to the other children. To all of this loose family group, Bushy came to be regarded as the nearest thing to home. One more boy who sometimes came to stay, and was loved and comforted by Dora, was FitzErnest, the Duke's nephew, and another illegitimate grandson of the King and Queen: his father, the Duke of Cumberland, took very little interest in him, and he seems to have been farmed out rather casually here and there, and to have envied his Clarence cousins their good fortune.

In January and February 1797, while the plans for Bushy were being made, and despite her advanced pregnancy, Dora was busy in the theatre. A new play, Frederic Reynolds's *The Will*, opened; it was somewhat creaking of plot and dialogue, but the public went to see her as Albina, a spirited girl obliged to disguise herself as a midshipman. She was applauded for herself, and no doubt the allusion to her lover's naval past provided an extra thrill for the audience. A perfectly fastidious Dora might have refused to go along with this, but she did not care enough to protest or withdraw. Perhaps she reasoned that it was harmless fun; it may even have made her, and the Duke, laugh. Secure in his affection as well as the public's, she could brazen out such things.

She enjoyed her successes, but she remained modest, and able to laugh at herself. When another Reynolds play again put her into breeches to represent a boy of fifteen, she expressed her doubts about it during a rehearsal: breeches and advanced pregnancy must have been especially difficult to reconcile. At this the company manager accused her of growing proud and attacked her with the obvious tease: 'Quite the Duchess,' he said. She could have stood on her dignity or thrown a fit of temper; instead, she giggled and told him a joke against herself, of how she had sacked her Irish cook that very morning for impertinence, and how the angry cook had banged a shilling on the table and said: 'Arrah, now, honey, with this *thirteener*, won't I sit in the gallery, and won't your Royal Grace give me a courtesy, and won't I give your Royal Highness a howl, and a hiss into the bargain!'[10] You can see why she was so much liked by most of her theatrical colleagues: she could no more resist capturing the lilt and vigour of her cook's speech than she could, as it turned out, refuse to play the part of the fifteen-year-old boy.

In February she had to retreat from Drury Lane. This time she chose to go to Petersham for her confinement, and there she gave birth to another boy. Henry Edward was born at eleven at night on 8 March, as his father carefully noted. *The Times* duly reported the birth of a son to 'Little Pickle'; and Little Pickle, or her Royal Grace, was back on stage again within weeks, and keeping Drury Lane full whenever she appeared.

In April, Gillray put out a 'Sketch from Life' called 'La Promenade en Famille', showing the Duke pulling a large perambulator decorated with a coronet over a chamber-pot, on the path from Richmond to Bushy; he is represented as a foolish-looking, thick-lipped creature, though – rather endearingly – he has a child's doll hanging out of his pocket. In the pram George is flourishing a toy whip at his father, Sophy has a large pet dog sitting in her lap and is half disappearing under an elaborate hat; Henry is, as he was, a featureless infant. The most striking thing about the print is the figure of Dora, who is walking apart, very trim, very severely dressed in a riding habit with a high-necked blouse and plain hat; she is taking no notice of either the Duke or her children, but is studying a play-script. Gillray really did this drawing from life, as the *ad vivam fecit* in the bottom left-hand corner indicates; and the feminine *vivam* also shows who was the most important figure in the picture in his view.

Gillray, in this instance at any rate, shows some respect for Mrs Jordan and her professional status; and the whole picture can be read as a sly topical comment on the rights and duties of the sexes. Its appearance coincided with two much discussed marriages that took place in London that April. One was between Mary Wollstonecraft and the philosopher William Godwin: Wollstonecraft, like Dora, had claimed the right to bear children without being married, for she too had a child by an earlier lover, and was already pregnant by Godwin. The other marriage was between Dora's colleague, the beautiful actress Elizabeth Farren who, this same April, gave up the stage to marry her admirer, the Earl of Derby. She was approaching forty, and had guarded her virtue resolutely for nearly twenty years while they waited for the death of the Earl's invalid wife; the marriage took place within weeks of the first Countess's funeral. Miss Farren had been the poorest of child actresses, beating the drum from village to village for her travelling company, and had risen entirely by her own merits; she excelled in playing fine, well-bred and elegant ladies. On leaving the stage of Drury Lane for the last time, she wept; but once she had become a countess she suffered no one to allude to her previous existence, and lived out a life of refined and blameless inactivity. Her behaviour won the warm approval of Queen Charlotte.

Before the end of the season Dora played several benefits, one for a fellow actor at Covent Garden, another for the widows and orphans of the sailors killed at the battle of Cape St Vincent in February. The Duke's friendship with Nelson, the hero of the battle in which he defeated the Spanish fleet, made this cause particularly appealing. William's pride in his association with the navy remained strong, despite being persistently passed over and excluded from naval matters. His rank of vice-admiral, his age and experience should have entitled him to a command, and his eagerness to find a real naval role of some kind broke out regularly. The year 1797 was particularly difficult for him. After Cape St Vincent came the mutinies at Spithead and the Nore; he wrote to Nelson expressing his horror at the 'state of democracy' into which the Fleet was falling.[11] The mutinies subsided and were brutally punished, to the Duke's approval; then came the news that Napoleon was appointed commander of forces for the invasion of England, and again William expressed his urgent wish to 'attack and distress the Gallic foe'.[12] Still no command was forthcoming; nor would his father make him Marine Minister, another ambition in which he persisted. The Duke might believe the country needed him, but those who made the decisions disagreed. Even his affectionate sister, Princess Augusta, had doubts about his capacities. She thought her brother 'had very good parts ... but was so indolent that he never did them justice ... If he has something of high importance to do ... he will exert himself to the utmost, & do it really well; but otherwise, he is so fond of his ease, he lets everything take its course.'[13] Dora, struggling to combine her own successful and demanding career with almost permanent pregnancy, might well have hoped he would be given a short spell at sea.

So he found himself unmanned professionally while her career prospered: just as Gillray had suggested. Both in public acclaim and in earning power, she was the man of the family. In the summer of 1797 she lent him £2,400 – a very large sum indeed – prompting him to a charming understatement in his correspondence with Coutts: 'Mrs Jordan has never been to me the least cause of expense.'[14] The fact that on stage too she was so often the man – or a woman disguised as a man, and more astute than her lover – may sometimes have struck her; she was certainly too good-natured and loving to make anything of it, and if he noticed, he was too easy-going, or too thick-skinned, to mind. Often, he stayed at home with the children while she went into town to work. Perhaps he cheered himself by considering that in the most private realm at least her masculine role was very regularly put aside, and his most thoroughly asserted.

Nor did she ever adopt an assertive tone with him in her letters. Like Fanny D'Arblay, though from a very different perspective, she could not formally allow that the King's son could be less than perfect in his conduct and character. Even when she offered him advice, as she did – not to get tipsy with his brothers, not to say indiscreet things, not to mind too much when he was passed over for the naval appointments he craved – she never forgot to defer to him. She asked his permission for trivial as well as important matters – whether she might stay in town overnight because of a changed rehearsal schedule, whether she might take one of the children with her, whether to accept or turn down offers of work – and she regarded herself as bound by his opinions and wishes. The law gave him entire rights over their children, though no legal rights over her; but in her eyes the fact of his princely status was probably more important than any legal consideration.

In the summer, as the work progressed at Bushy, William took himself off to a rented house at Dover, away from debts and builders, where he could at least look at the sea, even if he had no fleet to command. Dora joined him after Drury Lane closed in June, but did not stay for long; by July Bushy was habitable, and she installed herself there with the children, to prepare things for his arrival. She reported that her sister Hester was with her, and that Dodee and Lucy were comfortably lodged 'within a quarter of a mile'.[15] For the little girls, their mother being settled at Bushy must have meant a significant improvement in their lives; all the pleasures of the park and the farm could be shared with their half-brothers and sister. Haymaking and harvest, directed by young farmer Robin, and the activities surrounding horses, sheep, dairy and poultry were all entrancing for them. So the first summer at Bushy gathered together children of at least two mothers and three fathers, and the bonds between the groups became warm and close. Soon the Duke arrived and the pattern of their life began to be established. He was affectionate as always to the Gifford Lodge girls as well as his own brood; he was good-tempered and kindly, with what Dora called 'equal spirits', especially reassuring to step-children. He also entered enthusiastically into the estate activities, which from now on were a frequent subject of Dora's letters; harvest and lambing became important features of the year.

In September the Drury Lane season started again, and the coroneted carriage bearing her in and out of London for rehearsals and performances became a familiar sight along the Kingston Road. Blessedly, she was not yet pregnant again. That season she played Miranda in *The Tempest* and Beatrice in *Much Ado about Nothing* for the first time, calling Beatrice 'a very easy, quiet part', which may explain why it was never among her most popular.[16] In any case, Shakespeare took second place this season to the craze for the Gothic: ghosts and other horrors, statues spouting blood and ruined abbeys were what the public wanted, and Drury Lane obliged to the best of its ability. First they revived a play called *The Count of Narbonne*, a tale of divorce and incest partly inspired by Walpole's *Castle of Otranto*. There was no sharp comment on Dora's performance from Twickenham: Walpole, full of years and waspishness, had died in March.[17] She had played it twelve years before in Dublin, opposite John Kemble; now they repeated their performances, supported by Mrs Siddons and another Kemble brother, Stephen. Audiences loved it and asked for more Gothic business, which was provided by a young writer, Matthew or 'Monk' Lewis, who produced an entertainment called *The Castle Spectre*. Sheridan turned up his nose at a play which was no more than a series of tableaux with thrills, but that did not prevent it from running for forty-seven performances. Dora had the not very taxing part of Angela, her great scene a collapse in the moonlight when she is visited by the ghost of her mother; she shared Sheridan's view of its merits. 'The rage for the Castle Spectre is *astonishing*,' she wrote to the Duke from town, in a letter in which she expressed the hope that he might come to join her; whether he would or not, she assured him that she would 'contrive to see the dear children before the end of the week'. She went on, 'The House overflowed last night from every part, and there is the same prospect for the next performance of it.'[18]

She was also rehearsing *Knave or Not?*, a new comedy by Thomas Holcroft. He was a writer with advanced ideas about the organization of society and in particular the relations between the sexes; and a close friend of Wollstonecraft, who died in childbirth during the summer of 1797, leaving among her papers a half-finished comedy; in that small world, it seems a pity her widower did not get it submitted to Mrs Jordan, given her championing of plays by women. Wollstonecraft and Jordan were poles apart in many ways – the one political and intellectual, the other a performer and pragmatist – but they had important things in common too: personal experience of poverty that made them concerned to help their fellow women, and strength of character that allowed them to flout convention.

To some, Dora did embody social change. An article appeared at this time that presented her in this light, describing the domestic arrangements at Bushy as peculiarly admirable, and asserting that her children were likely to 'grow up cheerful, independent and happy'. It mentioned that she herself paid the Duke's chaplain, Lloyd, to instruct them, and that

> the noble sentiments flowing from a liberal education, will teach them to reverence the mother, without sprinkling the tender nomination with any unworthy reflections on the father. And the base ungenerous tongue that ignorantly reflects upon their own birth, that education will teach them to despise; whilst if necessary, it will also teach them to resent and chastise. The sense ingrafted in their youthful minds by the liberal and Christian principles of a Lloyd, will likewise teach them that one Being is the Great and Universal Parent of Mankind, and that Being will instruct them that next to him, they owe all their love and homage to a fond, a tender, and ever anxious mother.[19]

If not quite the voice of the Enlightenment, this is at least an attempt at an enlightened statement, with its rational and humane insistence that illegitimate children need not be ashamed of themselves or their parents. In practice Lloyd seems to have been an amiable man, who trod the delicate path between the church's dictates and the Duke's and Mrs Jordan's actual family situation with tact. The children were baptized; daily prayers were part of the routine at Bushy, and the whole family often attended divine service on Sundays at Hampton Church. 'The Great and Universal Parent of Mankind' did indeed appear to be watching over the little world of Bushy in a kindly way.

13

The Long Idyll: 1797–1806

Bushy gave Dora a place of comfort, beauty and continuity such as she had never known, an idyllic world within the busy outer world, an enclosed and self-sufficient rural paradise. Whatever the demands made on her by her profession and whatever the Duke's frustrations in attempting to pursue his, their domestic happiness, increased by their new home, was deeply felt. It brought out the best in both of them. Neither had enjoyed an easy childhood, both set out – at first at any rate – to ensure that their children's experience should be different. For a man of his class and generation, he gave his young children an unusual amount of fatherly love and attention.

There was no lack of scope. Judged by their productivity alone, they were remarkable parents, and made a striking contrast with the rest of William's generation of the royal family. The combined effects of the Royal Marriages Act and the King's reluctance to let his daughters have husbands meant that, having fathered fifteen children, he found himself with only one legitimate grandchild, Princess Charlotte, offspring of the Prince of Wales's official marriage; she was born in 1796 to already estranged parents. There were a few other miscellaneous and unblessed royal grandchildren; but William was the only one among his brothers and sisters to come anywhere near matching his parents' breeding performance. In thirteen years he and Dora produced ten children together; all survived, and all were healthy and good-looking, so that they presented a radiant spectacle of exactly the sort of *gemütlich* family life the King most approved – but for the drawback of their mother's status, history and profession.

There was no official royal acknowledgement of Dora's children; but a very slight unbending or softening towards them began to show itself from the time they settled at Bushy. A letter from Dora, written to William at Windsor, early in these years, shows there was some kind of gesture at least: 'A thousand thanks dear love for your kind letter . . . I am proud of their Majesties notice of the dear children,' she wrote; and later she mentions a proposal, emanating from the royal household, to do something unspecified, requiring the King's approval, which would be to the advantage of the boys – exactly what is not made plain.[1] The Princesses too, cloistered and childless in what one of them called the nunnery, were aware of the existence of these delightful nephews and nieces, and ready to take an interest in them; and as the years went by, it is clear that there were occasional meetings between some of the official and some of the unofficial members of the tribe. Charlotte rode in the park with her cousins, Princess Amelia sent messages to them and was visited by the older ones when she was ill. For the Duke's brothers, there was always less of a problem, and all showed friendliness; they called at Bushy and sometimes asked the children back to their homes; the Duke of Kent even invited Dora over to see his house at Ealing.[2] As William's best biographer has said, 'to the Prince of Wales and Duke of York, Mrs Jordan was to be treated as much like their brother's wife as the Royal Marriages Act would allow'.[3]

Although George had been privately christened as 'FitzClarence' at Petersham in 1794, it was during the Bushy years that the children began to be publicly known as the FitzClarences. There is a reference to them as such in a newspaper in 1802, and another in 1804, when the artist Henry Edridge reported on a visit from the Duke and Mrs Jordan, presumably to commission portraits of their offspring:

'It is sd. the Children are to bear the name of Fitz:clarence.'
This was between the birth of the eighth, Augusta, and the
ninth, Augustus. At the end of the same year another diarist
uses the name Fitz Clarence, in a passage that gives an
attractive view of the Duke as father, accompanying his
children to Christmas parties:

> Among the company were the Duke of Clarence and his
> eldest son by Mrs Jordan, Master Fitz Clarence, a fine boy of
> eleven, with a promising and even distinguished countenance.
> The next evening the Prince brought four, viz. this and
> another boy and two little girls, to Mrs Riddell's. His care of
> these children and marked affection for them is certainly very
> amiable. *Si sic omnia.*[4]

Once settled at Bushy, Dora had no more miscarriages, and
the rate of arrival of the babies speeded up to become almost
an annual event. No sooner did she get back to Drury Lane,
accompanied by the new one, than she was pregnant again;
small wonder that Sheridan was not always polite about the
Duke. Girls and boys alternated with perfect regularity. All
were named after the Duke's royal brothers and sisters except
Henry, who had his father's second name, but most were
given cosy pet names *en famille*. Henry was followed by Mary,
born at Christmas 1798, Frederick ('Freddles', a particularly
fine baby) at Christmas 1799, Elizabeth (Eliza) in January
1801, Adolphus (first 'Molpuss', then 'Lolly') in February
1802. Then, at a slightly slower rate, came Augusta ('Ta') in
November 1803, Augustus (briefly 'Stump', then 'Tuss' or
'Tus') in March 1805 and Amelia ('Mely' or 'Milly') two
years later, in March 1807. They were born in her bedroom
on the first floor, with the local doctor, Mr Nixon, in attendance, while the Duke sat composing letters to his friends and
brothers in his study; and even if it was late in the evening, he
would summon either Lloyd or a local clergyman to christen
each of 'the Babbs', as their mother called them, on its
arrival.

Dora mentions Nixon's distress over another of his patients dying in childbirth in one of her letters, and she must have felt, in common with all her contemporaries, that she was embarking on something hazardous and unpredictable with each pregnancy; but she was not faint-hearted. If she wrote letters of farewell before giving birth, as some women did, they were not preserved as Fanny D'Arblay's to her husband was, and the Duchess of Devonshire's to her son: these were letters to be read in the event of their death in childbed. They were both unnecessary, as it turned out, but are still affecting to read, because they make you understand how real the danger felt. For Dora the terrors and rigours of childbirth may have grown less by sheer force of repetition. There was no way of reducing pain, other than alcohol; and since antiseptic procedures were unknown, the best thing by far was for the mother to remain at home and for the doctor to intervene as little as possible, which is how she and Nixon managed things. The Duke generally seems to have kept calm. In one letter, written at eleven in the evening as a baby was about to be born, he merely mentions that she has been 'complaining' since six. On a different occasion, he wrote to the Prince of Wales: 'since seven this morning Nixon has been with Mrs Jordan who I sincerely trust and hope will be safe in bed before morning', though it seems to have taken rather longer than he expected.[5] Yet another time Dora had fever, and needed to be blooded and blistered, the all-purpose treatments of the age: then he did become anxious about her, and called in the Prince of Wales's surgeon, Mr Dundas. Luckily Dundas did no harm; but for a terrible moment William found himself wondering what he would do if his children should be made motherless: 'I need not inform you with nine children a mother is absolutely necessary: not forgetting an intercourse of uninterrupted happiness for more than thirteen years,' he wrote to his old friend and confidant, Coutts.[6]

Happily the absolutely necessary mother remained strong

and resilient. She rarely stayed in bed for long, and did not expect to take more than a few weeks off from work. The fact that every one of the babies arrived during the busy winter season in the theatre was a major inconvenience to her professionally, as well as an annoyance to Sheridan; it meant she usually missed the Christmas productions at Drury Lane, and may partly explain why she became willing to travel out of London to perform in the provincial theatres in summer. Yet if you look at the record of her Drury Lane attendances during her first ten years at Bushy, you would not easily guess she had another life as a mother in the country: during the years 1798 to 1805 she was still acting several times a week through the spring and the autumn. She added Miss Hardcastle in *She Stoops to Conquer* to her repertoire in 1800, Lady Teazle and Miss Sullen in *The Beaux' Stratagem* in 1802; and in 1803 and 1804 the Widow Belmour (*The Way to Keep Him*) and the Widow Cheerly (*The Soldier's Daughter*) – the last one of her most vivacious parts, played with Bannister for thirty-five performances in the season. On top of this, as always, she gave many extra performances for charity.

Charitable work was consistently important to her, particularly help to poor women, and women with children. She appeared in benefits to support lying-in hospitals; and it was while she was at Bushy that a free school for local girls was built and endowed close to the Hampton gates of the park. The girls were taught reading, writing and needlework under the supervision of a matron, and given clothes every Easter. The historian of Hampton, writing in the 1880s, says it was funded in 1803 and built in 1805 by the 'generosity of the Duchess': but since there was no Duchess at Bushy until 1818, the true founder of the school was surely the non-Duchess, Mrs Jordan. The same account is given of the foundation of a local Female Friendly Society in 1810, an insurance club for women, who paid in pennies and received help when they gave birth or fell ill; again, the benefactress must be the lady presiding over Bushy when the society was begun.[7]

Dora's own girls – the three eldest – were growing up: Fanny was twenty in 1802, and her mother bought a London house for her to share with Dodee and Lucy, in Golden Square. They kept Gifford Lodge too; Dora mentions their enjoyment of a day's boating party on the Thames, and their joining in many Bushy activities. But they began to find their aunt Hester's temper as trying as Dora had done, and refused to go on living with her; for some months they went to Wales without her, and enjoyed themselves so much they asked permission to stay longer than planned. They were accompanied on this occasion by a Mrs Sinclair, an aunt of Dora's on her father's side, who appeared at Bushy in the early days and remained in attendance for many years, further evidence of the Bland family's revised view of Dora. Another faithful attendant, something between nurse and governess, was Miss Sketchley, who became a permanent fixture: 'Poor soul, she has not much brains to spare but I think she always means well,' wrote Dora of her, divided between generosity and impatience.[8] There was also a Mrs Cockle, who wrote poetry, and helped with the girls' education.

By the time Dora was forty, in 1801, she had pretty well achieved the difficult feat of overcoming the scandalous stories and cartoons of ten years earlier. Her phenomenal energy meant that her fame still increased; her name was a household word, but not an automatic subject for sneers or chuckles. She was too industrious and, when not acting, lived too quietly and domestically at Bushy for that. In 1799 she played Cora in Sheridan's *Pizarro*, for which she had to appear on stage with a baby in her arms; Mary was then five months old, and by tradition at any rate she carried her on, and was painted with her in action by the theatrical portraitist Samuel de Wilde. At this point she was already pregnant again. The following May (1800), when Frederick was the baby and she was expecting another, she was in the royal command performance when the King was attacked in the theatre by a madman with a pistol. He had asked for *She*

Would and She Would Not, with one of Dora's best-known roles as the dashing Hippolita who disguises herself as an army officer to win her lover; and he came with the Queen and all the Princesses, 'who were naturally anxious to see Mrs Jordan in particular, who had appeared to justify a permanent attachment in one so dear to them, and to retain his respect, as well as his affection'.[9]

The Duke of Clarence was in the theatre, and Sheridan was officiating behind the scenes when, as the King and Queen entered their box, a man in the pit fired at the King, narrowly missing him; the Queen thought the noise came from backstage, until the King said, 'Do not come forward. A man in the pit has fired at me,' and himself advanced to the front of the box to show the audience he was unharmed – an act of considerable courage. After a period of confusion, 'an actress' (as the Queen wrote) announced the assailant was in custody. Then Sheridan, in a brilliant gesture, handed Dora a paper on which he had written down a new verse for 'God Save the King', and Dora passed it to Michael Kelly, who led the entire company and audience in singing. Sheridan's verse, beginning 'Our father, prince and friend' was repeated three times in a great burst of loyalty and relief, before the play proceeded. The Queen pronounced Sheridan 'un Ange', and the King invited him to come to court next day, and to bring his wife and son.[10] George III particularly enjoyed meeting children; although it does not appear that Dora was invited to bring hers.

The royals also came to see her at Richmond, in another of her popular parts, Letitia Hardy in Mrs Cowley's *The Belle's Stratagem*, in the autumn of 1802:

Their Majesties George III and Queen, accompanied by the Five Princesses ... honoured the Richmond Theatre, for the first time, with their presence, to see *The Belle's Stratagem* and *The Miser* ... The House was crowded with all the beauty and fashion of Richmond and its Neighbourhood and had to boast of the most brilliant audience that ever graced the Theatre.[11]

We may note in passing too that in 1801 Jane Austen commiserated with her sister Cassandra, who showed 'noble resignation' about having to put off her visit to London, 'Mrs Jordan and the Opera House'; the same year Fanny D'Arblay was pleased when her brother Charles 'procured a Family Box for the whole party to see Mrs Jordan tonight'.[12] Mrs Jordan was also the obvious choice for the ceremony when a silver cup was presented to Garrick's old comedian and her old friend Tom King, retiring at the age of seventy-two: he had been the original Sir Peter Teazle, and in his last appearance he played the part again to Dora's Lady Teazle.

Dora was in her prime: as busy as she had ever been, and with talents and interests ranging wider than ever. During these years, for instance, she turned composer. For a long time her name had appeared as a performer on printed songs, published with the words 'as sung by Mrs Jordan' and often 'to her own accompaniment on the lute' on the front page. Now, in 1800 and 1801, two of her own songs were published. One was a setting of a poem by William Shenstone, 'Go Tuneful Bird': 'The Melody compos'd by Mrs Jordan together with an Accompaniment for the Lute.'[13] It is an easy, attractive tune, with some birdlike jumps and trills, marked as optional on the score for those who could not manage them, that suggest her voice was a soprano. The Shenstone setting is quite forgotten, but the other song was an immediate and overwhelming success, became one of the most popular tunes of the nineteenth century, and is still well known today: 'The Blue Bell of Scotland', with patriotic words about the Highland Laddie going to fight the French for King George. The 32-bar melody, naïve but haunting, was printed and reprinted in edition after edition, in London and in Dublin, arranged for harp, flute and pianoforte and made into variations and duets of all kinds, and still appears in collections of popular songs. Curiously, it gradually detached itself from its composer and began to be ascribed to Anon. It is hard to see why, unless this is yet another piece of Victorian censorship.

Her interest in music and poetry was so well known that poets sent her copies of their work; and in this way two of the greatest young writers of the age made contact with her. In December 1800 Coleridge, who had admired her as an actress since he had begun theatre-going as an undergraduate in the early 1790s, told his publisher Thomas Longman that he and Wordsworth were sending her the second edition of *Lyrical Ballads*. She was the only actress so honoured; other copies went to Fox and the Duchess of Devonshire – 'people of eminence', Coleridge calls them – but the most interesting remark he makes is that Mrs Jordan has already said she 'intended to sing stanzas of the Mad Mother in Pizarro if she acted Cora again'.[14] The poem Coleridge calls 'the Mad Mother' is not by him but by Wordsworth (though the whole volume was published anonymously in its first edition). To find Dora acquainted with the work of Wordsworth, and ready to appreciate *Lyrical Ballads*, is another striking proof of her taste and range of interest. 'The Mad Mother' – more commonly known by its opening words as 'Her Eyes are Wild' – is quite a long poem, in ten stanzas, the first a description of a woman travelling alone with a baby; the rest is her monologue, a powerful and moving one. She has been abandoned by the child's father ('Thy father cares not for my breast,/'Tis thine, sweet baby, there to rest'); she has also been mad, and may be again, but she feels the baby and his needs now keep her sane. As he sucks at her breast, she says, he draws the pain away from her heart and loosens the 'tight and deadly band' she feels constricting her. It was a bold poem for Wordsworth to write and publish, with its theme of a suffering, poor, awkward, unglamorized female victim; and Dora's interest, and her idea of using some of it in her performance in *Pizarro*, is remarkable too. It shows both her

Title-page of 'The Blue Bell of Scotland', published in 1800, giving Mrs Jordan's name as composer.

openness of mind to the subject, and her readiness to listen to a new voice and manner in poetry.[15]

If she did ever use some of Wordsworth's lines when playing Cora, there is no record of it; but for Coleridge she remained a name to conjure with. In May 1804, when he was sailing to Malta, he had a dream of some wonderful words: 'abomination! The full moon came thundering down from Heaven, like a Cannon Ball; & seeing that nothing could be done went quietly back again!' He wrote them down in his notebook, adding: 'Put 'em into a Mrs Jordan's mouth, ridiculing some pompous moral or political Declaimer.'[16] Clearly he ranged her among the opponents of pompous and high-toned public declarations; and she remained a heroine to him to the end of her life. In 1815 he praised her verse-speaking, especially of Shakespeare, in a letter to Byron, as the best he had ever heard.[17]

Appearing in *Pizarro*, she had every excuse to have her most recent baby with her. It was what she liked. When she had to be away from Bushy without the children, she said every baby reminded her of her youngest, every boy and girl of George and Sophy.[18] A letter of 1802 shows she has the current one, Adolphus, with her in town, and some of the others too:

> The dear little ones committed to my care are very well particularly Adolphus – The play went off last night with increased Eclat – Sheridan was there and appeared highly pleased – I almost wish the weather would drive you to Town – I was very unwell during the play last night, and slept but little – I never heard so tempestuous a night, everybody talks of Peace – I am now going to lay down – I would have sent you Books, but I wont for that is providing amusement for you, and defeating my own wishes, however whether you come to Town or not – God bless you and the dear Children.[19]

This is a characteristic letter to the Duke, unstudied, light-hearted and affectionate, following her thoughts as they run from one subject to another and back.

In 1804 the baby in town with her was Augusta, 'a great comfort to me in my banishment'; in 1805 it was Tuss, 'the dear little Boy' whose health she reports on in her letter home, spiced with theatre gossip:

> Sheridan was at the theatre the whole evening and told me that Dr Pierson did not by any means think him out of danger as late as 8 oclock − I got through the night very well, and indeed I believe if I had not played something very serious would have taken place − Sheridan was very sensible of this and of course felt himself much served ... I play every night and therefore hope I shall see you in town − Sheridan wanted to see you last night − Fox was at the play and appeared much pleased − indeed the House was very great ... I am much obliged for the venison ...Frederick [at this time aged five] went with Mrs Sinclair and Lloyd to the Play and was in bed with me this morning by 7 and gave me a full account of my dress and part of the Play − he is certainly one of the most affectionate children in the world − he knows I am writing to Bushy and desires his love to all ...[20]

Her letters to the Duke were spontaneous and private, yet she often apologized for their hasty scrawl and asked the Duke to 'excuse the unconnected way in which I write ... I believe nobody but yourself could read my Letters.'[21] She had no eye on posterity; they were purely family letters, with family news. George, when aged three, asked by his mother to put a kiss in the note she is sending his father, 'immediately spit in it'.[22] Sophy wrote her first letter to her mother, away acting in Canterbury, at the age of six: 'I have recd. my dear Sophy's *first dear* letter.'[23] Mary became a particularly good and affectionate letter-writer, but Frederick could hardly put pen to paper, and George was reproached by his mother at the age of eight for his reluctance to write to her. Eliza was so proud of her own early attempt at a letter to her father that 'she said it over half a dozen times to me − no one dictated a word to her'. Lolly rejoiced in a letter from his absent father. Like all working mothers, Dora sent or brought back presents when she was away: a work-box for Sophy, a writing case for George, a new kind of lanthorn (i.e., lantern – they were made of horn) for Henry; on another occasion, two dolls for 'Ta and Milly', frocks for the girls, wooden soldiers for the boys, a parrot for the whole family.

Bundling children between Bushy and London was never easy, and required a good deal of support, but her enjoyment in combining her work with their visits to the theatre is obvious:

> We have got safe to town but too late for rehearsal . . . the children Mr Lloyd and Mrs Sinclair went to Covent Garden Eliza and all but Adolphus [Eliza was now three, Lolly two] – I joined them after the Country Girl, and never saw anything like the delight and attention of Eliza she kept awake to the very end of the whole – they go to Sadlers Wells tonight but I think it will be better for Mary Frederick and Eliza to stay at home as it was very late last night . . .[24]

Sometimes they were taken to see their mother perform in the Richmond Theatre by Bushy neighbours. One evening when she was giving a charity show for poor families in the district, 'two Temporary Boxes were erected on the Stage; in one of them sat the Earl of Athlone and his daughter, Lady Christiana Regina Ginkell, and the two Masters and the two Misses FitzClarence'.[25] This was in 1802, when George was eight, Sophy seven, Henry five and Mary three. Their father and mother also took them to Christmas pantomimes at Covent Garden and Drury Lane: *The Forty Thieves*, *Robinson Crusoe*, *Blue Beard*.

During her first autumn at Bushy, Dora made a short working visit to Margate, where there was a very good theatre; it is still standing today, although it is hard to believe that Margate once rivalled Brighton as a fashionable resort, where duchesses and admirals went for the bathing and the sea air blowing over the cliffs, and were glad to be entertained in the evening. The Duchess of Cumberland, widow of the King's brother, sent for twenty tickets for one of Dora's appearances, and the Devonshires and the Bessboroughs were Margate visitors, and were especially appreciative and civil to her.[26] She was such a success on her first visit that she returned many times, either in August or September, sometimes going on to Canterbury, Deal and once to Brighton.

The Duke did not accompany her on these visits; indeed, there is no evidence of them either taking a holiday or travelling together again after their stay in Dover in the summer of 1797. He would go to Brighton alone in August for the Prince of Wales's birthday; when she went on from Margate to Brighton in September 1801, it was strictly as a working woman. She noted that the Prince of Wales lent his box to the Duchess of Marlborough, who wrote her a polite note, but when she was invited to a ball 'by desire of *several Ladies* who will make a point of shewing her every attention', she declined. She may have felt uneasy about appearing professionally in the Prince's own territory, and being lionized there; and although she was warmly pressed to return to Brighton by the theatre manager, she declined.[27] The Duke sometimes took some of their sons to Brighton without her; Harriet Bessborough saw him there with 'three beautiful boys' in October 1805.[28] While they were enjoying the sea bathing, Dora was in London with Sophy and Mary, who were attending dancing lessons, and having their health checked by a court physician. Dora's letters also speak of their having their ears pierced – Eliza frightened Mary by telling her the man would bore through her lobes with a red-hot needle – and their teeth looked at. About such matters, and indeed about everything to do with the children's health and education, she was an extremely careful and conscientious mother.

She took none of the children to Margate; understandably perhaps, when you consider the difficulty of combining seaside holidays with her work schedule. There was also the fact that she was the object of so much attention she was sometimes forced to leave her lodgings by the back door to escape the crowd hanging about for a glimpse of her at the front. The person who did accompany her on the Margate visits, as well as her maid and manservant, was usually Lloyd. A clergyman may seem a curious companion for an actress, but he was eager to go; perhaps even a little stage-struck. His excuse was that his health required sea air, and he made himself useful and companionable. She gives a faintly satirical description of him, paddling on the beach by day and admiring the actresses backstage in the evening, but she liked him well enough. On one occasion he was with her in the coach, travelling late and after dark, near Sittingbourne, when they were threatened by two black-coated highwaymen; although they knocked Dora's manservant off his horse, they lost their nerve and were driven off. She was grateful for Lloyd's support on this occasion. Telling the Duke about it, she said she would not travel after dark again; but she only mentioned the incident to him for fear 'you might have heard it with additions'. She meant through press reports; and she added, rather peremptorily, 'Be so good as to write to the girls for the same reason, who may be alarmed.'[29] 'The girls' were her three eldest daughters; and no doubt the Duke complied.

It was on the Margate stage too that she was nearly burnt when her costume caught fire, in August 1802, as she was playing *The Country Girl*. 'I find by the papers of today that they have mentioned the accident that happened to me last Friday & which I was in hopes would not have taken wind,' she wrote coolly to the Duke a few days later; 'but as it is over, I may now tell you that I was near being burnt to death, my gown being in flames up to the waist so that I concluded my last scene in my petticoat. Notwithstanding all these disasters I shall come home safe to you & the dear children.'[30] At least she was not pregnant when it happened; even so, she was formidable in her refusal to show fear or fuss.

A few weeks later she was in Liverpool, still accompanied by Lloyd, and being pressed to go on to Preston and Ireland; she refused the latter, but agreed to stop at Preston on her way home. 'I never saw so pleasant an audience,' she wrote from Liverpool, adding, 'Notwithstanding all this I feel quite forlorn.' And a few days later, 'On Saturday ... I set out for dear dear Bushy. If the people of Liverpool knew how I long & pray for this day, they would think me very ungrateful ... You have not yet mentioned the £100 I sent. Do, if you can, think of it in your next.'[31]

In Margate she sometimes had her sister Hester with her, and her brother Francis is mentioned also; it may have been easier to see them there than at Bushy, where they risked disturbing the Duke. According to *The Times*, a paper that displayed consistent hostility towards Dora, she first went there to earn money to pay off her brother George's debts; and it implied there was something discreditable about this. She may well have been foolish not to resist his demands, but it is hard to see anything dishonourable about meeting them by her own exertions. If *The Times* felt she was a blot on the royal family, and her scrounging relations still more so, the facts of the matter were not as they imagined. She must have realized early in her relations with the Duke that, from a financial point of view, he was not much of a 'protector' – probably not as good as Richard Ford – but it made no difference to her affection for him. She was businesslike with theatre managers, but she was not at all businesslike, let alone mercenary, where he was concerned. He – or rather the King – provided her with a home, and he – or rather the taxpayer – gave her an allowance; but she was always sending and lending the Duke money, in small and large amounts, and he often depended on her earnings to keep up the way of life to which he felt he had a right, and to stave off disaster. In May 1803, for instance, he found himself unable to settle the £2,000 he owed his upholsterer, and his bank in Bond Street was refusing any payments; he managed to scrape up some, and Dora, 'whose benefit is on Monday, offered to give me the remainder, four hundred and fifty five'.[32]

Apart from money, everything flourished at Bushy: the Duke's constant building works, the gardens, the dairy, the green-house, the farm – above all, the children. There was always a fat new baby in the nursery, and often one – or two – in her bed: two-year-old Lolly 'having nearly escaped falling out of my bed twice on Wednesday night – I was obliged to put him in his own bed last night',[33] – she had a younger baby of one, and was just pregnant again. The top floor thundered with small feet running up and down the corridors; in the Family Room there were card games and billiards. There were peaceful evenings when they were all reading their books, or the girls singing and playing; Fanny helped Dora with their music lessons. There was another tutor, partly to replace Lloyd during his absence, a Monsieur Champeaux – surely a French émigré – and later Mr Daniell, to whom the children became strongly attached. The Duke also appointed a second chaplain, with a still stronger theatrical bent than Lloyd, being the son of the playwright O'Keefe, well known to Dora. But John Tottenham O'Keefe had a short career. He came to Bushy from Oxford, and the Duke then presented him with a rich living in Jamaica; he sailed out in 1803, only to die of a tropical fever on arrival.[34]

Summer and winter, the children lived much of their time outside in the park with their animals. There were dogs, and they all had ponies, and then horses, as they grew. They might help Robin the farmer bring in the hay, or enjoy Dora's tame pigeons with her. The boys went coursing for hares, and got covered in mud; no one thought of scrubbing them, she grumbled, until she came home. They also went to the races at Molesey and Ham. They fished, and later they learnt to hunt. Playing with them, Dora fell off 'a Jack Ass' one day; the donkeys were kept not only to work but also for their milk, prescribed by the royal doctors after the two great epidemics she nursed the children through: measles in 1805, whooping cough in 1807, with much rubbing in of embrocations, counting of 'boils', and many sleepless nights. George was at school in Maidenhead when the whooping cough struck, and Dora decided to take all the others over to visit him, and to spend the day at a nearby inn. The whole thing was a mistake: 'It is not the most agreeable thing in the world to be shut up on a rainy day in a small Inn, with 8 children in the Hooping cough, I do believe the people would give up all the profits of our visit, to get us out of the house – I hardly know what I am doing for the variety of noises.'[35]

The children got better, and life at Bushy continued as pleasantly as ever. Grapes, flowers and peaches came from the greenhouse, and many oysters were consumed, as well as turkey, venison, partridges, pheasants, the occasional turtle and vegetable broth for the invalids. There was cricket in the park in summer; sometimes the curate at Hampton Church brought over a team of local boys to play. Dora arranged entertainments for everybody: 'We are to have a *conjuror* here tomorrow evening from the fair at Kingston, he is to exhibit in the Hall, at 7 o'clock . . . I mean it as a treat for all the servants.'[36] When Polly the Parrot flew away, they spent the day coaxing him out of a tree. On another summer's day the colonel of a regiment stationed in the neighbourhood sent a message offering to send over his musicians to play for the family. It was accepted with delight. All the children 'danced to the Band and were very happy', she wrote to their absent father. 'I did not get to bed till past one – Jemmet and myself seeing everything safe and quiet.' Jemmet was a favourite, trusted old servant, and the image of the two of them going round the house together, the children sweetly sleeping in their beds upstairs after their day of sunshine, is one I like to think of as a high point of the family life.

'I did not go to London,' she added. Understandably, for she had spent the morning of the day of the dance with the builders working on the front of the house, and on the Duke's new library. It was all business he was pleased to have her supervise on his behalf. On one occasion she presided over the laying of eight thousand turfs in the garden; on another, over the rehanging of all the pictures in the house.[37]

As well as supervising the accounts and building works in the Duke's absences, she also intervened to preserve good relations with their neighbours. One of his many building projects on the outskirts of the park upset Mrs Garrick, who was still living on the small riverside estate her husband had laid out for his retirement; it was next to Bushy, and she felt threatened by the Duke's plans. Dora put all her persuasive powers into urging him to give them up:

> I have just had a visit from Mrs Garrick in the greatest distress about a building you are erecting opposite a principle [*sic*] Bow window of hers she says she is certain you do not know the detriment it will be to the Estate which cost her Husband so much money and pains to render beautiful or you with your goodness and condescension would not do it – if it can be done away I am sure you will do it and it will be a popular act to discontinue it, I wish you would let me say something handsome *from you* to the old woman who really seemed greatly agitated ... if you continue the building you will have all the old cats at Hampton Court on your back ... it would give me some pleasure, to be able to set the old soul's heart at ease about it.[38]

Dora's letter gives a precise impression of one aspect of life at Bushy, in which she had to juggle the Duke's wishes with the need to be friendly with their neighbours; she manages to be placatory and firm with him at the same time, and to show her affection for old Mrs Garrick.

In this case her wise counsels prevailed. There is another letter telling him about Mrs Garrick inviting her and the children over to see her house and gardens with the Shakespeare temple and grotto, and to 'stay as long as we pleased – this kindness you may be sure we availed ourselves of'. After this good relations flourished, because later she and Mrs Garrick took to going to the theatre together.[39]

Dora also intervened kindly in the matter of the Duke's son William. It was she who took him off to school in 1802, and cheered him up the following year when he cried as she was about to leave, and said he would rather live with her: 'However, I left him in very good spirits at last.' A year later she again expressed sorrow at the thought of not seeing him for a long time, and asked if he might spend the day with George and Henry at Bushy before leaving: this time he was not going to school, but to follow in his father's footsteps as a midshipman.[40] From his ship, young William sent her 'kind and affectionate letters', and asked her to intercede for him with his father about his leave; she told the Duke, 'I think Baptist [a Bushy gardener] might very easily send him grapes and peaches. You will of course let him come home when the ship is docked; he seems very anxious about it.'[41] There can be no doubt that she replied to William's letters with as much kindness and affection as he showed her.

Every summer the Duke had an attack of asthma. It varied in severity, sometimes responding to Nixon's ministrations, sometimes needing more important doctors, but during the first ten years at Bushy it was never very bad. There were other things to plague him. In 1803 he was put in charge of the Teddington volunteers, the Home Guard of the Napoleonic wars, and found them very troublesome. Dora wrote to him from London, 'I am sorry to hear that you are so plagued with the Volunteers I am afraid they are scarcely worth your trouble'; and then, 'if you cannot make them serviceable for God's sake let them go to the devil they are beneath your notice and example, neither the King nor his Ministers deserve it of you, and be assured you will make yourself unpopular in the neighbourhood when everybody was inclined to love you as you deserve.'[42] At Drury Lane Dora would sing the most patriotic songs and speak lines urging the women of Britain to their duties – 'Should British women from the contest swerve? We'll form a female army of reserve,' but she was too protective of the Duke, and too realistic, to want him to play at soldiers if it made him unhappy.[43]

In the summer of 1805 a young painter, George Harlow, a pupil of Lawrence and just making his reputation, came to paint the children. It seems likely he was commissioned to do them all in different groups, but the only one known to survive shows Frederick, Eliza and three-year-old Lolly. Eliza sat wearing a straw bonnet and a high-waisted dress with puff sleeves, and holding a posy; both her brothers wore wide frilled collars, and trousers under their knee-length jackets. Lolly has a mass of uncropped golden ringlets, and all of the children look as charming as any of those painted by Reynolds. Harlow showed them out of doors, Fred leaning on a large dog, Lolly holding a crimson banner with the royal arms of his grandfather the King blazoned on it.[44] About the same time Beechey came to paint Dora again, not this time as a theatrical character but as the *châtelaine* of a great estate. It is a full-length portrait set against a rural landscape; she is plainly dressed, a fine shawl draped around her high-waisted dress, a serious and dignified expression on her face, and neatly arranged hair.[45] In fact it is the nearest thing to a royal pose she ever adopted, and the two pictures prompt the question whether the Duke had serious thoughts of legitimizing their union. In 1805 he was forty, and could be presumed to be settled in his ways. They had lived happily together for thirteen years; when the Prince of Wales suggested in 1799 that Clarence might marry a daughter of the Landgrave of Hesse-Cassel in order to reduce the family debts, he had simply refused, 'being satisfied with Mrs Jordan'; and nothing had changed since 1799 except that she had given him five more children.[46]

Boaden, who had known her and the Duke since 1799, said that 'Whoever has had the happiness of seeing them together at Bushy, saw them surrounded by a family rarely equalled for personal and mental grace; they saw their happy mother an honoured wife, in every thing but the legal title, and uniformly spoke of the establishment at Bushy as one of the most enviable that had ever presented itself to their scrutiny.' He added his admiration for the way in which she 'devoted herself to [the Duke's] interests and his habits, his taste and domestic pleasures'.[47]

The Duke's career – or lack of it – apart, there seemed to be only one rift in his contentment, and that was her frequent working absences from Bushy. The loss of her company was not unbearable – he was often away himself – and he may have minded more that their children, and the household, and the whole royal family too, were so frequently reminded of her professional life and status. She might look like a duchess; she might be in most respects treated as his wife; she might behave in all respects as though she were his wife, as long as she was at Bushy; but at Drury Lane, or in Margate, she was unavoidably someone quite other. To many people – to Sheridan, no doubt, and to Coleridge and the young critics, to other managers, to all audiences – she was also someone greater than she could ever be at Bushy. If the Duke wanted her to approach more nearly to the status of wife, this may help to explain why, at the end of 1805, he decided she should devote herself entirely to their family life. He asked her to give up the stage. Other actresses – Elizabeth Farren, for instance – had done so unhesitatingly. It was the standard thing to do on acquiring a husband, and remained so throughout the next century; but where Dora was concerned, it was an extraordinary request. Nevertheless, for the next year and a half, she did as he desired, and became nothing more than the mistress of Bushy and the mother of his children.

14

The Serpent Enters Paradise

The happiness of life at Bushy, lasting like a long high summer for nearly ten years, could not entirely be proof against the world outside: against war, or death, or disapproval. The war in France came to a pause in 1802, but broke out again the following year; the Duke's Volunteers were called against an invasion scare, when Napoleon's troops massed on the channel coast, and this particular threat did not end until the autumn of 1805. At this time the Duke visited his old naval friend Nelson, his hero and now the whole nation's, who had achieved everything Clarence would have liked to have done. Dora was also invited by Nelson's mistress, Lady Hamilton, and drove to their house in Surrey, taking Lucy, Sophy and Henry with her.[1] Soon after these visits Nelson left. He was killed in battle at Trafalgar in October. The Duke was overcome with grief; he also decided to express his feelings in a piece of characteristic building work. At his request, part of the mast of Nelson's flagship, the *Victory*, was brought to Bushy, a mound was raised in the garden and a small round, classical temple built on the top to house the relic.[2] He also began to brood about going to sea again himself.

Nelson's state funeral in January 1806 marked the start of an altogether uneasy year. Pitt died, worn out, in January. Fox and Sheridan were in power for a few months, then Fox too died in September. The Duchess of Devonshire, not yet fifty, died, watched over by her adoring sister through the agonizing last days; so did Richard Ford, also in his forties, leaving a young family as well as his two daughters by Dora. Although he seems to have long since lost contact with them, still a father is a father, and they – and Dora – must have felt a pang and a sense of loss. Another loss – the departure of her brother George for America – was more of a blessing, although he left a tangle of debts for her to deal with, and she wrote irritably of 'the trouble, expence and vexation I have suffered on the account of my brother and sister since I was fourteen years old'; he too died within a year.[3]

John Bannister sent her some plays to read to lure her back to the stage, and she wrote back affectionately, saying her 'theatrical health' was on the decline; she did not take on the parts he suggested. 'The three tragedies you sent me I have read this day; and notwithstanding there's much pretty writing in the part you mention, I do not think I could do myself or the author any service by undertaking it. I think Mrs Siddons would do great justice to it,' she added magnanimously, adding, 'I find laughing agree with me better than crying.'[4]

So she sat out the spring and summer at Bushy. Fanny gave a 'rural fête' at Gifford Lodge in July, and in August the Duke was recovered enough from mourning Nelson to celebrate his own forty-first birthday with a large party. He prepared for it by installing a new dining room and redecorating the hall with clouds on the ceiling – a fashionable effect of the time – bronze pilasters and brilliant lamps suspended from an eagle. Two of his brothers, the Dukes of York and Kent, sent over bands to play on the lawn, and the pleasure grounds were open to the public. The music was worth listening to; one of the bands was a wind group that played parts of Haydn's *The Creation*, specially arranged. At five o'clock the Prince of Wales and four of the royal brothers – York, Kent, Sussex and Cambridge – arrived, with the Lord Chancellor, the Attorney-General, the Earl and Countess of Athlone and other aristocrats and dignitaries; everyone amused themselves in the grounds until seven, when the

Prince of Wales took Mrs Jordan by the hand and led her to the top of the table in the new dining room; the Duke of Clarence was at the other end. Later, the children were brought in, down to the youngest, Tuss, whose beautiful fair hair was much admired; there were toasts to the King and Queen, and a cannon was fired on the lawn.

From one point of view, this was a happy family party, a group of loving brothers and uncles gathered to celebrate on a summer evening. It also looked like Dora's social apotheosis; and as such there was something sham about it. There was nothing sham about Dora herself, but about the royal play-acting around her there was; and the whole occasion led to disaster. There were press reports. They attracted the attention of the most brilliant radical journalist of the day, William Cobbett; and Cobbett devoted a long attacking article to the Bushy party in his magazine, the *Political Register*.

First he claimed to believe that the report of the occasion must be untrue, since the royal family was known for its piety and morality, whereas the playing of music from *The Creation* made a blasphemous connection between God's creative work and the Duke of Clarence's creation of a large illegitimate family. After this ponderous piece of irony, Cobbett continued.

> We all know that the Duke of Clarence is not married, and that therefore if he had children, those children must be bastards, and that the father must be guilty of a crime in the eye of the law, as well as of religion, – and that he would exhibit a striking example of that vice and immorality which his Royal father's proclamation, so regularly read to us by our pastors, commands us to shun and abhor, and enjoins upon the magistrates to mark out and to punish whenever they shall find them existing among us.

The proclamation Cobbett referred to was a moral manifesto put out by King George at the beginning of his reign, 'For the encouragement of Piety and Virtue, and for preventing and punishing of Vice, Profaneness and Immorality'. It was read out four times a year in every church and chapel in the country, at the King's wish, as a reminder of his insistence that moral standards should be upheld, although it was unfortunately obvious that those closest to the crown were not much impressed by its urgings. Cobbett went on to say the unmarried Duke would be insulting the laws, manners and morals of the whole country if he really had a family at Bushy; and that 'Mother Jordan' ('who, the last time I saw her, cost me eighteen pence in her character of Nell Jobson') could not possibly be involved. He begged the royal family to deny the whole thing, for fear such reports should damage the throne, and make Parliament unwilling to vote taxes to maintain it.[5]

Cobbett's article was well founded as an attack on the royal Princes – rightly seen as the great drones of the nation – and the Duke must have been shaken. Whether it was fair also to go for Dora is another matter. He chose to insult her both as an actress and as a mother, without justification in either case, except that she was unmarried. She had surely earned her own keep more than any other woman in the land. Dora was wounded and frightened, and felt damaged in the eyes of the public.

Then came a private tragedy. In March 1807 the news reached them that William, the Duke's eldest son, was dead. He had been drowned at the beginning of February, when his ship, the *Blenheim*, disappeared off Madagascar in a cyclone; the wreck was never found. Dora loved the boy; he had been the playmate of all the other children, and his death, alone and far away, cast a chill over the whole family. Ten-year-old Henry in particular had a feeling for William, perhaps because he already knew he was to follow him into the navy; when a letter came from William to his father, Henry, recognizing the hand, had simply opened it and read it.

William's death made the question of her own sons' future suddenly much more ominous. Their father declared that the army and the navy offered not only the best, but the only possible professions for them all. 'I shall make five sons of mine fight for their King and Country,' he told a friend. To him, it was as though he were making a personal offering to the nation; he may even have seen it as an answer to Cobbett.[6] His sons were to be his justification and his war effort. He believed Britain needed every man – and boy – to fight off the threat of Bonaparte, and also that the services offered them their best chance in life, and a more honest and honourable one than the only possible alternatives of politics, the church or the law. By 1807 the Duke had already allocated the boys between the two services. George and Frederick were for the army, Henry and Adolphus for the navy; soon two-year-old Tuss was promised to the navy too.

The boys, brought up to believe that the army and navy offered the best of excitement and glory, and sent away to school with other lads destined for the same future, were not likely to protest. George returned to the military college at Marlow at the beginning of February and was immediately given a commission in the Prince of Wales's 10th Hussars, as a cornet, the junior officer who carries the colours in a cavalry regiment. His imagination was fired; he was a clever as well as a high-spirited boy, but he began to neglect his studies. All he could think of now was the prospect of joining his regiment and seeing action.

Before George had his wish, Henry started his working life at the age of eleven, as a midshipman. No doubt he went enthusiastically, aware that he was following in his father's footsteps, and reared on tales of Nelson and glory. He was sent to the Baltic to serve under the Duke's (and Nelson's) friend Admiral Keats, aboard the *Superb*. Keats had the reputation of caring for the boys aboard his ship more like a father than a master, but it was still a tough initiation: that winter they were frozen into the ice, and Henry did not return home for fourteen months. To Dora (and to us) he was still a child: 'Two years is a long time to lose the society of so dear a child as Henry,' she wrote before he went away a second time, 'but we must give up our children to the World, for our own sakes, and I will reconcile myself to the separation as well as I can.'[7] Henry was small for his age and he had a quick brain, for languages especially, and enjoyed reading; one of the things he asked his mother for was a copy of *Tristram Shandy*.

When the news of William's death came she was awaiting the birth of yet another baby. Bushy was, as usual, in the hands of the builders, and the Duke was away a good deal, leaving her to cope; she wrote to him expressing the hope the alterations to her bedroom would be finished by the middle of March ('which is the time I shall want it') and complaining mildly that 'I really don't know how to manage the brick-layers.'[8] In the event all went well. He returned, her room was ready, Nixon performed efficiently, and a fifth daughter for the Duke made her appearance on 21 March. She was named Amelia, after the Duke's youngest sister; but she was usually called Mely.

Dora was forty-five. We know this was her last child, and feel it as a relief. Naturally she did not share our knowledge, although she may have thought she had had enough: ten for the Duke, three for Ford, one for Daly. Lying with the little girl in her arms, she could go back in her mind over twenty-four years, to Fanny's birth in Hull, Dora's in Edinburgh, Lucy's in Gower Street; George and Sophy in Somerset Street; Henry at Petersham; Mary, Freddles, Eliza, Lolly, Ta and Stump all here at Bushy. To modern ears such a roll-call has a comic sound, and we have to remind ourselves that to her they were never an undifferentiated troop. Her heart's blood was in each of them, and each was entirely individual and precious, as is made abundantly clear in her letters. She had not handed them over as most great ladies did, to be brought up apart from her; she had fed them herself, nursed them through their illnesses, stayed up all night at their bedsides and put off her work when necessary, taken them with her into the theatre and entered into their pleasures and amusements. When she was parted from them, she dreamt of them, worried about them and wrote to them; and she took an intense pride in each of them.

Now, while she nursed Mely, she was busy arranging Fanny's marriage settlement. Fanny was going to marry Thomas Alsop, a young man who worked in the ordnance office, which dealt with military supplies. He was only a clerk, but a very presentable one. The ordnance office was full of young men like him, with the manners of gentlemen, but short of the income to support a gentleman's life-style. Dora thought he was 'a clever and honourably minded young man, but poor and proud, two sad things when united'.[9] He made himself agreeable, however, and was approved by the Duke as well as his future mother-in-law. Fanny was twenty-four, and had not received any suitable offers until now, perhaps because of her anomalous position. Alsop may well have been attracted to her; he also saw his chance. Her promised dowry of £10,000 was a huge fortune, and her connections could give his career the push it badly needed.

With the prospect of the money that would come with Fanny, Alsop took an expensive house in Park Place, Mayfair, and suggested that her sisters might like to share it with them after the marriage. Then he introduced Dodee to a charming colleague from the ordnance office, Frederick March, who, exactly like Alsop, was ambitious to escape from lowly clerking and aspired to a grander way of life. March had a good reason: he knew himself to be the son of Lord Henry Fitzgerald and the grandson of the Duke of Leinster; Lord Edward Fitzgerald was his uncle, Charles James Fox his cousin. The only drawback was that he was illegitimate. The Fitzgeralds acknowledged March and made something of a favourite of him; but that did not alter his material situation. No doubt March asked himself why he should not enjoy the same pleasures and privileges as his father, his cousins and his grandfather; when he saw his opportunity, like Alsop, he was not going to miss it. There was something else at work in his mind. Dodee and Fanny both came, like him, from the ranks of the illegitimates. However privileged they might be, they were also despised; the difference between them and him was that their mother had the power and the wish to make them rich. In the summer of 1808, when Fanny's wedding took place, he called at Bushy with his father, Lord Henry, and made himself extremely agreeable to Mrs Jordan and the children. Dodee was welcomed by the Fitzgeralds, and everyone at Bushy found March engaging. They married early in 1809. Both the Alsops and the Marches began at once to live beyond their means.

It was not too surprising. They found themselves in a society that offered expensive pleasures – horses, gambling, clubs, fine clothes and furniture, drink and drugs – and the temptation of easy credit. Debt was the condition of the age. Tradesmen were always ready to meet the demands of today against the promise of future payment; the flagrant example of so many members of the royal and aristocratic families availing themselves of tradesmen's willingness was naturally followed by anyone else who could get away with it. Thomas Alsop and Frederick March had the spectacle of the lavish life-style of Bushy before them, maintained – as far as they could see – by the royal purse. To them it must have seemed bottomless: why should they not have their share? Alsop and March saw their mother-in-law as a supplier of money, and not just what she had promised her daughters; they asked her charmingly for more when they needed it, and when March wanted to raise still more, he used her name without asking. With them, as with the Duke, she forgot to be cautious or businesslike.

She realized that it was necessary for her to earn more money; and when Mely was six months old she persuaded the Duke to let her return to Drury Lane. The theatre was in increasing difficulties under Sheridan's distracted management; she was older, and she accepted a drop in her fees

LUBBER'S-HOLE, alias _The Crack'd JORDAN.

The royal romance between the Duke of Clarence and Mrs Jordan gave every
caricaturist in the land a chance to do his worst, and the most brilliant, and the
cruellest, was James Gillray. His work was displayed in windows of print shops and
circulated very widely. Because a chamber-pot was known as a 'jordan', the chamber-
pot became the symbol of Mrs Jordan; the braided jacket and striped trousers of
a naval uniform stood for William. 'The Lubber's Hole, alias The Crack'd Jordan'
appeared on 1 November 1791, when Dora was performing almost nightly at
the Haymarket. Gillray, incidentally, had been a strolling player himself in his youth.
The attack was vicious; the surreal image he produced is unforgettable.

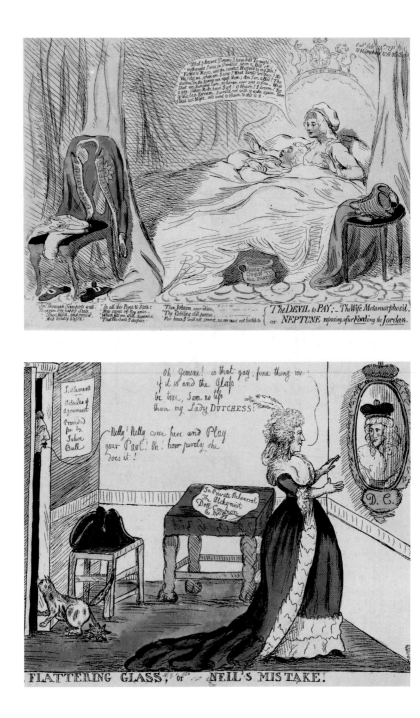

La Promenade en Famille. — a Sketch from Life.

(*above*) Gillray's finest drawing of Mrs Jordan and the Duke, done from life, as his '*ad vivam fecit*' indicates. It appeared in April 1797 as a comment on their move to Bushy; but its most striking aspect is the way in which Dora is walking apart, trimly dressed in a riding habit and studying her play-script, while the Duke, with a doll hanging out of his pocket, pulls the three children in their perambulator. Was it Gillray's contribution to the debate on the rights of women?

(*above, opposite*) Gillray shows William's naval jacket, draped over the bedroom chair, and the chamber-pot – labelled 'Public Jordan – Open to all Parties' – beneath the bed in this drawing of 24 October 1791; but his portrait of Dora is far from cruel – in fact it is very attractive. It has several captions: 'Neptune reposing after Fording the Jordan' is self-explanatory. 'The Devil to Pay' is the title of a well-known farce in which Dora often appeared as Nell, who finds herself magically transformed from the poor wife of a cobbler into the lady of the manor.

(*below, opposite*) 'The Flattering Glass, or Nell's Mistake' also refers to *The Devil to Pay*. This cartoon by William Dent appeared on 28 October 1791, in the same week as the two preceding ones, and many others. It shows Dora in her dressing room at the theatre.

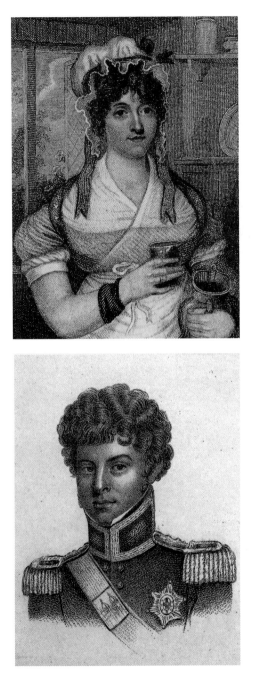

A late portrait of Dora in her role of Nell in *The Devil to Pay*. According to tradition, this was the part she was due to play in Cheltenham in the autumn of 1811 when she had a message from the Duke telling her he wished for a separation. She insisted on going on, although she could not prevent herself from crying on stage when she was meant to laugh.

Jane Austen was in the audience at Covent Garden on 7 March 1814 to see her play Nell, and was 'highly amused'.

George FitzClarence, the eldest son of Dora and the Duke, was brave, gifted and good-looking. Both his parents adored him, but he was put into the army and sent to fight in the Peninsular War at the age of fourteen: 'The distress of Mrs Jordan is not to be described: however, like what she is, one of the best and one of the ablest of women, she sees the propriety of his going,' wrote his father to the Prince of Wales. All the Duke's sons were sent into the army or navy, some as young as eleven.

CL___CE's DREAM, or. BINNACLE BILLY receiving an unwelcome visit from ye other world.

Isaac R. Cruikshank's cartoon appeared in 1821, three years after the Duke married Princess Adelaide of Saxe-Meiningen. It shows Mrs Jordan rising in her grave-clothes from a coffin inscribed 'Buried by Subscription at Paris' to rebuke him in Shakespearean words, while in the background the FitzClarence children appear, labelled 'Royal Bast . . . ds'.

William's remorse led him, once he was King, to commission a life-size statue of Dora from the country's leading sculptor, Francis Chantrey. The King intended it to be placed in Westminster Abbey, 'beside the monuments of the Queens', but instead it disappeared from public view for good.

(*above*) Lolly, who became Lord Adolphus FitzClarence, served in the navy and commanded Queen Victoria's yacht, chose to be painted not as an officer but as a corsair, in a highly theatrical pose, by Henry Wyatt. He preserved his mother's memory – and her letters – and always took a great interest in the theatre.

(*above, opposite*) William and Dora commissioned many paintings of their children, most of which have been lost. This one by George Henry Harlow shows Frederick, Eliza and Lolly, still ringleted and in pantaloons, in the gardens at Bushy with a pet dog, about 1805. Lolly is holding the royal standard bearing the arms of his grandfather King George III.

(*below, opposite*) Dora's two youngest daughters, Augusta and Amelia, known as Ta and Mely; they were thirteen and eight when their mother died. This drawing dates from the mid-1820s, before their marriages: Ta to a Scottish aristocrat, John Kennedy Erskine, in 1827, and Mely to Viscount Falkland – Byron's godson – four years later.

When the artist Charles Leslie saw Mrs Jordan in 1813 he remarked, 'Her face is still very fine, no print that I ever saw of her is much like,' and it is true that the scores of portraits that exist make her look confusingly different. Some have been wrongly ascribed; it must also be remembered that she was most often represented in theatrical roles, her appearance deliberately varied to suit them. This impression of her by George Romney, with its dark ambiguous gaze and half smile, is the more haunting because it shows her at ease, in an informal setting, and representing no one but herself – the tribute of one genius to another.

Probably dating from the mid-eighties, it was with a mass of unsold work at Romney's death in 1802, and was disposed of years later, in 1834, by his son, the Revd John Ramsey, for £13. It then remained at Northwick Park until 1965, when it was sold again for 17,000 guineas.

to £30 a week. Sheridan had brought in his son Tom, also newly married and needing a job, to help to run his theatre; he himself was in ever worsening personal financial trouble. When he entertained in London, his guests noticed that some of the 'servants' were theatre employees; others were even said to be debt collectors persuaded to put on livery for the evening: he could still charm even the most unlikely people. But he was on poor terms with Hecca, who had tired of his drinking and his unreliability, and they lived mostly apart. In moments of fantasy he was prepared to bet that he could restore the glories of the past: £500 that he would write and produce another play of his own. In harsh reality he was desperately seeking a new manager to put some money into Drury Lane and restore its fortunes.

The return of Mrs Jordan was a good augury, and he invited her to open the season, which she did. 'I am just return'd from the opening of Drury Lane! Mrs Jordan was received with boundless applause; she is terribly Large, but her voice and acting still delightful,' wrote Harriet Bessborough to an absent lover.[10] Dora's largeness became the subject of comment from this time on. For some it spoiled their pleasure when she played youthful parts; others found her size less than they had been led to believe and, since her powers as an actress were undiminished, thought nothing of it. But she herself mentions 'growing large' in some of her letters to the Duke, and jokes about people thinking she was pregnant when she was not; so perhaps she was a little sensitive on the subject.

She was in London working through the autumn and right up to Christmas 1807. Most of the children were with her, in a new house she had taken in Mortimer Street. In October the Duke was in Norfolk, and caused considerable surprise to the local post master, who spread it about 'that the Duke writes to *Mrs Jordan every day*'.[11] Sometimes she 'ran down to Bushy' in his absence, although the children obviously enjoyed being in London: 'I do not play next week and have used all my eloquence to persuade the children to go to Bushy and even tempted them with *no Book*, but I could not succeed – we all stay at home this evening, but they insist on being amused tomorrow – Lloyd is in town and I must contrive it.'[12] Frederick, Lolly and Tuss went with Lloyd to Greenwich for a day, and to the Tower for another. Mely had to be inoculated, but not until the weather was cold enough. Later George and Sophy were at Bushy with their father, and she took the younger ones to the pantomime in town, the 'worst I think ever exhibited and nearly caused a riot'. There are no letters covering Christmas, which must have been spent at Bushy all together.

The Duke now began to make his strongest bid yet to return to a command at sea. Alsop, in spite of his newly married condition, declared himself 'raving mad' (in Dora's phrase) to accompany him as his private secretary. Neither fulfilled his ambition; instead George was brought home in disgrace from the military college. He had been neglecting his studies; his father, who went to fetch him, said it was because he was so anxious to join in some fighting; and he promised to mend his ways on being told he might sail with his regiment to Portugal later in the year. It is possible that George's bad behaviour was aggravated because he was now old enough to be aware of his own anomalous position in the world, to be teased by other boys, and to worry about it. A poem published this year hailed the Duke of Clarence flatteringly as a second Rodney and likened his sons to the princely sons of Edward III:

> While in his lovely progeny I trace,
> The dauntless rivals of great Edward's race;
> Still crown'd with laurels on the embattled plain;
> Triumphant ever on the boundless main.[13]

But George and his friends knew he was not a prince, let alone crowned with laurels. On the one hand his father was a duke and he was the grandson of the King; on the other, there was something mysterious and shameful about his parentage. For a boy of fourteen, anxiety about such things would be enough to make him behave badly, stop working and decide he had to prove himself by heroic deeds.

Sophy also became difficult. Her mother was understanding, telling the Duke that his eldest daughter had headaches, that 'her constitution will shortly undergo a change' – she was thirteen – and that 'it is with the greatest difficulty that I can get her to stir out of her bedroom or hit on anything to amuse her'.[14] Sophy was upset by the departure of the two brothers who were her closest friends, and still more upset when she heard of the possibility of her father also going to sea. She too was old enough to understand that the idyllic life of Bushy was built on something the world disapproved. In a letter George wrote after her death about his 'oldest playmate', he made it clear that she had suffered: 'no one but myself knows the painfulness and difficulty of her *early* life', he wrote.[15] Her mother might give her love and attention, but she could not remove the difficulty for which she was responsible in the first place.

The serpent had entered paradise, at any rate for the older children, and they went willingly out of its gates. The Duke took George to Portsmouth, where he was to embark for Portugal; and told a party of naval officers that he devoted his son to the service of his country, having so far volunteered in vain himself. George sailed towards Corunna on a fair wind, in high health and spirits. 'The distress of Mrs Jordan is not to be described . . . however, like what she is, one of the best and one of the ablest of women, she sees the propriety of his going,' wrote the Duke to the Prince of Wales.[16] Dora sent her fourteen-year-old off with her blessing, assuring him he was a fortunate boy, and offering him one of the most unusual pieces of advice ever offered to an officer: 'as you are now a Lieutenant and employed on actual service it would be more appropriate if in future when you mention the Duke, that you should say *my father*, or *the Duke*: it may prevent any little ridicule that might be excited by your *saying Papa*'.

15

London and Dublin Disasters: 1809

Still in Portsmouth, the Duke sat down and wrote to Dora in London, where she was back at work. The letter, one of the very few from him to her to survive, shows him at his best. He sounds careful, affectionate and responsible. He enclosed a letter from George, described his last cheerful wave from the deck to his father below in a yacht, and said he himself was going to Windsor to press the King once more for a naval appointment. After that he and Dora would meet for dinner at 'dear Bushy'. Then he explained carefully, as though to forestall her distress, that if he should get a command in the navy, even though it meant 'separating from every domestic comfort possible', he would be earning something for the children. The letter went on,

> Thro' your excellence and kindness in private life I am the happiest man possible and look forward only to a temporary separation to make that happiness more compleat from having provided for our dear children. My love and best and tenderest wishes attend you all at Bushy... Adieu till we meet and ever believe me, dearest Dora, Yours most affectionately...[1]

The sweetness is meant to soothe, but the warmth is real.

The King was not able to help him; his mental health was increasingly precarious, he was taking little part in such decisions, and would not override his advisers. The Duke complained bitterly of not being considered trustworthy either in the Cabinet or in the field. Dora sympathized, then returned to her season at Drury Lane. Time hung more heavily for him, with two sons gone. To give himself something to do he started on yet another programme of changes to the house and garden. Here at least he could direct and control matters exactly as he wished, blocking and opening windows, putting in extra servants' quarters, installing bathrooms, redesigning and reallotting the function of rooms. Almost as soon as one improvement was finished, another was begun. Dora suggested tactfully that 'Bushy will be so thoroughly comfortable when the new room is finished that I do not think you will feel any wish to make any further alterations.' She was quite wrong: work on more new rooms and improvements to the grounds continued as long as she lived there. At St James's too there was much redecorating and furnishing. No connection between the enormous bills run up in this way and his anxiety about providing for his children seems to have occurred to him.

Did he cherish any hopes that the children might be more formally acknowledged and incorporated into the royal family than they were? He is reported as saying, 'Do you think that I and my brothers will ever suffer that girl to wear the Crown?', meaning the Prince of Wales's daughter, Princess Charlotte.[2] The report is only gossip, and sounds like drunken talk, but it is quite possible he said it, and that he sometimes compared Charlotte in his mind with his son George, her cousin and the grandson of the King. Even the Prince of Wales himself sometimes appeared to find George more interesting than his own daughter.

George FitzClarence arrived in Portugal to join Sir John Moore's army as it retreated before the French to Corunna. His first experience of action was consequently short and harsh, but he managed to distinguish himself. Late one evening the Prince of Wales burst in on Dora in Mortimer Street, full of news of her son's exploits, and delighted by the letter he had just had from him; he told her George had a horse shot under him, and was 'running in the road' until

Colonel Hawker found him another. Although it was after midnight, the Prince insisted on Dora getting nine-year-old Frederick out of bed so that he could tell him about his brother's exploits; no uncle could have been prouder, more friendly, less formal.[3] As the Prince left, he asked Dora to pass on his love and congratulations to the Duke: for once, through his son, he had done well. And when George arrived back in England in January 1809 he spent most of his time at Brighton, where his regiment was based, greatly in favour with Mrs Fitzherbert as well as the Prince. He came to London for a few nights with his mother, and then returned to Portugal in April, where he continued to win golden reports for his 'great quickness, Intelligence and Activity'.[4]

This time he was serving under Arthur Wellesley – the future Duke of Wellington – and experienced the horrors of a famously bloody and cruel campaign. He wrote his own vivid account of it later, based on the journal he kept. It started with the Portuguese ladies showering the young British officers with sugar plums and roses; soon the same young officers were being ordered, for the first time in their lives, to charge with bayonets. He describes how the French hanged the peasants and cut their ripe wheat and olive trees to make huts for themselves; how the Spaniards murdered the wounded; how everyone merrily looted the dead and dying. It is a remarkable impression of a war fought in an alien land by quarrelling and treacherous allies and guerrilla forces for whom the rules of honour no longer operated.[5] After reading George's narrative it is a shock to find Dora sending Lucy out to buy him wooden soldiers; but she insisted that he would still enjoy childish amusements, and she was right.

In July he was wounded at the battle of Talavera; the English were victorious, but at the cost of almost a third of their force. The Duke was in Brighton when the news came, and set off at five in the morning to ride to Bushy to reassure Dora that George's wound, though in the leg, was a slight one, and that he would be brought home to recover. Henry reappeared at last in July too, after fourteen months in the Baltic, a hardened twelve-year-old. George arrived in England suffering from dysentery. Soon Henry volunteered for another expedition, this time to Holland. The war ground on, Napoleon defeating the Austrians and threatening Holland, which he proceeded to take; Henry was lucky to get away alive.

Newspaper reports praised the FitzClarence boys in glowing terms for their courage and pointed out their extreme youth: 'It has seldom fallen to the lot of youths of their early age to have seen so much and severe service.'[6] Dora said George's reputation should be 'a fine soft pillow for his head, for many years to come': the turn of phrase is charming, but she also told a friend, 'I have five boys, and must look forward to a life of constant anxiety and suspense.'[7]

Now she worried about her child-warrior sons constantly, as her letters make plain; and above this ground of anxiety, other problems appeared. Three disasters struck in 1809. In January fire broke out at St James's Palace, destroying a great part of it, though not the Duke of Clarence's apartments, where she and the children had rooms; but it made her uneasy at what other members of the royal family, displaced by the fire, might feel. So she proposed to the Duke that he should buy a house in town for the children. It could be put in trust to Coutts or Adam, she suggested, and it was 'a measure that must be pleasing to every individual in your own Family', as well as saving her from mortification. 'There is nothing that can ever reconcile me to be at St James's ... Do take this into consideration, and by purchasing a House at once, give your children a home, that every author may not feel it in his power to dispute their right.'[8] Depending professionally on public good-will as she did, she worried about the possibility of more press attacks on herself, and on the children too. Her suggestion of a house was sensible and tactful on all counts, but the Duke did not follow it. He may have felt he could not afford to; he also saw no need to move his own children out of St James's, whatever Dora thought.

The second disaster of 1809 was the Duke of York's involvement in a scandal. He was the commander-in-chief of the army, and married to a virtuous wife; and he was revealed as having a married mistress who traded in commissions, and who, on top of that, made his love letters public. This set the press off in full cry against all the royal brothers. Gossip was passed round, some harmless, some vicious. It was said that the Duke of Clarence had seduced one of Dora's daughters. Further, that one of the Miss Fords was pregnant by him. Another report put about that the King was insisting on Mrs Jordan being removed from Bushy.[9] None of this was true; all of it was hurtful, some of it almost too much to bear just when Dodee Ford was about to be married. Dora wrote to Boaden complaining of the 'cruel and infamous reports' in circulation, and insisting that the Duke was 'an example for half the fathers and husbands in the world'.[10] The wedding went ahead at the beginning of March, and Dora and the Duke spent the rest of the month together at Bushy: 'Your mother . . . is reading by me,' he wrote calmly to George. Then the three grown-up daughters joined them at Easter, bringing Alsop and March with them. The gossip quietened down.

The third horror produced the worst and most lasting effects on Dora's life. Late in the evening of 24 February the 'new' Drury Lane – it had opened in the year of George's birth – caught fire. The huge building went up in a blaze, brightening the whole night sky of London. There was no hope of saving it. This was the occasion of Sheridan's greatest show of nonchalance; he refused to hurry from the House of Commons, and sat in the Piazza Coffee House answering his friends' urgings to action with, 'May not a man be allowed to drink a glass of wine by his own fireside?' A few of the staff and actors did, however, risk their lives bringing out the theatre's charter and some other pieces, the writing desk from Dora's dressing room among them; all her costumes were destroyed. Garrick's clock was lost, and the harpsichord belonging to Elizabeth Sheridan. No insurance could make up for these, but in any case the theatre was insured far below its value.

A joke was Sheridan's way of defying disaster; but it was undoubtedly an absolute disaster for him and for the many others whose livelihoods depended on his theatre – the 'extensive company' Dora immediately thought of and invoked in the warmly sympathetic and supportive letter she sent him. She offered to do anything she could to help, naming herself 'one who has the happiness of being ranked amongst your friends'. She also reminded him firmly of his past literary triumphs, and urged him to think that he at least had the power to recoup his losses, which lesser members of the company had not.[11] If she hoped he would be inspired to write more plays, she was being optimistic; he had lost the knack. For the moment the company was able to use its patent in other theatres, playing again at the King's Theatre in the Haymarket and at the Lyceum. Dora appeared with them, and took part in benefits for the stage-hands who had lost their jobs. Then the Duke again asked her to withdraw from the London stage entirely. At the same time Sheridan, who at first believed he could remain in charge and rebuild his theatre again, found that no one would back him; when a committee was formed to put up a new theatre royal, he was excluded from it.

Dora and Sheridan had been colleagues for twenty-three years. They had wrangled about parts and benefits, quarrelled over contracts and money; she had suffered from his deep-seated suspicion of actresses, he had been frightened by the tenacity with which she extracted her salary; but they had been part of the same team and the same world, one that extended from the Devonshire House ladies in their boxes to the lowliest scene-shifters and painters. She had known

Elizabeth, he had known her lovers, and they had shared many triumphs. The end of their Drury Lane careers meant they were both left without a professional base at ages – he approaching sixty, she in her late forties – when they most needed one. Not only did they never work together again; each of them became vulnerable, as creatures who have lost their supporting environment are vulnerable.

From now on the Duke opposed every invitation to appear in London received by Dora. No reasons are discussed in her letters; sometimes she asked his permission again, then obediently complied with his ban, even though she clearly wanted to accept, for instance, young Tom Sheridan's proposal that she should play at the Lyceum later that year. The Duke did not wish it, and that was that. His dignity took precedence over her convenience and career; very possibly he was thinking of the dignity of the children also. If Dora could be made less conspicuous, the children might seem less like her children and more like his; rather than there being any question of their moving out of St James's Palace, they might more easily take their place within the royal family. Dora, looking on the bright side, wrote of touring for four months of the year and spending the other eight months 'quietly settled with my dear family'; but it did not work out as she imagined.[12]

There was another darkening shadow of worry for her this year: money. Two hundred years later, her accounts are impossible to sort out; they were not much easier then. For decades she had earned more than she had ever hoped or expected to; she had spent as she needed, given generously, and saved for her three eldest daughters. In her letters she mentions debts, life insurance policies, tax problems and the setting aside of money for the children: she often sent cash to her sons, and this year she began to save for Sophy's future as she had done for her half-sisters. She was also known for spontaneous charitable gestures. Since she was almost always paid in cash, and often gave large sums to the Duke, estimating her tax must have been a nightmare. 'I do not think there is any occasion to fill up the Tax paper whatever I will write a line to Dalrymple and he and Barton can make the deductions together,' she told the Duke in April.[13] Colonel Dalrymple was a neighbour at Bushy as well as an adviser to the Duke; he and his daughter often dined with Dora, and she regarded him as a good friend. John Barton, another adviser, was not so friendly; and soon he would become a formidable enemy.

The letter about her tax was written from Bath. The effect of her anxiety about money, and the Duke's ban on London, was to make her agree to appear in the provinces. Instead of settling down quietly at Bushy, with the odd appearance at Richmond or Margate, she started on a series of strenuous tours. April was spent in Bath; in June she went, much against her inclination, to Dublin for six weeks; and in September she set off again for Leicester, Liverpool and Chester. Lucy, her third daughter, went with her on all these tours, and gave her loyal and loving support, sometimes in difficult circumstances. She was a good companion; her character shines out of Dora's letters as steadfast, sensible and intelligent. They made jokes together, simple family ones, ones to cheer themselves up when they felt low. About their poor lodgings, 'Lucy says we are like a couple of Pigs put up in a small place to fatten.' On hearing of the Duke having a new wig, 'Lucy is a TORY, and likes you best in your own hair, and I think if it was put to the vote there would be more *Tories* than *Wigs*.' She amused her mother with her clever vocabulary, saying they were 'two poor Itinerants' – Dora preferred 'pilgrims' – and amused herself by going out to see the sights, and sometimes drawing what she saw; the walls of Chester, with their double view over town and country, offered 'the most delightful walk she ever took'. She would go out in search of books from second-hand stalls, accompany Dora to church or to the Methodist services they found more entertaining, shop with her for presents for the younger children, write letters for her, sign and seal tickets for her benefits, and generally keep her in good heart.

For Lucy, it meant seeing her mother in a wholly new light, sometimes enjoying but more often enduring her celebrity. On the one hand admiring crowds gathered to look at Mrs Jordan when she left her lodgings; a hundred people might be 'waiting to put me into my Carriage'.[14] On the other it was a tiring way of life, often uncomfortable and never wholly predictable. It was pleasant to hear a cross-looking old man abruptly urging someone in the Bath Pump Room, 'Have you seen Mrs Jordan? If NOT, lose no time, SEE as much of her as you CAN,' especially when he was a 76-year-old chief justice, Sir James Mansfield. It was less amusing to find herself 'talked out' of visits to the market and the library, where she went to read the papers, 'for I heard nothing but *Mrs Jordan's* name, and tho' nobody knew me, I could not stand it and would not encounter it again on any account, therefore I shall stay at home except when I can get into the fields.' The letter went on to describe how she heard people discussing her private life, and even giving a detailed account of 'a most pathetic parting' between her and the Duke.

To get away from this, she 'slipped out yesterday with Lucy into the fields leading to Bristol, and walked, which procured me a good night, the only one I have had since I left Bushy'.[15] Walking in the country was always a solace to Dora when she felt at all bruised; but gossip is an inevitable part of fame, and she was too much of a realist not to understand that, and take most of it lightly. She had been hearing about her imminent parting from the Duke for years; in reality he was coming to meet her at Maidenhead on her way home, and their letters were full of affectionate teasing. She told him that he appeared 'just to have found out that we go on together very well. It was fortunate that you concluded the sentence with the hope that it would never be otherwise.

You may have your doubts about it; I have none. Mind, I only answer for myself.'[16]

How did Dora appear to the world as she approached fifty? She had lost her slim waist and slight figure, but she was still bright-eyed and seductive when she chose to be. She tired more easily, but was still able to summon up reserves of energy and spirits. Boaden, pressed to say whether she had been handsome by someone who never saw her, answered simply, 'Had you seen her as I did, the question would never have occurred to you!'[17] Leigh Hunt wrote still better,

> though she was neither beautiful, nor handsome, nor even pretty, nor accomplished, nor 'a lady', nor anything conventional or *comme il faut* whatsoever, yet was so pleasant, cordial, so natural, so full of spirits, so healthily constituted in mind and body, had such a shapely leg withal, so charming a voice, and such a happy and happy-making expression of countenance, that she appeared something superior to all those requirements of acceptability.[18]

Hunt was more than twenty years her junior, so he cannot have formed his judgement on her until she was in her midforties, and it is in these late appearances that he found her 'a performer who unites great comic powers with much serious feeling, ... not only the first actress of the day, but as it appears to me from the description we have of former actresses, the first that has adorned our stage'.[19]

The actor and stage-writer William Oxberry, another who did not see her until after 1807, also called her 'a wonderful woman ... with more natural genius for the profession she followed than any actress we ever saw'.[20] The great Victorian actor Macready received, as a very young player, some of his first lessons in acting from her after 1809, and wrote of her

> discrimination, an identity with her character, an artistic arrangement of the scene, that made all appear spontaneous and accidental, though elaborated with the greatest care. Her

voice was one of the most melodious I ever heard, which she could vary by certain bass tones, that would have disturbed the gravity of a hermit; and who that heard that laugh could ever forget it? . . . so rich, so apparently irrepressible, so deliciously self-enjoying, as to be at all times irresistible.[21]

John Bannister, after so many years playing opposite her, said, 'No woman, I think, ever uttered comedy like her. She was perfectly good tempered, and possessed the best of hearts.'[22] There is a great deal more along these lines, from fellow actors, critics and mere observers: Charles Mathews, Thomas Campbell, John Genest, Hazlitt. Byron called her 'superlative', Coleridge talked of the 'exquisite witchery of her tone'.

Strangers unconnected with the theatre – even hostile to it – were also struck by her sweetness of character. One of the most famous stories is of a Methodist preacher who observed her in Chester in 1809 as she was being thanked by a poor widow with three children whom she had rescued from a debtors' prison, giving a sharp reprimand to the lawyer who had increased her debt under the guise of helping her. Dora made light of what she had done and sent the woman away with another pound. The minister then came forward to praise her, and offered his hand. She drew back and refused, saying if he knew who she was, he would send her to the devil. He insisted until Dora said, 'I don't like fanatics; and you'll not like me, when I tell you who I am.' – 'I hope I shall.' – 'Well, then, I tell you. I am a player.' The preacher sighed. 'Yes, I am a player; and you must have heard of me. Mrs Jordan is my name.'

There was a pause, then the minister again put out his hand, saying, 'The Lord bless thee, whoever thou art; His goodness is unlimited; He has bestowed on thee a large portion of his spirit; and as to thy calling, if thy soul upbraid thee not, the Lord forbid that I should.' He offered her his arm and walked her back to her lodging, where he shook hands with her again, and said: 'Fare thee well, Sister; I know not what the principles of people of thy calling may be; – thou art the first I ever conversed with; but if their benevolent practices equal thine, I hope and trust, at the great day, the Almighty God will say to each – Thy sins are forgiven thee.'[23]

If Dora had any religious faith it is rarely in evidence in her letters beyond mentions of prayers at home, occasional church-going, and a sarcasm at the expense of two bishops sent to give the Duke an improving lecture during one of her absences; but clearly, as the Chester minister saw, she was a Christian in the sense that mattered most – in her practice.

She was also forthright, and capable of a sharp-tongued response to what she felt was false. When Sir Walter Scott told her he 'could not perceive the smallest alteration' in her since the last time he had seen her – some twenty years before – she found the flattery 'so gross' that she told him 'that that was very extraordinary, as you are said to be particularly sharp-sighted in this part of the world'.[24] But she was not a brilliant conversationalist, and some were disappointed, expecting her private talk to be a continuation of Wycherley's or Sheridan's dialogue – a common misconception where actors are concerned. Instead they found 'the animated, lively, brilliant mimic on the boards, was in the saloon retiring, quiet, nay, almost reserved. Mrs Jordan seldom spoke much in company, particularly in very large assemblies; but then she spoke well. She made no exertion to appear distinguished, and became more so by absence of effort.'[25]

Professionally she had the confidence of an actress who commands respect within her world and enthusiasm in her audiences, but personally she was not always so confident. In these later years she was torn between her pride in her absent sons and her fears for their safety. The fears were reasonable, but they sometimes drove her to the edge of hysteria in her letters home, particularly when she was without recent news, or when she knew that one of them was unhappy. This was the case with Henry, who began to hate the navy and asked to be transferred into the army. For many months she pleaded with the Duke to listen to him; it took a great deal of persistence before she succeeded. Anxiety about her sons became the danger point for her emotional well-being; her relations with the Duke, and their future together, caused her no worries, and were taken entirely for granted – at least within the context of Bushy. In her travels about the country she sometimes found her equivocal social position a strain. She did not talk of it directly to him, but she did mention both her reluctance to accept invitations, and her loneliness; reading between the lines of her letters, you pick up the painfulness of living between one layer of society and another. She might be amused when she overheard remarks about herself, but she was too intelligent not to be aware that some of her celebrity was as a royal mistress rather than as a working actress, and this could make her apprehensive of the sort of attention she was likely to attract. The Duke was never at her performances now; her life was absolutely divided between Bushy, where she was the good wife and mother, and the provincial theatres and lodging houses where she was the great, though not wholly invulnerable, Mrs Jordan.

The most adventurous of her journeys in 1809 was her trip to Dublin. She was persuaded to make it by the stage-manager of the Crow Street Theatre, Atkinson, with a promise of great houses and certain profits; but she was anxious about leaving the Duke in June, when he was often struck down by asthma, and she set off braced to resist the whole experience, from the choppy sea crossing to what she remembered of exuberant Irish hospitality. Dublin is a foreign city for a Londoner, and Dora, in spite of her Irish upbringing, was prejudiced enough to view it pretty well as such. Some of the past had been exorcized at least. Daly was dead, and the cruelty of the Blands towards her mother dimmed by the years; she was forgiving enough to take a Bland nephew under her wing on the journey, on his way to join his regiment, and only too glad to go with his famous aunt. Lucy went with her too, as well as a maid and her butler Thomas.

The sea did slop right into their beds during the crossing, and their first lodgings were dirty; she had to pay ten guineas to get out of them. The cook she hired presented herself in bare feet, declaring shoes 'a mightly nadeless custom'; but, as Dora said, she was not going to dress the dinner with her toes, so that was all right. She was warmly greeted by Atkinson at the Crow Street Theatre but found she had been double-booked with Kemble, which meant ten wasted days. The manager tried to make amends by sending round haunches of mutton, and butter and cream; but he failed in the more important matter of providing competent supporting actors, and the theatre's take had been exaggerated. All this was confirmation of her fears.

It was flattering that Dublin society was agog to see her, arranging elaborate picnic excursions and dinners in her honour; but so many people hung about her door that she began to feel under siege. She was forced to put up muslin curtains, and to wear a veil whenever she went out. Her celebrity brought some real and surprising dangers too. The first time she was carried to the theatre in her curtained chair, Thomas was surrounded by a crowd and roughly informed that unless she opened the curtains and let them see her, 'next time, they would throw stones into the chair'. Since they clearly meant it, she obliged; she also had to warn Thomas that he would be in danger himself if he did not mend his rude remarks about the Catholic faith.

There were some comforts too. She had an old friend in Sheridan's older sister, Alicia Lefanu, who came round to her lodgings to welcome her; the pleasure was only slightly less-ened when Alicia drew out a play-script she had written and asked Dora to read it. ('Pity me,' wrote Dora. It was her entire comment; later the play, *The Sons of Erin*, did reach the Lyceum in London, but it ran for one night only.) Scripts apart, the Lefanus were good people, and made much of

Lucy; their son, a clergyman, took a fancy to her, so strongly that Dora wondered whether there would be a match between her daughter and Sheridan's nephew. But Lucy would not consider a Dublin husband; she 'hates and detests the place as much as I do', wrote her mother, her pen at its most acerbic.[26] The Lefanus lived fully up to Dora's ideas of Irish hospitality as both generous and disconcerting. At dinner they served a salmon so large that 'the tail rested in my plate, and the head in the lap of my opposite neighbour, who, happening to be an Englishman, was, I believe, as much astonished as myself'. John Philpot Curran, the renowned politician, gave another great dinner for her, inviting 'all the blue stockings and wits in the town . . . I shall be very glad when it is over.' Dora wrote glumly, 'I am convinced they will think me very stupid. I cannot help it. There is to me nothing so tiresome as that eternal driving at wit, nothing so delightful when spontaneous and unaffected.' But later she called her host 'very gallant', so she may have enjoyed herself more than she expected. Another celebrated Dublin figure, Miss Sydney Owenson, author of *The Wild Irish Girl*, offended her by walking unannounced into her drawing room; their parents had been friends twenty-five years earlier, but Dora refused to accept her Irish spontaneity. She withdrew into a strict British formality, and refused to meet Miss Owenson.

Some encounters from the past moved her: a doctor, who remembered seeing her as a child with the measles, and a very old man who had been present – and indeed pushed her on to the stage – on the first night she ever performed at Crow Street. Others pleased her less; at one of the Lefanus' parties she met a general who had been at school with her father, now in his seventies, reputedly the largest man in Europe, and newly married to a beautiful girl about to have his child. 'I never saw such a monster. What will some girls do for money . . . God forgive her. I think of the two SHE is the greatest beast,' Dora wrote firmly to the Duke. You get the impression she was determined to see Ireland as a place of monsters, with its giant salmon and giant generals, shoeless cooks and stone-throwing street ruffians.

Yet there was great and friendly interest in her. People started calling on her at ten in the morning to ask how she was after performing on the previous night ('very obliging but very tiresome'), and she was up until midnight, when show and supper were at last over. As well as the Lefanus, she found other good friends in the family of Jonah Barrington, an Anglophile lawyer and theatre-lover. Dora needed his advice to deal with some bills of her brothers', dating from years back, which were suddenly presented to her. They totalled nearly £400, and Barrington advised her to settle them. Otherwise, he warned her, she would face being insulted in public and even prevented from playing, as had happened to Mrs Siddons in a similar situation. He also offered to advance the money. Dora paid, of course. 'This was an unexpected blow on me, tho' I must say I had some vague fears when I came here,' she wrote home, adding, 'Let us bury all this in oblivion.' She had the survivor's capacity to put things behind her. 'I will never mention, or if I can help it, think of it again.'

All this while she remained anxious about the Duke's health; Nixon kept her informed, and he got through the hay harvest without suffering a bad attack. There was Henry to worry about too, again at sea, and unhappy. She had bad dreams, and fears that she would never see any of them again; she said it was 'the most cruel separation I ever experienced', and when the Crow Street manager offered her another week at £100 a night and another benefit, she 'quietly but steadily refused it', to his considerable astonishment. She had made less than expected, only about £1,400, of which £400 was left for her brothers' bills; but she trusted that 'were it possible for me to return even poorer than I was when I left you, my welcome would not be less kind and sincere. It is the only recompence I look [for] for the vexations,

anxieties and disappointments and real miseries of mind I
have suffered.'

She did not tell the Duke of the most disconcerting episode
of her visit until just before setting out for England again. It
involved the Lord Lieutenant of Ireland, currently Charles
Lennox, fourth Duke of Richmond. All the Lennoxes were
descended from Charles II and his ennobled French mistress,
Louise de Kéroualle; they were a handsome, fiery family. The
present duke, a man of Dora's age, had been a soldier, hot
tempered enough to fight a duel with his own royal commanding officer, the Duke of York, in 1789, when he considered
himself slighted by him; later he was a Member of Parliament
and supporter of Pitt. He was known as a hard drinker, and
had a large family; the Duchess and their daughters came to
Dora's first night, when she played *The Country Girl*, but he
did not appear in his box until a later performance. The story
she had to tell of the Duke went like this. It was

an adventure, which I can laugh at now that it is over, tho'
at the time it had not so merry an effect. The Sunday evening
after the Command [performance], about 10 o'clock, Lucy
being at the Barringtons, I was sitting waiting for Atkinson,
who used to come at that hour to settle the weekly accounts,
he had hinted to me that the Duke of Richmond was so
delighted with my acting that he should not be surprised if
there was a second command. I was sitting quite alone when
Mr Parkhurst from the Castle was announced. It immediately
struck me that this was the command. He was therefore
shewn in. He talked for a long time but no mention made of a
command. I thought the man looked very foolish and nervous.
However, after a little hesitation he presented the Duke of R's
compliments to me, regretting that his situation prevented his
doing himself the pleasure of calling on me, but that he should
consider himself very much flattered and extremely happy if I
would allow him to call on me alone, at half past 12 that
night. It is impossible for me to give you any idea of the effect
this had on me. Yourself and the children down to Mele swam

before my eyes; speak I could not. At this very moment
Atkinson came in, and on his asking me what was the matter
I could no longer put any constraint on my feelings, and left
the room as quickly as I could. They went away together.
The latter returned in about half an hour, and when he saw
me (for I was really ill) the tears ran down his cheeks, and he
accused himself as the cause of all my vexations. He brought a
thousand apologies from Parkhurst, who said he was greatly
shocked at having distressed me so much, but that he could
not refuse to bring the message. It is now over and I can
really laugh at it ... Atkinson is frightened out of his senses
for fear I should mention it to you. To appease him I said I
would not, but it is too ridiculous to be kept as a secret.

So Dublin had not changed very much after all in the years
she had been absent. But Dora had, and the Lord Lieutenant
was no Daly; he had only attempted something ridiculous. Of
course she had to tell the Duke: he was the person with whom
she shared her secrets, and who should know that she could
still be paid even such a dubious sexual compliment as this,
and by a fellow duke. By waiting before she told him, she
allowed it to become more of a joke than an affront. 'Lucy
and I laugh at it whenever we think of it,' she added.
Surprising, perhaps, that she should have discussed it with an
unmarried daughter, but Lucy could clearly take these things
in her stride; and her mother was teaching her a basic lesson
of comedy. It could defuse humiliation and terror, and turn
tears into laughter. Instead of allowing the Duke of Richmond
to be a figure of menace, he was turned into a figure of fun.

Dora's account of the Lord Lieutenant's behaviour had a
close parallel in England this year, when Sheridan's old love,
Harriet Bessborough, went through a similar ordeal with a
still more highly placed admirer. She was the same age as
Dora, had been married for nearly thirty years, and was also
the mother of several children, two of them by Lord Granville
Leveson-Gower, who now decided to end their liaison and
take a young wife. On hearing this, the Prince of Wales

hurried round to Lady Bessborough, 'threw himself on his knees, and clasping me round, kiss'd my neck before I was aware of what he was doing,' – so wrote Harriet to her faithless lover.

> I screamed with vexation and fright; he continued sometimes struggling with me, sometimes sobbing and crying ... Then mixing abuse of you, vows of eternal love, entreaties and promises of what he would do ... had not my heart been breaking I must have laugh'd out at the comicality ... that immense, grotesque figure flouncing about half on the couch, half on the ground ... After telling him for two hours that ... I never could or would be on any other terms with him than the acquaintance he had always honour'd me with, we came to a tolerably friendly making up, and he kept me two more telling me stories ...[27]

Harriet Bessborough, like Dora, chose to make a funny story out of an experience that, at the time, was not so amusing. The two letters stand together as pieces of female reporting on a world in which men took themselves, and were taken, very seriously indeed. In one the Prince of Wales becomes a grossly comic figure, in the other the Lord Lieutenant of Ireland an absurd creature who demonstrates his supposed power by the crudest and most inept of insults to a celebrated visitor. Both were cases 'too ridiculous to be kept as a secret'. The men saw themselves as Lovelaces or Lotharios. The women presented them as Don Juans or Falstaffs, their great figures deflated by the scratching of that womanly weapon, the pen.

It is not too surprising that Dora missed the charm of Dublin, and was glad to see the last of it. She never went back again. The Barringtons saw her off, and she took their son with her; he was going to prepare for the army, starting at school with her younger sons. At Bushy she had the great joy of finding Henry home at last, and everyone well and in good spirits; Frederick, FitzErnest, the Duke of Cumberland's son, and all the girls were planning to go to the horse races, and there was cricket in the park. Although she and Lucy set off northwards once more, it was with a more comfortable feeling; and in October she was back, and put in some performances at Richmond again, while the Duke went to Windsor to cele-brate the jubilee of his father's accession with a roast ox, a water pageant, incense, fireworks and a grand supper, all organized by the Queen. The court ladies were got up in white satin cloaks, and a large crowd gathered, but the King himself went to bed early. His eyesight had almost failed, and he was tired.

16

'I am a better actress at this moment than I ever was': 1810

The Christmas of 1809 was one of rejoicing. 'My two beloved boys are now at home ... We shall have a full and merry house at Christmas; 'tis what the Duke delights in. A happier set, when all together, I believe never yet existed,' wrote Dora to Barrington. She was writing to let him know that her big sons had gone to visit his boy at school; Barrington was a friend, but not an intimate, and this was her formal, public voice. She was well aware that her letters to him might be quoted or shown to other people, and she added, 'The ill-natured parts of the world never can enjoy the tranquil pleasures of domestic happiness.'[1] For a moment she sounds more like a moralizing novelist than her usual self.

There is no doubt that Bushy was a place of domestic happiness that Christmas. Every room in the top floor had its complement of children, though two of the children were now seasoned fighting men. George was recovered from his wound and dysentery, and Henry had just been safely plucked back from the disastrous Walcheren expedition that had left so many others dead. The Duke and his sons could swap battle stories, and go out hunting and shooting together, and Dora would keep her dislike of guns and hatred of cruelty to herself. Indoors, firelight and candlelight cast their cheerful red and yellow circles all through the house, the maids and kitchen staff working at full tilt to keep every room bright and warm, and everyone well fed from morning to night.

There were frosty morning carriage rides across the park to

church at Hampton village, and great consumption of beef and pheasant, mince pies and plum pudding afterwards. Nixon and the Lloyd family were in attendance, and the curate Dr Morgan; Lucy played her part of good and helpful elder sister. The Duke's old friend, Colonel Hawker, who had suffered the double blow of losing his mistress and being wounded at Talavera with George, came to be cheered up, bringing his grown-up daughter Julia. There was music, dancing, whist, billiards, reading aloud and family games, and almost certainly an expedition to the pantomime at Covent Garden. Mely was just beginning to run about, a stout little figure in her red riding hood, Tuss and Ta were petted, curly-headed four- and five-year-olds; the older girls had new dresses and trinkets, and went out on their well-behaved ponies in the winter sunshine; tough Freddles raced his pony against all comers, went coursing for hares, and came in joyously covered in mud.

But now a paradox: from all this domestic happiness Dora departed even before the new year. She embraced the children and the Duke, and set off once again with Lucy; they were on their way to Manchester, then Halifax, Bradford, Leeds and York. She knew this was a perverse thing to do, and felt she had to explain to the Duke that it was neither 'avarice nor inclination' that impelled her; to leave 'the comforts of dear Bushy' and her adored children for long coach journeys, dirty lodgings and drudgery was something she did only because she felt she had to.

Why did she do it? She had given him part of a reason and part of a resolution before Christmas, when she told him she only wanted to get out of debt and stay at home, now that her three elder girls were provided for; and that, 'however you may joke about it you surely cannot doubt for a moment my being thoroughly tired of my profession'.[2] She also said she thought herself 'too burdensome to you' and was determined never to ask him for more than the allowance he gave her. The mystery is how she ran up debts, and why she was never able to pay them off. She went on talking about these eternal debts, and about her tax problems and life insurance policies; and she also went on sending the Duke money. She promised repeatedly that this would be her last tour, her last absence from home, her last self-inflicted misery; and it never was. After a few months, or weeks, or even days at home, she would set off again.

In 1810 she was away for the whole of January, then for June, and then again from September until Christmas. Sometimes she joked about it – 'it is a pity that like other professions I cannot have assistants'[3] – but on the whole her letters home offer a rich anthology of regrets. She invokes Goldsmith's *The Traveller*: 'I may well say that when I quit you all I drag at each remove a lengthened chain.'[4] 'I long to make this my last appearance more than ever I did to make my first,' she writes from her York dressing room, a portrait of Tate Wilkinson looking down on her.[5] Setting off northwards again, she explains, as though to reassure, 'I find I can by getting up at five and travelling till 10, go 130 miles a day. This will in some degree shorten this long absence.'[6] At Warrington she cannot 'help thinking of my dear little room at Bushy'. In Leeds she finds 'the only clean and good bed I have lain in since I gave up mine to dear Lolly,' but it is not enough to make up for what she is missing; even 'Lucy, with all her quietude and philosophy, begins to allow this is a very comfortless and weary life.'[7] They do their best to cheer themselves up: 'We have got books from Leeds, and are endeavouring to make this a little home for a few days.' More cheering even than books is the renewed 'idea that this is the last separation from you all'; it is 'a comfort to my mind beyond what I can express'.[8] But a false comfort, as it turns out. In Edinburgh, suffering from swollen ankles, she writes to George, 'I must soon give up the profession ... I have neither health nor spirits to continue much longer.'[9] Then to the Duke again, 'I merely want to get out of debt, but something always happens to prevent this long wished for event.'[10] She misses the children painfully, and reproaches herself for losing so much of Mely's development, and her 'dear innocent prattle'. And always, like a litany, 'Oh my God, how I do long to return home.'

If it was only money that drove her on, you have to ask why, after all her efforts, she remained always in debt, and why the Duke's advisers did not sort out the problems. It was a matter of understandable pride to her to have earned for her three elder daughters, but why was she trying to save money for Sophia too? Why was she sending the Duke money, and her sons?

For one thing, she could never resist the generous gesture, as her sons-in-law so quickly discovered and turned to their own account. Then, because she had always earned so much, she had not needed to insist on prudence and economy, and she had forgotten how to say no when asked for money. She saw herself as the provider, the benefactress who could solve everyone else's problems. For herself, she was not extravagant; she had no expensive habits, made her stage costumes last till they were in shreds, insisted on sobriety at Bushy. On the other hand she was clearly marked out as someone to be overcharged and exploited by family, tradesmen, servants, innkeepers and lodging-house people alike.

The Duke, by general agreement, had no sense or understanding of money at all. He relied on what he could squeeze out of Parliament, on the generosity of various bankers, on any credit he could raise; and he was wholly in the hands of his men of business. If they, who were in the counsels of the royal family, were beginning to think of how to separate the Duke from Mrs Jordan, they may have seen the question of their finances, joint and separate, as a promising area in which to operate. Since they were dealing with her tax, they must have had a good idea of her financial situation and problems, and been in a position to advise her; and even if she resisted their advice, they could surely have helped to disentangle her from debts once and for all. The fact that they did not choose to do so suggests that they were less than devoted to her interests.

Her money problems were real; which does not mean money was the only thing that kept her touring. When the Duke joked about whether she was really as tired of her profession as she claimed, he was making a shrewd point. Her letters to him naturally say more about the drawbacks than the pleasures and satisfactions; but she did sometimes touch on them too. When she does, you sense at once how important this other half of her life remained to her, where she was not a domestic creature, not an anxious, loving mother, not even a sexual being; where she was simply the best comic actress in the country. In that world she was among friends and fellow workers: Robert Elliston, who invited her to Manchester where he was running the theatre, had been Rolla to her Cora in Sheridan's *Pizarro* at Drury Lane; John Bannister was in Manchester just before her, and wrote for news of her as soon as he heard she was to be there. She took pride in what she could do with an audience; 'It is astonishing how good acting refines the mind of an audience,' she wrote.[11] She also felt revived when she acted: 'A fresh audience gives me fresh spirits. I suppose it has the same effect as you gentlemen experience in riding a fresh horse,' she explained to the Duke, seeking the right analogy to make him understand.[12]

At home, she was a matron. He saw her as the mother of his children, and no longer as the irresistibly seductive companion she had once been. She may have felt sexually weary herself by now. But on stage, in her working life, she was the same as she had always been; the inner self that remains, simultaneously child, girl, young woman and old woman, could find expression still as the Country Girl, as Beatrice, as Nell. It is not surprising that she did not want to suppress this part of herself; that there was a real battle going on inside her head between her wish to be at home with her family and her other wish – and need – to work.

One of the most important letters she ever wrote gives

expression to this division, her pride in what she had achieved in her profession and her acknowledgement of the price she and her family had to pay for it. It was sent to the Duke early in 1811, when she was acting in Bath.

> The Theatre last night was greatly crowded, and from the applause and admiration one would think that [I] had but *started* in the profession instead of being near the end of the race – but with regard to acting when I can for an hour or two, forget you all and the various anxieties that in general depress my spirits, I really think, and it is the opinion of several critics here that have known me from my first appearance in London, that I am a better actress at this moment than I ever was. You would be surprised to see with what eagerness all the performers treasure up any little instruction I give them at rehearsals; many of them make memorandums of them in their pocket books ... I drive you all from my mind as much as I can during the time I am employed, but then you all return with double force and my dreams are confused and disturbed to a degree.[13]

It is a statement that sounds like the exact truth: she was equally distressed at her separation from her family and proud of her achievement in the theatre.

Other people observed how acting put life into her. A man who saw her in Liverpool this year described how he

> accompanied Mrs Jordan to the green-room ... She went thither languid and apparently reluctant; but, in a quarter of an hour, her very nature seemed to undergo a metamorphosis; the sudden change of her manner appeared to me, in fact, nearly miraculous. She walked spiritedly across the stage two or three times, as if to measure its extent; and the moment her foot touched the scenic boards, her spirit seemed to be regenerated. She cheered up, hummed an air, stepped light and quick, and every symptom of depression vanished! The comic eye and the cordial laugh returned upon their enchanting mistress, and announced that she felt herself moving in her proper element.[14]

Macready's account of working with her at this period also shows what her stage presence and authority meant at a rehearsal to a novice, and an exceptionally intelligent and well-educated one:

> When the cue for my entrance as Felix was given, it was not without embarrassment that my few first words were spoken; but her good nature soon relieved me, for when I expressed the love that wrestled with a suspicious temper in the words, 'True love has many fears, and fear as many eyes as fame; yet sure – I think – they see no fault in thee!' she paused, apparently in a sort of surprise, and with great emphasis, said 'Very well indeed, Sir!' This gave me again my perfect self-possession, and I was able to attend to all her remarks and treasure up the points, in which she gave prominence to the text.

He went on, 'I have seen many Violantes since, but where was there one who could, like her, excite the bursts of rapture in an audience . . .? The mode in which she taught Flora to act her parts was a lesson to make an actress.'[15] To Macready and all her fellow professionals, as well as to her audiences, she was a fabled creature, as cunning in her arts, and as ageless, as Cleopatra.

Only at Bushy her magic was fading. It flickered for a last time in the summer of 1810, when the Duke remembered again that she was indispensable to him. She travelled up to Edinburgh at the end of May, anxious as ever about leaving, but getting good reports on everyone at home. The Duke was off to the races at Epsom; Alsop saw him looking very well. She wrote home teasingly saying he must expect her back like the bad penny, and that she trusted this would be her *very last* departure from home. In his reply the Duke took a new tone, saying he saw no reason at all for her to give up the stage just yet. This disconcerted her: 'I was sorry to perceive . . . that you do not seem to feel the necessity and propriety of my quitting the stage, as much as I could wish.'[16] But she moved on to Glasgow, as arranged. Suddenly, at the end of June, a message was brought, asking her to return to Bushy at once. The Duke was seriously ill; his annual asthma attack had come on so badly that he thought he might be dying. Fifteen-year-old Sophy was nursing him, but in his panic he wanted only Dora at his bedside.

Without a moment's hesitation she set off, travelling day and night without stopping for food or rest. The four hundred miles were covered in two and a half days – sixty-four hours, according to her own account to George – a journey that would have taxed anyone's strength, and for a woman of her age a remarkable feat. The Duke, mercifully, was no longer dying when she arrived at Bushy; he was already past the worst, and she was probably the more exhausted of the two. As soon as he was well enough, he wrote to George: 'Your most excellent mother flew to me from Glasgow in sixty three hours the moment she heard I was unwell.' He added that she had given up 'a very fine engagement' and was now tired. She thought of returning to Scotland, and it is a relief to know she did not, but remained at Bushy for the rest of the summer.[17]

The Duke, however, once fully recovered, departed without her for Brighton. If this was a trifle ungallant, 'les Princes . . . sont peu scrupuleux en tout ce qui regarde leurs plaisirs', as Harriet Bessborough observed, and his gratitude for Dora's dash to his sickbed was quickly dissipated.[18] At his brother's birthday celebrations 'he was on very hard duty as to drinking', she told George. He went on to Oatlands, the Duke of York's Surrey estate, for more festivities; and when it came to his own birthday there was, for the first time in many years, no celebration at Bushy.

Dora explained to George that his father had 'found it necessary to make some retrenchments in the family' and thought it prudent not to mark the day. Instead, the Queen graciously gave a fête at Windsor for him, and the Princesses presented him with some plate. What did Dora think of this? She is careful not to say; but she does tell her son that she is quite alone. The August sunshine is especially lovely over the park, she wrote, but Frederick has gone back to school, Henry is at sea; Tuss has been invited to his first party and Sophy has a message for her brother, but they are evidently absent, as are all the others. She does not say where they are; perhaps the Duke has taken them to see their aunts at Windsor. 'Even Mely has taken her flight, & the house is so still, that it does not appear like Bushy.'[19] It made an eerie end to the summer.

There were reasons, if not excuses, for the Duke's behaviour. The royal family was in a sad state. Princess Amelia was dying, slowly and agonizingly, from tuberculosis. The other Princesses were all miserable in varying degrees: Princess Sophia described them as 'poor old wretches ... old lumber to the country, like old clothes, I wonder you do not vote for putting us in a sack & drowning us in the Thames.'[20] The King, now over seventy, was blind and sinking into madness again, reopening the question of a regency. The Queen had every reason to be unhappy; and indeed Dora expressed her sympathy to the Duke for his mother's afflictions on several occasions, and shed some tears over them too.

The Duke was drawn closer to his mother and sisters by their unhappiness. He was with them more, and they welcomed him and, however cautiously, his children. While she still lived, Princess Amelia sent messages to George and Henry, and Sophy and Frederick were at Windsor when she died. Sophy was very kindly received by her aunts, the Princesses, and invited to attend the funeral. She did so, rather to her absent mother's consternation, because Dora thought it would upset her; Dora had, however, prepared mourning for all the children before going away again. Sophy was not distressed by the funeral, but her life became confusing. She and her father were now invited together to functions from which her mother was debarred. They went to stay with the Devonshires and Bessboroughs at Chiswick House, for instance, where there was waltzing every night, and the Duke made everyone laugh with his imitations of the Queen's outrage on hearing that Napoleon had married the Emperor's daughter: 'My Got! My Got! what will this come to? – the oldest House in Europe married to an Emperor of yesterday. My Got! My Got! married to *nothing* – he has no blood in his veins.' The Duke might mock his mother for insisting on the importance of blood, but Sophy saw that it was not entirely a laughing matter; her own blood put her in a very uncertain position.

Her mother had no blood in her veins at all, but she was generous. Dora realized that, if the Duke's children were to take their place in his world, she must let them go into it without her. So she sang Sophy's praises to him as 'charming in mind and person', said she would make a clever and accomplished woman, and encouraged the Duke to let her entertain for him. 'She is now old enough, to receive your friends – do Love, oblige me in this it is what I have long wished,' she wrote about this time, adding 'company may amuse you too ... I assure you it would give me great pleasure, during my absences.'[21] As a practical mother, she also urged him to give her daughter a proper dress allowance. Dora was right about Sophy; she was found to be just as charming as Dora said, and was welcomed into society.

The elder girls' problems were of a different kind. Lucy, the reasonable and sweet-natured, who had said she would never marry, suddenly announced she had accepted a proposal from the Duke's friend Colonel Hawker. He was a man of good family and well-to-do; he was also approaching fifty. Perhaps that was his charm to a fatherless twenty-one-year-old. Considering her mother's history, and Fanny's unsatisfactory marriage, and the Marches, Lucy may have reasoned that it was safer to be sensible than passionate; and considering the world in general, it also seemed better for a woman to be married than not. Like her fictional contemporary, Jane

Austen's Marianne, she settled for flannel waistcoats and emotional calm.*

Lucy was married at Hampton Church in April, in the presence of her mother, Henry and Sophy. Dora wrote, using her public voice, 'he is a most excellent man, and has a very good private property: she will make the best of wives – a better girl never yet lived: it makes me quite happy'.[22] What she felt privately is another matter; a few months later, after Hawker had carried Lucy off to Portugal as he rejoined his regiment, she wrote, 'I miss poor Lucy who has in her heart a Soldier and ought to have been a Colonel.' Dora wanted all her daughters to marry; she had never considered any other path in life for them, but this remark suggests that, when she thought about it, she saw that Lucy's capacities were greater than her opportunities.[23]

Fanny took over as her travelling companion, but where Lucy had been a support Fanny was more of a worry and a drain on her emotions. Alsop had become increasingly quarrelsome; he was ambitious and dissatisfied, and made Fanny suffer for it. She thought of trying to become a concert singer, or even following her mother on to the stage; Dora discouraged her as strongly as she could. Fanny was eager to help by looking after Dora's costumes, but there were disquieting aspects to her character. One night, without telling her mother, she poured 'white poppy syrup' into her bedtime wine and water; it was intended to give her a good night's sleep, she explained later. Dora said it had done her no harm, but Fanny's easy dispensing of poppy syrup – laudanum – was disturbing.

As Christmas approached again, nothing was quite right. Dora expected FitzErnest to stay with them, but he was not allowed to. Sophy's pious governess-companion, Miss Turner,

---

* *Sense and Sensibility*, Jane Austen's first novel, was published in 1811, and shows Marianne Dashwood settling for marriage to Colonel Brandon, a much older family friend suspected of fathering a natural child.

fussed about whether she should stay over the holiday, driving Dora to a rare outburst of temper:

> Miss Turner writes to Fanny today that you have asked her to stay over Christmas, but will not decide what she is to do, till she hears that it is agreeable to me, what nonsense ... I hate those unnecessary over refinements, if she will not squeeze my hand, or sit on my lap, she is heartily welcome to remain as long as it pleases you, or dear Sophy finds pleasure in her society.[24]

Fanny in turn was uneasy about whether the Duke really wanted *her* at Bushy for Christmas. Even Dora's servants were giving trouble, accusing each other of sexual misde-meanours and trying to embroil her in their feuds: the re-spectable Miss Sketchley, who sometimes looked after the children and sometimes travelled with Dora, accused Thomas of having women in his room. Since he was married, and the gossip got back to his wife, he was furious; he retorted by telling Dora he had found Miss Sketchley waiting for him in his bed at lunchtime one day. This is the world of *Tom Jones* rather than Jane Austen, but Dora was past seeing the funny side. Her letters this winter are full of anxiety and uncertainty, as though she sensed the approach of something bad, and as though those around her sensed it too.

And when it came, the Christmas of 1810 was 'far from what it used to be – thoughts of those absent spoiled all'.[25] George, Henry and Lucy were away. The Duke and Sophy were often out, sometimes until five in the morning if they had been to a ball, and then slept all day. The weather was cruel. The news of the King was bad, and the Prince of Wales was preparing to become Regent at last. Dora was home for a month, then set out for Bath, this time with no daughter for company. Arrived in Bath, she had a painful fall during a farce. She ate her meals alone: 'the servants are attentive and kind to me, but servants are not friends or *children*'.[26] Still her children were her consolation: Mary was a good little correspondent, Eliza too, Lolly was ever faithful, and always wanted to hear about her work in the theatre, her costumes, the other actors and the characters in the plays; to amuse him she kept up a joke about naughty Lord Foppington who got locked in the coal cellar. You can see from her letters to the little boy what a good and attentive mother she was, even in her absence.

She was given a moment of unexpected and overwhelming happiness during this Bath season, when George suddenly walked into her dressing room out of the blue. He had been given leave from Portugal, and decided to visit his mother before doing anything else. His good looks put all the young actresses in a whirl; he went out to buy 'a whole cargo of Toys' for his brothers and sisters. Then, with his mother watching and laughing, he went for a swim in the medicinal waters, with a straw bonnet on his head. She never forgot the joy of that moment in which her two lives fitted together for a brief two days.

He could not stay long, and she had to go on to Worcester and Coventry. On her way back to Bushy, she hoped to meet the Duke in the old way at Maidenhead; she was disappointed – he had a previous arrangement – but another of her sons made up for it. She spent the night with 'dear Frederick' instead: 'he desires to sleep in my room, and I do not feel inclined to refuse so gallant an offer'.[27]

She was a loving mother, but not a foolishly doting one. She lectured George on the dangers of smoking and drinking, and roundly told him bear-baiting was cruel 'and nothing can justify cruelty'. A few weeks after her happy meeting with him in Bath, she sent him two angry letters on the subject of his inattention to his father and, more important, the bills he was running up. She warned him solemnly, for his father's sake and for his own good name, never to live beyond his means or to subject himself to 'the insults of tradespeople'. She went on, 'I feel the smart of this every day, tho' not on my own account. Alsop has ruined himself and consequently poor Fanny by his unpardonable extravagance.'[28]

The list of her worries now was almost as long as the list of her children. Lucy was in Portugal, pregnant, and due to have the baby before she could return to England. Henry's detestation of the navy had become so strong that, despite his father's surprise and discomfiture, and after many eloquent pleas by his mother as well as himself, he was at last allowed to leave; now, at fourteen, he was going to Marlow to prepare for the army instead. Nine-year-old Lolly, willing or unwilling, was due to take his place in the navy and went off to school with Frederick: 'poor Lolly, but I think and hope it will do him much good, my Tus, is now my only boy, for from the moment they go to school, they begin to forget their mothers', she wrote, quite wrongly as it turned out.[29] The Marches had a baby daughter and another on the way; they were again sharing a house with the Alsops. Sophy and Mary were doing the social rounds with their father; the Prince Regent gave Sophy a dress to wear to Carlton House, where he was planning a fête more splendid than any yet given.

Now, when Dora was at Bushy, the Duke avoided being there except on Sundays. When she left, she wrote, 'I believe when I am out of the gate at Bushy Park I am very soon *forgot*. Well, I cannot help it – it is only a continuation of my strange fate.'[30] When she was due to return, she found things no better. She wrote from Yorkshire at the end of August 1811, 'If you are all to be out the 3rd Sept I will put off my return till the 4th, for I dont like to come to an empty house after so long an absence.'[31] The tranquil pleasures of domestic happiness had taken their flight from Bushy.

17

'My dear Mother . . . a Most Injured Woman': 1811

'My dear Mama,' wrote George from the army headquarters in Portugal to his mother as she toured Yorkshire in the summer of 1811,

> Lucy sailed on the 14th for England and cried at parting with me . . . I am soon to have my troop [i.e., become a captain] . . . Father suggests the poor old King will soon be dead . . . I hope to God I shall see you soon . . . Sophia I suppose is so proud tell her when I come home I will not *Chapron* her . . . tell her I understand walzes are going on in London and if she does so I shall be under the necessity of shooting all her Partners – It's not proper for a woman . . . I wish I was with you and Lucy to talk over our Campains – Give my love to all the children but [by] the by you are away at present – I hope the King will leave Papa a good round sum – Let me know all about it – Henry writes me word Papa expects something prodigious I trust in God he will leave him a good deal.[1]

Dora must have laughed at her soldier son's letter, naïve, affectionate, short on spelling and punctuation; sighed at his anxiety about money; and smiled too, with pleasure and pride. She had sent him the family news, about the Prince Regent inviting Sophy to his fête at Carlton House and giving her an elegant dress to wear for the occasion; about Frederick riding in Windsor Great Park with his friendly cousin Princess Charlotte of Wales and their aunts, Princesses Augusta and Sophia, a bishop in attendance – his father had roared with laughter on hearing this; about the cricket in the park at Bushy; about Henry enjoying his army training at Marlow, Lolly about to go away to school, her own eagerness to see Lucy with her baby. What else? His father's asthma attack had been less severe this year, but she had kept all his royal uncles informed, and they had responded kindly. She herself had played at Covent Garden for ten evenings in June, warmly greeted by the London audience, which had not seen her for two years: evidently the Duke had relented on this point.

George's understanding that the 'poor old King' was dying was mistaken, though the mistake was general; in truth he had only retreated into a private world of madness and had another nine years yet to live. But the Regent now ruled, and the fête at Carlton House to which Sophy was invited was given to mark his assumption of power. This was the party that enraged the young Shelley by its blatant extravagance – it cost £120,000 – when so many of the Prince's subjects were without work, and suffering and starving. Dora was not on the guest list of two thousand. She probably did not expect to be; Mrs Fitzherbert did not attend either. Sophy went on her father's arm, and was introduced to a pretty young woman who was attracting much attention. Her name was Catherine Tylney Long, and she had just come into a spectacularly large fortune. The Duke was immediately struck by her, and by the possibilities she suggested.

Soon after this Dora set off for Yorkshire, where George's letter reached her. The contrast with fashionable London could hardly have been greater. Tate Wilkinson's son John was doing his best to keep the old theatre circuit alive, but audiences were poor this year, both because of fears for the King's life and because so many were out of work. Pit- and gallery-goers could not afford tickets, and the gentry felt it disrespectful to visit the theatre at such a time. She and Wilkinson did their best, but it was hard going. She played in Leeds, taking lodgings out of town, beside the peaceful ruins of Kirkstall Abbey, opposite a farmhouse where she could go in and out without being seen, 'one of the solitary pleasures I enjoy'. In York she also enjoyed visiting an old actress who had been kind to her when she was a girl in the 1780s; she was now 'past 80, but cheerful and very pleasant. I let her have the newspaper every day and she walks out with me in the fields.'[2] She also visited the asylum, meant to be a model of its kind, with distressing results. One of the inmates had an obsession with the royal family, and when he found out who she was he 'grew outrageous' wanting to speak to her, and 'the poor devil was locked up'.[3] Later Dora was told he had tried to kill himself, and she blamed herself as 'the wretched, the innocent cause': this was the black side of fame and royal connections.[4]

Although audiences improved gradually at Harrogate and Wakefield, Wilkinson was in such difficulties he told her he could not pay what he had promised her. Reluctantly she decided she must agree to go to Cheltenham later in the month. Yet her letters had touches of light-heartedness. In one she described Thomas proclaiming, as he took her letters to the post, 'Here go letters to the best man and finest fellow that ever blood warmed.' She added, 'the next time he came into the room I could have given him a squeeze – but it would have been a very innocent one'.[5]

At Bushy the finest fellow that ever blood warmed was not at all himself. He was brooding over Miss Long and his future. For nearly twenty years he and Dora had been a married couple in all respects but the legal and religious. They were held together by profound mutual affection, by absorption in their children, by all the joint activities of their home. Here they shared a bed; here they joined in family prayers; here she had given birth to his sons and daughters, the eldest now seventeen, the youngest four; here too she had helped to carry out all his plans for the house, the garden and the farm. He respected her for her character and her judgement; she relied on his good temper and his fidelity, and never quite lost her sense of wonder at being chosen by a prince, and giving grandchildren to the King.

Common interests and pleasures held them together, and were reinforced by their social isolation; because their position was anomalous, they depended on each other more than couples who could mix freely with their peers. He might visit his family without her, enjoy bachelor dinners and sometimes yearn for the navy; and she might go on tour, and entertain her theatrical colleagues in London; but to both of them the family at Bushy was always the centre and heart of life.

Now the Duke's ideas were changing. He was in his mid-forties, an age at which even the staunchest of men sometimes feel they must seize a second chance of happiness before it is too late. He had the example of his friend Colonel Hawker before his eyes, carrying off young Lucy, with a dowry into the bargain. Dora had passed child-bearing age and may sometimes have seemed more like a mother than a mistress; in the last two years she had been away a great deal, leaving him to mope alone. Brooding on these things, he could summon up the knowledge that his mother had always disapproved of the relationship on moral and religious grounds; from time to time, bishops had been dispatched to talk to him about his way of life, not unnoticed by Dora.

Then, when his brother became Regent and took stock of the situation of the whole family, he almost certainly encouraged the Duke to think about changing his situation. There were financial incentives: Parliament would grant more money to a married prince. There were also dynastic ones: the royal family could do with some more legitimate children, there being still only the one – Princess Charlotte – in the younger generation. Unlike his mother, the Prince Regent cared not a straw for morality. He quite liked Dora and greatly approved of her children; on the other hand his liking gave none of them any reason to expect favourable treatment. He himself had seen no harm in ditching mistresses and making an advantageous marriage, so why should his brother not do the same? As far as that went, there was nothing to stop William keeping a mistress and taking a wife too.

William was a less sophisticated character than the Regent. He also found it hard to change the pattern of his life; he had nothing to reproach Dora with but that she was who she was, and chose to go on doing what she had always done. There are stories of attempts to blacken her name, of persons who 'affecting a high sense of public virtue and regard for the family on the throne, and its members within the probability of succession, spared no pains to excite distrust or disgust in the royal person connected with her'.[6] The Duke would not have believed a word of such insinuations. But he was ripe and ready to be corrupted.

His letters to Dora in Yorkshire suggest some uneasiness. He apologized for their being 'stupid', to which she answered, 'why do you say your letters are stupid – I don't find them so – don't they speak of everything that is dear to me?'[7] He told her the Queen was ill; her reply was full of sympathy for the Queen's afflictions. She asked him why the Duke of Cumberland seemed angry with her and would not let FitzErnest stay at Bushy: 'I loved the boy for his own sake.' He did not offer any explanation, but enthused instead about the gravel walk, his latest improvement. He also mentioned in passing that the family would all be absent on the day she proposed to arrive home.

She reached home on 6 September, whether to a full or empty house we don't know. Perhaps he avoided her eye, perhaps she pretended not to notice, and busied herself with children, house and garden. She appeared once at Richmond, where she gave two farces, and left again for Cheltenham on the 16th. Whatever the Duke had said or not said, she was aware of a change in their relations. 'I frequently feel myself a restraint on your pleasures, and this idea makes me unhappy even in the midst of my family,' she wrote to him now, adding, 'You see I already consider you as an old friend, and tell you everything I think.'[8] A few days later she put in a postscript, 'I see Miss Tylney Long is going to give another Ball, I hope you and Sophy will be invited.'[9]

If she had understood he might be looking for love elsewhere, she also seems to have thought, or hoped, it could be accommodated within their existing arrangements. Her letters show she was tired, and anxious about money; there were the usual problems, the weather turned rainy, Cheltenham audiences thinned, she developed a sore throat, and the manager who had offered her a short season at Exeter wrote to say he could not raise a company unless she would do the whole west country circuit. This she could not possibly undertake; so she was planning to return to Bushy when, on 2 October, she heard again from the Duke. He suggested they should meet at Maidenhead in three days' time.

The story goes that his letter came just before she was due to perform the part of Nell in *The Devil to Pay*, and that, though she guessed what it signified and was in anguish,

> with that kindness that always marked her conduct, she would not withdraw her name from the bills, though such was her state, when she arrived at the theatre, from continual hysterics, that we may literally say, she was saturated in sorrow... In her scene with Jobson... Nell laughs immoderately, on which Jobson remarks, 'Why, Nell, the conjurer has not only made you drunk, but he has made you laughing drunk.' When Mrs Jordan attempted to laugh, she burst into tears; and the actor, with great presence of mind, altered the text by saying, 'Nell, the conjurer has not only made thee drunk, he has made thee *crying* drunk,' and thus brought her through the scene. As soon as the play was over, she was put into a travelling chariot, in her Nell's dress, and started to keep her appointment with her royal lover.[10]

It is a good theatre tale, and gives powerful dramatic expression to the real shift from comedy to tragedy, laughter to tears, taking place in her life; but the last part at least cannot be literally true. There was no need for her to travel in her stage outfit, because we know she answered his letter, and had three days in which to prepare to go to Maidenhead, where they had often met, happily, in the past.

There is no record of what was said between them at Maidenhead. Dora now understood there was to be some sort of separation, but she still did not, and perhaps could not, grasp the full significance of the Duke's change of heart. In the next few days she was busy in London, seeing her beloved Lucy, not yet recovered from her confinement, and George, about to join his regiment again in Brighton; she also began negotiations with Covent Garden, which wanted her for the winter season. Then she went home to Bushy, the four younger girls and Tuss, and wrote affectionately to the Duke, describing the family's 'high health and spirits', and the planting and preparation of ground in the garden and trees around the dairy, which she discussed as usual with the gardener. All the dear little girls clamoured to send their love, she told him; none of the children of course knew anything of the proposed separation of their parents.[11] Fanny had been looking after them; Dora described going up to say goodnight and finding Eliza, Augusta and Mely all at 'proper prayers for the night, nor did my coming into and going out of the room take off their attention − the sight tho' it could not fail to give me pleasure yet it affected me very much'.[12] She said the family would be alone at Bushy until his return; either she really expected everything to go on as before, or she thought her best tactic was to behave as though it would.

But the Duke stayed away, dividing his time between London and Ramsgate, where Miss Long was taking the sea air. Princess Charlotte saw him 'in very high spirits & looking remarkably well'. Now that he had Dora's permission, as he saw it, he approached Miss Long's guardian with letters assuring her of his devotion and eligibility in terms that may not have produced quite the effect he intended. He explained he had adored Miss Long for 'four or five months', spoke of himself as 'the first unmarried man in the kingdom' and 'a man of honour', and added, 'Mrs Jordan has behaved like an angel and is equally anxious for the marriage.' 'Never *will* or *can* Miss Long meet with the man whose conduct either can or will be like mine,' he added.[13] The truth is, Dora did offer him some advice on his wooing of Miss Long; there is a curious letter from her in which she warns him to 'be cautious for fear of a disappointment. All women are not to be taken by an open attack, and a premeditated one stands a worse chance than any other.'[14] Perhaps she thought she could still help the man she had trusted for so long to avoid making a complete ass of himself before the world; but her counsel was in vain. Although Miss Long was flattered for a moment, she did not care for him at all. When he asked her to dance with him, she made the classic excuse that she had hurt her foot; she preferred a suitor of her own age.

Gossip raged. Lady Bessborough knew all about it: 'Lady Holland says the Duke told her he had the Regent's promise to withdraw the restrictions on Royal Marriages as soon as he was in power.'[15] A few days later she heard more. 'The story of the D of C and Miss Long is true. He propos'd in form, was rejected, but still has hopes founded on the Royal honours the Prince is to bestow, and on the chance of being the Mother of Kings. What will become of poor Mrs Jordan and all her Children, I wonder? for I have no doubt he will marry someone if he does not her.' Princess Charlotte heard the story too, and wrote of Mrs Jordan's excellent conduct and of how she had 'proved herself a true friend to him, & a most affcte. mother'.[16]

Sophy and George were the first of the children to hear of their father's plans. She objected strongly to the idea of his marrying and had to be coaxed into changing her mind. It did not take long; when only half your blood is good, it becomes all the more important to keep in with the good half. To George the Duke said little beyond that he had 'a thousand places to go to, and think I cannot be home at Christmas'.[17] He had decided – or been advised – not to see Dora face to face, perhaps because he knew he could not argue with her and would lose his resolve in her presence. When Miss Long turned him down, he immediately set about proposing to other rich women, though with no better luck; he continued to travel about, to Chatham and Portsmouth, and then Oatlands. He appears at his very worst during these months, like a parody of a wicked prince, as though whatever decency and kindliness he had acquired over twenty happy years had been blown to bits by excitement and vanity.

At Bushy Dora tried to understand his wishes. She had discreetly given up her negotiations with Covent Garden for the moment and made no further plans to work. She wrote to George in the middle of November that 'if he insists on taking all the children – I shall submit'.[18] As the law stood, she had a legal claim only to Tuss – for the next few months, until he was seven – and Amelia.[19] But she was not asked to give up the children. Perhaps the Duke's advisers saw that such a demand would be outrageous and hardly to his advantage. On 22 November – her fiftieth birthday – she wrote to him to say she had seen their lawyer Adam at Bushy, and that she was happy with all the arrangements he proposed. She asked to keep Miss Sketchley with the children, and the same teachers; she also hoped to be consulted about any new masters appointed. She seemed to think things were now settled and went into no further details.

But she was particularly grateful for the Duke's 'additional goodness to the *rest of my family*' – his acceptance of some continuing link with her three eldest daughters.[20] A week later he was still 'My dear friend'. She assured him she would defend his name against any attacks in the press; she cautioned him against unguarded talk and told him that his 'future credit shall be dearer to me than *my existence*'.[21]

She also wrote to Boaden, in her public voice, insisting that 'every branch of the Royal Family' was treating her very kindly, and that they all deplored 'this melancholy business'; the Regent in particular had praised her forbearance and said he would never forsake her. 'Do not hear the D of C unfairly abused,' she wrote. 'He has done *wrong*, and he is *suffering* for it. But as far as he has left it in his *own power*, he is doing everything *kind* and *noble*, even to distressing himself.'[22] But whose power was he in, if the royal family was so much engaged on her behalf? Dora was reluctant to find a villain, and unable to suspect she was being lied to by the highest in the land in order to keep her quiet.

Was there no one to tell the Duke to his face that his behaviour was that of a monster? Not a single adviser? Never mind his brothers, not even one of his sisters, the poor Princesses? Not a single bishop, to remind him of his duty towards the mother of his family, whether blessed by ceremony or not? Apparently not. Even some later historians have exonerated him, on the grounds that Mrs Jordan had grown 'plump, motherly and coarse' and that 'at the end she was not ungenerously treated and, during the twenty years she lived with the Duke, there were compensations for the lack of money in the shape of Royal favour and domestic bliss'.[23] Another, more sympathetic historian suggests that she had lost her sexual appeal: 'Mrs Jordan, stout, matronly, short of breath, could offer little stimulus to his flagging powers' and that, although his behaviour was 'inexcusable by any standards', he nevertheless behaved 'rather better than might have been expected'.[24]

No doubt this was the view from the royal family, but in lower circles there was unfavourable comment. The newspapers were not slow to get hold of the story. A paragraph appeared in *The Times* early in November, another in December. George Cruikshank published a drawing called 'Princely Piety', showing the Duke proposing, with Dora and children in the background; another showed her asking pathetically, 'What, leave your faithful Peggy?', again with a group of children about her. Peter Pindar, always her supporter, produced an illustrated poem, 'The R—l Lover, or The Admiral on a Lee Shore', poking merciless fun at the Duke. It began,

> What! leave a woman to her tears?
> Your faithful friend for twenty years;
> One who gave up her youthful charms,
> The fond companion of your arms!
>
> Brought you ten smiling girls and boys,
> Sweet pledges of connubial joys;
> As much your wife in honor's eye,
> As if fast bound in wedlock's tie.

– and went on with the suggestion that Miss Long herself had advised him to

> Return to Mistress J —'s arms,
> Soothe her, and quiet her alarms;
> Your present differences o'er,
> Be wise, and play the fool no more.

At this stage Dora wrote to the Duke telling him she was anxious to leave Bushy as soon as possible, finding it too painful to be there. She had asked her son-in-law March to take a house for her in London: 'The expense of the house could go into the general arrangement,' she suggested, adding, 'I could get the house sooner. I cannot describe how much I wish it as the only means of restoring me to any degree of comfort.'[25] Clearly she believed that an amicable agreement had been reached about the future; but now it suddenly appeared that everything was to be gone over again by John Barton. Dora took the children to St James's and had more talks about the settlement that was being drawn up. She was now faced not only by Adam and Barton, but also by the Prince Regent's secretary, John McMahon, and another lawyer called Wilks. She had no adviser of her own and had to fight her battles for herself, though her old friend Colonel Dalrymple – Barton's predecessor – seems to have tried to intervene in her favour; it may have been he who advised her to return to Bushy and remain there until the settlement was agreed; and this is what she did.

Dora had understood that the Duke shared her wish that the children should live with her. She was confident enough to write to Boaden to tell him everything was settled.[26] But when Adam came out to Bushy on Sunday, 15 December, to go through everything again, he denied any knowledge of such an agreement. This was the breaking point for her. She stopped writing in the old way to the Duke and for the first time ever addressed him formally as 'Sir', ending her letter 'I remain, Your Royal Highness's dutiful servant'.[27] When you have read through the hundreds of intimate, daily letters that cover their years together, the change of style is shocking. There is no direct reproach, she is simply distancing herself through her language. She had played enough dramatic heroines to see the force of that; and it is almost as though she were aware for the first time that posterity might read her letters. Until now, she had gone on believing some mutual love and trust remained; this was the formal marking of its end.

She wrote to McMahon, the Regent's man, protesting at the way she was being treated:

> I yesterday saw Mr Adam – and you may imagine my surprise – when he declared he knew nothing of the proposed arrangement or even of the Duke's wish that the children should live with me 'till they attained the age of 13. He had seen the Duke the Thursday before. All this, my dear Sir, you will allow must appear strange to one who has acted so firmly and openly as I have done. If they will *decidedly* say they cannot meet my fair demands – I should make up my mind on the subject and do the best I could for myself and children, but this is trifling most cruelly with my feelings and unfortunate situation. I now begin to feel the value of the advice of not quitting Bushy till something decided is done, but as a friend to both parties you will, I am sure, feel the advantage of an early decision in consequence of our last conversation, I told all those who are anxious about me that it was finally

settled; judge then of my disappointment. Mr Adam had not *seen* or *heard* of MY statement.[28]

George got a letter too, in which for the first time she treated him as an adult and complained of Adam's behaviour:

> I now begin to feel the value and prudence of the advice of not quitting Bushy, till I have a settled home to go to. Here I STICK and I will be well paid for leaving it. Generosity and liberality will not always do in this world – but I have justice on my side and shall be able to fight my own battles.

She told George that she had pointed out she might be forced to return to her profession if 'everything was not as I could fairly wish ... This seemed to give great alarm.'[29] From now on George was her chief confidant. It was not always an easy position for a boy of seventeen whose future prospects depended on the favour of the royal family.

Her second son, Henry, was not regarded as much of a letter-writer in the family; he had spent more time at sea, and fighting, than studying. In December 1811 he was at the Royal Military College when one of his friends showed him a newspaper story about his parents. This is what he wrote to George:

> Dear George,
>   Pray tell me all you know of this business mentioned in the papers between my Father and Mother I have really been in torments ever since I saw cursed papers I can never believe my Father would ever make proposals to Miss Long for god's sake write to me tell me all you know about I have not heard lately from Home ... If it is true that my Father did offer his hand to Miss Long I have no hesitation whatsoever in declaring my dear Mother right in separating if so I never more go near My Father ... were he not my father I could and would say more ... My God!! To think that our father such a father should have done such a thing I can assure you I have been literally very ill I find great consolation in writing to you for

god's sake write immediately I should like to see you before
the vacation . . . If this be true I will never more go home
except once to see my Dear Mother whom I consider as a
Most Injured Woman. Pray write as soon as you receive this –
I could not believe my eyes when I saw the paper which
contained Distressing truth I scarcely know how I write I am
nearly mad I think I shall run away home . . .

> Your affectionate brother
> Henry Edward Fitzclarence[30]

Henry's letter is striking for two reasons. One is its timelessness
– it could almost be a child of today writing about his
parents' separation. The other is that it was preserved by
George, surviving both Henry's and his own untimely deaths,
and has remained in a bundle of disregarded papers for
nearly two hundred years. When I opened the double sheet
with its crumbled edges and began to read, the clear, true
voice of Henry's outraged grief brought him to life before me
with all the force he put into the writing, and I found I had
tears in my eyes as I read.

Henry also wrote to his sisters' governess, Miss Sketchley,
for information, saying his delicacy would not suffer him to
write directly to his mother or sisters. Miss Sketchley, well
intentioned though ineffectual, handed the letter to Dora. 'I
answered it in the best manner I could, tho' I found it a cruel
task,' she told George. 'I told him to take the opportunity of
coming home on Saturday to tell dear Frederick.'[31] So the
children learnt, one by one; Mary was old enough to be
distressed; the younger ones understood little, but missed
their father's presence. Even to Boaden she now wrote that
she was 'heart-sick, and almost worn out with this cruel
business'.[32]

Dora had been a good fighter – 'I should make an excellent
soldier' she once told the Duke[33] – but in this battle she faced
too strong an opponent: not just the power of the royal family
and its servants, but also the respectful response of almost
everyone else to that power, which in practice exempted the

Princes from moral judgement. Pindar and Cruikshank were only jesters; they may have expressed what many people felt, but they could not affect what happened. She was trapped by her own history, by her affections, above all by her children. Any fight she got into was going to be conducted on such unequal terms that she was bound to lose.

Money was important, although there seemed little doubt that the Duke intended to make an adequate financial settlement. Her worries were as much for the children. What she wanted was to hold the family together, the small children to her *and* to their father, the older ones to the younger, sons and daughters to one another, the children of the Duke and her daughters by Ford and Daly, and their husbands too. This became her main endeavour over the next years. Her letters show how she kept the flow of information and affection circling round the many scattered members of the family. Most of them – she sometimes wrote as many as twenty a day – are lost. It is particularly sad that none to her daughters has survived; Mary, thirteen at the time of the separation, was a notably regular and affectionate correspondent. But two of her sons were able to preserve theirs, George and, more surprisingly, her fourth son, Lolly. He was a good correspondent even at nine – his age at the time of the separation – and passionately devoted to his mother. The forty letters he kept show that she used an especially fine and legible hand in her early letters to him, to make them easy for a small boy to decipher; and all of them breathe tenderness and a determination to say or show nothing that might upset him. From these letters you would not guess that she was undergoing humiliation and unhappiness. She writes gaily, she sends little presents, cakes, books and newspapers, she jokes about his brothers and sisters. She constantly assures him of her love and interest in what he is doing, and expresses her delight in his many letters to her. You can see what an adorable mother she must have been to a boy at boarding school, and why he not only wrote to her regularly, but also sent her gifts in return. The others may have done as much, but he is the only one of her children known to have taken the trouble.

Naturally she did not discuss the settlement with Lolly. The deed of separation was drawn up on 23 December, as formally as the settlement of November 1791 that had begun her association with the Duke. Then she had been chiefly concerned with the arrangements for her daughters; now they were again guaranteed £200 a year each from her income. The Duke's income is given as £12,000 a year (although it is likely to have been more), out of which he was to pay her £4,400.[34] This sum is subdivided, to cover house, carriage and horses, as well as the expenses of the four youngest daughters; Sophy would remain with her father. It was agreed that the Duke could take them at thirteen, and that he must have access to them whenever he wished to observe 'the progress of their Education, habits, behaviour and accomplishments'. The next clause stated that if 'the said Dora Jordan shall perform or act upon the Stage of any public or private Theatre or shall marry or form any other Engagement or connection which in the opinion of the [Duke] may be unfavourable to the morals manners or habits of the said children', she would lose that part of the allowance that relates to the children, leaving her with £2,100. This would still have been a very large income if she had chosen to withdraw from the world, to live simply and, more important, refused to go on helping her grown-up children; but it was not in her nature to do any of these things.

The question as to why her profession should suddenly now, after twenty years, become a reason for regarding her as an unsuitable guardian to her own children can only be answered in terms of the Duke's total reliance on his advisers. He let them impose the terms and conditions; for instance, he was quite prepared to allow his daughters to remain with Dora until they were sixteen, as he wrote to Sophy, firmly putting her off when she tried to insist that she wished to live with him immediately.[35] It was the lawyers and the Prince

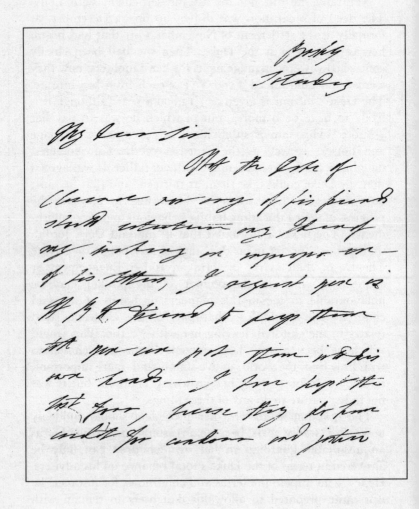

Letter from Mrs Jordan to John McMahon, adviser to the
Prince Regent, written before leaving Bushy in January 1812, with
which she returned all but four of the Duke's letters to her.

Regent's men who insisted the age should be thirteen. Judging from his correspondence over these months, he was absorbed in new activities. Sophy was worrying about what was to happen at Bushy, where inventories of the furniture were being made; and he was in fact considering exchanging Bushy for Oatlands with his brother Frederick. Apart from this, he was enjoying visiting friends, dancing, taking up fox-hunting in the New Forest, scattering proposals of marriage and penning character references for himself as a good-natured man. That he *was* normally a good-natured man was perhaps why he left the negotiations with Dora to other people who could be relied on to be less so.

On Christmas Eve the Prince Regent gave the Duke what he had always wanted, and appointed him Admiral of the Fleet. Dora had as yet been paid nothing of her promised allowance and was still at Bushy, negotiating the lease of a house in London ('any cheap and convenient one' would do, suggested the Duke to Sophy).[36] He remained inaccessible to Dora, and the lawyer Wilks, to whom she had been told to apply if she needed anything, failed to answer her letters. Remembering the kind words of the Prince Regent, she now wrote to him for help in getting and furnishing a house; at the same time she sent letters to all the other royal dukes who had been her guests at Bushy over the years. The Prince Regent did not answer her letter. He told Adam he considered her writing at all 'a very extraordinary proceeding' and suggested she should be paid some of her allowance in advance, 'if circumstances will at all admit it'.[37] This was not done, and none of the other dukes responded.

Now a story was put about that she was proposing to publish the Duke's private letters. Princess Charlotte was told this, and wrote to a friend,

What can the D. of Clarence expect from a discarded mistress? I own I am not in the least surprised at her procedure, nor should I at all wonder if she put her threat into execution. His children are so much distressed already, that it cannot be well added to, I fancy. Not that I mean to take her part, for if she really should publish his private letters, it will be abominable, but yet there is much to be said for her, & but little for him.[38]

The story was wholly untrue. When it reached Dora's ears, it caused her so much distress that she immediately packed up the Duke's hundreds of letters, saved over the years as he had saved hers, and sent them to one of the royal advisers (probably McMahon) with a covering note explaining her intention: 'That the Duke of Clarence nor any of his friends should entertain any idea of my making an improper use of his letters, I request you as HRH friend to keep them till you can put them into his own hands – I have kept the last four, because they do him credit for candour and justice.' A postscript apologized for the brevity and informality of the note: 'excuse this – for I am so ill that I write from my pillow'.[39]

She then wrote once more to the Duke, to say she was content with his arrangements and that she hoped he would never meet with 'a less sincere or more attached friend than she who now subscribes herself for the last time, Your Royal Highness's most dutiful servant'. She was 'on the eve of quitting this place for ever': she meant Bushy.[40] It was January, as it had been when they first drove delightedly into the park together, with George and Sophy, to inspect their beautiful home.

The Duke had not managed to persuade his brother to swap Oatlands for Bushy, but Dora's apartments were locked up, and he decided to make his bedroom in what had been the children's sitting room.

18

An Attack by The Times: *1813*

There is no established etiquette for a discarded royal mistress. When Clarence's brother, the Duke of Kent, was persuaded to give up his Madame de Saint Laurent, with whom he had lived happily for twenty-seven years, he was concerned that she should be provided with at least a proper household and carriage; he was miserable, but she went with dignity, choosing to retire into a convent, and was not heard of again. She had never been an actress; and if there were children, they were never seen in Britain; from the point of view of the royal family, she was easily disposed of. Mrs Jordan was bound to attract more attention. Her fame was an embarrassment to the royals, and her large family made things worse.

The plan was that she should lose both her home and her career. The Duke seems to have wobbled on the second point and 'kindly exonerated' her from the promise of not returning to her profession 'under the idea of its benefiting my health, and adding to my pleasures and comforts'.[1] But when she checked this with Adam, he wrote back firmly, 'As to the returning to the stage even in a limited way, HRH is very peremptory tho' very kind in his expressions of refusing it – and says it will be most painful to him, but he should think it his duty to enforce the condition of renouncing the children.'[2] And although the Duke spoke of their daughters remaining with Dora until sixteen in a letter to Sophy, the age was later fixed at thirteen. The impression is that the Duke, once the euphoria of his pursuit of Miss Long wore off, had no very definite plans or intentions, and mostly did as he was told by the Regent and his advisers. He was so heavily in debt that he could at first neither settle what he owed Dora nor begin her quarterly allowance, and needed to be bailed out. The first payment to her was not made until mid-February; after that payments were regular, although his financial problems continued to be so bad that within a year he was talking of selling up the contents of Bushy. A year later he was still desperate, begging the Regent to guarantee his credit and staking everything on a projected marriage to the sister of the Tsar – a plan that, like so many of his ventures, failed.

Dora had been allowed the right to care for her children until they were thirteen, but in practice the boys were sent away to school long before that. Lolly had already gone, and Tuss was to be sent, at seven, in the summer of 1812. The girls would also be divided. Warm-hearted and communicative Mary was thirteen just as the settlement was agreed. 'Dear Mary writes constantly, and I must shortly give her up,' her mother sorrowed. She was allowed to come to Dora at first, but would soon have to join Sophy in their father's care and come under the influence of governesses Dora disliked and mistrusted. Miss Turner in particular she considered 'an artful woman'; this governess told Sophy, whose religious education she had taken in hand, to reflect on the fact that her 'father and mother brought her into the world to please *themselves*', as though they should have had a higher reason such as duty to the state or fulfilling God's plan. It was a curious point to make to their unhappy sixteen-year-old daughter.[3]

Dora gathered her energies to prepare the house in Cadogan Place for the children. While she was busy with the practical matters of linen and beds, finding furniture and engaging servants, the Barrington boy came to stay, and her married daughters Lucy Hawker and Dodee March also descended on her. Lucy's husband was now a general and had been sent to Nottingham to crush the Luddite rioters;

whatever Lucy thought of that, she was glad to be with her mother again, and especially when her baby daughter became ill. Dora, with grandmotherly authority, took the child, 'clapped her into a tub of warm water up to the neck and in the course of two hours she began to breathe without much difficulty, and is now out of danger' and a grateful Lucy was able to rejoin her husband shortly afterwards.[4]

Dora's spirits were kept up by having too much to do. When a lull came, there was no protection against grief and bitterness: or, as she put it briskly, 'If it was not for the bustle of endeavouring to get the house ready for the dear little ones, I should be found hanging some morning in my garters.'[5] Frederick and Lolly came for dinner, on their way back to Bushy and then school. Then George failed to visit her on his eighteenth birthday, and she told him, 'I do not see a soul from night to morning – and absolutely feel myself quite an outcast.' She knew she would be better when the children came. She had 'worked and worried myself into illness to get the house ready for them,' but now 'I am almost tired of my life – and if it were not for the sake of the poor little ones I would not remain a week in the Kingdom – so disgusted am I with the whole affair – and time and reflection makes it appear worse every day.'[6] There was another very black moment when she proposed a day for their arrival and could get no answer from Bushy. All her unhappiness burst out to George again: 'I would not for the universe the world should know the cruel neglect I have been treated with. It would hardly be believed . . . If I had deserved it, it would be cruel, but that not being the case – I dare not give it a name.'[7]

And by now the Duke was hardly happier than she was. On 7 February he did deliver the children, Mary, Eliza, Ta, Tuss and Mely, coming to the back door of her house in order to avoid meeting their mother. 'He suffered greatly in parting with the children – and I am sure will ever prove himself, whether present or absent, an affectionate father,' she told George.[8] For a while she was content with the children, seeing their enjoyment of the new house and staying at home with them: 'I have not been out of doors these ten days.'[9] One evening the Duke, like a modern divorced father, took them to the theatre to see a Harlequin farce. Then she visited the boys at school. Henry went away to serve in the German Legion and was not expected to return for a year at least; Dora was annoyed to hear he did not write to his father. Neither she nor the Duke could quite stop feeling protective towards one another when there was no one else to interfere. She fussed when she heard he was ill or looked thin; and he had started to collect all the portraits of her he could find, to hang on the walls at Bushy.

She and the Duke were both shocked when the Regent, on assuming full power, turned his political coat and abandoned his old Whig friends. Jilting them, she called it in her frank language; she thought the Duke, who was 'disappointed and very much hurt' by his brother's behaviour, might go into opposition; but he was talked out of it. The Prince wanted to pursue the war vigorously, and he did not care about Catholic Emancipation; and now that he had supreme power at last, the Tories seemed closer to his views than he had ever realized, especially when their leader, Spencer Perceval, steered a bill to increase his income through the House of Commons. Sheridan was another casualty of the Regent's political about-face; already wounded at being excluded from the new Drury Lane, he now saw all prospect of power disappearing, and skidded from one defeat to another. He even lost his seat in Parliament this year. This meant he was no longer immune from arrest by his creditors, and he began to be a hunted creature.

The great spending spree of the nineties had to be paid for at last, and debts were the general affliction of the time. Dora's brother Frank surfaced again to torment her with his begging, and she had to warn her son George against him. The Alsops were overwhelmed by their unpaid bills, reduced to living in lodgings, and had no one to turn to but her.

Fanny's solution, which was to go on the stage, appalled her, and they had a painful row. Dora could see that she lacked the necessary talent; Fanny believed her mother was standing in her way and made such a scene that Dora felt she would have to stop seeing her: 'I have met with many cruel things – but this is a climax.'[10] As her eldest child, passionately loved and protected for so long, Fanny had a unique capacity to wound her; Dora could not bear – and did not fully understand – her anger against the world.

The demands on her as mother and grandmother multiplied. The Marches had a second child and came to stay again while their babies were christened. The first instalment of her allowance had been spent on moving and furnishing Cadogan Place; she had to supply the Alsops and keep up payments to her sister Hester, to the Marches and the Hawkers – these were the promised dowries. George made frequent demands, which were never refused, and the younger boys occasionally asked for money too. She may have been unwise in her generosity, but she was also paying £400 a year income tax and putting more than £1,000 a year into life insurance policies, which must have been intended to provide for her children after her death. She may also have been extravagant in ordering a carriage, although again it was for the children that she wanted it; when she thought she might not be able to afford it, she began to think of getting rid of it.

Servants are quick to smell trouble. In the spring a manservant spoke to her insolently and walked out without giving notice. The coming of summer brought an intensification of her problems. The children, accustomed to the freedom and fresh air of Bushy, were now confined in a small London house; she began to worry about the limited life she could offer them, and still more about their father's feeling for them. Tuss was soon sent, crying, to boarding school – not the school at Sunbury, but another at Pirbright Bridge, in Surrey. She asked Lolly to comfort him, sent him a cake, and wrote to both boys regularly. The fear that the younger girls, if they were not with their father, would be altogether 'out of his heart', grew when she heard that some of his entourage at Bushy were encouraging him to write them off; 'the less he sees them the less he will care for them'.[11] By the time his asthma attack came round in June she resolved it was best after all for them to return to Bushy.

It is not the thinking of a modern mother, but it seemed the correct course at that time. The same heartbreaking reasoning was followed by Claire Clairmont in giving up her only, and adored, child to Lord Byron: a father with a high social position could ensure that his daughter would be brought up to enter society, and the marriage market, at the right level – and what else was there for a daughter? Dora made her decision with her usual vigour, which does not mean it did not cost her pain; she said it 'would be death to me if I was not so strongly impress'd with the certainty of its being for their future advantage'.[12] She was fully justified in the event, although she never knew it: after her death all five daughters lived interesting and easy lives, and married men of rank and fortune, as every mother would then wish.

Barton came to discuss the return of the children in July. She took the opportunity to tell him she would have to go back to the stage, since she would be losing half the Duke's allowance, and needed to earn. He was unfriendly ('behaved very ill' was her phrase) and calmly contradicted what she had been previously told, saying the Duke had never had any objection to her acting. In fact, he insisted, the Duke was perfectly indifferent to anything she might do: it was a calculated snub as well as a lie.

The children remained with her until the day after their father's birthday in August, which was celebrated again this year at Windsor where, for the first time, George was invited. Dora's letter to him makes her feelings about the Duke and *his* mother, the Queen, abundantly plain without quite overstepping the mark:

I give you joy of this day [i.e., his father's birthday] and trust God you will all see the return of many of them. I hope your being at Windsor will be the means of introducing you to your *amiable grand mama* for I think she can scarcely leave you out on this day; if *she does* – if she does, it will only serve to confirm the opinion that I have ever had of her.

Since the next letter begins 'The old b—h conduct is just what I expected & I should have been surprised had it been otherwise', it looks as though George's amiable grand mama may not have treated him as nicely as Dora had hoped. Dora could not fail to blame her and suspect her influence on the Duke; she expended more sarcasm in a later letter, in which she called the Queen 'as beautiful in person as amiable and generous in disposition'.[13]

Now, after a break of a year – and one of the most painful and difficult of her fifty years – Dora again set about looking for work. Drury Lane was reopening in October, not under Sheridan as we have seen, but headed by a committee of rich businessmen and amateurs, one of them well known to her: the Regent's adviser, McMahon. The committee paid her £600 owing from before the fire, but made what she regarded as a shabby offer for the new season; she thought 'no single performer draws a single shilling anywhere but myself – this I may be allowed to say for it is truth', and so she decided she could make more in the country.[14] After seeing Frederick, she set off for Exeter, calling on Lolly and Tuss at school on the way. The old routine of the road established itself again, almost as though nothing had changed.

From Exeter she went on to Portsmouth; managers wrote to her wherever she was, and the tour prolonged itself into the winter, covering Gosport, Southampton, Salisbury, with Bath planned for January 1813. She enjoyed taking in the sights, including the dockyards, 'like the infernal regions', and Exeter Cathedral, worth seeing but 'at a disadvantage to me who have so lately seen York Minster'. Miss Sketchley, attentive but inept as ever, went with her; she became an irritating companion, so zealous in her care that Dora began to call her 'my jealous old husband', and even the innkeepers asked if she had been set to spy on her by the Duke. Everyone knew Dora's story, of course. There were good days, when she was entertained by an admiring clergyman and his wife, and taken on board Nelson's old flagship the *Victory*, where a band played for her and the Captain invited her to dine with him on board: 'but I did not like to encounter so many men – with only Miss Sketchley'. There were also bad days, when an admiral she knew well looked her 'full in the face & never touched his hat' – a contemptible gesture, as she said.[15]

She missed getting the newspapers – on her earlier tours the Duke had sent them to her – and she relied on George to keep her in touch with events in the great world: Napoleon's retreat from Moscow, Wellington's advance through Spain, and the war with the United States. And she missed the past. On 15 December she thought of 'the two dear boys' (Lolly and Tuss) going home from school: 'I used to long for this day – it now brings nothing but recollection and consequently pain.'[16]

The news from Fanny did nothing to cheer her. She and her husband were still in 'a shocking state', and Alsop had been obliged to resign his clerkship. The Duke very decently exerted himself to get him the promise of a voyage to India, but Dora thought Fanny would not let him go without her, and felt she could not afford to pay Fanny's passage – 'THEY have given me more trouble than all my family put together.' Henry was back from Germany, but there was some question of him going to India also, and George as well; much to their mother's relief the Duke opposed the idea, and after a 'very long and serious discussion' with the Regent it was agreed it was more in the interest of the boys to pursue their military studies in Europe. Lolly, however, was due to start his naval career as a midshipman in March, when he would be eleven.

At the end of the year Dora was in Salisbury, tired, with a sprained ankle, and painfully upset that George, who planned to visit her, had been advised that it was 'not prudent' to do so. She had to cheer herself with her professional success. The management of Covent Garden had invited her to do a season of thirty nights in the new year, at £50 a night. She was pleased and flattered by their offer, but she also knew there would not be many more like it; she was determined not to make a fool of herself and resolved that, 'as long as the power is left me to do it [i.e., act] with credit to myself I will not spare myself, and I think I may trust to my vanity not to continue one hour longer'.[17] She wrote a clutch of letters to her children ('dear Mary – this is her birthday') and asked George to 'give my love to all and [may] you all spend a happy Christmas & a great many of them together'.[18] She also sent him a post-dated cheque for £100, telling him her old friend Jones the ironmonger in Bond Street would cash it for him early if needs be. She wanted him to have 'efficient horses' and enough to pay for a picture of himself he proposed to send her; she knew young men needed money; and she told him he could pay her 'at some future time when I trust in God you will be a rich man – and probably I may want it then more than I do now'.[19]

On 10 February 1813 she appeared at Covent Garden in Susannah Centlivre's hundred-year-old comedy, *The Wonder: A Woman Keeps a Secret*. The great house was full, and she was warmly applauded as soon as she came on, and again at the end. The next day *The Times* attacked her, and the Duke, and the management – but mostly her. It began by suggesting that the audience had gathered to see Mrs Jordan for the wrong reasons – which was very likely true of some of them, including the critic of *The Times* – and went on to say how ludicrous most actors' and actresses' representations of fashionable life, as required in *The Wonder*, were. She, however, was different, because she had been 'admitted to the secrets of harems and palaces, seen their full exhibition of nude beauty, and costly dissoluteness, the whole interior pomp of Royal pleasure, the tribes of mutes and idiots, sultans and eunuchs, and lavish passion and lordly debility'. As an account of life at Bushy, this was on the purple side, but *The Times* was only getting into its stride.

It went on to describe her as a

> woman to whom nature has so few reserves -- whose 'proper study' as Pope says, has been 'man' – whose opportunities of study have been furnished in the course of a diligent life, from every rank and every age – who has adopted Shakespeare's conception in its fullness, and come 'home to the hearts and bosoms of men' with such unremitting assiduity – who has eminently, above all other women, deserved the renowned motto of 'humani nihil alienum'.

All this was an elaborate way of saying she had lived a promiscuous life. Then it suggested her stage representation of fashionable people consisted only of 'the perpetual lisp – the laborious lounge – the vulgar voice – the vacant expression – the inanity of mind' that she had learned 'during the long observation of twenty years', meaning, of course, from the Duke of Clarence.

Having laid about in this way, the article rose to a magisterial conclusion:

> The managers of a theatre are, of course, in some measure excusable for bringing forward any show that attracts a crowd, and we have no idea that they are likely to be restrained in this object by any voluntary zeal for public decency; but are there no other persons concerned? Is not the public forced to find the alternative for this degraded woman's appearance in the decline of life, either in her own vile avarice, or in her viler breach of stipulation by those who should never abandon her to poverty? We cannot believe that the latter is the case; and if the former, what share of public approbation should be permitted to one for whom it is impossible to feel any share of

personal respect? Whose sons and daughters are now strangely allowed to move among the honourable people of England, received by the Sovereign, and starting in full appetite for Royal patronage, while their mother wanders, and is allowed to wander, from barn to barn, and from town to town, bringing shame on the art she practises, and double shame on those who must have it in their power to send her back to penitence and obscurity?[20]

Whoever was behind this attack had judged the public as wrongly as they had judged Dora. The next evening, when one of the characters in the play spoke the lines, 'You have an honest face and need not be ashamed of showing it anywhere', the audience shouted its applause repeatedly until the tears came into her eyes. When, a few days later, she played Rosalind, she was again cheered even before she opened her mouth. Two critical opinions not remotely skewed in her favour show it was not just the pit that applauded her. Madame de Staël came to Covent Garden and was 'delighted with her', and Crabb Robinson, though he thought her voice less sweet, and her age and bulk a handicap when playing young girls, declared her acting in other parts 'truly admirable' and 'in no respect what it should not be'.[21] The rest of the press rallied to her defence, saying she should be judged only as a servant of the public, and suggesting the author of The Times's article must be feeling ashamed of himself.

Dora was never able to resist writing to the papers. She sent off a letter to a sympathetic journal, saying she would have endured the attack on herself silently, but could not let the insinuations against the Duke stand.

In the love of truth, and in justice to his royal Highness, I think it my duty, publicly and unequivocally to declare, that his liberality towards me had been noble and generous in the *highest degree*; but, not having it in his power to extend his bounty beyond the terms of his own existence, he has, with his

accustomed goodness and consideration, allowed me to endeavour to make that provision for myself, which an event, that
better feelings than those of interest, make me hope I shall
never live to see, would entirely deprive me of.

This, then, Sir, is my motive for returning to my profession.
I am too happy in having every reason to hope and believe
that, under these circumstances, I shall not offend the public
at large, by seeking their support and protection: and, while I
feel that I possess those, I shall patiently submit to that species
of unmanly persecution, which a female so particularly situ-
ated must always be subjected to. Ever ready to acknowledge
my deficiencies in every respect, I trust I may add, that I shall
never be found wanting in candour and gratitude – not
forgetful of the care that every individual should feel for the
good opinion of the public.[22]

Her letter had a good effect. As she told George, it was

copied into every paper in the kingdom, and the editor of *The
Times* was forced to put it yesterday into his own paper. I
have heard that a certain family are greatly pleased. This I
don't care a farthing about. It was at last but an act of justice,
& had I suffered in doing it I would have still done it. You
may suppose that I have been most harassed both in mind
and body, but I am getting over it. Thank God Lolly is quite
well and goes to school on Monday. I have very little time on
my hands. God bless you.[23]

You can't help hoping that George was properly proud of his
mother for this letter in which she showed herself, point by
point, at her best: shrugging off her own pains while tenderly
concerned for those of her children; forgiving where she might
have attacked, but properly elated at routing a mean and
cruel enemy; and just, and disinterested, in declaring the
truth.

19

'Bitter thankless': 1814

After the defeat of *The Times* there were no more public attacks. Dora had made her return successfully, and her career could now continue as before – or so she convinced herself. Some part of the audience came to see the celebrity rather than the actress of course; there is always this element in the theatre. There were a few private doubters: Boaden, loyal as he was, thought the distress of the separation had marked her performance, and that 'it was impossible for her to be a veteran on the stage'.[1] But there are enough solid tributes to prove she could still deliver something uniquely attractive. Byron, least gentle of critics, gave his unstinted praise to her Miss Hoyden in *A Trip to Scarborough*; and this was a year later, in 1814.[2] Another commendation came from an American painter, Charles Leslie, who saw her for the first time in 1813 in *As You Like It* and 'was quite as much pleased with her as I expected; indeed, more so, for I had been taught to expect an immensely fat woman, and she is but moderately so. Her face is still very fine; no print that I ever saw of her is much like. Her performance of Rosalind was, in my mind, perfect.'[3]

To Leigh Hunt she remained unsurpassed. He wrote about her in January 1815 from the prison to which he had been sent for libelling the Regent.

Of all the actresses whom we were in the habit of seeing before we came to prison, and who still keep possession of the

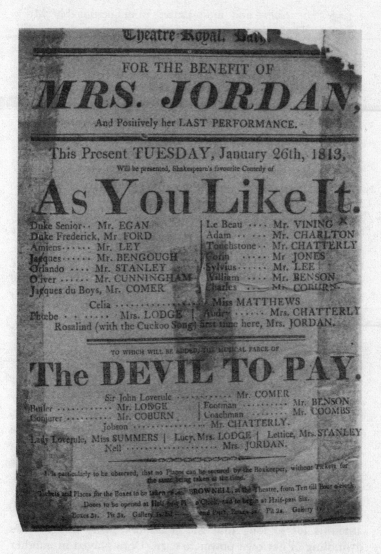

Theatre Royal, Bath

FOR THE BENEFIT OF

MRS. JORDAN,

And Positively her LAST PERFORMANCE.

This Present TUESDAY, January 26th, 1813,

Will be presented, Shakespeare's favourite Comedy of

As You Like It.

Duke Senior·· Mr. EGAN	Le Beau ···· Mr. VINING
Duke Frederick, Mr FORD	Adam ···· Mr. CHARLTON
Amiens······ Mr. LEY	Touchstone·· Mr. CHATTERLY
Jaques······ Mr. BENGOUGH	Corin ···· Mr JONES
Orlando···· Mr. STANLEY	Sylvius···· Mr. LEE
Oliver······ Mr. CUNNINGHAM	William ···· Mr. BENSON
Jaques du Boys, Mr. COMER	Charles ···· Mr. COBURN

Celia ········· Miss MATTHEWS
Phœbe ········· Mrs. LODGE | Audrey ···· Mrs. CHATTERLY
Rosalind (with the Cuckoo Song) first time here, Mrs. JORDAN.

TO WHICH WILL BE ADDED, THE MUSICAL FARCE OF

The DEVIL TO PAY.

Sir John Loverule ········· Mr. COMER
Butler ········· Mr. LODGE | Footman ········· Mr. BENSON
Conjurer ········· Mr. COBURN | Coachman ········· Mr. COOMBS
Jobson ········· Mr. CHATTERLY.
Lady Loverule, Miss SUMMERS | Lucy, Mrs. LODGE | Lettice, Mrs. STANLEY
Nell ········· Mrs. JORDAN.

It is particularly to be observed, that no Places can be secured by the Boxkeeper, without Tickets for the same being taken at the time.

Tickets and Places for the Boxes to be taken of Mr. BROWNELL, at the Theatre, from Ten till Four o'clock.
Doors to be opened at Half-past Five o'Clock, and to begin at Half-past Six.
Boxes 5s. Pit 3s. Gallery 1s 6d. ···· Second Price, Boxes 3s. Pit 2s. Gallery 0

Playbill for a performance of *As You Like It* and *The Devil
to Pay*, Mrs Jordan taking the lead in both, at the Bath Theatre
Royal in 1813, when she was fifty-one years old.

stage, the truest and most native is unquestionably Mrs Jordan. The last time we saw this charming actress she was of a size, however convenient for the widow, certainly obstructed a little the dancing vivacity of the hoyden; but such is the effect of native feeling, vivacity, and a tone of generous temper that even a portly young girl of forty hardly appeared an extravagance; and we had scarcely to shut our eyes in order to fancy ourselves in the middle of a school room when the governess had gone out of the way. Mrs Jordan is not only the first living actress in comedy, but we fear that when our readers consider the matter nicely, she will be found to be the only actress since the retirement of Miss Pope, who can any way be reckoned great and original.[4]

She had become an institution, with passionate admirers among critics, public and fellow actors alike; and she continued to give the roles she had made famous.[5] There were no good new ones being written – Sheridan still talked of another play, but there was no sign of it – and she would not consider making the transition to playing older women, although some advised her to do so.[6] Yes, there was probably a touch of the ageing actress's vanity here, but there was a real reason too: how many proper parts were there for middle-aged women? She did not see herself as Mrs Malaprop or Juliet's Nurse, although her Gertrude could have been interesting; more important, her public did not want her to change, and was still prepared to pay to see her in the old parts. In June 1813 she and Mrs Siddons, who had formally retired a year before, raised £1,000 between them in an evening for the Drury Lane Theatrical Fund, a charity for ageing actors. It would not have occurred to Dora that there was any element of irony here; she had made money in such large amounts for so long that she could not easily imagine the dwindling of her own power to earn. Dora played in another benefit to raise money for Isabella Mattocks, a retired actress whose son-in-law had swindled her out of all her savings, without stopping to think about what her own sons-in-law were doing with hers.[7] Dora saw herself, always, as a supporter and provider.

The Duke, with no earning power at all, viewed life differently, and was given to reminding his children of the 'great sacrifices' he had made for them. He was now in desperate difficulties. His debts stood at over £50,000, and he was threatening to sell up everything at Bushy and move his entire family to St James's. In May he applied to the Prime Minister and the Regent, and told Adam he feared public disgrace unless he was given immediate assistance. The combined efforts of Adam, Barton, the Regent and probably Coutts just kept him afloat, but it must have been an increasingly Micawberish existence at Bushy, with father, children and no doubt servants too all equally anxious for something to turn up. For the children what turned up mostly was a pound note in a letter from their mother. Everyone must have regretted the days when she contributed to the general funds. Although naturally she never came to Bushy any more, the Duke spent some time and energy that spring in acquiring portraits of her to hang on his walls. He wrote gratefully, if entirely ungrammatically, to Sir Henry Bunbury in April,

> Your servant has this moment brought me the picture. Mrs Jordan sat for your father, and which I particularly requested General Grey to express my wishes that you would have the goodness to permit me to possess, you cannot be surprized I should be anxious to have *all* the pictures of Mrs Jordan, knowing and therefore admiring her public and private excellent qualities, the only two I had before; they are both at Bushy, and this late valuable present from you compleats the whole except a small miniature that cannot be recovered by any means.[8]

The idea that he could comfort himself, or show his remorse, by collecting pictures of the living woman he had cast off is certainly odd; but it remained with him, and surfaced again when she was no longer living, and he commissioned the

Chantrey statue. Another difficulty for the Duke in 1813 was the ever widening gap between his mental image of the royal life he felt it necessary to maintain, and what was actually available for its maintenance. Sophy was invited to the great houses and, at eighteen, could be considered on the marriage market, and Frederick – the least intellectual and the most solidly conventional of the boys – was much in demand at royal fêtes and balls; both had to be kitted out properly. Meanwhile there was a plague of black beetles in the Bushy kitchens, and running skirmishes among the different factions of governesses and nurses.

Dora got news of everything at Bushy, and was able to see a good deal of her family during the spring and summer. She visited the boys at school, and the little girls came to stay over the Easter theatrical break; the Lloyds, who remained entirely devoted to her, not only kept her in touch but also offered their house as a cheerful meeting place with the children when she could get out of town for a few hours. Lucy was with her in May, and the Marches were increasingly inclined to use Cadogan Place as their home. Even Sophy came to dinner, in high beauty and health, showing a new mildness. She had her mother's musical gifts, and played the harp so well that her proud father forgot he was a pauper for long enough to lay out £100 on a new instrument for her. She was also enjoying the marked attentions of the young Duke of Devonshire, who invited her to Chiswick and Chatsworth, and idealistically took up the cause of all the FitzClarences, telling her that the way the Regent and the royal family neglected and undervalued her and her brothers made him furious.[9]

Sophy's success and prospects were everything her mother could wish for. They made a painful contrast with those of Fanny, now living alone in lodgings, with no husband, no harp, and nothing at all to do. Alsop had finally sailed for India. He left without any sign of regret or any indication that he meant to send for his wife later; he continued, however, to extract the instalments on Fanny's dowry. Meanwhile Dora had to maintain her, and found her 'a great trouble to me'. She was still hankering after a stage or concert singer's career and, rightly or wrongly, Dora was still opposed to it. At thirty Daly's daughter had become her problem child. Dora insisted that Fanny's heart was good, but her temper was growing more violent and unpredictable from month to month; she would never make a quiet companion for her mother's old age – which was in any case the last thing Fanny had in mind. She had the theatre in her blood from her bad, unknown father as well as her mother, and she envied what her mother had done for herself by working; probably she would have been happier if she had grown up backstage instead of being protected and turned into a lady – or half way to a lady. Rage and ambition burned inside her small frame; and she was driven to stoke her fires, and then damp them down again, by dosing herself with drugs, and then more drugs.

Of Richard Ford's two daughters, Dodee March had no ambitions and not much character: she remained sweet and bland, in thrall to her dashing and plausible husband, and overwhelmed with babies, pregnancies and miscarriages. She had a soft heart; when she met the Duke unexpectedly one day, and he shook her hand and spoke kindly to her, she burst into tears. He had been something like a father to her, and he was touched by the encounter too; but it was nothing more than a moment's indulgence in sensibility. Lucy, the one with the sense, calm and good, remained everyone's favourite; she had the knack of linking the different parts of the family. All the FitzClarence children loved her and were at ease with her, and she felt she was one of them; George stood godfather to her first son. As often as she could manage it, she was with her mother; but she was kept very steadily pregnant by her old General.

First Henry and then George went back to Spain in the spring of 1813. Their mother was a heroic correspondent, as always, and encouraged the other children to write to their brothers ('direct to Captain FitzClarence with Hussars, serving under Lord Wellington *Spain* – and then enclose this To the under Secretary of State *War* Department Downing Street London – it will be about 10 or 14 days going,' she told Lolly). Her own regular 'packet' letters – written in instalments – went off, full of family news and gossip; she described how she lay awake at night worrying about them, and working out in her mind what they might need. Some of her offers must have made the young men laugh: 'a very nice stewing canteen' was her suggestion in one letter; and could they do with 'anything warm in the flannel way'? Other gifts were received with delight: drawing books – George was a keen artist – and a map of France; a telescope; 'portable soup', which she had learnt to use in what she sometimes called *her* campaigns, while touring (you just added boiling water, as with today's stock cubes); and always, of course, money.

At the end of July both boys distinguished themselves in the victory over the French at Pamplona. They fought so bravely that even the Queen was told of it, and she congratulated the Duke on their bravery; the Princesses also 'inquired kindly' (in the royal phrase) after them. Hearing this, Dora almost softened: '[I] am glad to find that there is some feeling in your august family.'[10] It was just as well she was spared the sight, a few days later, of the Duke and his royal brothers celebrating the Regent's birthday. A fascinated Princess Charlotte described them drinking till they were so 'cut' (drunk) that they fell off their chairs one by one; the scene reached its culmination as the Duke of York 'fell over the back of his chair against a wine cooler & cut his head a good deal, & in recovering himself pulled the tablecloth & all the things upon him'.[11]

In September Dora started another of her campaigns, touring in the south-west and the Midlands again, and as far north as Chester. Her plan was to continue acting for eighteen months more and then retire in May 1815, by which time she was confident she would be able to afford to. Then she would give up Cadogan Place, settle in a small house within reach of Bushy, and live a quiet life: such was the dream. But before that, one more summer at Covent Garden, two more winters in the provinces. She remained extraordinarily resilient and tough, curious and interested in the world about her: finding herself in Lichfield, she set off at once to discover the birthplaces of Garrick and Dr Johnson. In Portsmouth she visited a Lancasterian school – they were set up by Quakers for educating orphans – and played a benefit performance for it. In Bath, in the freezing January of 1814, she plucked a wretched beggar boy from a snowdrift, bought him clothes and determined to send him to a charity school in London – only to have him turn on her and say he would rather be his own master and beg his way. All this she reported very frankly to Lolly, always passionately interested in whatever she was doing.

To Lolly she wrote of the wonderful new actor, Edmund Kean, who appeared at Drury Lane early in 1814, and whom she thought far better than Kemble; she sent her son a Sunday paper that gave a full account of Kean, and a likeness. She also kept him abreast of his father's travels, and of how his sisters were looking, and of how they had received presents from the Princesses. She joked with him, drawing little parcels marked 'kisses for Lolly' and 'blessings for Tuss'. She dug out and posted, obviously at his request, 'an account of the first appearance of Mrs Jordan'. She made her letters fun, sending 'Mrs Jordans Compts to the Masters A and A FitzClarence', and continuing in the same mock formal style, 'She likes Covent Garden very well, and what is better, Covent Garden likes her.' She sent him writing-paper and books. Anyone who remembers lonely days at boarding school will see that what she did for the two youngest boys was just as important as her letters to her soldier sons. She was giving Lolly and Tuss a lifeline. She was giving herself one too: in her imagination, she still held them all together as a united group. 'What would I not give to see you both safe at home!' she wrote to George and Henry. 'I dare say I sd not know Henry – for he remains on my mind a little fat, chubby boy. Tus grows very like him – & Lolly is a compleat fine gentleman.'[12]

Outside the safe place in her imagination, the world grew less comfortable. She was not earning as much as she had expected. She told George, 'Don't be uneasy about me, or my money matters – I am determined to wry myself out of all embarrassments before I quit the profession,' but she also wrote, 'All my excursions begin in necessity and end in the sweat of my brow.'[13] There were some frightening examples before her now of what could happen to friends who failed to keep a grasp upon money matters, and had lost their protectors. Lady Hamilton was arrested early in 1813 for debt and was living within the confines of the King's Bench Prison. In August Sheridan too was arrested for the same reason; Whitbread, chairman of the Drury Lane committee, paid for his freedom, but made him wait in the sponging-house where he was being held on the way to the Fleet prison; and it was only a holding measure.[14] Sheridan wept at the humiliation. The Regent would do nothing more for his old friend. Sheridan's debts may have seemed a bottomless pit to him, but his behaviour does him little credit. Power had made the Prince into a creature of cruelty and caprice.

Early in 1814, while Dora was in Bath, the Duke persuaded the Regent to give him £1,000 to finance a trip to Holland to woo the young widowed sister of the Tsar Alexander I. Whether Dora knew the object of his journey or not, she worried about the children being left without either parent – something she had always tried to avoid in the old days – and wrote with a touch of caustic to George, 'your father's expedition to Holland I do not understand – nor how it can be of any use to himself & his family. The weather is greatly against it, or the change of scene & air might have done his health good, but in no other point of view can I perceive the advantage.'[15] The Duke thoroughly enjoyed himself seeing Brussels and Antwerp, and felt he was somehow taking part in the final defeat of Napoleon; but the Grand Duchess found his manners not up to scratch, and turned down his proposal of marriage. His brother forgave him the wasted £1,000 and offered consolation in the form of a naval job: that of ferrying the restored Bourbon King of France, the fatuous Louis XVIII, across the channel.

At once sentimental and unimaginative, the Duke acquired the buffoon's knack of passing unscathed through all his adventures. Dora, though she believed she always landed catlike on her feet, was less lucky. In April there was a family crisis when she was summoned away in the middle of her Covent Garden season to Essex, where Lucy appeared to be on the point of death after giving birth to her second child. Having made one of her dashes to be with her daughter, she poured out her emotion in a letter to George:

> We have been in the greatest misery and distress − expecting to see one of the most sensible young creatures in the World breathe her last − she received the sacrament − and awaited her doom with the resignation of an Angel, she was again bled and blistered, and today fresh hopes are held out − but the suspense is almost too much to bear − the General is the most pitiable object you can picture to your mind, − and she is just in the state I was in when you were born, with inflammation in the side − but she has not the constitution I then had.

Lucy, however, had a better constitution than she thought, and recovered from childbirth, and bleeding and blistering. The worst fears over, Dora remembered she was a working woman as well as a mother. 'This has been been . . . a most cruel occurrence on me − for much depended on my playing, both in respect to money matters and keeping up the Ball, so fairly poised – but, in the reflection that I am performing a sacred Duty, all other considerations vanish – my philosophy can stand buff to every thing but the loss of what I love . . .'[16]

Just as Lucy was getting well again, there was another drama: George was wounded in the fighting outside Toulouse. The first news meant panic, then came reassurance; it was only a flesh wound, and he was well enough to be sent back to England to convalesce. Henry had already arrived home with a bad arm. Since neither was seriously hurt, and the war was virtually over, Dora could surely now breathe a sigh of relief and regard them as safe. What she did not know was that the two of them were planning a course of action that would turn to catastrophe both for them and for her.

They had decided, with the support of twenty-two of their fellow officers – all young men – that they were going to bring formal accusations against their commanding officer of the 10th Hussars, Colonel Quentin, charging him with incompetence and neglect of duty in France over the four months between January and April of that year. They spent June and July preparing their accusations with great care. The charges were detailed, and related to particular incidents and battles; they included hazarding the safety of his men and allowing them to be taken prisoner, failing to give orders during battle, and failing to maintain proper discipline. These were charges that would inevitably lead to a court martial.

No group of officers would mount such an exercise unless they felt strongly that their officer had let them down, and unless they could produce good evidence; but it was a very unusual action, and as soon as it was started, those in authority over the army began to show they were worried by it. Captain George FitzClarence and Lieutenant Henry FitzClarence were very young, but they were clearly ambitious. They felt themselves to be able; they chafed against their uncertain status and their poverty, surrounded as they were by officers with well-established families who purchased their commissions for them. They had grown up in a world at war, and had taken early – while they were still children – and with exemplary courage to life in the services. France was the enemy, but it was an admired enemy, and one of acknowledged brilliance, as George's writing makes quite clear; and it offered the example of a meritocratic army, led by a man who had risen through that army to become an emperor. Their own commander, Wellington, likewise, from being the younger son of an obscure Irish peer, had become the idol of his country through military prowess. Their father's hero, Nelson, had made the same ascent. These were the models and heroes of their generation. George especially was impatient for promotion, and for command.

His father had warned him that he must not expect to advance quickly, and that his best course was to please the Regent; the Duke was

> sorry to see you always grumbling about the regiment: remember you are not one and twenty, and near three years a captain and without purchase. Recollect how much the Prince is your friend and attached to the regiment . . . the Prince expects you to attend to the regiment; besides, should those captains you expect leave the regiment, and you become the senior captain, with the reduction of two Field Officers you will occasionally be in command. The Prince will take care of you if you are attentive. . . [17]

The Duke's insistence on the Prince, and the absolute importance of pleasing the Prince, underlined his own entire dependence on his brother; the only advice he could give his sons was to seek favour and bow their necks, exactly as he had always done.

When the Duke sent this letter, he had no idea that George and Henry were preparing their attack on Colonel Quentin. In any case his advice was not palatable. They presented their accusations in mid-August. George told his mother what they had done as soon as it was public, writing from his regimental quarters in Brighton. She was then in Margate, appearing there and at Ramsgate, and feeling lonely and unwell. Her first reaction was a slight uneasiness, because she worried about what the Duke would think of his sons' action; but there seemed no cause for serious anxiety, since this was an internal army matter, and both George and Henry were acknowledged to be good officers and favoured by the Regent. She trusted their good sense. So she went ahead with a trip she had planned, crossing the channel and visiting Bruges, Ghent and Brussels; she even acted for three nights in Brussels 'with great *éclat* & was called the *belle actrice*'.[18] It was her first visit to the continent; she found it reviving and enjoyable, and was away for three weeks.

When she got back she heard that the court martial was scheduled for 17 October, and that the Regent was displeased with the whole business. The Duke began to sound anxious in his letters to his sons; still Dora had no idea – why should she? – that there was any risk for them. She was due to set off again at the end of October for a three-month tour to the north. It was to be her last; she sent a cheerful letter to Henry from Stafford to say she was saving up – 'making up a purse' – for a continental holiday with him and George when she returned. Her next letter, from Sheffield, suggests that George had sent her a gloomy account of the proceedings, and that he had been singled out by Quentin as the ringleader of his accusers. Still there was no reason for alarm: 'the worst they can say of you all [is] that you acted from too nice & quick a sense of honour'.[19]

She was wrong. The court martial was presided over by the Duke of York as commander-in-chief of the army, and he made it clear that, in his view, the real offence was not Colonel Quentin's but that of the junior officers who had dared to criticize him; and while he allowed that the Colonel had indeed been neglectful of his duty in some respects and should be reprimanded, it was the accusers who were to be punished. Unbelievably, all twenty-two of them were stripped of their swords and dismissed from the regiment; and to bring home York's disapproval, the prosecuting officer at the trial was given the same treatment.

The bizarre injustice of the outcome suggests that something else was at work beneath the surface. The idea of George as a ringleader, trying to make his mark by attacking his colonel and supported by a group of sympathetic young officers, must have given his uncles serious twinges of alarm. George and Henry were only twenty and seventeen, but if they were prepared to topple their colonel, might they conceivably go on to greater rebellion? The bad bastard is one of the most strongly established stereotypes in history and literature: envious, plotting against the legitimate line, building up a rival court. Absurd as the comparison might be, the shadow of Monmouth, Charles II's illegitimate son who rose in arms against his uncle James II, may have hovered in the Regent's mind.

All the disgraced officers were instructed to hold themselves ready to join such other regiments as they should be appointed to. George and Henry's first reaction was that they would leave the army altogether. Their mother, now on the Scottish borders, wrote passionately consoling letters, reminding them of the purity of their motives and assuring them the whole thing would soon blow over; she asked how their father bore the disappointment and, at her most maternal, suggested it was perhaps after all for the best. Even as she was writing, the two young men were informed of their fate: they were to go to India, and to remain there for four or five years at least.

Their first reaction was to refuse outright what they both regarded as a sentence of banishment. In truth they had hardly any choice in the matter. Once the Regent had decided, their father immediately caved in. There was nothing else for them to do, unless they were prepared to break with their family and the only career they had been trained for. The Duke, terrified of what might happen if they did not obey, suddenly began to insist that India offered them a golden future, and that the Regent was acting out of kindness;

at the same time, he nervously forbad them to go anywhere near the Regent or any of their uncles.

India was a land of opportunity, their father told them, where they could make their fortunes; the Regent was all goodness, McMahon was their friend and would smooth their paths. The truth was, McMahon was already composing a letter to the Governor-General in India, Lord Moira, 'begging that the strictest discipline, not to say severity, should be exercised towards them in consequence of their share in the business of the 10th Hussars'.[20]

The Duke also urged his sons not to see their mother before they went; he said he felt most sincerely for her distress, but 'Believe me, it is better for your mother and you two *not* to meet: it will only make her more unhappy and do no good.'[21] And their departure was to be hurried; they must go as soon as possible and not wait for the spring, which was the usual time of embarkation. George and Henry, like Dora, had failed to keep their heads down as they were expected to by the royal family; this was an offence not to be forgiven.

At Bushy the younger children were taken aback, and dismayed. Mary thought at once of her mother: 'Poor Mama I will write to her tomorrow it will be the bitter thankless seeing it first in the Papers for I am sure it will worry her to death – What does Henry say – When shall you come how I long to see you God bless you my dearest George.'[22] She was right. Bitter thankless it was for Dora in Carlisle to hear of the sacrifice of her sons. The news must have reached her for her ill-fated November birthday. In the evening she had to be led weeping from the stage, and for a day she was ill with grief, and took to her bed. Miss Sketchley, writing frantically to George, had great difficulty in preventing her from abandoning her tour immediately. She felt as much for the Duke as for herself and the boys. As soon as she was well enough, she wrote, 'It is your dear father that I feel for; surely on this occasion I may judge of his feelings by my own, and bitter, very bitter they have been,' she told George.[23]

She rallied her spirits again, began to make plans, and sent off volleys of letters. Were George and Henry to be together in India? The answer was no, their stations were to be 700 miles apart, George in Calcutta, Henry in Madras; but at least they had now been granted permission to travel out together. Then Dora asked, would they consider taking Fanny with them, to join Alsop? George refused with great firmness: 'I cannot take her on board the King's ship. It will be impossible; I would not shackle myself with her. McMahon gives me the most certain assurances of Alsop being provided for. I will do all I can; but I cannot take Fanny out with us. It will cost £3,000 to get us out to India – where is all this to come from?'[24] Where indeed? Dora began at once to think what she could raise, and wrote to Barton offering to contribute; when he declined, she told Henry, 'I sd hope the £3,000 comes from any source but your dear father, it ought for the misery they have occasioned him.'[25] It is not clear who did pay, and likely she did contribute a good deal of the cost.

In London Colonel Palmer brought a motion in the House of Commons against the court martial's verdict, and Lord Egremont, whose son was one of the young officers, enraged the Regent by threatening to do the same in the Lords. The Duke advised his sons, 'I hope you and Henry will be quiet and recollect the thing is over and that the law of the land makes the Sovereign absolute with his Army.' He added that he never spoke to the Regent now on any business but what was absolutely necessary.[26]

Dora accepted George's refusal to take Fanny with good grace. Alsop had revealed himself as an unfeeling and unprincipled man who had cheated her out of a large amount of money before abandoning his wife to her care. Fanny was currently living in Cadogan Place with the Marches, and causing fresh trouble by writing hostile letters to the Duke; she may have seen this as a demonstration of love and loyalty to her mother, but the letters brought Barton, supported by Wilks, one of the lawyer signatories of the settlement, round to Cadogan Place in a fury. Frederick March was questioned, and denied any involvement or knowledge of the letters; Dora, outraged by what Fanny had done, asked March to tell her she must leave London and go to one of her uncles in Wales, and stay there until her husband sent for her. She would continue to give her an allowance.

> If she refuses this, I here swear, by the most heart-breaking oath that presents itself to my tortured mind, that 'may I never again see those two sacrificed young men, if I ever (if possible) think of her again as a child that has any claim on me'. And I shall be led to doubt the affection of any one who may, by a mistaken motive, endeavour to make me break an oath so seriously and solemnly taken. If she has an atom of feeling, and wishes to regain any part of my affection, she will instantly agree to this: if not, the £90 a year shall be regularly paid to her so long as I have it to give. Let her not look on this as a banishment: let her look on the fate of two gallant young men submitting to a cruel exile without a murmur, whatever they may feel.[27]

Two days later she wrote to March again, 'I trust in God you will exert yourself in pointing out to Fanny the absolute necessity of her prompt compliance with the proposal; in which case she shall ever find me her mother and friend.' Fanny did not relish getting messages of this kind from her mother. Her response was to walk out of Cadogan Place and break off all communications. She surfaced later, as we shall find, but her mother never saw her again. Dora reproached herself bitterly for having 'almost deprived myself of the means of affording to two amiable children [Dodee and Lucy] by having lavished them on *one*'.[28]

With one grief piling on another, Dora was absolutely determined to see her sons before they left. The next day – 4 December 1814 – she wrote to George again to say, 'If you go soon I shall instantly set out – if not till the spring I will endeavour to finish my engagement – but by the hopes of our meeting again, dont deceive me – my mind is too unsettled to bear a disappointment.'[29] At this the boys disobeyed their father and told her the truth, that they were scheduled to leave early in the new year of 1815. She fulfilled one more engagement, in Newcastle, then cancelled the rest of her tour, and travelled south. Arriving at Cadogan Place at Christmas, she had a month in which to see them before their departure; they were to sail from Portsmouth on 21 January. The journey to India took from five to six months; they would arrive in the summer, and she might hope to hear from them in a year's time. She would be able neither to help them nor to communicate in the easy, comfortable to-and-fro fashion that was so precious to her. For years the Duke had been her confidant, to whom she could complain, argue, boast, lament, gossip, joke and give family and theatre news; when he abandoned the role, she gave it primarily to George – Henry being a less assiduous correspondent, as well as younger. Now that comfort too was taken from her.

Once they had gone, she sat down to consider her situation. Money, for so long an easily solved problem, was becoming a more stubborn one. In fact it was so short that she began to think of disposing of the lease of her house and of finding somewhere out of town, 'but not farther from the children than I am at present' – although the children were an ever diminishing band.[30] Lolly, having reached twelve, had been sent to sea and was somewhere in the Atlantic aboard the *Newcastle*. Frederick, just fifteen, was preparing to join his regiment in France where, in March, Napoleon reappeared and the war was resumed. Fanny had disappeared. Sophy, on the point of her official 'coming out', was busy with her young life. Tuss was away at school, and also promised to the navy. Lucy was taken up with her family at Woodbridge, expecting another child. Mary and Eliza were always loving, but they too were much occupied, being carefully prepared for their confirmation by the Bishop of London; the Duke was no fonder of religion than before, but someone was making sure all his daughters should be well drilled in its precepts.[31]

To the little ones, Ta and Mely, their mother had become an increasingly episodic and mysterious presence, appearing and disappearing unpredictably, unrelated to their daily life, likely to evoke sour looks and comments from their governesses: she must have seemed more fairy godmother than parent.

Yet Dora was determined not to lose her girls; she found a small house at Englefield Green, intended to replace Cadogan Square. Only the Marches were now in permanent residence there, with their three thriving but noisy babies. Dora had always had a soft spot for Frederick March, and when he mentioned that he was in slight financial difficulties, she gave him some 'notes' that appear to have allowed him to draw on her bank account. It was the sort of generous gesture she was used to making without a second thought; and it was a mistake.

Her judgement was not as good as it had been. She was sometimes confused, and her energy was running out. She had planned to retire in the spring of 1815, and in effect she did; but there was no triumphant and emotional last performance, no speeches and tears, no appreciative crowd making a formal farewell, no presentation from fellow actors. Perhaps she could not face it, or perhaps the committees of Covent Garden and Drury Lane thought it inappropriate. She went to Dover and Deal to give some performances in their small theatres, then to Boston in Lincolnshire for a few more. She visited Tuss at school, and saw as much as she could of the girls. Lolly delighted her with his letters and presents of oranges from Madeira, where his ship was stationed, although some of her letters to him, which she had asked the Duke to forward, went mysteriously astray at Bushy.

In the summer came the great news of Waterloo; England was triumphant but exhausted. Perhaps Dora felt she was lucky after all that George and Henry had not been able to fight; and that Frederick's regiment was not involved. As she said, it was time for the heroine of *The Soldier's Daughter* to become a full-time soldiers' mother. Her professional life was at an end; there was a final flicker when she gave ten performances in Margate in July and August and three in Oxford on 25, 27 and 28 August. This was the very last time she appeared on a stage. She was fifty-three; she had been acting for nearly forty years; and she had less than a year to live.

At the end of August she was in Gosport, saw in the papers that Lolly's ship was back in English waters, and sent off a letter to Bushy. 'My darling Lolly,' she wrote,

> I see the Newcastle is arrived, and that this may meet you, surrounded by your dear Sisters at Bushy I pray God – I have been miserable about you, I shall return to Englefield Green on Sunday – and hope to see you, as soon as you can be spared – if you write immediately I shall get a letter in answer to this before I leave this place give my love to your dear Sisters and God Bless you my dear Boy prays your affectionate and anxious mother DJ.[32]

We don't know whether she went to Englefield Green, or whether she managed to see Lolly or any of the others. The person she did see in September was Barton. He was surprised to be summoned by letter, and found her 'in tears, and under much embarrassment, from a circumstance that had burst upon her, as she said, "like a thunder storm".'[33] The circumstance was the discovery of the extent to which Frederick March had been drawing on her Coutts account, and not only that: he had borrowed in her name, and run up a terrifying tangle of debts that were now out of control and impossible to conceal any longer. Once again, she had been betrayed where she had most put her trust.

Barton's account says she was fearful of immediate arrest, wished to treat all her claimants fairly, and to save 'the wife and children of the person who had so deceived her, from utter ruin'. Since she could not negotiate with creditors if she was under arrest, her idea was to go abroad while things were sorted out. Barton seized on this plan and encouraged her in it enthusiastically. There was no fight left in her; yet again, she gave her trust too readily. She had to believe Barton was acting in her best interests, and to accept his seeming kindness at its face value, though the obvious truth is he was eager to get her out of the way before she and her awkward children and crooked son-in-law could bring more embarrassment on the royal family. Had he chosen to exert himself to help her, she could almost certainly have avoided leaving the country; as it was, he did not choose even to inform the Duke. She went relying on Barton to arrange matters and summon her home as soon as possible; ten days abroad, she believed, might be enough.

Before she left, she called in an auctioneer to value the contents of Cadogan Place; once more, she let herself be swindled, allowing furniture and lease to go for a sum far below their value.[34] Then, accompanied only by Miss Sketchley, she took ship, landed at Boulogne, and found a modest and isolated cottage. The name Mrs Jordan was now a liability; after this crossing of the water she changed it again, and chose to be called Mrs James. She asked for her letters to be delivered to the Post Office, Boulogne.

Two of her children were in Paris at this time: Frederick was there on regimental duty, and Sophy had just arrived for a holiday. None of Sophy's letters to her former companion Miss Turner makes any reference to her mother; she talks mostly of being very happy, of sightseeing and riding, and of her great social success. Metternich was kind to her, the Duke of Wellington gave dinners and concerts; she visited Talleyrand, went to Lady Castlereagh's balls, and was hotly pursued by a Prince Royal of Bavaria, who turned out to be married. Through all these adventures Sophy kept her 'horror of impropriety and irreligion', she assured Dot Turner, and was delighted to find her letters gave 'dear Papa' pleasure.[35] We know she met Frederick only because he wrote to his mother in Boulogne to say so.[36] Both brother and sister were cast down by the news about the Marches. Sophy told her brother she was about to write to her mother; so perhaps she was not so entirely taken up with her social triumphs as the letters to Miss Turner suggest. Frederick was homesick, but his regiment was not due home for a long time: 'I long to see dear Lucy,' he told his mother; but she could no longer hold the family together.

On 18 October a new actress appeared at Covent Garden as Rosalind in *As You Like It*. She was small, and sang well; she was also visibly pregnant. Crabb Robinson described her in his diary as 'the plainest woman, I should think, who ever ventured on the stage'.[37] This was Fanny Alsop. William Hazlitt went to see her on 22 October and was inspired to write as follows:

A lady of the name of Alsop, a daughter of Mrs Jordan (by a former husband), has appeared at Covent Garden theatre, in the character of Rosalind. Not only the circumstances of her relationship to that excellent actress, but the accounts in the papers raised our curiosity and expectations very high. We were unwillingly disappointed. The truth is, Mrs Alsop is a very nice little woman, who acts her part very sensibly and cleverly, and with a certain degree of arch humour, but no more like her mother, 'than I to Hercules'. When we say this, we mean no disparagement to this lady's talents, who is a real acquisition to the stage in correct and chaste acting, – but simply to prevent comparisons, which can end only in disappointment. Mrs Alsop would make a better Celia than Rosalind. – Mrs Jordan's excellencies were all natural to her; it was not as an actress, but as herself, that she charmed everyone. Nature had formed her in most prodigal humour, and when nature is in the humour to make a woman all that is delightful, she does it most effectually. Mrs Jordan was the same in all her characters, and inimitable in all of them, because there was no one else like her.

Her face, her tears, her manners were irresistible. Her smile had the effect of sunshine, and her laugh did one good to hear it. Her voice was eloquence itself: it seemed as if her heart was always at her mouth. She was all gaiety, openness and good nature. She rioted in her fine animal spirits, and gave more pleasure than any other actress, because she had the greatest spirit of enjoyment in herself. Her Nell – but we will not tantalise ourselves, or our readers. Mrs Alsop has nothing luxurious about her, and Mrs Jordan was nothing else. Her voice is clear and articulate, but not rich or flowing. In person she is small, and her face is not prepossessing. Her delivery of the speeches was correct and excellent, as far as it went, but without much richness, or power; – lively good sense is what she really possesses. She also sung the Cuckoo song very pleasingly.[38]

Between mother and daughter, it is hard to imagine which of them would have found Hazlitt's sincere and entirely good-hearted criticism more piercing and painful.

20

Heartbreak: 1816

If you have ever been poor, the stratagems of poverty come back to you like old friends when it looks you in the face again. Dora's life with her mother in Dublin and Yorkshire thirty years earlier was there to draw on as she set up a frugal existence in France with Miss Sketchley at her side. Expecting, or at least hoping, it would be only a short stay, she took a small cottage on the coast, ten minutes' walk out of Boulogne, in a hamlet called Marquetra. There was a garden planted with flowers and fruit trees, the landlady lived next door, and the landlady's maid Agnès was happy to act as their servant. Agnès quickly understood that Madame James was a great personage fallen on hard times; or so she said afterwards. When pressed for detail, she also reported that the unhappy lady played her guitar to herself to pass the time, and that she appeared anxious. Communication was difficult, but it was obvious that she was waiting for letters; life was punctuated by Miss Sketchley's visits to the post office in Boulogne. Madame James lived very economically, but she paid her rent regularly; and endeared herself to both landlady and maid as the ten days prolonged themselves and turned into as many weeks. There was no summons to return to London. When December came, she told them she was leaving, though not for England.

All biographies come to sad ends, but this must be one of the saddest. 'I begin to feel that acting keeps me alive,' Dora wrote to George when he was still near enough for such day-to-day confidences, 'in fact it keeps me from thinking.'[1] There was nothing to keep her from thinking now, and less and less to keep her alive. At least a cheerful letter came from him at the end of the year, full of the wonders of India: 'every house a palace, and the climate beautiful'. Frederick wrote too, from Paris, where he was stationed with his regiment; and it was probably to be near him – the only one of her sons she could hope to see – that she decided to move, first to Versailles and then to Saint-Cloud, both places with barracks and officers' quarters attached to their palaces. The palace of Saint-Cloud, set on a terrace above the Seine, amid steeply rising gardens and woods, with a magnificent view over Paris on the other side of the river, had been a favourite residence of Napoleon, and was used by General Blücher as his head-quarters in 1814. Both the barracks and the village of Saint-Cloud were clustered on the slope between the palace and the river, and here she found lodgings at Nº 1, rue d'Angoulême.[2]

Jonah Barrington, who, after her death, visited the house where she had lodged and was shown round by the landlord, described it as 'large, gloomy, cold, and inconvenient' with 'scanty, old, and tattered' furniture and a dank, unweeded garden. Barrington is an unreliable witness, but he was clearly shocked to find how comfortless her surroundings had been. The rooms she had used were, he said, shabby, and 'in her little drawing room, a small old sofa was the best-looking piece of furniture; on this she constantly re-clined,' he was told.[3] Reclining on a sofa had never been her habit, and suggests she was physically ill as well as unhappy.

The Marches were now occupying her house in Englefield Green; since none of the debts he had accumulated were in his name, he was safe from arrest. In January Dora sent Miss Sketchley to England to collect her settlement money from Coutts, and also deputed her to see March and get his solemn word that he had no more outstanding bills or other claims on her estate. He objected rudely to Miss Sketchley's asking him anything at all, and refused to answer; and with this depressing news she went back to Saint-Cloud.

Dora then wrote to Barton, from whom she had heard nothing, to say she was worried that March was keeping back the names of more creditors. Previously March had promised that the list was complete, but she had reason to suspect it was not: 'he declines making an oath to that purpose: this has caused me much uneasiness, for it appears to me vague, if not equivocal. I can solemnly declare that the names I sent you, are the only ones I know of, and the greater part utter strangers to me . . . What interpretation can be put on his refusal?' The interpretation was unfortunately all too obvious: he had not confessed to everything yet; and this meant she could not safely return to England, unless Barton took some action to help her.

She went on, 'It is not, believe me, the feelings of pride, avarice, or the absence of those comforts I have all my life been accustomed to, that is killing me by inches; it is the loss of my only remaining comfort, *the hope I used to live on from time to time, of seeing my children.*'[4]

Barton did nothing. He did not attempt to clear the debts or to pin down March; and apparently he did not even inform the Duke. March was no better. He accused Barton of dragging his feet, claimed to have written to his mother-in-law himself, and later said his letter must have been prevented from reaching her by some persons unknown. It is clear that this, like almost everything March said, was a lie.

Though she was sinking into illness and despair, Dora still showed only her bright face to her children. The day after her letter to Barton, she wrote to Lolly, at sea again, thanking him for his 'kind and affectionate letters', passing on news of India, of Bushy, even of Fanny, who was acting in Bath, and Dodee, who was leaving Englefield Green, and moving into Fanny's London lodgings. She urged him not to worry about her at all. She often dined with Frederick, she said, and he was all kindness and attention. In London General Hawker was active on her behalf, and Barton was kindly trying to sort out her 'unfortunate affair'. 'Make yourself, my dear Lolly, quite easy about me – I shall do very well . . . We shall all meet again, and I trust be very happy.'[5]

On the back of this letter Lolly wrote, 'This is the last letter I ever received from my dear departed and lamented Mother. Adolphus.' It is not only the last to him, but the last of all her letters to survive. The absence of any more after January leaves a mystery over her last months. Many letters have been lost, of course – none of hers to George and Henry in India survives, nor any to her daughters – but it is unthinkable that she would have stopped writing to her children had she been able to hold a pen, or even to dictate to Miss Sketchley. In February Frederick had to leave Paris with his regiment for Cambrai, a hundred miles away; as far as we know he never said or wrote anything of his last contact with his mother. In her letter to Lolly, she said she planned to follow Frederick; but she did not. Miss Sketchley was not sent to England again, though she might have been expected to go in April, since Dora's allowance was paid quarterly; but she remained in Saint-Cloud. However well intentioned, she was not capable of planning or initiating action.

Dora's health had been deteriorating for some time; she suffered from bilious attacks, pains in her side, swollen ankles, shortness of breath and increasing general weakness. Now her skin became discoloured. It was thought she might have a form of jaundice, *la maladie noire*. She was observed to be ill by her landlord, and she was visited by a physician, for what it was worth. She may have been suffering from liver disease or from slowly progressive heart failure, about neither of which could anything then be done.

Apart from the doctor, Dora's visitors now were not friends or family but fans, with their flattering and exhausting curiosity: an English hotel proprietor and wine merchant, Mr Greatorex, who had discovered the true identity of 'Mrs James', and Helen Maria Williams, one-time poet and radical, who had lived in Paris since the Revolution and was now a journalist, and curious to interview the celebrated actress. She called once, appeared sympathetic, and was allowed to come again; and the two women, who were of an age, talked of the theatre and gossiped about Napoleon, at any rate according to Miss Williams's account, which was not published until after her own death a decade later.[6] Miss Williams wrote that Dora was modest about her own achievements, and warm in her tributes to her friend and former leading man, John Bannister; she also spoke gratefully of her audiences, and said she wished she had been able to play more pathetic parts. The most interesting of her remarks, perhaps, as recalled by Miss Williams, were about the effects of applause. Dora described them as 'internal exultation' and 'delight bordering upon extasy': a stimulus or restorative she knew she would never experience again. It is unfortunate that Miss Williams's four interviews are overwhelmingly made up of her own contributions to the conversation, and Dora's are given in stilted literary prose: enough to make you long for an anachronistic tape-recorder. At her fourth visit Dora presented her visitor with a small book of poems she had written herself, and then sent a note excusing herself from the next meeting, being too tired and melancholy to see anyone.

The collection of Dora's poems seems to have been lost, and Miss Williams gave no dates for her interviews, although she said the last took place a few weeks before Dora's death; Mr Greatorex also said he visited her a few days before her death, and found her ill but as charming, and as uncomplaining, as ever. The puzzle is that she should have been entertaining when she was not well enough to carry out the one activity that meant more to her than any other, writing letters to her children. March, April, May and June, when the woods and slopes of Saint-Cloud are freshly green and beautiful, remain an unexplained blank in this respect. She had already told Lolly that she found Paris 'an odious place'.

Now, as the trees came into leaf, she turned her face to the wall.

In May the Duke was in London, assigned the task of leading his niece, Princess Charlotte, to the altar at Carlton House, where her wedding to Prince Leopold took place. They made an odd pair. She held her uncle in contempt; he resented her for standing between himself and the throne.[7] She, at twenty, was happy to be marrying a husband she had chosen for herself; he, at fifty, had still not found himself a wife.

Near by, in a house in Savile Row, Sheridan was lying sick in an upstairs room, his wife almost as badly afflicted with cancer downstairs. Too ill to move himself, he was in terror of the bailiffs carting him off bodily to prison; desperate notes of appeal to friends show how frightened he was. At this stage the Regent was informed of the condition of his old adviser, supporter and friend, and did arrange for some money to be sent round; it is said that Mrs Sheridan refused it proudly. Then Harriet Bessborough sent inquiries, and followed them up with a visit. She made her way into the house in the wake of a bailiff. The whole place was filthy, the ground floor occupied by more bailiffs, smoking and playing cards. Mrs Sheridan welcomed her and sent her up to her husband, begging her not to let her expression betray what she felt at the sight of him; and in his bedroom Harriet sat down on a trunk – there was no chair – beside his truckle bed. He fixed her with brilliant eyes, gripped her hand and told her he was determined she should never forget him; he would, he said, visit her after his death. She was frightened, and went away much distressed, both by his circumstances and his words.[8]

A few days later, on 7 July, he was dead. Death somewhat restored his popularity in society. On 13 July – a Saturday – he was buried in Westminster Abbey, though not among the statesmen, as he had hoped, but in Poets' Corner, which some might think a better place. Peers and bishops attended as mourners, and offered to serve as his pall-bearers; but the Prince Regent did not come to the Abbey, having given one of his large parties at Carlton House the night before. On the evening of the funeral, there was a performance of Mozart's *Così fan tutte* at Covent Garden.

Posthumously, Sheridan did better than his leading lady. Dora died two days before him, on 5 July: as lonely, as distressed, and ten years younger. Two men registered her death at the town hall in Saint-Cloud, at nine o'clock in the morning; they said she had died before dawn, at two. Neither of the men was a doctor: one was her landlord, Jean-Jacques Mongin, the other a young infantry officer in the French army named Suard, perhaps a fellow lodger. Mongin and Suard produced a curious mixture of fact and fiction for the *Acte de décès*. They called the dead woman 'Dorothée Blamd' and said she was 'native de London (Capitale d'Angleterre)'. They reduced her age by six years to forty-eight ('âgée de quarante-huit ans'), made her a widow and provided her with a businessman for a husband: she was 'Veuve de Jordan – négociant'.

Miss Sketchley must have been the source of this information. There are many stories surrounding Dora's death, some of them stemming from Miss Sketchley's confusion. At the beginning of July she wrote to Lucy Hawker – who had just given birth to her fourth baby – informing her of her mother's death. While Lucy was in a state of shock, another letter arrived, saying she had made a mistake and that, although Mrs Jordan was very ill, she was still alive. Lucy immediately prepared to set off for France; but before she could leave, a third letter came, informing her that her mother was after all dead. While this private correspondence was going on, someone was also keeping the newspapers informed. On 1 July *The Times* reported the death of Mrs Jordan on 27 June, attributing it to a violent inflammation of the chest, which led to the rupture of a blood vessel; on 2 July it printed a correction:

The death certificate of Mrs Jordan, calling her 'Dorothée Blamd, native de London . . . âgée de quarante-huit ans . . . Veuve de Jordan, négociant' from the archives at Saint-Cloud, dated 5 July 1816.

> We entertain hopes that this interesting woman still lives. The letters which announced her death last week were received on Thursday. Letters of a subsequent date, received in town this morning, from a lady who accompanies Mrs Jordan, state, that her life had been despaired of, but that severe blisters had been applied, and hopes were entertained of her recovery.

Either Miss Sketchley was writing to *The Times*, or to someone in London who passed on the information. On 4 July *The Times* reported 'The letter received on Tuesday from a lady who resides with Mrs Jordan states, that she was alive on Friday morning, but that a few hours would probably terminate her existence. The slight hopes which the physician entertained had entirely vanished.' It was almost another week before, on 10 July, the newspaper said it had received papers from Paris that 'mentioned her death'. She had 'lingered in a state of insensibility until Friday last'.

So farce took over from pathos at the end. It sounds as though Dora was in a coma during her last days, which was perhaps as well, since none of her children was with her, nor anyone she loved. George and Henry were in India, Lolly at sea, Tuss at school, Frederick – the only one of the boys who might have reached her – with his regiment. Fanny, struggling to establish herself as an actress, with a baby not her husband's, and a drug problem, was in severe difficulties; so was Dodee March, who had to live with the knowledge that her husband had helped to bring her mother to ruin. Only Lucy, as we have seen, prepared to go to her when she heard she was ill; and it was her husband who travelled to Paris when the death was confirmed, the sole person to do so.

The five FitzClarence girls were not in a position to travel abroad without their father's permission and financial support. Whatever he felt privately, the Duke appears to have remained silent on the subject of her death. There is not a word of it in his letters to George and Henry, though he wrote regularly to both; incredibly, he seems to have relied on Barton to break the news to them. Eighteen months went by before he made his first reference to it, not with a word of regret or sympathy, but simply blaming March and Fanny for their bad behaviour, and Hawker for his 'extreme folly'.[9]

Barrington, who went in due course to Saint-Cloud to find out what had happened, said he got the details of Dora's death from her landlord, whom he calls Mr C —, and who told him that her chief interest during her last weeks had been the arrival of letters from England; and that she grew very distressed when there were none for several days, and died in a sort of fit after he had told her one morning that there were still none. Boaden attributed her death to *la maladie noire*. He also introduced a note of ghastly frivolity into his account by suggesting she may not have died at all, saying he was certain he had seen her in Piccadilly later in the year, looking into a bookshop window through a concealing veil. Fanny also saw her in the Strand, he said.

In Saint-Cloud Miss Sketchley found herself responsible for organizing the funeral. According to one of several conflicting accounts, Dora was at first denied Christian burial by the Catholic church – as an actress and a Protestant – and only by 'the strenuous interference of an English gentleman of some weight' was she allowed to be placed in the Saint-Cloud Cemetery at all. One version says the Reverend Foster, chaplain to the British Embassy, officiated; another says he was unwell, and his place taken by Monsieur Marron, a French Protestant pastor. A third says the Mayor officiated, resplendent in his uniform. The numbers attending are also variously recorded. According to *The Times*, there were only two Englishmen present, and they were there only because they were passing 'by accident': Mr Greatorex and a London sculptor, William Henshall. A different version says Mr Greatorex found the pastor and gathered eight or nine English gentlemen from Paris. One English paper reported two hundred people present. The coffin was described as deal, a mere shell painted black, according to *The Times*, and without any sort of ornament or lining; alternatively, it was decently lined and embellished in white, and covered with a light blue cloth.[10] She was buried beneath an acacia tree in the cemetery close to the park and near the top of the hill above the river.

After the funeral Miss Sketchley is said to have served a cold collation of fruit and wine. She then left Saint-Cloud, just possibly taking the diamond ring Dora always wore, and returned to London, where she is said to have drawn the last instalment of her late mistress's allowance before disappearing for ever; the next report is of the dead woman's few remaining possessions being auctioned by order of the French police.[11] Dora's life insurance policies had presumably been allowed to lapse, and she left no will. When General Hawker arrived, three days after the funeral, there was apparently nothing more to be done. No one seems to have told him that the funeral expenses had not been paid.

They remained unpaid for the next three years, when the municipality of Saint-Cloud announced publicly that sixty francs (£2.12s.6d) were still due. Boaden says there was a plan to move her remains to the Père Lachaise Cemetery in Paris, and put up a marble monument, but that what he calls 'mistaken ideas of delicacy' prevented this; and he bursts out into indignation that she was not taken home to 'the noblest cemetery of the world', to lie alongside other great actresses in Westminster Abbey. His suggestion may have stirred something in the Duke's mind later.

What happened was that a memorial stone was ordered for the grave by an English couple, a Mr and Mrs Henry Woodgate of Dedham in Essex, who are supposed to have visited Dora shortly before her death. Their respect for her memory was such that, on returning to England, they asked the theatre historian, John Genest, to write an epitaph, which he did. Cypresses were planted around the grave, and in 1818 Genest's dignified tribute was engraved on a large, plain stone and placed over the tomb, despite the unpaid funeral dues. In twenty-three lines of Latin he praised her outstanding skill as an actress, her wit and sweetness of voice, her ability to play men as well as women, and her goodness and generosity of heart. The epitaph ended with the words 'Mementote Lugete': remember her, and weep.[12]

Dora's death, like Sheridan's, still has the power to shock us today. His was made more terrible by his debts, and she was driven abroad by debts incurred in her name; but it is not the question of money that makes them so painful. The Duke defended himself later, half-heartedly, by insisting that her allowance was always paid. So it was; but how little that signifies. It is the failure of love, friendship, imagination and simple decency that appals. A woman who should have been honoured and supported, surrounded by her family, comforted in her illness, was instead first driven out of her home, then separated from the sons who were her natural protectors, and divided from her young daughters, who were encouraged to forget about her while she lived. No one took up the case against her swindling son-in-law; no one lifted a finger to help her in practical matters; no one spoke for her in her isolation and illness. The most loving of her adult daughters, Lucy Hawker, was tied down by three babies and another pregnancy; in any case she depended on her husband's permission to do anything, and the General, though well intentioned, was also interested in retaining royal favour. Both Sheridan and Dora died from physical causes that would in all likelihood have killed them wherever they were and however they were treated; but the misery of the conditions in which they found themselves – Dora especially, in a foreign country with no real friend even to understand what she said – made their last months infinitely more cruel. No one dies of a broken heart, perhaps; but they were both of them broken-hearted when they died.

21

The Children: 'with the King they die'

As for Dora's children, their stories make up as broad and striking a map of human experience as you would expect to find in some great panoramic novel of the nineteenth century: from a suicide in Greenwich Street, New York, to a glittering life as viscountess and wife of a governor of Bombay; from a remote village vicar, building a school for his parish children, to a distinguished oriental scholar. One daughter became mistress of Penshurst Place; one son helped to found the Garrick Club. Several have descendants in the House of Lords today, and Rupert Hart-Davis is one of Dora's most brilliant sprigs. Others faded into obscurity, like the Marches, who went to ground in Wales. Their aunt Hester – Dora's little-loved sister – outlived several of them, dying in 1848 at the age of eighty-eight, pensioned by Queen Victoria to the end.

On the day of Dora's funeral – 13 July 1816 – the Duke wrote to Henry from Bushy as though nothing had happened.

> I have had my annual attack lightly ... Frederick and Tus are both at home ... It looks like war in India and so much the better for you ... All your sisters unite with me in every sincere and good wish for your health and welfare; I hope you mind the climate and do not expose to the sun ... Do not spend more money than is requisite; we are a large family and must take care of ourselves.[1]

Henry must have received his father's letter round about Christmas 1816, along with the one from Barton informing him of his mother's death. We don't know what he thought.

He was well liked in Madras, and gave 'unceasing satisfaction' to his commanding officer, as did George in Calcutta, but neither had anyone to share their grief with them.[2] In September the Duke wrote again from Bushy,

> Frederick is quite well at Cambray; I am anxious to hear of Adolphus and the fleet under Lord Exmouth; Augustus is very kindly noticed by the Duke and Duchess of Gloucester and I dined with the dear boy there last week ... I hope to enclose letters from your sisters ... our weather is lamentable ... tho' not so bad as on the Continent ... I think having nothing in fact to say I have written a pretty good letter.[3]

With this sort of thing his sons had to be content. Only in November of the following year (1817) did the Duke make any allusion to their mother, in a letter to George. 'Barton has written the particulars attending your mother's misfortunes and death: the infamy and rascality of March and Mrs Alsop and the extreme folly of Hawker permitting himself to be made a Cat's paw by them will prevent my future intercourse with them. I pity Mrs March and Mrs Hawker.' He went on, 'Henry is or has been with you and I shall expect home about this time twelvemonth.'[4]

Henry was being sent home because of his health. Of all the children, he had led the toughest life physically – locked into the Baltic ice at eleven, serving with the ill-fated Walcheren expedition at twelve, with the Mediterranean fleet at thirteen, the German legion at fourteen, the Peninsular War at fifteen, and to India before he was eighteen. He never grew very tall; he was brave and passionate in temper, a good linguist but not much of a letter-writer, and always overshadowed in the family by the favourite eldest son, George; it had taken him years, and his mother's persistent championing, to get out of the navy after he came to detest it. He hated the idea of going to India, and was furious at his father's treatment of his mother. There was not much joy in Henry's life. After the news of his mother's death reached him, his health began to give cause for alarm; and before he was due to start the long journey home from Madras, before he could even visit George, he became ill. For four days the fever raged in him; and after four days he died.

This was at the beginning of September 1817. His father did not get the news until the following February; by then George was on his way home. Perhaps Lord Moira feared a second tragedy; George was sent bearing dispatches, by an overland route, setting off in December. He had been away for nearly three years, and in the course of them he had lost both his mother and his closest brother.

Fanny is supposed to have learnt of her mother's death through Barton's summary stopping of the payment of her allowance. He may have had the law on his side, but Dora had surely earned every penny of the allowance for her awkward daughter. Fanny went, grieving and fuming, to Englefield Green to collect what she could of her mother's possessions; she came away with a portrait, a mirror that had once belonged to Garrick, a half-knotted rug started by Dora, a few letters. Because her mother had died intestate and was declared illegitimate, the King's solicitor collected her effects, which were estimated at less than £300; a few years later, in 1823, the Treasury announced that her creditors would receive five shillings in the pound.

There was vengeance in Fanny's heart, and she was almost certainly involved in a publishing project announced in June 1817 to bring out the *Authentic Memoirs of Mrs Jordan* 'in one Vol. octavo, with original letters'.[5] The book did not appear, doubtless stopped by royal intervention: Fanny's threats against the Duke were mostly futile gestures, but she remained a thorn in his side. For a while she pursued her stage career; in 1817 she was again seen in London, acting at Drury Lane at the same time as Kean.[6] Then, in 1820, the Duke paid her passage to America, where she had offers of work and was billed as 'the Grand-Daughter of the late King of Britain'. Whether she took her child with her is not known. Nine months later, in June 1821, she swallowed an overdose of laudanum in her Greenwich Street lodgings. The register of deaths makes her thirty-one; really she was thirty-nine. What became of the child? We don't know. The cause of death is bleakly given as 'suicide'. Little Fan, adored, cherished and misunderstood by her mother, had outlived her by only five years.

As for Lucy Hester Hawker – good, sensible Lucy – she settled into a busy life as wife of a general and mother of a large family. She gave her husband ten children, the youngest born when he was in his seventies. The Hawkers were the backbone of England, sending their strong and healthy sons into the army and the navy. One of Lucy's boys – Adolphus Octavus – died in 1921, in his ninety-first year. Lucy became Lady Hawker, and must have lived many years as a widow. In 1847, when she was nearly sixty, and free, she travelled to Saint-Cloud to visit her mother's grave. By then she could have taken the train for part of the journey at least; she may even have passed the hours reading the popular newly published books of the year, *Vanity Fair* or *Jane Eyre*, with their warnings against bold, adventurous women; or she may simply have sat and thought of her mother and the rapidly fading past. Whatever sadness she felt as she climbed the hill to the cemetery above the Seine, whatever memories came crowding back, she kept them all to herself.[7]

For the Bushy girls, the death of their mother allowed them to be drawn more closely into royal circles. This was a relief to Sophy, who suffered most acutely from her ambiguous status. In October 1816 Princess Augusta wrote to her, conveying the Queen's thanks for her letter, and after this there was a steady correspondence between her and the Princesses. They sent presents to all the girls: garnet and malachite earrings, gold chains and lockets for Sophy, Mary and Eliza, muslin dresses for Augusta and Amelia.[8] The Duke was often with his mother; he was at her side in Bath when Princess

Charlotte died in childbirth at the end of 1817, and the whole pattern of the succession changed. The old King could not live much longer; now only the Prince Regent and the Duke of York stood between the Duke of Clarence and the throne. Parliament voted some money to repair Bushy House, and £1,000 for each of the girls, and he set about looking for a wife once again. In 1818 he was finally found an acceptable and willing German princess, Adelaide of Saxe-Meiningen. She was not much older than his daughters. The Duke himself, showing more imagination than was usual with him, was somewhat appalled at the idea of her fate: 'She is doomed, *poor, dear, innocent young* creature to be *my* wife. *I cannot, I will not, I must not* ill use her,' he wrote to George, newly returned from India.[9]

The Duke shared a wedding with his brother Kent, each marrying a German princess in July 1818. Now Queen Charlotte could, and did, go to her grave in peace, secure in the knowledge that some of her sons had at last settled into a correct way of life. Six months later the Kents produced a healthy daughter, and named her Victoria. Adelaide too bore two daughters, both of whom died. She found consolation in becoming a model stepmother, good-hearted and generous, and won the hearts of all the FitzClarence girls by her kindness. At her insistence the portraits of their mother remained in place at Bushy.* She made no attempt to keep

* In November 1826 the actor Charles Mathews was asked to perform for the Duke and Duchess of Clarence at Bushy and invited to spend the night. As he breakfasted with his hosts, he was somewhat surprised to see a large painting of Mrs Jordan over the chimney-piece. The Duke noticed Mathews looking at it and when the Duchess left the room said, 'I know you have a collection of theatrical portraits, Mr Mathews, which I shall like to see one day. I hope you have not one like *that?*' – meaning, he explained, that he would not want anyone else to possess so good a likeness as his. Mathews replied that he did not, and the Duke, gazing at the picture and clearly much moved, said, 'She was one of the best of women, Mr Mathews.' He spoke with so much feeling that tears came to Mathews's eyes; at which the Duke reached out and pressed his hand, saying, 'You knew her, Mathews; therefore must have known her excellence.'[10]

either sons or daughters away from their father. He adored all his daughters, and he and Adelaide took groups of them on several foreign holidays. In 1826 Ta and Mely went with them to visit the Queen of Würtemberg – George III's eldest daughter – who declared they were pleasing, sensible and modest as well as handsome, and added that their brother Colonel George FitzClarence was so nice that she regretted he was not legitimate.

One by one, the girls found aristocratic husbands. Eliza was the first; she became Countess of Errol at St George's, Hanover Square, in December 1820. 'What a handsome, spanking creature Lady Errol is, and how like her mother. She looks as if she was quite uncomfortable in her fine cloaths and wanted to have them off,' wrote Thomas Creevey in his sneering way.[11] After Elizabeth's marriage the four remaining girls lived together in Audley Square, chaperoned by a Mrs Harpur, 'a respectable Lady, who accompanies the elder daughters when they go into company,' observed Farington in his diary, adding, 'The Duke of Clarence shews great attention to them. They dine with the Duke and Duchess every day when there is no particular engagement.'[12] Charles Fox, the illegitimate eldest son of Lord and Lady Holland (and great-nephew of Charles James Fox), had been in love with Eliza, but when she jilted him he turned to Mary, and they married in 1824: Mary had grown into 'a fine looking, brown girl with a pleasant countenance and manners', and remained considerate and charming. The next year Sophy married Sir Philip Sidney of Penshurst Place in Kent; ten years later her father made him Baron De L'Isle and Dudley. Augusta took the son of the Marquess of Ailsa, who died of tuberculosis after only four years; from a second husband, Lord John Frederick Gordon Hallyburton, she also had children. Lastly Mely married Byron's godson, Viscount Falkland; she went with him to Bombay when he was appointed governor-general; and she wrote and published a lively account of her travels in India, Egypt and Palestine, which show her as adventurous and unconventional, full of curiosity, always ready to meet and mix with the people among whom she found herself, and to go exploring wherever she pleased, sketch-book in hand.[13]

So the FitzClarence girls, charming, clever and pretty, were assimilated by the establishment, bad blood or no, their matrimonial chances aided, no doubt, by the prospect of their father becoming king, as he did in 1830. For their brothers things were more difficult. All of them felt their anomalous position; they were jeered at and humiliated in the press, verbally roughed up as 'the Fitzjordans' and 'the Bastards', and treated with contempt by many of the nobility as well as by journalists. In 1832 a book called *The Great Illegitimates* offered the public a spicy account of their origins. Princess Victoria's mother established a firm line early in their father's reign: 'I never did, neither will I now associate Victoria in any way with the illegitimate members of the Royal family. – With the King they die; did I not keep this line how would it be possible to teach Victoria the difference between Vice and Virtue?'[14] How indeed?

George FitzClarence arrived back from India in March 1818, having travelled through the deserts of Egypt, explored the pyramids and descended the Nile. He was promoted to brevet lieutenant-colonel; and at the same time he prepared an account of his travels, with his own drawings as illustrations, which he published as *Journal of a Route across India, through Egypt to England, in the latter end of the year 1817 and the beginning of 1818*. It does not have quite the immediacy of his journal of the Peninsular campaign, but was a considerable achievement for a young man trained to fight rather than to choose his words; and after this he went to work in the field of oriental studies. He collected a mass of material for a projected *History of the Art of War among Eastern Nations*; he worked with a scholarly secretary, and promoted the translation of oriental texts. He became a member of the Royal Society and other learned bodies, and helped found the Royal Asiatic Society, all suggesting an inclination for study. Had he been able to concentrate entirely on the quiet life of a scholar, he might have been a happier man than he was. Instead he was made miserable by a sense of grievance. It was not due to domestic unhappiness, for he married, shortly after his father, the sister of one of his army friends, the daughter of Lord Egremont, and they had a large family.

All the FitzClarence brothers were stirred into action when their father became king in 1830. While William was still at Bushy he seemed disposed to give George some official tasks – he was sent, for instance, to make the arrangements for the visit to London of the King of Würtemberg, husband of his approving aunt Charlotte; and he was clearly believed to have influence with his father, since the following year the editor of the *Morning Post* wrote to him asking him to intervene in the matter of Coleridge's pension.[15] George asked to carry the crown at the coronation: 'Who is more fit than your own *flesh and blood*?' It is even said that he asked his father to make him Prince of Wales; the King refused, saying that if he encouraged George's pretensions, he would lower himself in the estimation of the country and injure the interests of the monarchy.[16] More reasonably, all four sons petitioned their father together, complaining of 'the cruel position in which we are placed as natural children . . . in the eyes of the Law we are at present nameless and devoid of many rights and advantages of our Fellow Subjects'.[17] They were asking for titles and pensions; they were also surely expressing their rage against the system that had destroyed their mother and set them in limbo. The King was angry. George foolishly threatened suicide, and Frederick more effectively proposed to stand for Parliament. After several months of wrangling, in which they all left their father's house and resigned their appointments, the King gave way and conferred on George two of his own subsidiary titles, Earl of Munster and Baron Tewkesbury; the rest of his children were granted the rank of children of a marquis – i.e., they could call themselves Lords and Ladies. The sons continued to ask for money. George was accused of meddling in politics where he had no right to, and of giving bad advice to the King over the Reform Bill.

Tuss, who had pleaded his way out of the navy faster than the others, and been sent to Oxford and Cambridge, was installed as Vicar of Mapledurham. He became an unusually devoted and enthusiastic clergyman, and built a village school, very probably inspired by the girls' school established at the Bushy gates in his mother's time; he provided uniforms and meals for the children, and was much loved by his parishioners. His other interest was the theatre. When not at Mapledurham he spent a good deal of time standing in the wings at Covent Garden and Drury Lane, sometimes waving his gloves about in sympathetic dumb show when, for instance, Fanny Kemble played Juliet; later he danced with her at a ball, where he spoke of his father, uttering 'an expression of his filial disrespect for the highest personage in the realm, of such a robust significance as fairly took away my breath', she noted.[18]

Lolly served in the navy for thirty-nine years, but when he had his portrait painted, it was not as a naval officer but as a Byronic corsair, resplendent in plumed and jewelled hat, with pistol, cutlass, striped collar and buckled belt: a very handsome young man in fancy dress, with black flashing eyes and curly hair like his mother's. He was another devoted theatre-goer, and was said to 'cling to the minutest recollection of his gifted mother'.[19] He went out of his way to assist Madame Vestris when she set up as manager of the Olympic Theatre, getting the King to allow her stage designers to study the rooms at Hampton Court; and he was also involved in the founding of the Garrick Club, intended as a meeting place where those two distinct groups, gentlemen and theatrical people, might be able to meet.

Frederick remained in the army all his life, without ever

seeing active service. He married a daughter of the Earl of Glasgow, and was generally liked for his 'frank and generous disposition'.[20] It was to him that Queen Adelaide gave the hundreds of letters written by his mother that she found at Bushy after the death of his father. In 1852 Frederick was sent to India to command the forces in Bombay, and there he died within two years. The letters were presumably left in England, which helps to explain how they became scattered; his only daughter did not marry.[21] Lolly remained a bachelor, and preserved all his mother's letters most carefully. Tuss, at the age of forty, married the sixteen-year-old Lady Sarah Gordon and took her to Mapledurham. He named their first child Dorothea after his mother, fathered several more, then died suddenly of blood poisoning in 1854, greatly mourned in the village.[22]

And George, the infant Hercules, darling of both his parents? He embittered his father's life and his own by quarrels and demands that were never satisfied, and could not be satisfied: what he was asking for was a replay of his life, with different circumstances. I believe George kept alive a hope that somehow he would after all find himself on the throne of Great Britain: he so clearly had the physique, the intelligence, the courage, the will; he was the right sex, *and he was the son of the King*. When he saw his cousin, little Princess Victoria, ascend in his place, he may have told himself that she could easily go the way of his other cousin, Princess Charlotte. There was another cousin now, young George Cambridge, but who could tell what might yet happen? George had sons of his own; but Princess Victoria married; she had a daughter; then, in November 1841 she gave birth to a son, Edward, the first male heir born to a reigning monarch in living memory. In December he was created Prince of Wales, amid national rejoicing. George Munster was abroad, settling his two elder sons in a military college. In late November he had written from Paris to the Prime Minister, Sir Robert Peel, asking if he might be found public employment of some kind in Europe, in order to earn money for his sons, who could expect almost nothing. The letter referred to 'my *very* peculiar Position', said the Queen was fully aware of it and had 'expressed herself, with relation to its improvement, in the most gracious and feeling manner, through Lord Melbourne'; and it went on to say Peel should simply refuse his request if it caused him the least embarrassment, and that George would call on him on his return to London.[23]

Evidently Peel did nothing for him. George returned to London and, four months later, on 20 March 1842, as he sat alone in his library late on a Sunday night, he killed himself. The footman told the inquest that he heard a shot, went to see what had happened, and found his master with his right hand blown to bits; Lord Munster said he had had an accident, and as the footman went for help there was a second shot. This time George put the gun in his mouth, with his left hand, and blew out his brains. The gun was one given him by his uncle, George IV.[24] Two days later Peel wrote to Adolphus, expressing his regret, explaining that 'The Queen has this day put into my hands a Letter connected with that sad Event – which I believe was delivered by you at the Palace for Her Majesty' and adding, 'I will communicate personally with you upon the subject of it.'[25]*

Lord Melbourne told the Queen that George had always been 'an unhappy and discontented man, and there is something in that unfortunate condition of illegitimacy which seems to distort the mind and feelings and render them incapable of justice and contentment'.[27] On the face of it, he was right. The jury returned a verdict that the 'deceased destroyed himself by his own hands whilst labouring under temporary mental derangement'. The funeral left his house in Belgrave Square at eight o'clock in the morning, followed by

* On 23 March, Charles Greville wrote of George's death, 'The horror of the deed excited a momentary interest, but he will soon be forgotten.'[26]

carriages bearing kind Queen Adelaide and members of George's family. It proceeded through Knightsbridge, through Fulham, through Wimbledon and Kingston; and at last, at eleven thirty, it arrived at the parish church at Hampton, where George had attended with his father and mother and all his brothers, sisters and half-sisters on Sunday mornings, riding or driving across Bushy park to get there. He was laid beneath the nave of the church, in a vault under a plain slab; whether he chose his burial place himself or left it to his family, it seemed the right spot.[28]

When his closest sister, Sophy, had died in childbirth early in 1837, George wrote to his father, using a striking phrase: 'Death has already commenced his havoc amongst us.'[29] He was a man who thought about death, and also thought much of his family. Some time in the 1820s he had himself painted by George Hayter with all his brothers and sisters, gathered together in a room in Bushy. He called it 'the great family picture', and it is very curious.[30] They form a group around a bust of their father, set on a high plinth above them in the middle; on the wall, still higher, but far away to one side, is the Romney portrait of their mother (inexplicably reversed); and behind the bust is another painting, showing a boy with his dogs: it is plainly Henry, who could not be missed out. When George asked his father for titles, land and money, it was not so much simple acquisitiveness as compensation, a desire to fix something that eluded him, that he felt was denied him – a solidity, a sense of belonging.

In the aftermath of his death, his sister Mary went to Saint-Cloud to visit their mother's grave; it is tempting to think George had made the same pilgrimage while he was in Paris. The FitzClarences remained close to one another; George's two elder sons both married first cousins, one Ta's daughter Wilhelmina, the other Sophy's daughter Adelaide. But they were not a long-lived family. Frederick died in India in the same year as Tuss at Mapledurham; Lolly and Eliza – Lord Adolphus and the Countess of Errol – two years later, in

1856. The only ones to reach sixty, Mary and Augusta, followed them in 1864 and 1865: the last relics of an age and a scandal no one then wished to remember.[31] When *The Life and Times of William IV* was published in two volumes in 1884, Dora Jordan's name had disappeared, her twenty-year presence and ten children reduced to half a sentence: the King had 'formed a connection with a well-known actress . . . there is no need to do more than to chronicle the fact, as the subject is a distasteful one'.[32]

22

The Statue's Story: 1830–1980

This is not quite the end of the story. Chantrey's statue of Mrs Jordan, commissioned by King William and intended for Westminster Abbey, was still in the artist's studio, unclaimed by either the royal family or Dora's children, at the artist's death in 1841. Then at last a home was found for it, rather more modest than had been intended, but at least a welcoming one. The Revd Lord Augustus FitzClarence – Tuss – had his mother's statue crated and carried – probably by boat – to his parish of Mapledurham, and placed in his church there. St Margaret's is a tiny building, divided into two sections, one Roman Catholic and one Anglican, so there was not much space for a life-size monument. We do not know whether he attempted to explain its presence to his flock. If an inscription had ever been cut, it was removed, leaving it without a name – it has none now – and perhaps the parishioners took it for a representation of Mary with St John and the infant Jesus on her lap. There it stood, and there or thereabouts it seems to have remained for another sixty years, many decades after Tuss himself had gone to his rest in the churchyard outside, and his widow and children had departed to Ireland.[1]

Whether it stayed in the church, or more likely was removed into a shed or outbuilding, nobody claimed the statue or took any interest in it.[2] Dora's story was not wholly forgotten, but the virtues she embodied – independence of spirit, devotion to her profession – were troubling to the Victorian age, and her private behaviour still more so. Her frankness looked like flagrance, defying a society dedicated to moral improvement, or at any rate moral cosmetics; where Mrs Fitzherbert and the Whig ladies had at least allowed their men to get off unscathed and paid their tribute to public morality by concealing the existence of any inconvenient children, Dora was remembered for parading her pregnancies on the stage, carrying her babies round London with her and showing pride in these many inconvenient sons and daughters. The Chantrey statue revived this flagrance, which was perhaps the main reason for its rejection.

It remained unclaimed until the early years of the twentieth century. Then the fourth Earl, Aubrey – Dora's great-grandson – a quiet bachelor with a court appointment who succeeded to the title in 1902, discovered where it was, sent for it and had it installed in his London house; and again nothing was heard of it until the 1950s, when it appeared in another private house, or rather on the veranda of the fifth Earl's country place, Sandhills, in Surrey.[3]

Yet although it was lost to the public for which it was intended by the penitent King, there was another way in which it could, in theory at any rate, be seen. The statue had a twin sister in the plaster cast prepared by Chantrey as a preliminary to sculpting the marble. He preserved all his casts in his studio, to show to visitors; and after his death his widow decided to present them to the newly founded Ashmolean Museum in Oxford. Here they were set up in a gallery in 1843; and the Keeper, Joseph Fisher, recorded them in 1847 in a small book of etchings, one of which shows Mrs Jordan and her children.[4] As the years went by, however, and Chantrey fell out of fashion, the casts were demoted, first to a 'sunk court' and then to a storeroom in the basement. Successive curators grew less and less interested in conserving them; one even noted, with evident satisfaction, that the whole collection was deteriorating. So it continued for nearly a century. No one wanted to see them, it seemed, and very few people knew of their existence.

The outbreak of the Second World War gave an especially zealous curator the chance to provide a solution to the 'problem'. Claiming that the basements of the Ashmolean might be needed as air-raid shelters, he made this the excuse for smashing up the whole collection. A grisly scene followed, in which the casts were broken, one after another, like so many aristocrats of the *ancien régime* meeting their fate. The parallel became even closer when the curator, struck with a sudden doubt, ordered that a few of the casts should after all have their heads sawn off and preserved. Dora Jordan was one of those selected for the process; and this is why the Ashmolean possesses a plaster cast of her severed head.[5]

Happily, the marble twin survived in one piece. Tastes changed; the fifth Earl was proud enough of her to think she should be seen. So she made her first public appearance, more than a hundred and twenty years after she was sculpted, in 1956. At this time not a single likeness of her was on public display anywhere in the country; but now at least the statue was shown at the Royal Academy in an exhibition of British Portraits. Afterwards the fifth Earl had a garden house or temple specially built for her at Sandhills, an architectural echo of the Duke's temple to Nelson at Bushy. She was protected by a green blind in winter and open to the birds in summer; one art historian who went to see the statue there found the surface marked and rather rough, and she needed cleaning before her second public showing, again at the Royal Academy, in the Neo-classical exhibition of 1972.[6]

Three years later the fifth Earl of Munster died.[7] He was childless, and had decided to bequeath the statue to the Queen, perhaps with the idea that this would be the best way of ensuring its safety and good preservation. Her Majesty was pleased to accept the bequest, and in May 1980 Mrs Jordan was brought to Buckingham Palace and given a royal welcome. There she now sits in splendour, with two of her sons, among the tall portraits of the kings and queens: Queen Charlotte, King George III, King George IV, King William

IV, Queen Adelaide, Queen Victoria and her consort, Prince Albert. Two exquisite chairs made for the Prince Regent, in pink silk and gilt, and with snakes wound about their legs, stand beside her in the corner of the Picture Gallery; above her is a wall hanging showing the Annunciation, and on a staircase not far away hangs Hoppner's allegorical portrait of her as the Comic Muse fleeing from the satyr.

As an actress, Dora Jordan knew all there was to know about reversals of fortune and transformations of appearance and personality. She might have seen the story of her own statue as a comic drama in its own right, starting from the King's sentimental but noble *arrière-pensée*, in which he at last made exactly the right gesture by offering her back to the nation that had loved her work. She would have smiled at the power of the church and the establishment to kill the gesture, shrugged, and said it was only to be expected. She would have understood and forgiven poor George for being embarrassed by her statue and not wanting anything to do with it; and she would have blessed dear Tuss, who was able to show his love and give her a home. After that, the sheer awkwardness of there being no appropriate place for her in the whole of Victorian England, and her statue's total disappearance for many decades, provided a long interval in the comedy. The sub-plot of the twin or double, deteriorating and then decapitated, contributed a few scenes of black farce; and the Surrey garden temple added a fine touch of the pastoral-historical-elegiacal. The fifth Earl was Dora's direct descendant; he had grown up in South Africa, come to England as a young man, married a wealthy wife and become Lord Lieutenant of Surrey and a pillar of the establishment. His decision to introduce the statue of his great-great-grandmother and great-grandfather to the legitimate royal line was the climax or apotheosis of her long history. Mrs Jordan came to rest at last in the heart of the very building into which the living Dora was never, and never could have been, invited to set foot. The smile on the face of the statue appears at last entirely appropriate.

This drawing by Henry Edridge, signed and dated 1808, shows Henry FitzClarence at the age of eleven, wearing his brand-new midshipman's uniform. It is the only known portrait of him, and must have been commissioned by his parents shortly before he went to sea. (Drawing in private possession.)

Afterword

Little has been known of the family of Mrs Jordan's mother, Grace Phillips, beyond the fact that she was connected with Trelethyn in Wales, was the daughter of a clergyman, and one of three sisters. The researches of local historians Peter Davies and David James have revealed a good deal more. They have studied wills, baptismal registers and the archives held in the National Library in Aberystwyth, the Haverfordwest Record Office, the Cathedral Library of St David's and the Reference Library at Haverfordwest, from which all the following information is derived.

Trelethyn is a Pembrokeshire hamlet (known today as Treleddyn) close to St David's and not far from Haverfordwest. Grace Phillips was the youngest of the three sisters, born in 1736 and baptized at Haverfordwest, her two elder sisters being Anne, born 1734, and Margaret (who used the name Mary or Maria later and especially in her stage career), born in 1735. Their father was the Revd George Phillips, rector of St Thomas's, Haverfordwest, from 1735 to 1743, their mother Margaret, about whom nothing is known. George Phillips died in 1743, leaving his three daughters aged seven, eight and nine.

The little girls had an older cousin Blanch, who took an interest in them. She was the daughter of their father's elder brother, Thomas Phillips of Trelethyn, and she too had lost her father early; he died in 1728, when Blanch was only eight. In 1758 (aged thirty-eight) she married a local gentleman, Thomas Williams, and in 1760 she inherited money and property from her elder sister Mary. Blanch had no children of her own. She seems to have been a strong-minded and generous woman, establishing something of a matriarchal pattern in the family. Both Blanch and her cousin Grace lost their fathers early; then when Grace and her children were abandoned by their father (Francis Bland) Blanch gave support to the family. It was at her home that Grace's invalid daughter Lucy Bland died, aged fourteen, in 1778. Dora's recollections of her childhood days in Wales also presumably relate to periods spent with Aunt Blanch. And when Blanch died in 1788, she left her property at Trelethyn to two of Grace's children, Dora's brother Nathaniel Bland and her sister Hester ('Ester') Bland. (Grace herself died a year later.)

Nathaniel Phillips Bland was an Oxford graduate. He settled at Trelethyn and married in 1812 Phebe James, daughter of a prosperous local family. When Dora sent her three eldest daughters to Wales from 1803 to 1804, it seems likely it was to be near Nathaniel and Phebe, who were childless; they are said to have lived in Cloister Hall in the Close in St David's. Certainly when Fanny was proving difficult in 1814 Dora wrote of sending her 'to her uncle in Wales'. Nathaniel, highly respected in the community, died in 1830. Hester Bland, who settled near him in due course, also died there in 1848. Another brother, Francis Bland, is also said to have lived for some time in the Chancellor's House in the Close.

Blanch Williams and Lucy Bland are buried in the same grave. The inscriptions read as follows:

In memory of Lucy Bland of Trelethin, who departed this life the 4th of May, 1778, in the 14th year of her age. Not lost but gone before.

For here I am free from sickness, free from pain,
But with my God in endless pleasure reign.

> This life is past, therefore rejoice
> That I am now in Paradise.
>
> My soul with Angels sweetly sings;
> 'Hosanna to the King of Kings.'

and

> In memory of Blanch Scudamor, the Wife of Thos. Williams of Trelethin, Esq. who departed this life on the 6th day of January, 1788, aged 68 years.

Nathaniel Bland's gravestone reads:

> In memory of Nathaniel Philips Bland, of Trelethin, in this parish, Esq. who departed this life May 31st, 1830, in the 63rd year of his age. He was a man, possessed of rare endowments of mind, dignified manners, inflexible integrity, unfeigned benevolence, with every social and amiable virtue. Having lived respected and beloved he died sincerely lamented by all who knew him. 'Manet post funera virtus'.

With the additions, 'Also of Hester Bland of Trelethin his sister, who died March 4th, 1848, aged 88' and 'Also of Phoebe, his widow, who died June 23rd, 1852, aged 77'.

Local legend has it that the Duke of Clarence stayed at the Castle Hotel in Haverfordwest, but there is no documentation for this. It is also said that Mrs Jordan visited Trelethyn from time to time during the years of her fame, which seems perfectly possible, although not recorded in any currently known letters of hers. A Major Harries of Travaccoon is supposed to have sent his carriage for her personal use when she did.

'Treleddyn' is the modern spelling for what was known variously as 'Trelethyn' (as I give it), 'Treleddin', 'Trefflethin' and 'Treffleddin'. It is close to the sea, with St David's Head to the north-west, and consists of two houses, Upper Treleddyn, the solid Georgian farmhouse associated by tradition with Mrs Jordan, and Lower Treleddyn, also a farm.

The house at Upper Trelethyn, where Dora Jordan and her brothers and sisters sometimes stayed as children. It passed to her brother Nathaniel and sister Hester. (Photograph courtesy of Peter Davies.)

Although Dora Jordan herself never contradicted Tate Wilkinson's account of how he suggested her stage name (p. 27), it may also have had a Welsh family origin. In her mother Grace's native Pembrokeshire there were many Jordans, and among them several Dorotheas, Dorothys or Doras scattered through the sixteenth, seventeenth and eighteenth centuries. One Dorothy Jordan married in 1642; another died unmarried in 1714. Yet another was born about 1775, her mother being a Phillips; she married a Joseph Clare of Haverfordwest and lived until 1858. It is possible that Grace and Maria Phillips's mother was born a Jordan, or connected with the Jordans, and that the name suggested itself for that reason.

THE FITZCLARENCE-DANIELL LETTERS

After the original publication of this book, I was kindly offered the chance of examining a collection of about 150 letters written by the FitzClarence children, or connected with them, between 1813 and 1854. The letters were addressed to their one-time tutor, James William Daniell (1773–c. 1855). As well as tutoring the boys, Mr Daniell served as librarian to their father and later as his steward at Bushy at least until 1826. Daniell preserved his letters from the FitzClarences carefully and they have been handed down through the family to his great-great-great-niece, Diana Daniell, who showed them to me.

They include George's instructions to his old tutor about preparing the Upper Lodge at Bushy for himself and his bride on returning from their wedding tour in 1820, and letters from Frederick, Eliza, Adolphus, Augusta and Amelia, some giving family news of deaths – Amelia wrote of that of Sophia – and marriages, Augusta announcing her own first wedding; but the bulk of them are from Augustus, the youngest son.

As a clergyman, Tus had the pleasant privilege of conducting his former tutor's wedding ceremony in December 1829. The Daniells lived in London, and most of Tus's letters were written from his vicarage at Mapledurham, although, as the years went by and he acquired a family of his own, some came from seaside lodgings at Weston-super-Mare, Torquay and Broadstairs. He gave family news, complained of a chronic shortage of money and asked Mr Daniell to perform small chores for him. In 1835, while his father was on the throne, he wrote from 85 Eaton Square, saying that most of his brothers and sisters were in Brighton, but George was in Paris and 'great friends with Louis Philip' (sic). But after the death of King William things changed. There is no mention of George's suicide in 1841. In 1844 he described a visit to Windsor and expressed annoyance at having to write down his name before being allowed entrance. He visited the room where his father died and observed that the Queen was 'in the family way'.

He announced his own marriage in Kensington Church the following January (1845) and thereafter the births of his children. His eldest daughter, Dora, became a source of great pride; at the age of thirteen her achievements in reading the Bible and doing arithmetic were far beyond his at the same age, he reported. He saw this as evidence of the '*March of intellect*', like a true Victorian. His politics were proclaimed in a letter of March 1847 when he wrote, 'Where is the promise of the poor man's better days? Not in this world – you may depend upon it: we give them a pull at the whistle every 100 years & make them pay well for it.' In the same year he adorned a letter with a disrespectful sketch of Queen Victoria.

Money was always a problem. He took to selling off possessions, among them his fine dinner services and, in 1847, dismantling his conservatory. Describing this, he wrote, 'The *figure* is removed – and the Conservatory will soon be down' – perhaps a reference to the Chantrey statue, and if so a tantalizing one which offers no clue as to where he put it next. The following year, when Frederick was offered a highly paid place in India, he in turn offered Augustus £1,800 a year to go with him as his secretary, but Augustus, in spite of his difficulties, refused it unhesitatingly. He preferred to stay at Mapledurham with his young family, choosing England on a lower income rather than India on a higher one: 'this dear old country with a few *hundreds* – bright days – cool nights and a good pump of clear water – and I will never give her up'. It is perhaps worth noting that, despite his money problems and constant talk of retrenchment, the 1851 census records eleven servants at Mapledurham vicarage.

Also in 1851 Augustus mentioned a visit from his half-sister Lucy, Lady Hawker, now a widow: no doubt they had much to recall together about Bushy and their mother. In the same year, on 11 October, Frederick wrote to Daniell to say he was going to Madeira for his daughter's health (she died young of tuberculosis) and asked him to 'write to Tus, & say I take

Dora Jordan, 'so pleasant, so cordial, so natural, so full of spirits, so healthily constituted in mind and body, had such a shapely leg withal . . . and such a happy and happy-making expression of countenance' – Leigh Hunt's words are borne out by William Beechey's portrait of Dora as Rosalind in her delightful yellow knee breeches. She first played the part in April 1787, when Beechey was building his career as a fashionable, and no doubt flattering, portraitist, and the picture probably dates from the late eighties. 'The Rosalind of both art and nature; each supplies its treasures in her performance of the character, and renders it a perfect exhibition,' wrote her fellow actress, Elizabeth Inchbald. She continued to play the part for twenty-seven years; in 1813 an American artist, seeing her for the first time, commented, 'Her performance of Rosalind was, in my mind, perfect.' This painting was used by Chantrey when working on his statue of her, according to Lord Melbourne, who told Queen Victoria that it was 'done after the picture Beechey did of her when she was quite young and thin'.

(*above*) The Theatre Royal, Drury Lane, as Dora Jordan first saw it. It held 2,000, and drew its audience from all social classes; no other theatre was so big, so splendid, so conscious of a long and great tradition.

(*above*) The Revd Matthew Peters, painter and chaplain to the Prince of Wales, specialized in Shakespearean scenes, and this portrait shows Dora on stage in 'Elizabethan' costume, perhaps as Beatrice in *Much Ado*, or as Mrs Ford in *The Merry Wives*, or even Ophelia: 'Nell of Clarence plays Ophelia tonight at Richmond,' wrote Horace Walpole in August 1795.

(*below, opposite*) While Drury Lane was rebuilt in the 1790s, Sheridan's company moved to the King's Theatre in the Haymarket. It was from this stage that Dora faced a hostile audience in December 1791, booing and hissing her for her association with the Duke of Clarence, and won them over by her courage and good humour. 'Nothing in the play that night was quite so good as that moment,' wrote James Boaden, who was present.

John Russell's pastel of Richard Brinsley Sheridan dates from 1788, showing
him much as he was when he became Dora Jordan's employer at Drury Lane in
1785. Their lives ran strikingly parallel outside the theatre as well as in: he was
ten years older than her, but they died in the same week, having worked together
for a quarter of a century. Both came from Irish backgrounds, both were scarred
by the humiliations of their early years, both put aside their griefs and relied on
their skills, charm and toughness to make the world do their bidding. Befriended
by Charles James Fox and the Prince of Wales, Sheridan rose with unprecedented
speed and grace through the layers of English society; he was acclaimed for his
plays in the 1770s, appointed by Garrick to succeed him at Drury Lane in 1780
and found a seat in Parliament in the same year. His tragedy was that, unlike
Dora, he felt ashamed of the theatre and put his best energies into politics and the
social round of the Whig aristocrats, fatally neglecting Drury Lane and his genius
as a playwright.

Another John Russell pastel, of Mrs Jordan, dated 1792, is one of the most attractive of all the portraits of her. She looks gentle and serene, partly perhaps because she is pregnant, although the pregnancy ended in a miscarriage in August 1792. By framing her face in pale powdered hair and a high-necked white bertha, Russell focuses on her dark eyes and bright cheeks and mouth; the long nose and chin are recognizable, but softened. This is the face, you feel, that her children knew best.

(*above*) Romney's painting of Dora as 'The Country Girl' was begun in November 1786. 'Jordan-mania' made her much in demand as a sitter, and he made at least three copies, selling one to the Duke of Clarence in 1791 for seventy guineas.

(*above, opposite*) Bushy House, standing in its own vast park next to Hampton Court. In this idyllic setting Dora and the Duke settled in 1797 and brought up their large extended family; seven of their children were born here, while she continued her career in London and the provinces, and he remained unemployed.

(*below, opposite*) 'The great family picture by Hayter', a group portrait of the FitzClarences, children of Dora and the Duke, was painted at Windsor after the Duke became King in 1830. His bust stands in the middle; Henry, the only one to die young, appears in a portrait on the wall, and the Romney represents their lost mother. It went to Augustus on the death of the King.

This Beechey portrait of Dora wearing a white Empire dress with a golden stole is of particular interest because it shows her in nontheatrical costume, quietly dignified, standing against a background representing her country estate. The effect is to assimilate her image to portraits of aristocratic – or even royal – ladies. As in his earlier portrait, he gives her hair a reddish tinge. This picture was in the family of the Earls of Munster, descendants of her eldest son George, until 1984, and is now owned by the De L'Isle family, into which her daughter Sophia married.

all the papers to sort when at Madeira, except one box with my mother's letters to my Father which Adolphus has sealed with my seal and his'. An added note reads, 'Should anything happen to me, I wish Tus to have my rights in them and that anything disparaging be in them about my Father (which there is) I wish them to be burnt.' This was presumably done; but the fate of the letters after the deaths of Augustus and Frederick in 1854, and Adolphus two years later, remains obscure until they reached the sale rooms early in the next century.

Mr Daniell received a final letter from Mapledurham in 1854, announcing the death of Lord Augustus. Later in the year Frederick also died in India, and his widow sent him a lock of his 'dear hair'. The very last letter seems to be from the youngest FitzClarence daughter, Amelia, Viscountess Falkland: she wrote asking if he could trace the record of her baptism, wanted by her husband's lawyer. No record of it had been found at either Teddington or Hampton, and it appears that Mr Daniell was unable to help the anxious Viscountess, doubly stigmatized by illegitimacy and no evidence of baptism. Probably she had been baptized privately at Bushy in 1807, and no proper record made.

James Daniell was clearly held in affection by the FitzClarence children, even though George took a rather high-handed tone with him. I have noted that there are no references to George's suicide, either because it was too upsetting to mention, or because the letters were destroyed later. Henry's death is not mentioned either, but I have seen a letter from Henry to Daniell in the De L'Isle Archive written from Portsmouth just before his embarkation for India in January 1815: perhaps Daniell gave it to Sophia as a memento of her brother. Another link with the Bushy days appears in a letter from Jane Lloyd, daughter of the Duke's chaplain, the Revd Thomas Lloyd, who was good friend to Mrs Jordan from the early 1790s on. Jane wrote to Daniell from Richmond Park, where she was with Lord and Lady Errol (formerly

Eliza FitzClarence); this letter does not give the year but has an 1834 watermark, so evidently the family connection remained for several decades.

The earliest letter of all is from Colonel Butler at the Royal Military College, dated 30 June 1813, asking for news by return of the Duke's health, of which he has read bad accounts in the newspapers: Frederick was his pupil at the time. Daniell was at Bushy then with the girls but no boys, for in the summer of 1813 George and Henry were fighting in the Peninsular War, Adolphus had started his naval career, and Augustus was away at school. Mrs Jordan had left Bushy eighteen months earlier and was based in Cadogan Street. She had just given a benefit with Mrs Siddons at Drury Lane which raised £983 for their Theatrical Fund. The Duke was in dire financial difficulties, threatening to close Bushy and move his family to St James's.

Although Daniell could not help with baptismal certificates, he kept two copies of the Duke's list of the place and date of birth of each of the ten children Mrs Jordan bore to him. And finally, there is some correspondence in the 1840s in which Daniell asked both Frederick and Adolphus to assist his nephew, who was seeking a clerkship at the Home Office. Both seem to have done what they could, but without success; evidently their power of patronage was very limited.

The place held by their tutor in the hearts of the FitzClarence children – girls as well as boys – is clearly demonstrated in these letters. It suggests he was a stable figure for them in what was otherwise a bumpy and unpredictable world.

In 1996 Captain Hugh Owen RN published his research into the Duke of Clarence's son William in *The Mariner's Mirror*. He found from the muster book of the *Blenheim* that his full name was William Henry Courtney and that he was sent to sea in July 1803. The identity of his mother remains unknown, and the pitiful pay due to him after his drowning was returned to the Crown because he was intestate and 'a Bastard'.

An ambrotype of a watercolour miniature showing Mrs Jordan's daughter Lucy, Lady Hawker. The resemblance to her father, Richard Ford, is striking, but the spectacles – an unusual feature in a portrait of a woman – suggest she inherited her mother's short sight. It seems likely from her mourning clothes that the original was painted some time after 1838, when her husband, General Sir Samuel Hawker, died. She was then fifty. Lucy was much loved by her half-brothers and sisters, and family bonds remained close despite the behaviour of the Duke of Clarence and tragic death of their mother. According to family records the Duke stood as godfather to her son Henry, who was born in the year of Mrs Jordan's death. The boy followed family tradition by starting his naval career at the age of twelve under Lord Adolphus FitzClarence, who gave him daily lessons and 'was quite a father to him'.

Lucy's portrait, the only one known to exist, came to light recently among the family papers of a direct descendant, Mr Claude Swain.

Sketched on the spot by J. BENNETT, Comedian. May 4th 1824.

INSCRIPTION
on the Tomb of Mrs. Jordan
at St. Cloud

M. S

DOROTHEÆ JORDAN,

QUÆ PER MULTOS ANNOS
LONDINI INQUE ALIIS
BRITANNIÆ URBIBUS
SCENAM EGREGIE ORNAVIT,
LEPORE COMICO,
VOCIS SUAVITATE,
PUELLARUM HILARIUM
ALTERIUS QUE SEXUS
MORIBUS HABITU IMITANDIS
NULLI SECUNDA;
AD EXERCENDAM EAM
QUA TAM FELICITER
VERSATA EST ARTEM,
UT RES EGENORUM
ADVERSAS SUBLEVARET
NEMO PROMPTIOR;
EVITA EXIIT
3TIO NONAS JULIE 1816,
ANNOS NATA. 50.
MEMENTOTE!
LUGETE!

Burke Sculpt

Note that both her age and the date of her death are given wrongly. This
inscription is now illegible and is covered by a bronze plaque (see p. 383).

Appendix:
Mrs Jordan's Roles

Although various lists have been compiled of the parts played by Mrs Jordan, it would be hard, if not impossible, to produce a complete one. The theatre historian John Genest lists her first appearances in each role at Drury Lane, the Haymarket and Covent Garden; but during her early years in Ireland and Yorkshire she covered a wide repertoire and took many supporting roles. Among them are Lady Anne to Kemble's Duke of Gloucester in *Richard III* (in Dublin early in 1782), Emilia in *Othello* and Octavia in Dryden's *All for Love* with Tate Wilkinson's company; and there were of course many more. There are no complete records of these years or of her many later provincial tours that took her to all but the most remote parts of the country: Liverpool, Dublin, Edinburgh, Newcastle, Bristol, Bath, Cheltenham, Birmingham, Coventry, Canterbury, Margate, Carlisle, Hull, York, Leeds, Manchester, Portsmouth, Salisbury, etc.

The three roles in which she was most admired were, first, Rosalind in *As You Like It*, which she played in London from 1787 to 1814 – a remarkable span of twenty-seven years. Second, Hippolita, the spirited Spanish heroine who appears dressed as an army officer throughout all five acts of Colley Cibber's comedy of 1702, *She Would and She Would Not*. Hippolita is the pivot and controller of the plot, winning her lover by a series of tricks, among them a wedding ceremony with the heiress he is supposed to marry. Her maid is also disguised as a boy, leading to the exchange,

Is this gentleman your friend, sir?
This friend, madam, is my gentlewoman.
Gentlewoman! What, are we all going into breeches, then?

When Genest was introduced to her in 1814 and complimented her on her playing of Hippolita, she answered him, 'Aye, that was one of the parts on which I used to pique myself.'[1]

The third role with which she was always associated was that of the Country Girl in Garrick's mid-century adaptation of Wycherley's *Country Wife* (1675): Garrick cleaned up the jokes and watered down the humour in the process, but Mrs Jordan's performance as an innocent nineteen-year-old (her opening line is 'Pray, sister, where are the best fields and woods to walk in in London?') whose jealous guardian dresses her as a boy for a walk in St James's Park became and remained a hit. Jane Austen used the notion of the 'Country Girl' as a point of reference in a letter to her sister in 1799; Mrs Jordan played her for fifteen seasons at Drury Lane, from 1785 to 1800, and continued to play occasionally elsewhere up to 1814; even when she was too old and large to be convincing as a young girl, people still wanted to see her in the role.

After Rosalind, her most famous Shakespearean role was Viola in *Twelfth Night*, the first she played at Drury Lane (in 1785). Her Imogen in *Cymbeline* was not a success, but her Helena in *All's Well that Ends Well* was singled out for praise by Charles Lamb. She played Mrs Ford in *The Merry Wives of Windsor* by royal request at Cheltenham in 1788. She was Ophelia in *Hamlet* during the 1790s, both at Richmond and in London; in a letter written after a performance to the Duke at the end of the decade she says she 'never got so much applause as last night – but the particular friend of Mr Kemble will not allow me any merit in Ophelia': the particular friend was almost certainly his sister, Mrs Siddons, who often played Gertrude in the same production.

Mrs Jordan played Juliet for a few performances in 1796. Her Beatrice in *Much Ado* was popular, and she was still playing the part in 1804, at Margate; she was also briefly Miranda in *The Tempest* in 1797. She seems never to have played Cleopatra, either Shakespeare's or Dryden's version. For its single performance she acted Flavia in *Vortigern*, the famous Shakespeare forgery, her part especially conceived by young Samuel Ireland to suit her, with boy's costume and a song.

From Shakespeare's contemporaries Beaumont and Fletcher she acted Bellario, the page's part in *Philaster* (1609) and Second Constantia in *The Chances* (adapted by Garrick); and the high-spirited Estifania in their *Rule a Wife and Have a Wife* (1624) was one of her standard roles. The Restoration dramatists gave her many of her best parts. She was Miss Prue in Congreve's *Love for Love*, and in five of Farquhar's plays: as Bizarre in *The Inconstant*, Sir Harry Wildair in *The Constant Couple*, Silvia in *The Recruiting Officer*, Mrs Sullen in *The Beaux' Stratagem* and Fidelia in *The Plain Dealer*. She was Corinna in Vanbrugh's *The Confederacy*, and Miss Hoyden in Sheridan's adaptation of Vanbrugh's *The Relapse* – another watered-down version. As Boaden wrote, complaining of the failure of contemporary writers to provide her with decent parts, 'Wycherley, and Congreve, and Cibber, had conceived something, perfectly in *nature*, which she appropriated to herself.' And he called Drury Lane 'this political and bankrupt theatre' for not providing her with a comedy as good as any of Congreve's.[2] Horace Walpole took a similar line when he contrasted the excellence of her performance with the poor material in which she so often had to work, in a letter written on 1 July 1789, from Strawberry Hill:

Nothing has happened within my beat, but the arrival of Mrs Jordan at the theatre at Richmond, which has raised its character exceedingly: our Jews and Gentiles throng it. I have not been there, for though I think her perfect in her walk, I cannot sit through a whole play ill performed to see her play however excellently in such wretched farces as *The Romp* in which I have seen her.[3]

In spite of Walpole's scorn, the operatic farce called *The Romp*, in which she played Priscilla Tomboy, was continuously popular with the general public; she played it in York for Wilkinson, and then at Drury Lane in her first season, at which she introduced her own business, boxing Watty Cockney right off the stage. It was based on Isaac Bickerstaffe's play *Love in the City* (1778). Bickerstaffe was a prolific writer of farces, who started his career as page to Lord Chesterfield during his Lord Lieutenantship of Ireland, and ended it like Oscar Wilde, fleeing to the continent from English intolerance of his homosexuality. *The Sultan* was another enormously popular farce of his, in which Mrs Jordan played Roxalana, an English girl who puts down the harem system single-handed by a combination of courage and outrageous cheek.

Garrick's farce *The Irish Widow* gave her a good part as Mrs Brady; according to Genest she had an Irish brogue when she started acting in York, which she lost, but no doubt recovered as needed: there were many 'Irish' farces. She was Helena in Aphra Behn's *The Rover*, again not in its original version, but reworked by John Kemble, and renamed *Love in Many Masks*. Another woman playwright, Susannah Centlivre, provided her with a triumphant role as Donna Violante in *The Wonder: A Woman Keeps a Secret* (1714); it seems to have been the last play in which she appeared, at Margate in 1815. Violante is the daughter of a Portuguese nobleman; she falls in love with Don Felix, whose sister takes refuge with her to escape a hateful marriage; and Violante risks losing Felix by keeping the other woman's secret even when her own reputation is at stake.

She played Miss Hardcastle in Goldsmith's *She Stoops to Conquer* and appeared in two of Henry Fielding's one-act farces: Lettice in *The Intriguing Chambermaid*, Lucy in *The Virgin Unmasked*. She was one of the great Nells in Charles Coffey's *The Devil to Pay*, written in 1731, half opera and half farce, and perennially popular. Among playwrights of her own generation, John O'Keefe's plays gave her roles early in her career: Cowslip in *The Agreeable Surprise*, Araminta in *The Young Quaker* (performed in Hull in 1783), Caroline Sandford in *Dead Alive*. O'Keefe also had a hand in *The Fugitive* in which she played Julia Wingrove in 1796, and the farce *She's Eloped* in which she played Arabel to Bannister's Plodden in 1798. She first appeared as Letitia Hardy in Hannah Cowley's *The Belle's Stratagem* four years after it was written, in Hull in 1784.

The only original role Sheridan gave her was Cora in *Pizarro* – and he detested her performance – but she played Lydia Languish in *The Rivals* and Lady Teazle in *The School for Scandal*: this was her last London appearance, on 1 June 1814, with Charles Mathews in the cast. Elizabeth Inchbald wrote the farce of *The Wedding Day* especially for her, and she also played Amanthis in Inchbald's *The Child of Nature*. She was in several of Thomas Holcroft's plays – Susan Pole in *Knave or Not?* in 1798, Sophia in *The Road to Ruin* in 1792, Susan in *Follies of a Day*, his adaptation of Beaumarchais's *Le Mariage de Figaro*, and Eliza in *Hear Both Sides* in 1803: the play was a flop, but the song sung by Mrs Jordan was a hit.

Singing was an important aspect of her skill and success, although her voice was untrained. She sang the Shakespearean songs, and many of the works in which she appeared were more like musicals or operettas than plays: James Cobb's *Strangers at Home* was her first original singing part at Drury Lane, in December 1785; she had already scored a hit as William in *Rosina, or Love in a Cottage*, as well as Rachel in *The Fair American*, an 'opera', and *Lionel and Clarissa*, a musical version of Bickerstaffe's *School for Fathers*, all given in Yorkshire in 1783; and her Matilda in *Richard Cœur de Lion* in 1786 depended more on singing than acting ability. *Pizarro* also contained several songs.

Other contemporary writers who wrote especially for her were 'Monk' Lewis in his Gothic entertainments: she was Angela in his *The Castle Spectre* and Innogen in his *Adelmorn the Outlaw*. Kemble's three-act farce *The Pannel* gave her an often repeated success; it was an adaptation of Bickerstaffe's *'Tis Well It's No Worse* (1770), set in Spain, the plot depending on a movable panel behind which characters are concealed, and her part that of another strong-minded servant maid, Beatrice. Richard Cumberland gave her his sentimental play *First Love* in 1795, in which she played Sabina Rosny, an orphan of the French Revolution, and *The Last of the Family* in 1797; Andrew Cherry wrote *The Soldier's Daughter* for her in 1804, a patriotic play produced during the invasion scare, in which she played the young Widow Cheerly and spoke the epilogue, 'Should British women from the contest swerve? We'll form a female *army of reserve* – /And class them thus. Old maids are pioneers – /Widows, sharp-shooters – wives are fusileers; / Maids are battalion,' etc. Boaden describes this as one of her very good parts, 'attractive from vivacity, knowledge, and goodness' and acted with zeal and skill. (Cumberland tried to rival it with his *Sailor's Daughter*, with Dora as Louisa Davenant, but it failed.) Frederic Reynolds wrote the part of Albina Mandeville for her in his *The Will* in 1796, and of the fifteen-year-old Sir Edward Bloomly in *Cheap Living* in 1797.

Arthur Murphy's *The Way to Keep Him* (1760) gave her the role of the Widow Belmour, which she acted from her Yorkshire years until her Dublin visit of 1800; she was Lady Restless in his *All in the Wrong* (1761) in 1784, Maria in his *The Citizen* (1761) in 1798, and in 1801 Lady Racket in his *Three Weeks after Marriage* (1764).

There were a few more plays by women: Mary Robinson's ill-fated *Nobody*, which Dora championed bravely in 1794; Miss Cuthbertson's *Anna*, in whose text she may have had a hand herself, another failure early in 1793. *The School for Friends* by Miss Chambers (1805), in which she played the part of Mrs Hamilton, was more successful, running for twenty-five nights; Genest calls it 'on the whole a tolerable play'.

Other parts she played in Yorkshire include Zara in a translation of Voltaire's tragedy of that name; Fatima in Garrick's Arcadian romance *Cymon*; Rutland in Henry Jones's tragedy *The Earl of Essex* (1745); Calista in *The Fair Penitent* by Nicholas Rowe, adapted in 1703 from Massinger, and also Rowe's *Jane Shore* (1713); Lady Alton in Colman's *The English Merchant*; and Indiana in *The Conscious Lovers* by Steele (1721).

In London she was Augusta in *Better Late than Never* by the MP Miles Peter Andrews (1790); Little Pickle in *The Spoiled Child* in 1790; Mrs Sneak in the farce of *The Mayor of Garratt* in 1791; Clara – disguised as Lucio – in *The Female Duellist* in 1793; Cowslip in Colman's *The Agreeable Surprise*; Isabella Plinlimmon in Jerningham's *The Welch Heiress*, a farce, in 1795; in the same year 'Old Maid' in the farce of that name; Rosa in Morris's *The Secret* (1799); Julia in Colman's *Surrender of Calais*; Julia in *Indiscretion* by Prince Hoare in 1800; Biddy Tipkin in *The Tender Husband* in 1801; Miss Racket in *The Fashionable Friends*, with Kemble as Sir Dudley Dorimant, author unknown, a flop, in 1802; Emma Harvey in *The Marriage Promise* by John Allingham, with music by Michael Kelly (1803); Clara in *Matrimony*, a farce translated from the French in 1804; in the same year Rosetta in *The Foundling* (1748) by Edward Moore, and Grace Gaylove and Lady Bab Lardoon in two farces, *Review* and Burgoyne's *The Maid of the Oaks*; Mrs Beverley in *The Gamesters* and Mrs Doggerel in *The Register Office* and Lady Flutter in *Discovery*, all in 1805; Helen Worrett in *Man and Wife* by S.J. Arnold (1809); a part in another farce known as *The Parrot*; and so on.

The list, which grows tedious on the page, represents an amazing range. It also underlines the way in which her distinction lay in her double appeal: for the beauty of her verse-speaking and integrity of her performance she was applauded by such as Coleridge, Hazlitt, Lamb and Macready; for her humour, frankness and simplicity she drew the general, and largely uneducated, public. She was the least pretentious of beings, but she saw the role of the actress, and of the theatre, as a civilizing one; and having none of Sheridan's ambivalence, she pursued her art with passionate dedication.

Notes

1. George Jones, *Personal Recollections of Sir Francis Chantrey* (1849), pp. 118–19.
2. Chantrey's ledger is in the library of the Royal Academy.
3. Two preliminary studies for the statue survive in the Ashmolean Museum, Oxford. See Nicholas Penny's catalogue No. 456 and Appendix, p. 649 (Catalogue of European Sculptures in the Ashmolean Museum, vol. 3, 1992). According to Penny, the statue was not completed until 1834. The mask is usually associated with Thalia, Muse of Comedy, the pipes with Euterpe, Muse of Music and Lyric Poetry – both appropriate to Dora Jordan, who also wrote verse and sang.
4. Ireland's bust is in the Bodleian Library.
5. 'The Old Actors', *London Magazine* (October 1822) about Charles Mathews's collection of portraits (bequeathed to the Garrick), reprinted in E.V. Lucas (ed.), *The Letters of Charles Lamb*, vol. 2 (1935), pp. 294–5.
6. There is no record at Westminster Abbey of the King's request, but Chantrey's ledger note suggests it was made. Mary Hopkirk wrote in her book on Queen Adelaide (1956), that the King tried the Dean of St Paul's in 1833, and that he too turned down the statue (pp. 131–2); but she gives no source, and here again there is no confirmation from the chapter minutes of St Paul's. Thomas Campbell's statue of Sarah Siddons was put in the Abbey in 1845.
7. 25 July 1839, Lady T. Lewis (ed.), *Journals and Correspondence of Miss Berry*, vol. 3 (1865), pp. 463–4. Miss Berry met Chantrey

at Sir William Dundas's, and said Lord Munster had made some objection to another proposed site for the statue.

8. 28 December 1838, journal of Queen Victoria, RA, p. 122. Some of this is printed in Lord Esher, *The Girlhood of Queen Victoria*, vol. 1 (1912), p. 84.

9. Sir William Beechey (1753–1839) was appointed official portrait painter to Queen Charlotte in 1793; he naturally painted her and George III and their sons. Two portraits of Mrs Jordan are believed to be by him, one showing her seated, as Rosalind, in yellow knee breeches, the other a full length of her standing; neither is an obvious source for Chantrey, but the seated one is possible.

10. If there was an inscription, it has been removed. Another version of the alleged inscription is 'To Dora Bland, by one who loved her' (Lewis Melville, *More Stage Favourites of the Eighteenth Century*, 1929, p. 253).

11. Esher, 16 January 1839, *The Girlhood of Queen Victoria*, vol. 2, pp. 101–2, gives part of the conversation between Queen Victoria and Lord Melbourne, which I have supplemented from the RA copy of Queen Victoria's journal for 16 January 1839. On 16 January there was a further bit of conversation. '"She lived with Sir Richard Ford by whom she had a number of children before she lived with the King," said Lord M. It's with 2 of the children, and done after the picture Beechey did of her when she was quite young and thin, and not like what Lord M remembers her.'

12. ibid.

13. *Journals and Correspondence of Miss Berry*, vol. 3, pp. 463–4.

1 THE SINS OF THE FATHERS: 1761–1782

1. See Parson James Woodforde's diary (John Beresford, ed., 1924–31) between 1758 and 1797 for the many entries about his theatre-going, from the time he was an undergraduate and through his days as a clergyman. He managed to see a large repertoire of plays put on by strolling players in Somerset villages, by the troupe that played regularly in Norwich, and at Drury Lane and Covent Garden whenever he was in London.

2. George Faulkner's *Dublin Journal*, 30 October 1756.

3. See R. Hitchcock, *An Historical View of the Irish Stage*, vol. 1 (1788), p. 274. 'Several performers of merit were brought out, amongst whom were two sisters, Miss G. and Miss M. Phillips, young ladies of a good family, who for many years afterwards were well received in a variety of characters, both in tragedy and comedy.' See also pp. 279, 283, 307.

4. See *An Historical View of the Irish Stage*, vol. 2 (1794), p. 53: 'the two Miss Phillips's returned to England in autumn 1760'.

5. For Thomas Sheridan in Henrietta Street, see James Boswell's *London Journal 1762–3* (F.A. Pottle, ed., Penguin edition, 1950), p. 60, etc.

6. The Coronation shows were played as afterpieces to the main play of the evening. Garrick did not take much trouble with his, and is said to have used the costumes left over from the 1727 coronation show: see W. Macqueen-Pope, *Theatre Royal Drury Lane* (1945), p. 177.

7. The information about the arrival of the Princess comes mainly from Olwen Hedley's *Queen Charlotte* (1975).

8. A 'court drawing room' is a formal reception held by a member of the royal family at which ladies are 'presented' at court.

George Villiers, second Duke of Buckingham in the 1670s, wrote *The Rehearsal*, probably in collaboration with others; it was a satire on the heroic tragedies of his time, but remained very popular throughout the eighteenth century, and was often played with topical references. Garrick played Bayes, the author of the mock play.

9. *Queen Charlotte*, pp. 47, 65.

10. See J. Hemlow (ed.), *The Journals and Letters of Fanny Burney*, vol. 4 (1973), p. 79, where Madame D'Arblay reports her conversation with the Queen in February 1798.

11. Information from Pedigree of Family of Bland, compiled by J.F. Fuller (London, 1907), reprinted from *Miscellanea Genealogica et Heraldica*, and from Peter Davies and David W. James, both of St David's.

12. DJ to the Duke of Clarence, 30 January 1811, Arthur Aspinall (ed.), *Mrs Jordan and Her Family, being the Unpublished Letters of Mrs Jordan and the Duke of Clarence, later William IV* (1951), p. 183:

> an old Welsh acquaintance called on me the other evening of the name of Harris I had not the least recollection of him, till he reminded me of a Little Boy, that I whipped once very smartly for drownding a Mouse, I then remembered the circumstance very well and we both laughed very heartily, he appears a very gentlemanly young man and says he is not a little vain of having been whipped by Mrs Jordan – he was then about 5 years old and I ten.

13. *An Historical View of the Irish Stage*, vol. 2, p. 23.

14. The phrases are from DJ's poem of July 1789 on her mother's death.

15. See letter from DJ to James Boaden, 22 April 1809, in James Boaden, *The Life of Mrs Jordan*, vol. 2 (1831), p. 242.

16. DJ to the Duke of Clarence, 10 November 1810, *Mrs Jordan and Her Family*, p. 166.

17. See her letter to the Duke of Clarence from Dublin, 10 June 1809, in which she describes rehearsing and being 'addressed by a very *old man* who was standing at the *wing* . . . It was the very person that brought me on to the stage the first night I played. He reminded me of my running off the stage behind the scenes, and his following me, and bringing me forward by *main force*. He is not a little *proud of this*' (cited in Philip H. Highfill, *A Biographical Dictionary of Stage Personnel, London 1600–1800*, 1982, p. 256).

18. John Williams, writing as 'Anthony Pasquin', referred to her 'keen sable eye' in 1792. Her short sight is well attested, and the Hoppner portrait of her in the National Portrait Gallery shows her carrying a pair of spectacles.

19. Tate Wilkinson said 'she sported the best leg ever seen on the stage'.

20. Leigh Hunt, in Roger Ingpen (ed.), *Autobiography*, vol. 1 (1903), p. 150. Although Hunt did not see her until later in her career, this description catches something about her performance that seems to have been there from the first.

21. According to Clare Jerrold, *The Story of Dorothy Jordan* (1914), p. 42.

22. *The Life of Mrs Jordan*, vol. 1, p. 14. Boaden also says that Grace was advised by a fellow actor, Richard Owenson (father of the writer Lady Morgan), who must have made his own estimate of Dorothy's talents.

23. ibid., p. 11.

24. ibid., pp. 11–12.

25. ibid., p. 360.

26. See H. Baker, *John Philip Kemble* (1942).

27. See letter by Lady Carlow dated November 1781: 'I was quite charmed with Mrs Daly at the play. She acted Miss Hardy in *The Belle's Stratagem* and the opera singer in the *Son-in-Law*, which she did most admirably, notwithstanding her being ready to lye in.' Mrs Godfrey Clark, *Gleanings from an Old Portfolio*, vol. 1 (1895), p. 166.

28. All quotes in this section from Tate Wilkinson, *The Wandering Patentee; or a History of the Yorkshire Theatre from 1700*, vol. 2 (1795), pp. 132–40.

29. *The Life of Mrs Jordan*, vol. 1, p. 23.

30. Brian Fothergill, *Mrs Jordan: Portrait of an Actress* (1965), p. 52; this version comes from John Bernard's *Retrospections of the Stage* (1830).

2 THE YORKSHIRE CIRCUIT: 1782–1785

1. So Elizabeth Inchbald reported. See S. R. Littlewood, *Elizabeth Inchbald and Her Circle* (1921), p. 23.

2. Tate Wilkinson, *The Wandering Patentee; or a History of the Yorkshire Theatre from 1700*, vol. 4 (1795), p. 14.

3. This story is not in Wilkinson, who accuses Swan of behaving meanly to Dora by failing to leave her anything in his will; but it may well come from Dora herself, since it appears in the anonymous *Life* published in 1832 (see Bibliography), p. 9 of 1886 edition.

4. James Boaden, *The Life of Mrs Jordan*, vol. 1 (1831), p. 31.

5. ibid., p. 41: 'the quick study of Mrs Jordan could at any time supply her place at a day's notice'.

6. According to William Wilberforce, who grew up in Hull in the 1780s; quoted in Gordon Jackson, *Hull in the Eighteenth Century* (1972), p. 267.

7. *The Wandering Patentee*, vol. 2, p. 173. Wilkinson wrote that she set off from Sheffield on 2 November, 'but did not despatch her business to be ready to do mine until Thursday December 26'.

8. The registration of births was not compulsory at this date, and

if Fanny was baptized, no record exists in Hull. Later she went by the name 'Frances Jordan', then changed her name to 'Frances Bettesworth' in circumstances that remain obscure.

9. *The Life of Mrs Jordan*, vol. 1, p. 43.

10. Quoted in the anonymous *Life* (1886 edition), p. 112. No source given.

11. *The Life of Mrs Jordan*, vol. 1, p. 48.

12. When Mrs Robinson, a cast-off mistress of the Prince of Wales, sent Mrs Siddons some poems, she wrote to a friend that she *might* 'long for the possibility of being acquainted with her. I say, the possibility, because one's whole life is one continued sacrifice of inclinations, which, to indulge, however laudable or innocent, would draw down the malice and reproach of those prudent people who never do ill . . . The charming and beautiful Mrs Robinson! I pity her from the bottom of my soul!' Sarah Siddons to John Taylor, 5 August 1793, Lewis Melville, *More Stage Favourites of the Eighteenth Century* (1929), pp. 131–3.

3 DRURY LANE

1. The house is considerably changed but has kept many of its original features from the 1730s, when it was built (on the site of an earlier house). It is now a publishing office.

2. DJ to the Duke of Clarence, n.d., Huntington Library MS: 'I saw Fox this morning who came over to take a Box for tomorrow – he made several Ah—s when the scene came down and I never saw him afterwards, but I heard he had sat down in a pot of paint and damnd the Prompter and disappeared.'

3. See Dora's letter: 'I must be at the Theatre by 11 tomorrow to sign the Books by the order of the Lord Chancellor [a slip for Chamberlain] therefore I think I had better not go out of Town tonight.' RA Add. 40/86, n.d. but watermark 1801.

The company with which Shakespeare was most closely associated and for which he wrote most of his plays was known as the Chamberlain's Men; under James I they were appointed Grooms of the Chamber and renamed the King's Men, coming under direct patronage of the sovereign. This remained so until theatres were closed in 1642; and in 1660, with the restoration of Charles II, the Lord Chamberlain – a political appointee, and the highest court official – began to intervene directly in the regulation of theatres. The Lord Chamberlain's Warrant books for 6 October 1660 show that the leading actors were 'not only actors but sworn servants as well', some appointed Grooms of the Chamber, and entitled to wear livery of scarlet and crimson velvet. Mrs Jordan's contemporary, Robert Baddeley (1733–94), appears to be the last actor to have worn the livery; he was the first Moses in *The School for Scandal*.

4. This and quotes in the next paragraph come from Richard Brinsley Sheridan to Thomas Linley, 1775, draft letter, Cecil Price (ed.), *The Letters of Richard Brinsley Sheridan*, vol. 3 (1966), pp. 293–307. He goes on for pages in this vein in order to persuade Linley to reject Garrick's offer to Mary, saying the theatre was the nursery of vice, that no decent man would marry an actress, that 'nine out of ten' bitterly regretted ever going on the stage, that he would rather see her dead, that Garrick could not be trusted, etc., etc.

5. James Boaden records these remarks, which sound authentic enough, *The Life of Mrs Jordan*, vol. 1 (1831), pp. 68–9.

6. The Bruntons were a large theatrical family, and this Miss Brunton was probably the aunt of Elizabeth and Louisa Brunton, whose careers began fifteen years later.

7. Quoted by W. Fraser Rae, *Sheridan: A Biography*, vol. 2 (1896), pp. 12–13. Sheridan's drama with songs, *The Foresters*, was often mentioned but never finished; at his death drafts of it were found. Mary Tickell also points out that the Country Girl was the part Garrick had offered her, so enraging Sheridan.

8. *Sheridan: A Biography*, vol. 2, pp. 13–14.

9. ibid., p. 14.

10. Kitty Clive's joke about the man-midwife was much reported. For Ford's delivery of Princess Amelia, see Olwen Hedley, *Queen Charlotte* (1975), p. 127.

11. Reginald Blunt (ed.), *Mrs Montague, Queen of the Blues*, vol. 2 (1923), p. 203.

12. Mrs Inchbald's edition of *The British Theatre* (1808) contains introductory remarks to classic plays, several of which refer to Dora Jordan's performances. This is from the Introduction to *The Country Girl* in vol. 16, pp. 4–5.

13. Boaden says 'the whig club' gave her 'a very handsome present', *The Life of Mrs Jordan*, vol. 1, p. 84; the anonymous *Life* of 1886 (see Bibliography) names Brooks's and the sum as £300, p. 15; but there is no record of this in the archives at Brooks's.

4 PROPRIETOR AND PRINCE

1. See Madeleine Bingham, *Sheridan: The Track of a Comet* (1972), p. 343, quoting (presumably) Anne Mathews's life of her actor husband, who remembered Sheridan entering 'his own theatre as if stealthily and unwillingly ... his appearance amongst his performers never failed to act like a dark cloud ... one particular afternoon ... Miss de Camp, after a somewhat *animated* colloquy with him, closed it by telling him "that the performers were all very happy before he entered the room, and that he never came but to make everybody uncomfortable" '.
2. Richard Brinsley Sheridan to Thomas Grenville, 24 February 1773, cited by W. Fraser Rae, *Sheridan: A Biography*, vol. 1 (1896), p. 249.
3. The letter she wrote him in 1809, when Drury Lane burnt down, is evidence of friendly and respectful feelings. See p. 209.
4. *Diary and Letters of Madame D'Arblay*, edited by her niece, vol. 1 (1842), pp. 170–71. This was in 1779, when he tried to persuade Fanny Burney to write a play. Her description of him follows a still more admiring one of his wife.
5. Quoted by W. Fraser Rae in *Sheridan: A Biography*, vol. 2, p. 69; he gives the reference to Gibbon's *Miscellaneous Works*, vol. 2, pp. 421–2.
6. Lord Holland's account, told him by Mrs Fox, quoted by Arthur Aspinall (ed.), *The Correspondence of George, Prince of Wales*, vol. 1 (1963), p. 174.
7. His name was Robert Burt, and he died in 1791, before he could get his bishopric, and confessed on his deathbed (*The Correspondence of George, Prince of Wales*, vol. 1, p. 174).

5 ADMIRERS: 1786–1787

1. *Public Advertiser*, 3 May 1786, cited in W. McKay and W. Roberts, *Hoppner* (1914).
2. It was for many years at Hampton Court, but is now in the collection of H.M. the Queen, at Buckingham Palace. See O. Millar, *The Later Georgian Pictures in the Collection of Her Majesty the Queen* (1969), pp. 52–3. The painting measures 93 × 57½, and the engraving was made 1 August 1787.
3. Sir Henry Russell's MS notes, cited *Connoisseur* (April 1953), p. 147. The portrait is often said to have been commissioned by the Duke of Clarence, but the date makes it impossible; the Duke commissioned copies from Romney later, so he made a good profit on his venture. There are currently four versions of this picture, one in private ownership in Detroit (probably the original), one at Waddesdon Manor, and two more in private ownership. There are at least two other striking Romney portraits of her that I have seen only in reproduction.
4. The anonymous *Life* of 1886 (see Bibliography), pp. 42–4, quoting *Morning Herald* for 1 March 1786.
5. Tate Wilkinson, *The Wandering Patentee; or a History of the Yorkshire Theatre from 1700*, vol. 2 (1795), pp. 262–3.
6. In Edinburgh she recited her own verses, the first piece of her writing to be preserved. It shows she had a decent command of language, an ear for verse and a sense of humour. She refers to Edinburgh priding itself on its clever and learned citizens, to herself as 'a twinkling star', and to Mrs Siddons, who was in Edinburgh before her, as a 'planet':

> Presumption 'tis, in learning's seat,
> For me the Muses to entreat;
> Yet, bold as the attempt may be,
> I'll mount the steed of poesy;
> And as my *Pegasus* is small,
> If stumbling, I've not *far* to fall . . .
>
> 'Tis true such *planets* sparkled here,
> As made ME tremble to appear;–
> A *twinkling star*, just come in sight,
> Which, tow'rds the *Pole*, might give no light!

> *Melpomene* has made such work,
> Reigning despotic like the Turk,
> I fear'd *Thalia* had no chance
> Her laughing standard to advance;
> But yet, her youngest Ensign, I
> Took courage, was resolv'd to try,
> And stand the hazard of the *die*.

7. There are letters between Dora and Miss Ford in the possession of Sir Brinsley Ford.

8. This is Charles Reade's account, in his novel about Peg Woffington, of what it was like to be in love with a leading actress; he wrote it in 1853, when he was in love with Fanny Stirling.

9. According to Frederic Reynolds, 'the love scene between him and Miss Prue, when, this latter part was acted by Mrs Jordan, was probably never surpassed in rich natural comedy', *The Life and Times of Frederic Reynolds, written by himself*, vol. 2 (1826), p. 319.

10. This Beechey portrait appears on the first page of the third inset of this book. It is in private possession and has never been shown. Beechey, born in 1753, painted Queen Charlotte in 1793, the year he became an Academician, and was knighted in 1798. He painted Dora again about twenty years later, this time not in theatrical costume. There is another fine Rosalind painting now at Penshurst Place by William Hamilton, Academician and theatrical portraitist, showing her in a feathered and pearled hat, yellow with white feathers and green brim, upturned at front, dark hair peeping out, pearls on arm; she has a long nose, quizzical expression, dark eyes. There is also a Charles Knight engraving, published 20 December 1788, after a painting by the amateur artist Henry Bunbury, showing the Drury Lane performance of *As You Like It*, Dora in her boy's costume, feathered hat, trousers, boots, spotted jacket, sword, etc.

6   A VISIT TO CHELTENHAM: 1788

1. *Diary and Letters of Madame D'Arblay*, edited by her niece, vol. 4 (1842), p. 200.

2. She first met the Sheridans in January 1779, and formed a very

favourable impression of both. Sheridan asked her for a play on this occasion, and although she said she immediately began to imagine the horrors of a first night at Drury Lane, she also began to think of writing for it, and her play *Edwy and Elgiva* was put on at Drury Lane in March 1795, with Kemble and Mrs Siddons. It failed.

3. *Diary and Letters of Madame D'Arblay*, vol. 4, p. 207.

4. *Morning Post*, cited by Brian Fothergill, *Mrs Jordan: Portrait of an Actress* (1965), p. 101.

5. James Boaden's account is given in *The Life of Mrs Jordan*, vol. 1 (1831), pp. 126–9. Another account is in J. Adolphus, who describes her playing with John Bannister as Beau Clinch, and writes that 'no scene palled in her performance, and not a sentence missed its due effect' (*Memoirs of John Bannister*, 1839).

6. Anonymous, taken from E. Humphris and E. C. Willoughby, *At Cheltenham Spa* (1928), p. 81, no source given.

7. Fanny Burney's diary for 13 January 1788, *Diary and Letters of Madame D'Arblay*, vol. 4, p. 34.

8. *Diary and Letters of Madame D'Arblay*, vol. 4, p. 210. The next quotations follow on from this one.

9. 25 March 1789. Sir Joshua Reynolds says in his 'Sitter Book' that a Mrs Jordan called on him at 3 o'clock: information from David Mannings, who says this is the only entry relating to DJ, and that the reference to 23 March in Groves's and Cronin's *History of Works of Sir Joshua Reynolds* (p. 530) is incorrect.

10. Boaden reports this as a conversation he had with Reynolds, and confirms that he never painted her (*The Life of Mrs Jordan*), vol. 1, pp. 220–21.

11. John Kemble in December 1789, H. Baker, *John Philip Kemble* (1942), p. 132.

12. Cecil Price (ed.), *The Letters of Richard Brinsley Sheridan*, vol. 2 (1966), p. 61n., taken from the Farington diary for 25 February 1804.

7 CARNIVAL: 1789–1791

1. Note by Lady Elizabeth Foster on 15 December 1788, cited by Olwen Hedley, *Queen Charlotte* (1975), p. 163.

2. Betsy Sheridan to Mrs Lefanu, 21 November 1788, cited by W. Fraser Rae, *Sheridan: A Biography*, vol. 2 (1896), pp. 94–5.

3. It was Parson James Woodforde.

4. BM Print Room, no. 7514, by Rowlandson, 6 March 1789.

5. The Duchess of Buccleuch to Lady Louisa Stuart, July 1789, in Mrs Godfrey Clark, *Gleanings from an Old Portfolio*, vol. 2 (1896), pp. 149–50.

6. James Boaden prints the whole poem in a section called 'Illustrations' at the end of vol. 1 of his *Life of Mrs Jordan* (1831), pp. 367–8.

7. The letter is partly paraphrased in the anonymous 1886 *Life* (see Bibliography); it then gives a direct quotation, as reproduced here, pp. 46–7.

8. Bannister's own account, from J. Adolphus, *Memoirs of John Bannister*, vol. 1 (1839), p. 81.

9. Betsy Sheridan's journal, quoted in *Sheridan: A Biography*, vol. 2, p. 36. Mrs Inchbald had already satirized the Dr Marmadukes in her farce of 1788, *Animal Magnetism*, and Dora had played in it: but the satire failed to affect fashionable behaviour.

10. Michael T. H. Sadler, *The Political Career of R. B. Sheridan* (1912), p. 83.

11. ibid., p. 81.

12. Elizabeth Sheridan to Mrs Stratford Canning, 27 January 1791, cited in *The Political Career of R. B. Sheridan*, p. 85.

13. See, for example, Chapter 10 in Frederic Reynolds's *The Life and Times of Frederic Reynolds, written by himself*, vol. 1 (1826). For the Prince of Wales's mimicry of Kemble, see R. Fulford, *George IV* (1935), p. 101.

14. See *Sheridan: A Biography*, vol. 1, p. 195n.

15. Thomas Moore, *Memoirs of the Life of R. B. Sheridan*, vol. 2 (1858 edition), p. 87.

8 A ROYAL EDUCATION: PRINCE WILLIAM

1. See, among many sources, R. Fulford's *George IV* (1935), pp. 19–20.

2. Philip Ziegler, *King William IV* (1973), p. 34.

3. ibid.

4. Prince William to the Prince of Wales, 23 July 1784, quoted in *King William IV*, p. 51.

5. Prince William to the Prince of Wales, 12 August 1784, Arthur Aspinall (ed.), *The Correspondence of George, Prince of Wales 1770–1812*, vol. 1 (1963), p. 155.

6. ibid., p. 222.

7. Prince William to the Prince of Wales, 10 February 1786, *The Correspondence of George, Prince of Wales 1770–1812*, vol. 1, p. 219.

8. *King William IV*, p. 63.

9. Prince William to the Prince of Wales, 24 January 1789, *The Correspondence of George, Prince of Wales 1770–1812*, vol. 1, pp. 454–5.

10. In *King William IV* Ziegler quotes on p. 69 from RA 44850 an expression of remorse made by William on 26 October 1788: 'I have been living a terrible debauched life of which I am heartily ashamed and tired. I must in the West Indies turn over a new leaf, or else I shall be irrevocably ruined. I have made a determined resolution to abstain from excess of all kinds.'

11. Fanny Burney, 2 May 1789, *Diary and Letters of Madame D'Arblay*, edited by her niece, vol. 5 (1842), pp. 24–6.

12. 4 June 1791, *Diary and Letters of Madame D'Arblay*, vol. 5, p. 205.

13. *King William IV*, p. 73.

14. Elizabeth Sheridan to Mrs Canning, quoted by Madeleine Bingham, *Sheridan: The Track of a Comet* (1972), p. 276. She assigns it to the autumn of 1789, but gives no source.

15. This appears to cast some doubt on the authenticity of the wine coolers that bear the inscription 'His Royal Highness the Duke of Clarence to Dora Jordan, New Year's Day, 1790.'

16. On 2 May 1792, Parson James Woodforde was at Norwich Theatre, where a Miss Edmeads was acting in her own benefit: 'there saw Tragedy of Hamlet and the new Entertainment called the spoiled Child, a droll thing enough. She acted the part of Hamlet and young Pickle and performed both her parts very well.' John Beresford (ed.), *The Diary of a Country Parson*, vol. 3 (1927), p. 348.

17. Charlotte Papendiek (V.D. Broughton, ed.), *Court and Private Life in the Time of Queen Charlotte*, vol. 1 (1887), p. 250.

18. Elizabeth Sheridan to Richard Brinsley Sheridan, n.d. but attributed 1790, when the production was done on 16 April. W. Fraser Rae, *Sheridan: A Biography*, vol. 2 (1896), pp. 129–30.

19. James Hare to the Duchess of Devonshire, 9 February 1790, Earl of Bessborough (ed.), *Georgiana: Extracts from the Correspondence of Georgiana, Duchess of Devonshire* (1955), p. 167. Hare is quoting Mrs Hobart.

20. Duke of Clarence to the Prince of Wales, 15 May 1790, *The Correspondence of George, Prince of Wales 1770–1812*, vol. 2 (1964), pp. 71–2.

21. Frederic Reynolds, *The Life and Times of Frederic Reynolds, written by himself*, vol. 2 (1826), pp. 79–80. DJ was supported by Bannister, Dodd, Palmer and Kemble; the audience was doubtful but during the last scene 'the acting of Mrs Jordan produced so powerful an impression, that on the termination of the comedy, the voices of the few non-contents were drowned in the applause of the vast majority'.

22. Duke of Clarence to the Prince of Wales, 17 August 1790, *The Correspondence of George, Prince of Wales 1770–1812*, vol. 2, pp. 88–9.

23. Footnote, *The Correspondence of George, Prince of Wales 1770–1812*, vol. 2, p. 176. The conversation is as reported by Lady Elizabeth Foster.

24. Point of law reported in Annual Register for 19 April 1791.

25. The Duke of Clarence to the Prince of Wales, 13 October 1791, Petersham; quoted in Arthur Aspinall (ed.), *Mrs Jordan and Her Family, being the Unpublished Letters of Mrs Jordan and the Duke of Clarence, later William IV* (1951), p. 10, from 'Windsor Archives 44892'.

26. The originals of these letters have disappeared. They are partly quoted direct and partly paraphrased by Michael T. H. Sadler, *The Political Career of R. B. Sheridan* (1912), pp. 83–4. In fact William was still twenty-five in January 1791.

27. Years later, in May 1810, when Harriet Duncannon was Lady Bessborough, she wrote thus to her lover. Lady Granville (ed.), *Private Correspondence 1781–1821, Lord Granville Leverson-Gower*, vol. 2 (1916), p. 355.

28. Ziegler quotes Walpole thus on p. 45.

29. The silhouette is plate xxxiv in E. N. Jackson's *History of Silhouettes* (1911), and is attributed by both Mrs Jackson in her *Silhouettes: A History and Dictionary of Artists* (1938) and Mrs S. McKechnie's *British Silhouette Artists and Their Work 1760–1860* (1978) to Mrs Millicent Brown, an amateur cutter living in Portman Square from the 1770s until 1809. Among her other subjects were Edward Gibbon and the Duchess of Devonshire. It is thought to be in Mr J. Cullen's album in New Jersey, USA, amongst other silhouettes of DJ.

30. British Museum Print Room, M.D. George Catalogue, no. 7835, published 15 March 1791.

31. The play is Fletcher's *The Greek Slave*.

32. This was the theatre known as the King's, no longer in existence, although the present Her Majesty's is built on part of its site.

33. *Diaries and Letters of Madame D'Arblay*, vol. 5, pp. 205–11, for a full account of William's behaviour.

34. James Boaden, *The Life of Mrs Jordan*, vol. 2 (1831), p. 269.

35. There is a long account of this visit to Yorkshire in Tate Wilkinson's *The Wandering Patentee; or a History of the Yorkshire Theatre from 1700*, vol. 3 (1795), pp. 237–68.

36. Both Wilkinson and Boaden (vol. 2, p. 193) give this information.

37. Horace Walpole to Mary Berry, 16 September 1791, Mrs Paget Toynbee (ed.), *The Letters of Horace Walpole*, vol. 11 (1904), p. 352.

38. *The Life of Mrs Jordan*, vol. 2, p. 269.

39. The Duke of Clarence to the Prince of Wales, 13 October 1791, in *Mrs Jordan and Her Family*, p. 10, from 'Windsor Archives 44892'.

9 SCANDAL: 1791

1. 3 November, quoted in the anonymous *Life* of 1886 (see Bibliography), p. 51.

2. Quoted in ibid., p. 54.

3. See letters written between November 1791 and February 1792, the Duke of Clarence to William Adam, 27 November

1791, the rest undated, the Duke of Clarence to William Adam, William Adam to John Palmer, the Duke of Clarence to William Adam, the Duke of Clarence to William Adam, the Duke of Clarence to William Adam, all in Arthur Aspinall (ed.), *Mrs Jordan and Her Family, being the Unpublished Letters of Mrs Jordan and the Duke of Clarence, later William IV* (1951), pp. 11–13, 18–19.

4. Quoted in Brian Fothergill, *Mrs Jordan: Portrait of an Actress* (1965), p. 148.

5. Both letters are cited in *Mrs Jordan and Her Family*, p. 12.

6. Dr James Ford to Richard Ford, Rouen, 18 January 1792, summary from Brinsley Ford MS in Cecil Price (ed.), *The Letters of Richard Brinsley Sheridan* (1966), vol. 3, p. 288.

7. DJ's letter, which was printed in several newspapers, is quoted in James Boaden, *The Life of Mrs Jordan*, vol. 1 (1831), pp. 209–11; he says 'I have not preserved any of the ill-natured sneers at this clear and candid explanation', and that it was a vain attempt to satisfy everybody. The comment in *The Times* of 2 December is in *Mrs Jordan and Her Family*, p. 3.

8. C. B. Hogan, *The London Stage* (1968), p. 1, 410.

10 'THE ONLY RIVAL YOU CAN EVER HAVE'

1. R. Fulford, *The Royal Dukes* (1933), p. 206.

2. From 'Anthony Pasquin' (John Williams), *The Children of Thespis*, published in June 1792.

3. James Boaden, *The Life of Mrs Jordan*, vol. 2 (1831), p. 235n.

4. Hester Bland to DJ, n.d. but late 1791, Arthur Aspinall (ed.), *Mrs Jordan and Her Family, being the Unpublished Letters of Mrs Jordan and the Duke of Clarence, later William IV* (1951), p. 14; the anonymous *Life* of 1886 (see Bibliography), p. 28.

5. Hester Bland to DJ, n.d. but late 1791, *Mrs Jordan and Her Family*, p. 15.

6. Hester Bland to DJ; her three letters written during the crisis are given in *Mrs Jordan and Her Family*, pp. 14–18.

7. DJ to William Adam, January 1795, RA Add. 21/128/23 and DJ to William Adam, February 1795, Sir Brinsley Ford Archive.

8. The two wills are in the possession of Sir Brinsley Ford.
9. The survival of Dora's side of the correspondence is explained in Chapter 21. William's papers were largely destroyed by his executors. Quotations and paraphrases in this section are taken from three sources: MSS in the Royal Archives; the Huntington Library MSS; and *Mrs Jordan and Her Family*, pp. 4–11.
10. DJ to the Duke of Clarence, 1791, *Mrs Jordan and Her Family*, p. 7.
11. DJ to the Duke of Clarence, n.d. but autumn 1791, *Mrs Jordan and Her Family*, pp. 4–8.
12. *The Life of Mrs Jordan*, vol. 1, p. 309.
13. Cited in *The Life of Mrs Jordan*, vol. 1, p. 216.
14. Michael T. H. Sadler, *The Political Career of R. B. Sheridan* (1912), p. 84.
15. Richard Brinsley Sheridan to Harriet Duncannon, March 1792, Cecil Price (ed.), *The Letters of Richard Brinsley Sheridan*, vol. 1 (1966), p. 239; Richard Brinsley Sheridan to the Duchess of Devonshire (in Geneva with Harriet Duncannon), May 1792, vol. 1, p. 245; Richard Brinsley Sheridan to Harriet Duncannon, 14 May 1792, vol. 1, p. 247.
16. He became Lord Grey, the Prime Minister of the Reform Bill.
17. Further information about Eliza Courtney in Appendix IV, Earl of Bessborough (ed.), *Georgiana: Extracts from the Correspondence of Georgiana, Duchess of Devonshire* (1955), pp. 294–5.

11 NELL OF CLARENCE: 1792–1796

1. Tate Wilkinson, *The Wandering Patentee; or a History of the Yorkshire Theatre from 1700*, vol. 1 (1795), p. 22.
2. Lord Edward took her to Ireland, where he became an active revolutionary and died in the violence of 1798. For the Duke and Pamela, see the Duke of Clarence to Thomas Coutts, 21 March 1798, Arthur Aspinall (ed.), *Mrs Jordan and Her Family, being the Unpublished Letters of Mrs Jordan and the Duke of Clarence, later William IV* (1951), p. 42.
3. The Duke of Clarence to Thomas Coutts, 6 November 1793, *Mrs Jordan and Her Family*, p. 21.

4. The Duke of Clarence to Thomas Coutts, 5 January 1794, *Mrs Jordan and Her Family*, pp. 23–4.

5. This and the baptism of Lucy Hester (Ford) are both in Ewell Parish Register in the Surrey Record Office. The Duke himself made a clear and careful note of the time and place of birth of each of the children borne to him by Dora; several copies are still preserved in private possession.

6. Cecil Price (ed.), *The Letters of Richard Brinsley Sheridan*, vol. 2 (1966), p. 51n., information from Hodgson's Catalogue, 26 April 1911, lot 588.

7. Quoted in Brian Fothergill, *Mrs Jordan: Portrait of an Actress* (1965), p. 166.

8. RA Add. 40/41, 42, 44.

9. Cited in *Mrs Jordan: Portrait of an Actress*, pp. 168–9.

10. DJ to the Duke of Clarence, n.d. but winter of 1794–5, RA Add. 40/48–52, and *Mrs Jordan and Her Family*, p. 30.

11. The words were written by the Prince of Wales in January 1796, when he wrote his will, leaving everything to Mrs Fitzherbert except for one shilling to the Princess of Wales.

12. The Prince of Orange's visit was in August 1795, noted by Horace Walpole, 25 August, Lewis Melville, *More Stage Favourites of the Eighteenth Century* (1929), p. 233.

13. Lord Glenbervie, *Diaries* (1928), pp. 58, 71.

14. Horace Walpole to Mary Berry, 19 August 1795, Lady T. Lewis (ed.), *Journals and Correspondence of Miss Berry*, vol. 3 (1865). The *Telegraph* (25 August 1796) and the *Morning Chronicle* (5 September 1796) also noted her appearances at Richmond, cited in *The Letters of Richard Brinsley Sheridan*, vol. 2, p. 61n.

15. James Boaden, *The Life of Mrs Jordan*, vol. 1 (1831), p. 292n.

16. Miss De Camp married Kemble's brother Charles and became the mother of Fanny Kemble. Information from H. Baker, *John Philip Kemble* (1942), p. 192; the quotation is from the Piozzi letters.

17. Richard Brinsley Sheridan to William Adam, September 1796, *The Letters of Richard Brinsley Sheridan*, vol. 2, p. 52.

18. Richard Brinsley Sheridan to John Grubb, n.d. but November or December 1796, *The Letters of Richard Brinsley Sheridan*, vol. 2, pp. 60–61.

19. Samuel Taylor Coleridge to Mary Evans from Jesus College, Cambridge, 7 February 1793, E. L. Griggs (ed.), *The Collected Letters of Samuel Taylor Coleridge*, vol. 1 (1956), p. 51.

20. Lamb, *On Some of the Old Actors* (1822) printed in E. V. Lucas (ed.), *The Letters of Charles Lamb*, vol. 2 (1935), pp. 132–3. The passage reads in part,

> Those who have only seen Mrs Jordan within the last ten or fifteen years can have no adequate notion of her performance of such parts as Ophelia; Helena in All's Well . . .; and Viola . . . Her voice had latterly acquired a coarseness, which suited well enough with her Nells and Hoydens, but in those days it sank, with her steading melting eye, into the heart. Her joyous parts – in which her memory chiefly lives – in her youth were outdone by her plaintive ones. There is no giving an account of how she delivered the disguised story of her love for Orsino. It was no set speech, that she had foreseen, so as to weave it into an harmonious period, line necessarily following line to make up the music . . . but when she had declared her sister's history to be a blank, and that she never told her love, there was a pause, as if the story had ended – and then the image of the worm in the bud came up as a new suggestion – and the heightened image of Patience still followed after that, as by some growing (and not mechanical) process, thought springing up after thought, I would almost say, as they were watered by her tears. So in those fine lines – Write loyal cantos of contemned love – Hollow your name to the reverberate hills – there was no preparation made in the foregoing image for that which was to follow. She used no rhetoric in her passion; or it was nature's own rhetoric most legitimate then, when it seemed altogether without rule or law.

21. So she said to Helen Maria Williams at the end of her life; see Chapter 20.

22. *Mrs Jordan and Her Family*, pp. 34–5.

12 THE MAN OF THE FAMILY: BUSHY, 1797

1. See 31 January 1794, K. Garlick and A. Macintyre (ed.), *The Diary of Joseph Farington*, vol. 1 (1978), p. 151, reporting a conversation with Hoppner relating to an earlier summer.

Hoppner had a sharp tongue, but it did not prevent him from asking the Duke to be godfather to his daughter, Helen Clarence Hoppner (information from unpublished D. Phil. thesis by John Human Wilson, June 1992). Wilson offers further evidence of intimacy between the two families in an undated letter from DJ to Phoebe Hoppner from Petersham Lodge (i.e., written between 1792 and 1797), quoted in Dobell's *Catalogue of Autograph Letters*, p. 18, No. 214.

> I never intentionally forfeited your friendship. I am of that unfortunate disposition that, when I once form a friendship I cannot relinquish it without much uneasiness ... I could no longer resist the strong inclination I felt of writing to you, some unpleasant words that passed between you and my brother in the street, [?] alone prevented me at first ... I have another motive: – that no misunderstanding between you and me should prevent a continuation of His Royal Highness's regard and attention to Mr Hoppner ...

2. Lord Glenbervie, *Diaries* (1928), p. 122, remark attributed to Lord Liverpool.
3. Queen Charlotte's letter to William when he was still a boy at sea is quoted in Philip Ziegler, *King William IV* (1971), p. 35.
4. 31 January 1797, Lord Glenbervie, *Diaries*, p. 123: 'saw the Duke of C yesterday at the Great Lodge with Mrs Jordan and two children', etc.
5. Bushy House has been since 1900 part of the National Physical Laboratory, used partly as the home of its director and partly as offices. It has never been open to the public, but is being restored. I was shown round by the present director and his wife.
6. Unfortunately only three examples survive today.
7. J. Hemlow (ed.), *The Journal and Letters of Fanny Burney*, vol. 4 (1973), p. 25. The aide-de-camp was Colonel Dalrymple, who remained a firm friend to Dora for many years and is frequently mentioned in her letters.
8 The Duke of Clarence to Thomas Coutts, 22 January 1797, Arthur Aspinall (ed.), *Mrs Jordan and Her Family, being the Unpublished Letters of Mrs Jordan and the Duke of Clarence, later William IV* (1951), p. 37, and 22 August 1797, p. 40.
9. 6 July 1798, letter from Soane to Treasury (Private Corr.

XI.A.1.1–3). He writes of works done at Bushy, not yet completed, in which he finds very defective workmanship, materials by no means durable, bad carpentry, mortar made of unfit loam and river sand, extravagant charges 'much beyond any experience of mine', unworkmanlike and expensive, etc. Lead on gutters deficient – no supervision – 'enormous charge' for bell hanging – carpenters and iron workers charge for material they already have (from steps, iron taken from colonnades). The steps to the north and south entrances have been taken down, stone from them valued at 16d. per cubic foot, then used again in house, charging 3/6 per foot cube. 'In the course of the investigation I have had frequent occasion to observe that all the Works have been done without any arranged or general Plan ... carried out by workmen as their individual opinion suggested without any effective control whatever whereby many alterations and much expence has been incurred.' Soane reduces the bill, item by item, from £3,789.17s.1½d. to £3,154.14s.8½d. – saving the Treasury over £600.

10. Anonymous *Life* of 1886 (see Bibliography), p. 35.

11. The Duke of Clarence to Horatio Nelson, 1797, cited in Tom Pocock, *Sailor King: The Life of King William IV* (1991), p. 158.

12. The Duke of Clarence to Thomas Coutts, 7 February 1797, cited in *Mrs Jordan and Her Family*, p. 38.

13. 3 November 1797, *Journals and Letters of Fanny Burney*, vol. 4, p. 25.

14. The Duke of Clarence to Thomas Coutts, 3 September 1797, cited in *Mrs Jordan and Her Family*, p. 36.

15. DJ to Miss Turner, 9 July 1797, MS letter, Sir Brinsley Ford Archives.

16. She wrote this later, when playing in Dublin in 1809; DJ to the Duke of Clarence, 17 June 1809, cited in *Mrs Jordan and Her Family*, p. 95.

17. Walpole wrote a tragedy called *The Mysterious Mother*, printed in 1768, which was found too shocking and disgusting for performance, because it showed the Countess of Narbonne bearing a child to her own son. *The Count of Narbonne* was Robert Jephson's 1780 tragedy based on *The Castle of Otranto*, and it was very popular.

18. DJ to the Duke of Clarence, n.d. but ?23 January 1798, *Mrs Jordan and Her Family*, p. 41.
19. Anonymous writer in York, quoted in the *Life* of 1886, p. 112. The article says Fanny is Daly's child, and calls her Miss Jordan; it includes her and Ford's daughters in its discussion of Lloyd's pupils.

13 THE LONG IDYLL: 1797–1806

1. DJ to the Duke of Clarence, n.d. but watermark 1801, Huntington Library MS; the second reference is also in Huntington Library MS, in a letter from DJ in Edinburgh dated 12 June 1810 that speaks of some kind of offer 'respecting the dear boys. . . with the King's approbation, it would be desirable, as it would give them some distinction in society as your Sons'.
2. DJ to the Duke of Clarence, n.d., Huntington Library MS.
3. Philip Ziegler, *King William IV* (1971), p. 80.
4. The first reference is from K. Garlick and A. Macintyre (eds.), *The Diary of Joseph Farington*, vol. 6 (1979), p. 2,222, an entry for Friday, 20 January 1804, reporting what the artist Edridge told him after a visit from the Duke and Mrs Jordan. The second is from Monday, 31 December 1804, Lord Glenbervie, *Diaries* (1928), p. 414. The Latin tag means 'If only all were like him.' But George himself said later that his father stopped kissing him on his tenth birthday, telling him he was no longer a boy 'and that he did not like kissing men' (S. Leslie, *The Letters of Mrs Fitzherbert*, 1940, p. 246).
5. The Duke of Clarence to the Prince of Wales, 19 March 1807, *The Correspondence of George, Prince of Wales 1770–1812*, vol. 6 (1969), p. 152.
6. The Duke of Clarence to Thomas Coutts, 5 March 1805, cited in Arthur Aspinall (ed.), *Mrs Jordan and Her Family, being the Unpublished Letters of Mrs Jordan and the Duke of Clarence, later William IV* (1951), p. 60.
7. Henry Ripley, *History and Topography of Hampton-on-Thames* (1885), pp. 12, 30, 131. The school – funded 6 October 1803 and built 1805 – is credited to the Duchess, the Friendly

Society – set up 25 October 1810 – to Queen Adelaide. No doubt she gave her support and patronage when she came to Bushy, first as Duchess in 1818, then as dowager Queen in 1837.

8. DJ to the Duke of Clarence, 23 June 1809, *Mrs Jordan and Her Family*, p. 98.

9. James Boaden, *The Life of Mrs Jordan*, vol. 2 (1831), pp. 54–5.

10. Queen Charlotte's account from Olwen Hedley, *Queen Charlotte* (1975), pp. 201–2; see also J. Adolphus, *Memoirs of John Bannister*, vol. 2 (1839), p. 58.

11. Notice of 23 October 1802, reprinted in the *Richmond & Twickenham Times,* 19 February 1821.

12. Jane Austen to Cassandra Austen, 8 January 1801, R.W. Chapman (ed.), *The Letters of Jane Austen*, vol. 1 (1952), p. 30; *Diary and Letters of Madame D'Arblay*, edited by her niece, vol. 4 (1842), p. 494.

13. British Library H 1650.j. (no. 2). The cover says the song was sung by her at the Theatre Royal Drury Lane, published for the Author at 1s. and sold by Buckenger, 443 Strand. It is dated 1801.

14. Samuel Taylor Coleridge to Thomas N. Longman, Monday, 15 December 1800, E. L. Griggs (ed.), *The Collected Letters of Samuel Taylor Coleridge*, vol. 6 (1971), p. 1,013. See also Samuel Taylor Coleridge to Thomas Poole, 19 January 1801, vol. 2, p. 665, in which Coleridge again mentions sending a copy of *Lyrical Ballads* to DJ.

15. The following is the text of 'Her Eyes are Wild' from Wordsworth's *Lyrical Ballads*:

I

Her eyes are wild, her head is bare,
The sun has burnt her coal-black hair;
Her eyebrows have a rusty stain,
And she came far from over the main.
She has a baby on her arm,
Or else she were alone:
And underneath the hay-stack warm,
And on the greenwood stone,
She talked and sung the woods among.
And it was in the English tongue.

II

'Sweet babe! they say that I am mad
But nay, my heart is far too glad;
And I am happy when I sing
Full many a sad and doleful thing:
Then, lovely baby, do not fear!
I pray thee have no fear of me;
But safe as in a cradle, here
My lovely baby! thou shalt be:
To thee I know too much I owe;
I cannot work thee any woe.

III

A fire was once within my brain;
And in my head a dull, dull pain;
And fiendish faces, one, two, three,
Hung at my breast, and pulled at me;
But then there came a sight of joy;
It came at once to do me good;
I waked, and saw my little boy,
My little boy of flesh and blood;
Oh joy for me that sight to see!
For he was here, and only he.

IV

Suck, little babe, oh suck again!
It cools my blood; it cools my brain;
Thy lips I feel them, baby! they
Draw from my heart the pain away.
Oh! press me with thy little hand;
It loosens something at my chest;
About that tight and deadly band
I feel thy little fingers prest.
The breeze I see is in the tree:
It comes to cool my babe and me.

V

Oh! love me, love me, little boy!
Thou art thy mother's only joy;
And do not dread the waves below,
When o'er the sea-rock's edge we go;
The high crag cannot work me harm,
Nor leaping torrents when they howl;

The babe I carry on my arm,
He saves for me my precious soul:
Then happy lie; for blest am I;
Without me my sweet babe would die.

VI

Then do not fear, my boy! for thee
Bold as a lion will I be;
And I will always be thy guide,
Through hollow snows and rivers wide.
I'll build an Indian bower; I know
The leaves that make the softest bed:
And, if from me thou wilt not go,
But still be true till I am dead,
My pretty thing! then thou shalt sing
As merry as the birds in spring.

VII

Thy father cares not for my breast,
'Tis thine, sweet baby, there to rest:
'Tis all thine own! – and if its hue
Be changed that was so fair to view,
'Tis fair enough for thee, my dove!
My beauty, little child is flown.
But thou wilt live with me in love;
And what if my poor cheek be brown!
'Tis well for me, thou canst not see
How pale and wan it else would be.

VIII

Dread not their taunts, my little Life;
I am thy father's wedded wife;
And underneath the spreading tree
We two will live in honesty.
If his sweet boy he could forsake,
With me he never would have stayed:
From him no harm my babe can take;
But he, poor man! is wretched made;
And every day we two will pray
For him that's gone and far away.

IX

I'll teach my boy the sweetest things:
I'll teach him how the owlet sings.

My little babe! thy lips are still.
And thou hast almost sucked thy fill.
– Where art thou gone, my own dear child?
What wicked looks are those I see?
Alas! alas! that look so wild.
It never, never came from me:
If thou art mad, my pretty lad,
Then I must be for ever sad.

x

Oh! smile on me, my little lamb!
For I thy own dear mother am:
My love for thee has well been tried:
I've sought thy father far and wide.
I know the poisons of the shade;
I know the earth-nuts fit for food:
Then, pretty dear, be not afraid:
We'll find thy father in the wood.
Now laugh and be gay, to the woods away!
And there, my babe, we'll live for aye.'

16. Kathleen Coburn (ed.), *The Notebooks of Samuel Taylor Coleridge*, vol. 2 (1962), Note 2,059.

17. Samuel Taylor Coleridge to Lord Byron, 17 [15] October 1815, *The Collected Letters of Samuel Taylor Coleridge*, vol. 6, p. 1,038. Coleridge is talking of players he has seen in Calne, and mentions a Mrs Hudson, 'who pronounced the blank verse of Shakespeare, & indeed Verse in general, better than I ever heard it pronounced, with the solitary exception of some verses by Mrs Jordan'.

18. DJ to the Duke of Clarence, n.d. but watermark 1799, RA Add. 40/100.

19. DJ to the Duke of Clarence, n.d. but watermark 1802, RA Add. 40/104.

20. DJ to the Duke of Clarence, n.d. but probably 1805, Huntington Library MS.

21. DJ to the Duke of Clarence, ?1801, Huntington Library MS.

22. DJ to the Duke of Clarence, n.d. but probably 1797, quoted in *Mrs Jordan and Her Family*, p. 41.

23. DJ the Duke of Clarence, ? 1 September 1801, *Mrs Jordan and Her Family*, p. 47.

24. DJ to the Duke of Clarence, n.d. but probably 1804, RA Add. 40/122.

25. See Note 11 above.

26. DJ to the Duke of Clarence, n.d. but ?3 September 1802, *Mrs Jordan and Her Family*, p. 50:

> I thought it proper as the Duchess of Devonshire sent to know how long I stayed to let her know that my night was fixed for Friday, on which she sent me the most civil letter, highly pleased with the attention, desiring me to keep both stage boxes, & if her name would be of any use, to say by her desire. The Duke is very unwell, but if it is possible he will come that night; if not, she will quit him on that occasion, tho' she goes nowhere. Was not this handsome?'

27. An unpublished letter (Huntington), probably from the autumn of 1801, indicates that she was playing in Brighton, and speaks of the Prince's box. DJ to the Duke of Clarence, September 1802, says the Brighton manager has made her a very good offer from 20 September. She does not take it up, but goes to Liverpool instead. See *Mrs Jordan and Her Family*, pp. 51–3.

28. Lord Duncannon became Viscount Bessborough on the death of his father. Lady Bessborough to Lord Granville Leveson-Gower, 10 October 1805, Lady Granville (ed.), *Private Correspondence 1781–1821, Lord Granville Leveson-Gower*, vol. 2 (1916), p. 120.

29. DJ to the Duke of Clarence, n.d. but ?August 1802, *Mrs Jordan and Her Family*, p. 48.

30. DJ to the Duke of Clarence, n.d. but 31 August 1802, *Mrs Jordan and Her Family*, pp. 49–50.

31. DJ to the Duke of Clarence, n.d. but October 1802, *Mrs Jordan and Her Family*, pp. 52–3.

32. The Duke of Clarence to Thomas Coutts, 7 May 1803, *Mrs Jordan and Her Family*, p. 54. See also gossip – and of course it is only gossip – retailed on 22 November 1804 (*The Diary of Joseph Farington*, vol. 6, p. 2,452) when at the Academy Club James Heath (official historical engraver to George III) 'spoke of the situation of Mrs Jordan with the Duke of Clarence as being far from happy. She is now *pregnant* with her *9th Child*. The Duke takes Her money and she finds it difficult to manage

for the Children she had before she lived with the Duke. – Heath said she makes more than £3000 a yr.'

33. DJ to the Duke of Clarence, n.d. but watermark 1803, RA Add. 40/107.

34. John Tottenham O'Keefe became a chaplain to the Duke probably in 1798 when he completed his studies at Oxford, and died in Jamaica in 1803.

35. DJ to the Duke of Clarence, n.d. but late 1806, Huntington Library MS.

36. DJ to the Duke of Clarence, n.d. but early 1800s, Huntington Library MS.

37. In another letter she says, 'The builder says the Duke does not mean to sit in his library in the winter, as it is to be only a kind of shew Library.'

38. DJ to the Duke of Clarence, n.d. but ?1801, Huntington Library MS.

39. DJ to the Duke of Clarence, n.d. but early 1800s, Huntington Library MS. For a visit to the theatre, DJ to the Duke of Clarence, n.d. but ?9 October 1804, *Mrs Jordan and Her Family*, p. 59.

40. DJ to the Duke of Clarence, n.d. but 1803, *Mrs Jordan and Her Family*, p. 54; then Huntington Library MS.

41. DJ to the Duke of Clarence, n.d. but September 1804, *Mrs Jordan and Her Family*, p. 57.

42. DJ to the Duke of Clarence, n.d. but 1803, Huntington Library MS.

43. She spoke these words in the epilogue to Cherry's *The Soldier's Daughter* in 1804, when there was an invasion scare.

44. Sadly, I have been unable to trace the whereabouts of this painting. It was advertised for sale by a New York gallery in the English art journal *Apollo* in 1968, no. 12, p. lxxxiii. The gallery has disappeared.

45. This painting, for many years in the family of the Earls of Munster, is now the property of Lord De L'Isle, and can be seen at Penshurst Place.

46. Lord Minto, in letter to his wife, cited in *The Correspondence of George, Prince of Wales 1770–1812*, vol. 4 (1967), p. 91n.

47. *The Life of Mrs Jordan*, vol. 2, p. 270.

14 THE SERPENT ENTERS PARADISE

1. Undated Huntington Library MS letters mention the visit to Merton Place with the children and the invitation to both a dinner and a ball, both of which DJ seems to have refused; it is clear she did not become a close friend of Emma Hamilton, about whom there is a later unsympathetic reference, giving gossip about a drunken party Hamilton attended when she was confined for debt.

2. Some of the columns from the colonnades were used; the temple is still there, but the piece of mast was moved, first into the house, then to Windsor and then to the United Services Museum; it is now in storage in the National Portrait Gallery.

3. DJ to the Duke of Clarence, n.d. but 1807, Arthur Aspinall (ed.), *Mrs Jordan and Her Family, being the Unpublished Letters of Mrs Jordan and the Duke of Clarence, later William IV* (1951), p. 66.

4. DJ to John Bannister, 26 February 1806, J. Adolphus, *Memoirs of John Bannister*, vol. 2 (1839), p. 151. The letter goes on, 'Do come out soon, and re-establish my health – I mean my – *theatrical* health, which without you, is certainly on the decline. My best compliments to Mrs Bannister and your fair daughters. Yours very sincerely D. Jordan.'

5. Cobbett's article is quoted in the anonymous *Life* of 1886 (see Bibliography), pp. 63–6.

6. The Duke of Clarence at Bushy to Samuel Hawker in Portugal, 28 September 1810, De L'Isle Archive.

7. DJ to the Duke of Clarence, n.d., Huntington Library MS.

8. DJ to the Duke of Clarence, n.d. but March 1807, Huntington Library MS.

9. DJ to the Duke of Clarence, n.d. but 1810, Huntington Library MS.

10. Lady Bessborough to Lord Granville Leveson-Gower, 19 September 1807, Lady Granville (ed.), *Private Correspondence 1781–1821, Lord Granville Leveson-Gower*, vol. 2 (1916), p. 284.

11. 15 October 1807, K. Cave (ed.), *The Diary of Joseph Farington*, vol. 8 (1982), p. 3,127.

12. DJ to the Duke of Clarence, n.d, but ?December 1807, Huntington Library MS.

13. Thomas Maurice, *Richmond Hill* (1807), p. 149.

14. DJ to the Duke of Clarence, October 1808, *Mrs Jordan and Her Family*, p. 69.

15. George Munster to De L'Isle, April 1837, De L'Isle Archive, Sydney MSS U1500 C221–229.

16. The Duke of Clarence to the Prince of Wales, n.d. but 1810, *Mrs Jordan and Her Family*, p. 67.

15 LONDON AND DUBLIN DISASTERS: 1809

1. The Duke of Clarence to DJ, 1 November 1808. Aspinall prints this in *Mrs Jordan and Her Family, being the Unpublished Letters of Mrs Jordan and the Duke of Clarence, later William IV* (1951), p. 70, but he gives no source, and says he did not see the MS, though he does not doubt its authenticity. Since DJ returned almost all the Duke's letters to the royal family in 1811, this is probably one of the few she kept, regarding it as particularly precious. It is not in the Huntington collection or the Royal Archives.

2. Lord Glenbervie, *Diaries*, vol. 2 (1928), p. 26.

3. DJ to the Duke of Clarence, n.d. but Wed. half past one, Mortimer St, ?1809, Huntington Library MS.

4. Tom Pocock, *Sailor King: The Life of King William IV* (1991), p. 172.

5. George's *Account of the British Campaign* was first published anonymously in parts in the *United Service Journal*, 1829, and reprinted in 1831.

6. Newspaper cutting of 1808 included among Huntington Library MS.

7. DJ to the Duke of Clarence, n.d. but 1809, Huntington Library MS. DJ to James Boaden, 17 August 1809, James Boaden, *The Life of Mrs Jordan*, vol. 2 (1831), p. 253.

8. DJ to the Duke of Clarence, 'Bushy Thursday', n.d. but 1809, Huntington Library MS.

9. 14 February 1809, K. Cave (ed.), *The Diaries of Joseph Farington*, vol. 9 (1983), p. 400: the portrait painter Thomas Phillips told him 'it had long been mentioned that the Duke of Clarence

had seduced a daugr. of Mrs Jordan'. 19 February 1809, *The Diary of Joseph Farington*, vol. 9, p. 3,403, 'General Morse had told him of the report that Miss Ford a daughter of Mrs Jordan is pregnant by the Duke of Clarence.' Lady Spencer to Lady Bessborough, 20 March 1809, Earl of Bessborough and Arthur Aspinall (eds.), *Lady Bessborough and Her Family Circle* (1940), p. 184.

10. DJ to James Boaden, n.d. but 1809, *The Life of Mrs Jordan*, vol. 2, p. 237.

11. DJ to Richard Brinsley Sheridan, 2 March 1809, Bushy House, cited in G. Raymond, *The Life and Enterprises of R. W. Elliston, Comedian* (1857), p. 152.

12. DJ to the Duke of Clarence, Bath, Sunday, n.d., ?April 1809, *Mrs Jordan and Her Family*, p. 84.

13. DJ to the Duke of Clarence, Bath, n.d., Huntington Library MS.

14. DJ to the Duke of Clarence, n.d., but 1809, Huntington Library MS.

15. DJ to the Duke of Clarence, n.d. but April 1809, *Mrs Jordan and Her Family*, p. 80.

16. DJ to the Duke of Clarence, n.d. but ?26 April 1809, *Mrs Jordan and Her Family*, p. 84.

17. *The Life of Mrs Jordan*, vol. 1, p. 275.

18. Leigh Hunt, in Roger Ingpen (ed.), *Autobiography*, vol. 1 (1903), p. 148.

19. Leigh Hunt, in N. Archer and R. Lowe (eds.), *Dramatic Essays* (1894), p. 84.

20. William Oxberry, *Dramatic Biography and Histrionic Anecdotes*, vol. 1 (1835), pp. 197–205.

21. W. C. Macready in Frederick Pollock (ed.), *Reminiscences*, vol. 1 (1875), p. 63.

22. J. Adolphus, *Memoirs of John Bannister*, vol. 2 (1839), p. 261.

23. Boaden tells this story, without attribution, in an appendix to vol. 1 of his *Life*, pp. 362–4. He can have heard it only from Dora herself, which seems a little improbable, or from Lucy. I favour Lucy. She was with her mother in Chester; she was the most likely to have talked to Boaden after Dora's death, being adult, married to a man who respected her mother, and deeply attached to her herself.

24. DJ to the Duke of Clarence, n.d. but June 1810, *Mrs Jordan and Her Family*, p. 139.

25. Sir John Barrington, *Personal Sketches of My Own Time*, vol. 2 (1827), p. 45.

26. This and all further quotations from DJ's letters in this chapter are taken from *Mrs Jordan and Her Family*, pp. 88–104.

27. Harriet Bessborough to Lord Granville Leveson-Gower, n.d. but probably December 1809, Lady Granville (ed.), *Private Correspondence 1781–1821, Lord Granville Leveson-Gower*, vol. 2 (1916), pp. 349–50.

16 'I AM A BETTER ACTRESS AT THIS MOMENT THAN I EVER WAS': 1810

1. DJ to Jonah Barrington, n.d. but winter 1809, Sir Jonah Barrington, *Personal Sketches of My Own Time*, vol. 2 (1827), pp. 235–6.

2. DJ to the Duke of Clarence, n.d. but September 1809, Arthur Aspinall (ed.), *Mrs Jordan and Her Family, being the Unpublished Letters of Mrs Jordan and the Duke of Clarence, later William IV* (1951), pp. 108–9.

3. DJ to the Duke of Clarence, n.d. but January 1810, *Mrs Jordan and Her Family*, p. 134.

4. DJ to the Duke of Clarence, n.d. but January 1810, *Mrs Jordan and Her Family*, p. 134. She knew she was misquoting Goldsmith's beautiful lines from *The Traveller*, which go:

> Where're I roam, whatever realms to see,
> My heart untravell'd fondly turns to thee;
> Still to my brother turns with ceaseless pain,
> And drags at each remove a lengthening chain.

5. DJ to the Duke of Clarence, n.d. but January 1810, *Mrs Jordan and Her Family*, pp. 132–3.

6. DJ to the Duke of Clarence, n.d. but June 1810, *Mrs Jordan and Her Family*, p. 136.

7. DJ to the Duke of Clarence, n.d. but January 1810, Huntington Library MS and *Mrs Jordan and Her Family*, p. 130.

8. DJ to the Duke of Clarence, n.d. but June 1810, *Mrs Jordan and Her Family*, p. 144.

9. DJ to George FitzClarence, n.d. but July 1810, RA Add. 40/147.

10. DJ to the Duke of Clarence, n.d. but October 1810, Huntington Library MS.

11. DJ to the Duke of Clarence, n.d. but January 1810, *Mrs Jordan and Her Family*, p. 131.

12. DJ to the Duke of Clarence, n.d. but February 1811, *Mrs Jordan and Her Family*, p. 188.

13. DJ to the Duke of Clarence, n.d. but January or February 1811, Huntington Library MS. *Mrs Jordan and Her Family* quotes part of this letter on p. 184, but misreads 'crowded' and omits the last sentence quoted, as well as a good deal else relating to the family and her anxieties about them.

14. Diprose, *Diprose's Book of the Stage and Players*, (n.d.), p. 61.

15. W.C. Macready, in Frederic Pollock (ed.), *Reminiscences*, vol. 1 (1875), p. 63.

16. DJ to the Duke of Clarence, n.d. but 19 June, *Mrs Jordan and Her Family*, p. 142.

17. His account in *Mrs Jordan and Her Family*, pp. 146–7; hers in RA Add. 40/147.

18. Harriet Bessborough to Granville Leveson-Gower, n.d. but 1810, Lady Granville (ed.), *Private Correspondence 1781–1821, Lord Granville Leveson-Gower*, vol. 2 (1916), p. 375.

19. DJ to George FitzClarence, Friday ye 24th [August 1810], *Mrs Jordan and Her Family*, pp. 150–51.

20. Cited in Olwen Hedley, *Queen Charlotte* (1975), p. 254.

21. DJ to the Duke of Clarence, n.d. but February 1811, Huntington Library MS.

22. DJ to Jonah Barrington, April 1810, *Personal Sketches of My Own Time*, vol. 2, p. 238.

23. DJ to the Duke of Clarence, n.d. but September 1810, Huntington Library MS.

24. DJ to the Duke of Clarence, n.d. but December 1810, Huntington Library MS.

25. DJ to George FitzClarence, n.d. but January 1811, *Mrs Jordan and Her Family*, p. 180.

26. DJ to the Duke of Clarence, n.d. but February 1811, *Mrs Jordan and Her Family*, p. 187.

27. DJ to the Duke of Clarence, n.d. but stamped 4 March 1811, Huntington Library MS.

28. DJ to George FitzClarence, n.d. but April 1811, *Mrs Jordan and Her Family*, p. 192.
29. DJ to the Duke of Clarence, n.d. but August 1811, Huntington Library MS.
30. DJ to George FitzClarence, n.d. but summer 1811, Huntington Library MS.
31. DJ to the Duke of Clarence, n.d. but August 1811, Huntington Library MS.

17 'MY DEAR MOTHER . . . A MOST INJURED WOMAN': 1811

1. George FitzClarence to DJ, 21 August 1811, Huntington Library MS. George's spelling is terrible, but no worse than Princess Charlotte's, and he soon got it up to scratch.
2. DJ to the Duke of Clarence, n.d. but August 1811, Arthur Aspinall (ed.), *Mrs Jordan and Her Family, being the Unpublished Letters of Mrs Jordan and the Duke of Clarence, later William IV* (1951), p. 197.
3. ibid.
4. DJ to the Duke of Clarence, n.d. but September 1811, *Mrs Jordan and Her Family*, p. 202.
5. ibid.
6. James Boaden, *The Life of Mrs Jordan*, vol. 2 (1831), p. 281.
7. DJ to the Duke of Clarence, 'York Sunday' n.d. but August 1811, Huntington Library MS.
8. DJ to the Duke of Clarence, Sunday [22 September 1811], *Mrs Jordan and Her Family*, p. 203.
9. DJ to the Duke of Clarence, Cheltenham Sunday [2 September 1811], Huntington Library MS, omitted by Aspinall in transcript on p. 203 of *Mrs Jordan and Her Family*.
10. William Oxberry, *Dramatic Biography and Histrionic Anecdotes*, vol. 1 (1835), pp. 202–3. The story was credited to an actor who was present, and was told also by Boaden, but it had been handed on verbally for twenty years before it was written down.
11. DJ to the Duke of Clarence, n.d. but 13 October 1811, Huntington Library MS. *Mrs Jordan and Her Family* prints part of this letter on p. 206, but omits everything about the plans for the garden and the children.

12. DJ to the Duke of Clarence, n.d. but November 1811, Huntington Library MS.

13. The Duke of Clarence to Lady de Crespigny, aunt of Miss Tylney Long, n.d. but October 1811, *Mrs Jordan and Her Family*, p. 212.

14. DJ to the Duke of Clarence, Bushy, Sunday [13 October 1811], *Mrs Jordan and Her Family*, p. 206.

15. Lady Bessborough to Granville Leveson-Gower, 2 November 1811, Lady Granville (ed.), *Private Correspondence 1781–1821, Lord Granville Leveson-Gower*, vol. 2 (1916), p. 413.

16. Princess Charlotte to Miss Mercer Elphinstone, 23 November 1811, cited in Arthur Aspinall (ed.), *The Letters of Princess Charlotte* (1949), p. xiv.

17. The Duke of Clarence to George FitzClarence, Ramsgate, n.d. but November 1811, *Mrs Jordan and Her Family*, pp. 212–13.

18. DJ to George FitzClarence, Monday [November 1811], *Mrs Jordan and Her Family*, p. 216.

19. 19 April 1791 point of law reported in Annual Register that mother of child born out of wedlock has no right as guardian after age of seven.

20. DJ to the Duke of Clarence, 22 November 1811, Huntington Library MS.

21. DJ to the Duke of Clarence, St James's Friday [29 November 1811], *Mrs Jordan and Her Family*, p. 217.

22. DJ to James Boaden, n.d. but November 1811, *The Life of Mrs Jordan*, vol. 2, pp. 273–5.

23. R. Fulford, *The Royal Dukes* (1933), pp. 124–5.

24. Philip Ziegler, *King William* (1971), pp. 110–11.

25. DJ to the Duke of Clarence, n.d. but before mid-December 1811, Huntington Library MS.

26. Boaden quotes her letter in *The Life of Mrs Jordan*, vol. 2, p. 278.

27. DJ to the Duke of Clarence, n.d. but 16 December 1811, *Mrs Jordan and Her Family*, p. 219.

28. DJ to John McMahon, n.d. but 16 December 1811, *Mrs Jordan and Her Family*, pp. 219–20. Aspinall found this letter among the Prince Regent's papers in the Royal Archives.

29. DJ to George FitzClarence, n.d. but 16 December 1811, *Mrs Jordan and Her Family*, p. 220.

30. Henry FitzClarence to George FitzClarence, 7 December 1811, Birkbeck MS.

31. DJ to George FitzClarence, n.d. but 10 December 1811, *Mrs Jordan and Her Family*, p. 218.

32. *The Life of Mrs Jordan*, vol. 2, p. 276.

33. DJ to the Duke of Clarence, n.d. but December 1810, Huntington Library MS.

34. In 1806 the royal Princes were reported as having their allowances increased from £12,000 to £18,000 a year, plus a special grant each of £20,000 to settle their debts.

35. The Duke of Clarence to Sophy FitzClarence, n.d. but late 1811, from Portsmouth, RA Add. 4/148.

> I never wish either to say or write an angry word to you: but I cannot approve of your *now* wishing to live with me: I must be the best judge and am your best friend: you will *of course* live with me as *must all* my daughters as they attain the age of *sixteen*: the boys *must* live with me and will occasionally visit their mother: till everything is settled between me and your mother there is not any hurry about her taking a house unless a very cheap and convenient one offers: Tus may remain till next April twelvemonth with his mother if she wishes to keep him . . .

36. ibid.

37. John McMahon to William Adam, 30 December 1811, *Mrs Jordan and Her Family*, p. 223.

38. Princess Charlotte to Miss Mercer Elphinstone, 5 January 1812, *The Letters of Princess Charlotte*, p. 25.

39. DJ to John McMahon, n.d. but early January 1812, Huntington Library MS. It is curious that Aspinall did not print this letter.

40. DJ to the Duke of Clarence, n.d. but early January 1812, *Mrs Jordan and Her Family*, p. 226.

18 AN ATTACK BY *THE TIMES*: 1813

1. DJ to James Boaden, n.d. but January 1812, James Boaden, *The Life of Mrs Jordan*, vol. 2 (1831), p. 277.

2. William Adam to DJ, 24 January 1812, cited in Arthur

Aspinall (ed.), *Mrs Jordan and Her Family, being the Unpublished Letters of Mrs Jordan and the Duke of Clarence, later William IV* (1951), p. 230.

3. DJ to George FitzClarence, n.d. but September 1812 (from Exeter), RA Add. 40/196.

4. DJ to George FitzClarence, n.d. but January 1812, Huntington Library MS.

5. DJ to George FitzClarence, n.d. but January 1812, *Mrs Jordan and Her Family*, pp. 228–9.

6. DJ to George FitzClarence, n.d. but January and February 1812, *Mrs Jordan and Her Family*, pp. 230–31.

7. DJ to George FitzClarence, 'Tuesday ye 3d' but slip for 4 February 1812, *Mrs Jordan and Her Family*, p. 230.

8. DJ to George FitzClarence, n.d. but ?7 February 1812, *Mrs Jordan and Her Family*, p. 232.

9. DJ to George FitzClarence, n.d. but spring 1812, RA Add. 40/179.

10. DJ to George FitzClarence, n.d. but ?March 1812, *Mrs Jordan and Her Family*, p. 235.

11. DJ to George FitzClarence, n.d. but June 1812, RA Add. 40/184, and DJ to George FitzClarence, n.d. but June 1812, *Mrs Jordan and Her Family*, p. 236.

12. DJ to George FitzClarence, n.d. but June 1812, *Mrs Jordan and Her Family*, p. 235.

13. DJ to George FitzClarence, ye 21st (i.e., 21 August 1812), *Mrs Jordan and Her Family*, p. 237; then two September letters, ibid., pp. 237, 238–9.

14. DJ to George FitzClarence, n.d. but September 1812, RA Add. 40/195, and DJ to George FitzClarence, n.d. but watermark 1812, RA Add. 40/222.

15. DJ to George FitzClarence, November and December 1812, *Mrs Jordan and Her Family*, pp. 239–43.

16. ibid., p. 244.

17. ibid.

18. ibid., p. 246.

19. ibid., pp. 245–6.

20. *The Times*, Thursday, 11 February 1813.

21. Lord Melbourne recalled Madame de Staël's verdict to Queen Victoria; Crabb Robinson's entry is in his diary for 18 March

1813, Eluned Brown (ed.), *Henry Crabb Robinson on the Theatre* (1966), p. 53.

22. *The Life of Mrs Jordan*, vol. 2, pp. 348–9.
23. DJ to George FitzClarence, n.d. but February 1813, *Mrs Jordan and Her Family*, p. 249.

19 'BITTER THANKLESS': 1814

1. James Boaden, *The Life of Mrs Jordan*, vol. 2 (1831), p. 363.
2. L.A. Marchand (ed.), *Byron's Letters and Journals*, vol. 3 (1974), p. 249.
3. Quoted in W. Clark Russell's *Representative Actors* (n.d.), pp. 275–6.
4. *Sketches of Performers*, No. 187, 7 January 1815, cited in the anonymous *Life* of 1886, pp. 108–10.
5. At Covent Garden this year she played Cora in *Pizarro*, Rosalind in *As You Like It*, Nell in *The Devil to Pay*, Miss Prue in *Love for Love*, Miss Hoyden in *A Trip to Scarborough*, Violante in *The Wonder*, Lady Teazle in *The School for Scandal*, Beatrice in *The Pannel* and created the role of Barbara Green in Kenney's *Debtor and Creditor*.
6. 'Before she left the stage some of her real friends wished her to take up elderly characters, such as Mrs Malaprop.' John Genest, *Some Account of the English Stage from the Restoration in 1660 to 1830*, vol. 8 (1832), p. 432. Brian Fothergill in *Mrs Jordan: Portrait of an Actress* (1965), p. 261, says Charlton, the manager at Bath, tried to persuade her to play old women in farces in January 1813, but she refused on the grounds that they were vulgar, and out of her line.
7. H. Simpson and Mrs C. Braun, *A Century of Famous Actresses 1750–1850* (n.d.), p. 289.
8. The Duke of Clarence to Sir Henry Bunbury, 5 April 1813, Arthur Aspinall (ed.), *Mrs Jordan and Her Family, being the Unpublished Letters of Mrs Jordan and the Duke of Clarence, later William IV* (1951), pp. xvii–xviii. Sir Henry was the son of the Bunbury who saw Dora in Cheltenham in 1788, and painted her in a scene from *As You Like It*.
9. DJ reports this to George and Henry FitzClarence, 13

November 1813, *Mrs Jordan and Her Family*, p. 255. Sophy took the attentions of the Duke quite calmly. He was Georgiana's son, and therefore part of a tangle of legitimate and illegitimate half-brothers and sisters, although himself the heir. It was widely expected he would propose to Sophy, but she was not disappointed when he failed to do so. He never married.

10. DJ to George and Henry FitzClarence, n.d. watermark 1812 but ?1813, RA Add. 40/223.

11. Princess Charlotte to Miss Mercer Elphinstone, August 1813, Arthur Aspinall (ed.), *The Letters of Princess Charlotte* (1949), pp. 62–3.

12. DJ to George and Henry FitzClarence, 18 December 1813, *Mrs Jordan and Her Family*, p. 257.

13. DJ to George and Henry FitzClarence, 6 January 1814, *Mrs Jordan and Her Family*, p. 263, and DJ to George and Henry FitzClarence, n.d. but watermark 1812 and ?1813, RA Add. 40/223.

14. Sheridan appears to have been arrested several times in 1813 and 1814; W. Fraser Rae gives the August 1813 date (*Sheridan: A Biography*, vol. 2, 1896, pp. 277–8), Cecil Price mentions March 1814 and August 1815 (*The Letters of Richard Brinsley Sheridan*, vol. 3, 1966, p. 187n.), and prints a reproachful letter from Sheridan, detained in the Sheriff's office in Tooke's Court, Cursitor Street, to Whitbread, dated May 1814.

15. DJ to George FitzClarence, 26 January 1814, *Mrs Jordan and Her Family*, p. 265.

16. DJ to George FitzClarence, n.d. but April 1814, RA Add. 40/235.

17. The Duke of Clarence to George FitzClarence, n.d. but summer 1814, *Mrs Jordan and Her Family*, p. 269.

18. DJ to George FitzClarence, 19 September 1814, *Mrs Jordan and Her Family*, p. 272.

19. DJ to George FitzClarence, n.d. but November 1814, *Mrs Jordan and Her Family*, p. 274.

20. This is Boaden's paraphrase (*The Life of Mrs Jordan*, vol. 2, p. 295). He said the contents of the letter were made known to him by the officer who received it. His story is confirmed by Lord Moira's letter from Calcutta of 6 October 1816 to John McMahon:

It is singular that in my last letter I should omit what had really been prominent in my mind. I was solicitous, because I know how earnestly the Prince feels on the subject, to tell you that I continue to have every reason for being satisfied with Capt. FitzClarence's conduct. He is perfectly attentive to his duty, strictly correct in his maners, & much liked by all the officers in my family. The Prince feared that if he were not kept in order he would be apt to run riot. I do assure you I have not seen any thing of that disposition in him. We go steadily & regularly; but, were there even more opening, I do not think he would have any propensity to avail himself of it.

Arthur Aspinall (ed.), *The Letters of King George IV 1812–1830*, vol. 1 (1938), p. 170.

21. The Duke of Clarence to George and Henry FitzClarence, n.d. but November 1814, *Mrs Jordan and Her Family*, p. 282.

22. Mary FitzClarence to George FitzClarence, n.d. but December 1814, Birkbeck Archive.

23. DJ to George FitzClarence, n.d. but December 1814, quoted in *Mrs Jordan: Portrait of an Actress*, p. 277.

24. George FitzClarence to DJ, 2 December 1814, *The Life of Mrs Jordan*, vol. 2, pp. 302–3.

25. A letter from John Barton to DJ, dated 6 December 1814, says 'That the Expense of the Equipment will be heavy is pretty certain, but I presume H.R.H. will, if not otherwise assisted, be able to divise the means of defraying the same, and will not on any account permit it to be [word illeg.] in the same manner you suggest.' Barton also assured her that her sons were going out 'with the strongest recommendation to the Governor General'. Birkbeck Archive. DJ to George and Henry FitzClarence, n.d. but December 1814, *Mrs Jordan and Her Family*, p. 284.

26. The Duke of Clarence to George and Henry FitzClarence, n.d. but December 1814, *Mrs Jordan and Her Family*, pp. 284–5.

27. DJ to Frederick March, 3 December 1814, *The Life of Mrs Jordan*, vol. 2, p. 303.

28. DJ to Frederick March, 3 December 1814, *The Life of Mrs Jordan*, vol. 2, p. 298.

29. DJ to George FitzClarence, n.d. but 4 December 1814, *Mrs Jordan and Her Family*, p. 284.

30. DJ to George FitzClarence, n.d. but December 1814, *Mrs Jordan and Her Family*, p. 285.
31. The Duke of Clarence to Henry FitzClarence, 5 May 1815, RA Add. 39/250.
32. DJ to Adolphus FitzClarence, 30 August 1815, unpublished MS in private possession.
33. Boaden quotes Barton's own account, written nine years later, *The Life of Mrs Jordan*, vol. 2, pp. 343–56.
34. This is the story given by Robert Huish, *History of the Life and Reign of William IV* (1837), p. 395: Charles Wigley, who ran public exhibitions in Spring Gardens, was asked by DJ if he wanted to buy her furniture; he approached the auctioneer Fisher (father of the child actress Clara), and asked him to go to Sloane Square to estimate value of goods, not naming the vendor. Fisher looked, went to coffee house with Wigley, said the goods were worth £300 in place, if moved £220. The two men returned to the house, Fisher met DJ, then left. Wigley then offered her 100 guineas, with lease of house thrown in (it was worth £500). DJ was anxious to conclude, and easily swindled.
35. Typed copies of Sophy's letters are in the De L'Isle Archive.
36. Frederick FitzClarence to DJ, n.d. but September 1815, *The Life of Mrs Jordan*, vol. 2, p. 325.
37. Cited in *Mrs Jordan: Portrait of an Actress*, p. 280.
38. William Hazlitt, *View of the English Stage* (1818), p. 168.

20 HEARTBREAK: 1816

1. DJ to George FitzClarence, 6 January 1814, RA Add. 40/230.
2. The palace was destroyed in 1870, and the rue d'Angoulême disappeared under modern buildings in the mid-twentieth century; but the site of the palace is clearly marked, and many of the service buildings are still there.
3. James Boaden, *The Life of Mrs Jordan*, vol. 2 (1831), p. 328, and Sir Jonah Barrington, *Personal Sketches of My Own Time* (1827), vol. 2, p. 58.
4. DJ to John Barton, 18 January 1816, *The Life of Mrs Jordan*, vol. 2, pp. 354–6 (March gives the date as 16 January 1818).

5. DJ to Adolphus FitzClarence, 19 January 1816, MS in private archive, partly printed in Brian Fothergill, *Mrs Jordan: Portrait of an Actress* (1965), pp. 305–7.

6. Miss Williams died in Paris in 1827, and her account of her talks with Mrs Jordan were printed in *The Great Illegitimates* of 1832 (see Bibliography), pp. 198–239.

7. Philip Ziegler, *King William IV* (1971), pp. 117–18.

8. The story is given by both Lewis Gibbs (*Sheridan*, 1947) and Madeleine Bingham (*Sheridan: The Track of a Comet*, 1972), both of whom believe it.

9. The Duke of Clarence to George FitzClarence, 6 November 1817, RA Add. 39/288.

10. Information about her last days and funeral from *The Life of Mrs Jordan* and *Mrs Jordan: Portrait of an Actress*.

11. According to John Barton, quoted in *The Life of Mrs Jordan*, vol. 2, pp. 341–2, the last payment of the Duke's allowance was drawn after her death by 'a lady, formerly a governess at Bushy, and afterwards resident with her as a companion in France, who came over to London for the purpose'.

12. In 1943 the municipality of Saint-Cloud decided to raze the old cemetery on the Rue Gounod. Some of the tombs were moved to a tidy new one in the Avenue Foch, among them that of Mrs Jordan. John Genest's inscription had weathered into illegibility, but it read:

> Memoriae Sacrum
> DOROTHEAE JORDAN,
> Quae per multos annos
> Londini, inque aliis
> Britanniae Urbibus,
> Scenam egregie ornavit;
> Lepore comico,
> vocis suavitate,
> Puellarum hilarium,
> Alteriusque sexus,
> Moribus, habitu, imitandis,
> Nulla secunda:
> Ad exercendam eam,
> Qua tam feliciter
> Versata est artem,
> Ut res egenorum

adversas sublevaret,
Nemo Promptior.
E vita exiit
Tertio nonas Julii, 1816,
Annos nata 50.
MEMENTOTE.
LUGETE.

(Sacred to the memory of DJ who for many years, in London and other cities of Britain, outstandingly adorned the stage. For comic wit and sweetness of voice, for imitating the manners and customs of laughing girls as well as the opposite sex she ranked second to none in the display of that art wherein she was so pre-eminently skilled; and no one was more prompt to relieve the needy. She departed this life, etc.) Other versions have been printed but this is Genest's own.

The date of her death and her age are wrongly given. In 1971 the late Thomas Goff, Dora's great-grandson, and grandson of her youngest son, Augustus (Tuss), had a round bronze tablet fixed over a stone, with a French inscription:

Ci-gît
Dorothy Jordan
La plus grande interprète anglaise
de la Comédie de 1782 à 1815.
Bien-aimée de
William Henry, Duke of Clarence
par la suite William IV
Roi de Grande-Bretagne et d'Irlande
et mère de ses dix enfants,
décédée à Saint-Cloud
5 juillet 1816.

21 THE CHILDREN: 'WITH THE KING THEY DIE'

1. The Duke of Clarence to Henry FitzClarence, 13 July 1816, RA Add. 39/273.
2. Sir John Hislop to John McMahon, 28 April 1816, Lord Moira to John McMahon, 26 October 1816, both in Arthur Aspinall (ed.), *The Letters of King George IV 1812–1830*, vol. 2 (1938), pp. 164, 170.

3. The Duke of Clarence to Henry FitzClarence, 12 September 1816, RA Add. 39/274.

4. The Duke of Clarence to George FitzClarence, 6 November 1817, RA Add. 39/288.

5. The anonymous *Life* of 1886 (see Bibliography), p. 107, gives the announcement, by Colburn of Conduit Street, Bond Street, on 13 June 1817. It is likely the book was suppressed by royal intervention.

6. 5 February 1817, Eluned Brown (ed.), *Henry Crabb Robinson on the Theatre* (1966), p. 75. Crabb Robinson wrote,

> The pleasure I had was in being reminded of old times and in having old enjoyments brought back to my mind – I saw for the first time Mrs Alsop – Mrs Jordan's daughter – the ugliest woman I should think who ever ventured on the stage – ill-made almost to deformity – cross-eyed and ill-complexioned – she nevertheless delighted by the sweet tones of her voice which frequently startled me by their resemblance to her mother's – Mrs Alsop has the same or nearly the same hearty laugh and much of the frolicsome antics of Mrs Jordan – Only one is apt to conceive that so ugly a creature has no right to take such liberties – And how I should have enjoyed her acting if I had not recollected her mother I cannot tell.

7. A Lucy Hawker died at Alverstoke, Hampshire, in 1850, but appears to have left no will.

8. Princess Augusta to Sophy FitzClarence, 4 October 1816, De L'Isle Archive, Sydney MSS U1500 C212.

9. The Duke of Clarence to George FitzClarence, 21 March 1818, Arthur Aspinall (ed.), *Mrs Jordan and Her Family, being the Unpublished Letters of Mrs Jordan and the Duke of Clarence, later William IV* (1951), p. xxiii.

10. Anne Mathews, *Memoirs of Charles Mathews*, vol. 3 (1839), pp. 574–5.

11. Cited in Mary Hopkirk, *Queen Adelaide* (1956), p. 55.

12. 6 April 1821, *The Diary of Joseph Farington*, vol. 16 (1984), p. 5,644.

13. Amelia's book was called *Chow-Chow; being Selections from a Journal Kept in India, Egypt and Syria* by the Viscountess Falkland. She chose the title, she explains, because the pedlars in India carried among their wares one basket which they called the

Chow-Chow basket, in which there were all sorts of odds and ends; 'and in offering *my* Chow-Chow basket to the public, I venture to hope that something, however trifling, may be found in it, suited to the taste of everyone'. It was published in 1857, the year of the Indian mutiny; and Mely died the following year, aged only fifty-one.

14. The Duchess of Kent, reporting conversation with the Duchess of Northumberland, 7 February 1831, RA M5/19.

15. For the King of Würtemberg's visit, see 11 July 1830, George FitzClarence to Lord Aberdeen, British Library Add. MSS 43040. Daniel Stuart, editor of the *Morning Post*, wrote to George, 19 July 1831, about Coleridge's pension. He had been given £100 annually since 1824 from the Privy Purse of George IV, through the Royal Society of Literature, and was supposed to read an annual essay in return (only one had been delivered). George promised Stuart he would lay his letter before the King, but warned that his income was only half that of the previous monarch; and the pension was discontinued. It was made up by others; but Coleridge complained that his gold had been taken to 'emblazon d'or the black bar across the Royal Arms of the Fitzclarences'. See E.K. Chambers, *Samuel Taylor Coleridge* (1938), p. 322.

16. *Mrs Jordan and Her Family*, p. xxv.

17. Philip Ziegler, *King William IV* (1971), p. 158.

18. Fanny Kemble, *Record of a Girlhood*, vol. 2 (1878), p. 74.

19. According to a Mr Bunn, who records a conversation with him on 28 April 1838, cited in Clare Jerrold, *The Story of Dorothy Jordan* (1914), pp. 420–21. Wyatt's splendid portrait of Lolly (Lord Adolphus FitzClarence) now belongs to Viscount Falkland, and hangs in Brooks's Club.

20. Obituary notice in *Illustrated London News*, 23 December 1854.

21. Frederick kept the letters until his death, and left all his property to his wife; and it is after this they began to be dispersed.

22. He is buried in Mapledurham Churchyard, and the clock which his father the King presented to his school can be seen on the tiny church.

23. Lord Munster to Sir Robert Peel, 25 November 1841, British Museum Add. MSS 40495, f. 372.

24. Report of inquest in *The Times*, 29 March 1842. In the report

of George's death *The Times* stated that 'Mrs Jordan withdrew from the protection of the Duke of Clarence ... soon after the death of Princess Charlotte', which was of course untrue – Princess Charlotte's death was in 1818, seven years after the separation, and more than two years after the death of Mrs Jordan. *The Times* praised George's military career, saying he had taken part in twelve engagements, but made no mention of the court martial of 1814.

25. Sir Robert Peel to Lord Adolphus FitzClarence, 22 March 1842, British Museum Add. MSS 40505, f. 27.

26. 23 March 1842, R. Fulford and L. Strachey (eds.), *Memoirs of Charles Greville*, vol. 2 (1938), p. 20.

27. *Queen Adelaide*, p. 187.

28. The church had been rebuilt since his childhood. It is now impossible to see his tomb, as a carpet has been fixed down over it, and there is no record of the inscription; but Mr Francis C.E. Atkins, for many years church warden, recalls that there was an inscription. Lady Munster died in December of the same year, and is also buried there.

29. George Munster to William IV, ?n.d. but after 10 April 1837, De L'Isle Archive, Sydney MSS U1500 C221.

30. George Munster to Minney Dawson-Damer, 22 June 1837, quoted in S. Leslie, *The Letters of Mrs Fitzherbert* (1940), p. 321. George says the picture is in the possession of his younger brother Augustus, so presumably it went to Mapledurham. He mentions 'water-colour drawings' of himself, and one of Henry by 'Eldridge' (presumably Edridge); and also says he has taken 'two seals of my poor mother ... with which she has often sealed hundreds of letters to me full of that entire affection and excellent feeling she so greatly possessed'.

31. Amelia had one son who died childless, Mary no children. Sophy died in childbirth in 1837, leaving five children, and her descendants are still at Penshurst Place. Eliza and Augusta also have many descendants; and Eliza's grandson married into the legitimate royal family in 1889 when he became the husband of Queen Victoria's granddaughter, Princess Louise, and was created first Duke of Fife. See Family Trees.

32. Percy Fitzgerald, *The Life and Times of King William IV*, vol. 1 (1884), p. 121. The royal family was embarrassed throughout

the century by a situation that paralleled that of Mrs Jordan and William in the next generation. Prince George, cousin of Queen Victoria, and considered a possible husband for her, fell in love with another theatrical figure, the dancer Louisa Fairbrother, fathered three sons on her, married her – unconstitutionally, but otherwise correctly – and lived with her in Queen Street, Mayfair, until her death. The Fairbrothers were a theatre clan: Robert Fairbrother was Sheridan's servant, another Robert was prompter at Drury Lane, Samuel Fairbrother printed playbills. Louisa, born in 1814 (and christened Sarah), started dancing at sixteen, gave birth to two children by Charles Manners Sutton, grandson of the Archbishop of Canterbury, and continued her career. She met Prince George after a command performance on the evening of the Queen's wedding in 1840. George's closest friend was his older cousin Lord Adolphus FitzClarence, and they shared a passion for the theatre. Many efforts were made to break up the relationship between George and Louisa; he was sent to Corfu in the summer of 1843, just as she gave birth to their first child, another George. She returned to the stage but as soon as he was back in England they resumed their affair, and in January 1846 she bore another son, Adolphus. A year later she was pregnant again, and she and George were married at St John's, Clerkenwell. So Louisa achieved respectability, but she paid a price. Obliged to give up the stage, she found life empty: and she was never accepted by any of her husband's family, so that he lived a double life, attending state occasions and visiting the Queen as a bachelor, and sometimes lectured on his morals by Albert. George was a kindly man and enjoyed domestic life; he was good to Louisa's two elder children, who called him Papa, and put the boy into the army, as he did his own sons. Louisa was sometimes jealous, both of his royal duties and his wandering eye. She complained that the Queen was always sending for him just when she wanted him at home; but as the years went by she gradually accepted her shadowy half-life as 'Mrs FitzGeorge', and his regular departures for shooting parties and royal holidays in Germany without her. He succeeded his father as second Duke of Cambridge in 1850; six years later he was appointed commander-in-chief of the army. In the same year he paid his first visit to Balmoral, and suffered the death of his dearest friend, Adolphus FitzClarence. In this year also Louisa made a last attempt to get permission to take part in a play. He wrote to her, 'As regards the question you put to me about your taking part in some private theatricals, I never thought darling that you put that question to me seriously, but now that I find you do, I must confess that I have a *very great objection* to it and hope you will *not* do so.'

1.   In 1878, when the FitzGeorge sons were all in their thirties, George's mother, the old Duchess – now eighty-one – asked to meet her grandsons for the first time. She found them charming, and they continued to visit her regularly at St James's, without their mother of course. Mrs FitzGeorge died in Queen Street in 1890, unacknowledged by her husband's family, although Queen Victoria wrote a note of sympathy to George after her death, 'which would have been such a joy to my beloved one, had she known the fact,' he wrote in his diary.

22 THE STATUE'S STORY: 1830–1980

1. The *DNB* says it was at Mapledurham Church in 1851. In 1913 Philip Sergeant wrote (*Mrs Jordan, Child of Nature*, p. 329), 'after his [WIV's] death next year it was taken down to the Rev. Lord Augustus FitzClarence's rectory at Mapledurham and forgotten'. Harold Armitage's book on Chantrey, published in 1915, also mentions 'the monument of Mrs Jordan that may be seen now in the church at Mapledurham in Oxfordshire' (p. 86). Neither the parish nor the bishop's archives has any record of it being there, nor do any of the local people have any recollection of it. Lord Augustus's widow left Mapledurham after his death in 1854; the church was heavily restored and altered in the 1860s by Butterfield, and it seems likely the statue would have remained *in situ* during these operations. Clare Jerrold (*The Story of Dorothy Jordan*) in 1914 says it 'was for a considerable time at Mapledurham' and that although it 'had to go begging for a resting place in earlier days [it] now holds an honoured place in the house of the present Earl of Munster': perhaps Sergeant's

reference spurred him to collect the statue from wherever it being kept. This was the fourth Earl, Aubrey, who succe in 1902, aged forty, lived in London, and died 1 January 1 he also visited Dora's grave at Saint-Cloud and had it put good order. Jerrold obviously saw the statue – she sho photograph of it – and says there was no inscription on it.

2. Mapledurham Church was restored and enlarged by Butter in the 1860s under the Revd Ernest Coleridge, who offici from 1862 to 1883, so that it looks quite different from church over which Augustus presided; and the statue have been moved out during the building work.

3. Miss Mary Birkbeck, niece of the fifth Earl, remembers cle seeing it on the 'stoep' – the Earl's word for the vera because he had been brought up in South Africa – and excitement of its arrival some time in the 1950s.

4. Joseph Fisher, *Etched Reminiscences* (1847).

5. It also has the modello for the statue, a very interesting p The whole story of the Chantrey plasters is told by Nich Penny in 'Chantrey, Westmacott and Casts after the Anti in the *Journal of the History of Collections*, vol. 3, no. 2 (19 pp. 255–64. The curator responsible for the destruction E. T. Leeds; curiously, he was an archaeologist.

6. Information from John Kenworthy-Browne, who inspected

7. The Earls of Munster were (1) George (2) his son Will who married a first cousin, Wilhelmina, daughter of Aug (3) their third son Geoffrey, who died without issue (4) 1 fifth son Aubrey, who died without issue (5) his nephew, so William and Wilhelmina's seventh son, another Geoffrey always known as Boy, also childless (6) Edward Charle grandson of the second Earl's younger brother George) and his son, the present Earl, Anthony Charles, who is the sev and last, having no male heir; nor do there appear to be male descendants of Frederick or Augustus FitzClarence.

APPENDIX

1. John Genest, *Some Account of the English Stage from the Restor in 1660 to 1830*, vol. 6 (1832), p. 382. Genest also notes

Cibber spelt his heroine's name 'Hypolita', which Drury Lane amended to 'Hippolita' on its playbill of 1 January 1787 (*Some Account . . .*, vol. 7, p. 241). Confusion has reigned ever since.

2. James Boaden, *The Life of Mrs Jordan*, vol. 2 (1831), pp. 67–8.
3. Horace Walpole to Lady Ossory, W. S. Lewis (ed.), *The Correspondence of Horace Walpole*, vol. 34 (1965), p. 51.

Bibliography

1. Unpublished Material

Letters of Mrs Jordan and miscellaneous papers relating to her in the Huntington Library, California

Letters of Mrs Jordan and the Duke of Clarence in the Royal Archives; also the journal of Queen Victoria

British Library manuscripts: letters by Mrs Jordan; letters by the FitzClarences; typescript by Hoppner's granddaughter Mrs Cromarty

Letters of the Duke of Clarence, Sophia FitzClarence and others held in the De L'Isle Archive at Maidstone

Royal Physical Laboratory Archive

Sir John Soane's workbook and other papers held at the Sir John Soane Museum

Ledger of Sir Francis Chantrey in the Royal Academy

Other letters by Mrs Jordan and the FitzClarences in private possession

2. Newspaper

The Times

3. Biographies of Mrs Jordan

Boaden, James, *The Life of Mrs Jordan* (2 vols., 1831). Boaden knew his subject personally, printed some of her letters to him, and wrote with great warmth and feeling, even though he felt obliged to be circumspect in his remarks about the reigning monarch. His book is an indispensable source, vivid and sympathetic. There are inaccuracies, and he gives rather more theatrical information than most readers could possibly want, but he is a good, companionable writer and brings his subject to life.

Anon., *The Great Illegitimates, or Public and Private Life of that Celebrated Actress, Miss Bland, otherwise Mrs Ford, or, Mrs Jordan, late mistress of H.R.H. the D. of Clarence, now King William IV* by a confidential friend of the departed (1832?). This is less scurrilous than its title makes it sound. It offers some information and documentation not found in Boaden, and is generally sympathetic to its subject. A shorter version appeared in 1886(?), still anonymous, and less offensively called *The Life of Mrs Jordan*; this edition is not illustrated, and lacks the appendix containing Helen Maria Williams's interviews.

Sergeant, Philip, *Mrs Jordan, Child of Nature* (1913). Straightforward but uninspiring.

Jerrold, Clare, *The Story of Dorothy Jordan* (1914). Established Mrs Jordan's date and place of birth for the first time, and printed some unpublished letters. Jerrold, previously a royal biographer, was stirred to passionate indignation on behalf of her subject.

Aspinall, Arthur (ed.), *Mrs Jordan and Her Family, being the Unpublished Letters of Mrs Jordan and the Duke of Clarence, later William IV* (1951). A pioneering edition of Mrs Jordan's letters, done at the behest of the fifth Earl of Munster, and using the letters then in his possession (which later passed to the Royal Archives) as well as those from the Huntington Library. The notes are excellent, but the letters are cut – in the case of one letter culpably – and set in an unsympathetic narrative: see my Foreword.

Fothergill, Brian, *Mrs Jordan: Portrait of an Actress* (1965). Written at the suggestion of Thomas Goff, descended from Mrs Jordan through her youngest son Augustus, this is a sympathetic and scholarly account of her life, with much stress on the theatrical aspect. It relies, however, on Aspinall's edition of the letters.

There are also many essays on Mrs Jordan in collections on eighteenth-century actresses and others, among them Gerard, Frances A., *Some Fair Hibernians* (1897); Simpson, Harold, and

Braun, Mrs Charles, *A Century of Famous Actresses 1750–1850* (1913); Melville, Lewis, *More Stage Favourites of the Eighteenth Century* (1929) – none reliable but all entertaining.

4. Journals and Letters

Burney, Fanny, *Diary and Letters of Madame D'Arblay*, edited by her niece (7 vols., 1842–6) and Hemlow, J. (gen. ed.), *Journals and Letters of Fanny Burney* (12 vols., 1972–1984). Unparalleled account of the court, its activities and personalities, by one of Mrs Jordan's most intelligent contemporaries, shocked by some aspects of the actress's life and activities, but able to do her justice.

Lewis, Lady T. (ed.), *Journals and Correspondence of Miss Berry* (1865). Gossip with Horace Walpole.

Clark, Mrs Godfrey, *Gleanings from an Old Portfolio* (3 vols., 1895–8). Letters of Lady Louisa Stuart, a shrewd observer of the late eighteenth-century scene, theatrical and social.

Granville, Lady (ed.), *Private Correspondence 1781–1821, Lord Granville Leveson-Gower* (2 vols., 1916). Valuable for Lady Bessborough's marvellous letters.

Bessborough, Earl of, and Aspinall, Arthur (eds.), *Lady Bessborough and Her Family Circle* (1940). More of the same.

Woodforde, James, *The Diary of a Country Parson*, Beresforde, John (ed.), (5 vols., 1924–31). Woodforde's many visits to the theatre in Norwich, Somerset and London are particularly interesting.

Glenbervie, Sylvester Douglas, Lord, *Diaries* (1928). Trivial but lively.

Chapman, R.W. (ed.), *The Letters of Jane Austen* (2 vols., 1932). For general background, also reference to the Country Girl and to her sister Cassandra's enviable proposed visit to the theatre to see Mrs Jordan.

Lewis, W.S. (ed.), *The Correspondence of Horace Walpole* (48 vols., 1937–83). Walpole's correspondence has been edited many times, but this Yale edition makes all others superfluous.

Boswell, James, *London Journal*, Pottle, F.A. (ed.) (1950). Sets the scene of mid-eighteenth-century London, streets and lodgings and theatres, better than any other source.

393

Bessborough, Earl of (ed.), *Georgiana: Extracts from the Correspondence of Georgiana, Duchess of Devonshire* (1955). Lady Bessborough's younger sister, another important contemporary of Mrs Jordan and Sheridan.

Griggs, E.L. (ed.), *The Collected Letters of Samuel Taylor Coleridge* (6 vols., 1956–71). There are several references to Coleridge's admiration for Mrs Jordan.

Coburn, Kathleen (ed.), *The Notebooks of Samuel Taylor Coleridge* (4 vols., 1957–90; vol. 4 ed. with M. Christensen).

Aspinall, Arthur (ed.), *The Correspondence of George, Prince of Wales 1770–1812* (7 vols., final vol. published 1971). Essential background material on the royal family. Also
   The Letters of King George IV 1812–1830 (3 vols., 1938).
   The Letters of Princess Charlotte (1949).
All these contain references to Mrs Jordan and the Duke of Clarence.

Marchand, Leslie A. (ed.), *Byron's Letters and Journals*. For general background, and in particular vol. 3, *Alas! The Love of Women 1813–1814* (1974) has reference to Mrs Jordan's performance.

Garlick, K., and Macintyre, A. (eds., vols. 1–6) and Cave, K. (ed., vols. 7–16), *The Diary of Joseph Farington* (1978–84). Another rich source of gossip.

5. Memoirs

Wilkinson, Tate, *The Wandering Patentee; or a History of the Yorkshire Theatre from 1700* (4 vols., 1795). Vol. 2 is especially good on Mrs Jordan. Wilkinson knew and worked with her mother and her aunt before he saved her from destitution and helped to make her a star. Everything he writes is delightful, and he gives a wonderful account of the relatively closely knit world of the eighteenth-century theatre, about which he knew as much as anyone.

Boaden, James, *Memoirs of the Life of John Philip Kemble* (1825). Boaden's first theatrical biography, flattering to Kemble and with many references to Mrs Jordan.

Kelly, Michael, *Reminiscences* (1826; 1975 edition Fiske, R., ed.). Kelly worked with Mrs Jordan and knew her well, but is very circumspect in mentioning her, perhaps because by the time he wrote his memoirs he prided himself on his friendship with King George IV.

Reynolds, Frederic, *The Life and Times of Frederic Reynolds, written by himself* (2 vols., 1826). Jolly, self-regarding account by London playwright, born in 1764, of his varied experiences in the theatre and society, some involving Mrs Jordan.

Barrington, Sir Jonah, *Personal Sketches of My Own Time* (2 vols., 1827). Barrington knew Mrs Jordan in Dublin in 1809; his son went to school with hers, and he made inquiries at Saint-Cloud after her death.

Mathews, Anne, *Memoirs of Charles Mathews* (4 vols., 1838–9). A treasure trove of information, with some letters from Mrs Jordan and several stirring tributes to her from the best known and best loved of her acting contemporaries.

Adolphus, J., *Memoirs of John Bannister* (2 vols., 1839). An account of Mrs Jordan's favourite leading man, who was said to resemble her in voice and appearance.

Bulow, Gabriele von, *A Memoir* (1897). Gives a view of King William IV in later years.

Greville, Charles, *Memoirs*, Fulford, R., and Strachey, L. (eds.) (1938). More gossip.

Hart-Davis, Rupert, *The Arms of Time* (1979). Tells of his descent from Elizabeth FitzClarence and the Earl of Errol.

6. Sheridan

Moore, Thomas, *Memoirs of the Life of R. B. Sheridan* (2 vols., 1858). The first biography, loyal and funny.

Rae, W. Fraser, *Sheridan: A Biography* (2 vols., 1896). Excellent account of his subject, and also gives many quotations from letters by the Linley sisters describing Mrs Jordan.

Sadler, Michael T. H., *The Political Career of R.B. Sheridan* (1912). Gives in an appendix Mrs Sheridan's letters to Mrs Canning about the Duke of Clarence.

Gibbs, Lewis, *Sheridan* (1947). Good short biography.

Lefanu, William (ed.), *Betsy Sheridan's Journal* (1960).

Price, Cecil (ed.), *The Letters of Richard Brinsley Sheridan* (3 vols., 1966). Packed with information and evidence of the often strained relations between Sheridan and his theatrical employees.

Bingham, Madeleine, *Sheridan: The Track of a Comet* (1972). Another sympathetic and thoughtful study, but sources not always given.

7. Biography and History

Hitchcock, R., *An Historical View of the Irish Stage* (2 vols., 1794). Information about Mrs Jordan's mother and her working world.

Genest, John, *Some Account of the English Stage from the Restoration in 1660 to 1830* (10 vols., 1832). See vols. 7 and 8 in particular, which give summaries of Mrs Jordan's career.

Oxberry, William, *Dramatic Biography and Histrionic Anecdotes* (vol. 1, 1835). Oxberry saw Mrs Jordan act, and reported his impressions.

Huish, Robert, *History of the Life and Reign of William IV* (1837). A hostile account of the King, with lots of gossip.

Walsh, J. E., *Sketches of Ireland Sixty Years Ago* (1847, 1911 edition). Good on the background from which Mrs Jordan came.

Raymond, George, *The Life and Enterprises of Robert William Elliston, Comedian* (1857). More background to the stage world.

Russell, W. Clark, *Representative Actors* (n.d. but after 1870 and before 1880). Handy potted information.

Fitzgerald, Percy, *The Life and Times of King William IV* (2 vols., 1884). The standard work for many years, it omitted any reference to Mrs Jordan or the King's ten children by her.

Littlewood, S. R., *Elizabeth Inchbald and Her Circle* (1921). Old-fashioned biographical study, almost no sources given, but still useful.

Fulford, R., *The Royal Dukes* (1933). Witty and good on the royal background; entirely unsympathetic to Mrs Jordan.

George IV (1935). Makes the best case he can.

Hanover to Windsor (1960). A trace of sympathy for Mrs Jordan has crept in at last.

Leslie, S., *Mrs Fitzherbert* (1939) and *The Letters of Mrs Fitzherbert* (1940). Gives letters from George FitzClarence to Mrs Fitzherbert's adopted daughter.

Baker, H., *John Philip Kemble* (1942). Full and scholarly.

Macqueen-Pope, W., *Theatre Royal Drury Lane* (1945). Enthusiastic theatre history.

Hopkirk, Mary, *Queen Adelaide* (1956). A sympathetic account.

Watson, J. Steven, *The Reign of George III* (1960). Ever useful.

Clark, William S., *The Irish Stage in the Country Towns 1720–1800* (1965). Good specialist study.

Ziegler, Philip, *King William IV* (1971). Scholarly and readable apologia, entirely fair to Mrs Jordan although less so to her children.

Hedley, Olwen, *Queen Charlotte* (1975). Superbly researched, with a mass of fascinating detail.

Highfill, Philip H., *A Biographical Dictionary of Stage Personnel, London 1660–1800* (1982). Essential reference work.

Kendall, Alan, *David Garrick* (1985). Informative, with many illustrations.

Fraser, Flora, *Beloved Emma* (1986). The most recent and excellent life of Lady Hamilton.

Pocock, Tom, *Sailor King: The Life of King William IV* (1991). Especially good on the naval background.

8. Art History

Fisher, Joseph, *Etched Reminiscences* (1847). Fisher recorded the Chantrey cast of Mrs Jordan in the Ashmolean.

Jones, George, *The Personal Recollections of Sir Francis Chantrey* (1849).

Jackson, E. N., *History of Silhouettes* (1911). Plate xxxiv is of Mrs Jordan as Hippolita.

McKay, W. and Roberts, W., *Hoppner* (1914).

Armitage, Harold, *Francis Chantrey* (1915). Describes the statue of Mrs Jordan and locates it in Mapledurham.

Millar, O., *The Later Georgian Pictures in the Collection of Her Majesty the Queen* (1969). Essential information and references.

Penny, Nicholas, *Catalogue of European Sculptures in the Ashmolean Museum*. Vol. 3 (1992). Gives the story of the destruction of the Chantrey casts.

9. Places

Ripley, Henry, *History and Topography of Hampton-on-Thames* (1885). Anecdotes of Bushy and Hampton village.

Law, E., *History of Hampton Court Palace* (3 vols., *c.* 1900). Section on Bushy.

Humphris, E., and Willoughby, E. C., *At Cheltenham Spa* (1928). Much good material, but few sources given.

George, Dorothy, *London Life in the Eighteenth Century* (1930). Describes many aspects of the city in which Mrs Jordan was born and to which she returned in 1785.

Maxwell, Constantia, *Dublin under the Georges* (second edition, 1956). The town in which Mrs Jordan grew up.

Hart, Gwen, *History of Cheltenham* (1965).

Jackson, Gordon, *Hull in the Eighteenth Century* (1972). The background to the Hull theatre.

Foster, Peter, and Pyatt, Edward, *Bushy House* (1976). A most valuable source of information in pamphlet form.

10. Miscellaneous

Carey, G. S., *The Dupes of Fancy* (1792). A short play dedicated hopefully to Mrs Jordan, with a frontispiece of her.

Maurice, T., *Richmond Hill* (1807). The poem mentions Bushy, the Duke and his family, as well as lamenting the deaths of Nelson, Pitt and Fox.

Inchbald, Elizabeth (ed.), *British Theatre* (25 vols., 1808) and *British Farces* (1815), with introductions. Two formidable pieces of editorial work. Several of the introductions refer to Mrs Jordan's performances.

FitzClarence, George, first Earl of Munster, *An Account of the British Campaign of 1809 under Sir A. Wellesley, in Spain and Portugal*, first published anonymously in the *United Service Journal*, 1829, reprinted 1831 in volume of *Memoirs of Late War*. This is Mrs Jordan's eldest son's vivid narrative of his first weeks in the Peninsular War as a fifteen-year-old officer serving under Wellington.

Journal of a Route across India, through Egypt to England, in the latter end of the year 1817, and the beginning of 1818, 1819. His account of his return journey.

Reade, Charles, *Peg Woffington* (1853). A fictionalized version of Woffington, written when Reade was in love with the popular but unhappy Victorian actress Fanny Stirling, and fascinated by the combination of genius and sexual levity he saw in both the dead and the living woman. He also wrote a charming sentimental play about Woffington, *Masks and Faces*.

Falkland, Viscountess (Amelia), *Chow-Chow: being Selections from a Journal Kept in India, Egypt and Syria* (2 vols., 1857). Mrs Jordan's youngest daughter's lively account of her time in India as wife of the Governor of Bombay, and her return journey through Egypt.

FitzClarence, Wilhelmina, *My Memories* (1904). Mrs Jordan's granddaughter, eldest child of Augusta Kennedy Erskine (née Fitz-Clarence), married her first cousin William, son of George Fitz-Clarence, and became the second Countess of Munster. Her reminiscences go back to her grandfather King William IV and describe some of her uncles. She also wrote novels, including *Dorinda* (3 vols., 1889).

Brown, Eluned (ed.), *Henry Crabb Robinson on the Theatre* (1966).

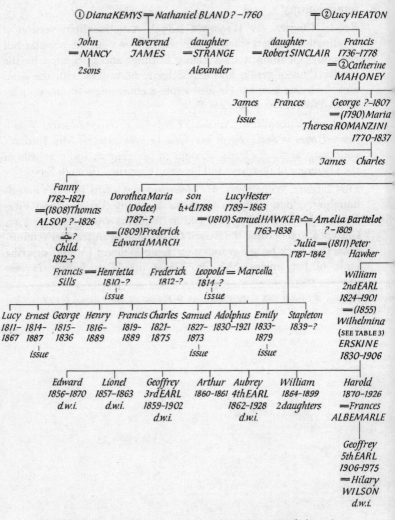

KING WILLIAM granted a special remainder, in his son George's male descendants,
to Lords Frederick, Adolphus and Augustus FitzClarence, primogeniturely,
and to their male heirs. The present Earl (the seventh) will, however, be the last.

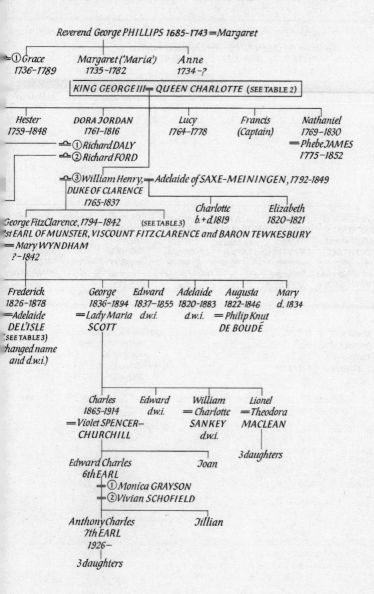

Reverend George PHILLIPS 1685–1743 = Margaret

= ① *Grace*
1736–1789

Margaret ('Maria')
1735–1782

Anne
1734–?

KING GEORGE III = QUEEN CHARLOTTE (SEE TABLE 2)

Hester
1759–1848

DORA JORDAN
1761–1816

Lucy
1764–1778

Francis
(Captain)

Nathaniel
1769–1830
= *Phebe JAMES*
1775–1852

① *Richard DALY*
② *Richard FORD*

③ *William Henry,* = *Adelaide of SAXE-MEININGEN, 1792–1849*
DUKE OF CLARENCE
1765–1837

Charlotte
b. + d.1819

Elizabeth
1820–1821

George FitzClarence, 1794–1842   (SEE TABLE 3)
1st EARL OF MUNSTER, VISCOUNT FITZCLARENCE and BARON TEWKESBURY
= *Mary WYNDHAM*
?–1842

Frederick
1826–1878
= *Adelaide*
DEL'ISLE
(SEE TABLE 3)
changed name
and d.w.i.)

George
1836–1894
= *Lady Maria*
SCOTT

Edward
1837–1855
d.w.i.

Adelaide
1820–1883
d.w.i.

Augusta
1822–1846
= *Philip Knut*
DE BOUDÉ

Mary
d. 1834

Charles
1865–1914
= *Violet SPENCER–*
CHURCHILL

Edward
d.w.i.

William
= *Charlotte*
SANKEY
d.w.i.

Lionel
= *Theodora*
MACLEAN

3 daughters

Edward Charles
6th EARL
= ① *Monica GRAYSON*
= ② *Vivian SCHOFIELD*

Joan

Anthony Charles
7th EARL
1926–

Jillian

3 daughters

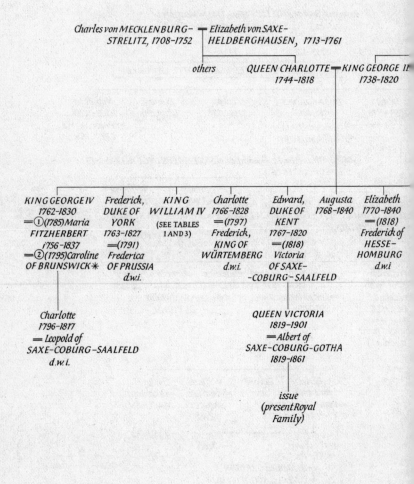

Charles von MECKLENBURG- ══ Elizabeth von SAXE-
STRELITZ, 1708-1752　　　HELDBERGHAUSEN, 1713-1761

　　　　　　others　　　QUEEN CHARLOTTE ══ KING GEORGE II
　　　　　　　　　　　　1744-1818　　　　　　1738-1820

KING GEORGE IV　Frederick,　KING　Charlotte　Edward,　Augusta　Elizabeth
1762-1830　　DUKE OF　WILLIAM IV　1766-1828　DUKE OF　1768-1840　1770-1840
══①(1785) Maria　YORK　(SEE TABLES　══(1797)　KENT　　　　══(1818)
FITZHERBERT　1763-1827　1 AND 3)　Frederick,　1767-1820　　Frederick of
1756-1837　══(1791)　　　KING OF　══(1818)　　HESSE-
══②(1795) Caroline　Frederica　　WÜRTEMBERG　Victoria　　HOMBURG
OF BRUNSWICK✱　OF PRUSSIA　　d.w.i.　OF SAXE-　　d.w.i
　　　d.w.i.　　　　　　-COBURG-SAALFELD

Charlotte　　　　　　QUEEN VICTORIA
1796-1817　　　　　　1819-1901
══ Leopold of　　　══ Albert of
SAXE-COBURG-SAALFELD　SAXE-COBURG-GOTHA
d.w.i.　　　　　　1819-1861

　　　　　　issue
　　　　　(present Royal
　　　　　Family)

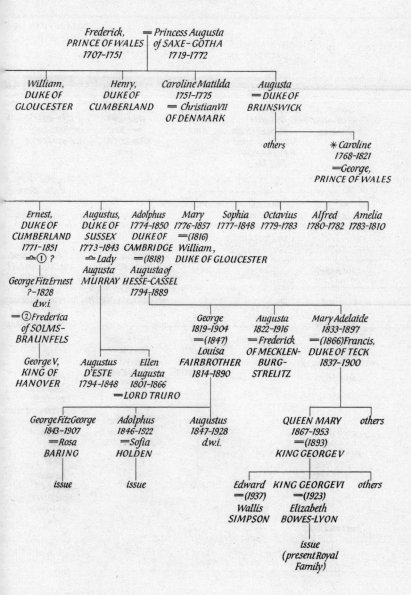

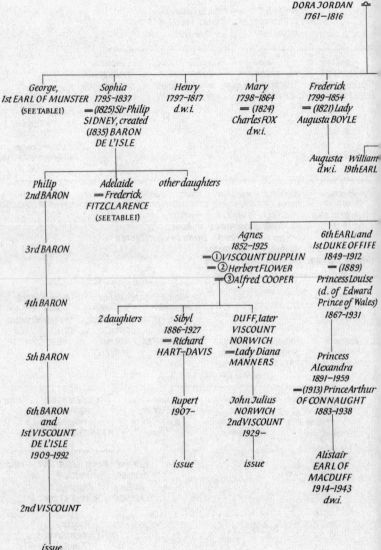

TABLE SHOWING THE YOUNGER CHILDREN OF MRS JORDAN

DORA JORDAN
1761–1816

George,
1st EARL OF MUNSTER
(SEE TABLE 1)

Sophia 1795–1837
= (1825) Sir Philip
SIDNEY, created
(1835) BARON
DE L'ISLE

Henry
1797–1817
d.w.i.

Mary
1798–1864
= (1824)
Charles FOX
d.w.i.

Frederick
1799–1854
= (1821) Lady
Augusta BOYLE

Augusta   William
d.w.i.   19th EARL

Philip
2nd BARON

Adelaide
= Frederick
FITZCLARENCE
(SEE TABLE 1)

other daughters

3rd BARON

Agnes
1852–1925
= ① VISCOUNT DUPPLIN
= ② Herbert FLOWER
= ③ Alfred COOPER

6th EARL and
1st DUKE OF FIFE
1849–1912
= (1889)
Princess Louise
(d. of Edward
Prince of Wales)
1867–1931

4th BARON

2 daughters

Sibyl
1886–1927
= Richard
HART–DAVIS

DUFF, later
VISCOUNT
NORWICH
= Lady Diana
MANNERS

5th BARON

Rupert
1907–

John Julius
NORWICH
2nd VISCOUNT
1929–

Princess
Alexandra
1891–1959
= (1913) Prince Arthur
OF CONNAUGHT
1883–1938

6th BARON
and
1st VISCOUNT
DE L'ISLE
1909–1992

issue

issue

Alistair
EARL OF
MACDUFF
1914–1943
d.w.i.

2nd VISCOUNT

issue

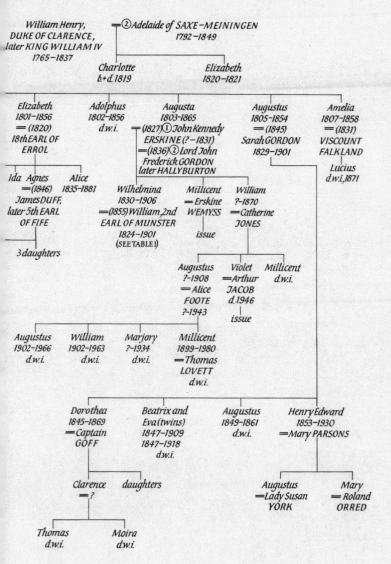

William Henry, **②** Adelaide of SAXE–MEININGEN
DUKE OF CLARENCE, *1792–1849*
later KING WILLIAM IV
1765–1837

Charlotte
b.+d.1819

Elizabeth
1820–1821

Elizabeth
1801–1856
= (1820)
18th EARL OF
ERROL

Adolphus
1802–1856
d.w.i.

Augusta
1803–1865
= (1827) ① John Kennedy
ERSKINE (? –1831)
= (1836) ② Lord John
Frederick GORDON
later HALLYBURTON

Augustus
1805–1854
= (1845)
Sarah GORDON
1829–1901

Amelia
1807–1858
= (1831)
VISCOUNT
FALKLAND

Lucius
d.w.i, 1871

Ida Agnes Alice
= (1846) *1835–1881*
James DUFF,
later 5th EARL
OF FIFE

Wilhelmina
1830–1906
= (1855) William, 2nd
EARL OF MUNSTER
1824–1901
(SEE TABLE 1)

Millicent
= Erskine
WEMYSS

issue

William
?–1870
= Catherine
JONES

3 daughters

Augustus
?–1908
= Alice
FOOTE
?–1943

Violet
= Arthur
JACOB
d.1946

issue

Millicent
d.w.i.

Augustus
1902–1966
d.w.i.

William
1902–1963
d.w.i.

Marjory
?–1934
d.w.i.

Millicent
1899–1980
= Thomas
LOVETT
d.w.i.

Dorothea
1845–1869
= Captain
GOFF

Beatrix and
Eva (twins)
1847–1909
1847–1918
d.w.i.

Augustus
1849–1861
d.w.i.

Henry Edward
1853–1930
= Mary PARSONS

Clarence
= ?

daughters

Augustus
= Lady Susan
YORK

Mary
= Roland
ORRED

Thomas
d.w.i.

Moira
d.w.i.

Index